Philosophies of Organizational Change

Philosophies of Organizational Change

Perspectives, Models and Theories for Managing Change

SECOND EDITION

Aaron C.T. Smith

Institute for Sport Business, Loughborough University London, UK

James Skinner

Institute for Sport Business, Loughborough University London, UK

Daniel Read

Institute for Sport Business, Loughborough University London, UK

 Edward Elgar
PUBLISHING

Cheltenham, UK • Northampton, MA, USA

Published by
Edward Elgar Publishing Limited
The Lypiatts
15 Lansdown Road
Cheltenham
Glos GL50 2JA
UK

Edward Elgar Publishing, Inc.
William Pratt House
9 Dewey Court
Northampton
Massachusetts 01060
USA

Paperback edition 2021

A catalogue record for this book
is available from the British Library

Library of Congress Control Number: 2020944679

This book is available electronically in the **Elgar**online
Business subject collection
http://dx.doi.org/10.4337/9781839105098

ISBN 978 1 83910 508 1 (cased)
ISBN 978 1 83910 509 8 (eBook)
ISBN 978 1 80088 843 2 (paperback)

Printed and bound by CPI Group (UK) Ltd, Croydon, CR0 4YY

Contents

1. Introduction: 'changing philosophies'

INTRODUCTION

Enacting successful organizational change could well be the most important—but also most difficult—task a leader can undertake. Academics and business commentators have been talking about organization change in various forms since the 1950s. The prolific resulting literature since has proven divergent in approach and emphasis, but beginning in the early 1990s, a shared observation started re-appearing: 'the world is changing, traditional bureaucracy is bankrupt and the future is now—or at least soon' (Nohria and Berkley, 1994, p. 108). Unfortunately, the consensus stopped at an agreement that managing organizational change is more important than ever before; an axiom that has only escalated in repetition with the passing years. How to make change happen successfully, however, depends on a myriad of other assumptions and variables, like an organization's readiness for change (Weiner, Clary, Klaman, Turner and Alishahi-Tabriz, 2020), the political, institutional and technological context (Waeger and Weber, 2019), human responses and commitments to change (Raeder and Bokova, 2019) and resilience in the face of upheaval (Brown and Abuatiq, 2020).

The need for change features prominently in organizational ambitions, as its success or failure can lead to decisive consequences, from transformational improvements in productivity to catastrophic plunges towards insolvency (Brandt, Andersson and Kjellstrom, 2019). Research also reveals a disconcerting chasm between leaders' change ambitions and their tangible effects on organizational performance (Oreg and Berson, 2019). Perhaps most concerning, the evidence informing organizational change is scant and tends to rely on unvalidated theories, models and cases (Evans, 2020). This second edition aims to inventory and explain the diverse, pluralistic organizational change approaches that have attracted research and practitioner interest. It reveals the 'philosophies' that guide change theories and models on the presupposition that a better understanding of these underpinning perspectives provides valuable insight for the research and practice of change. We assume that organizational change can be best studied and applied when the philosophies that structure an approach are clearly exposed. Making sense of change means making sense of all the different ways that have been employed to bring about change (Cameron and Green, 2019). In this second edition, over the forthcoming chapters, we explore 12 different organizational change philosophies.

AN UNPRECEDENTED IMPERATIVE

At the same time as the diversity of organizational change theory and practice proliferated, the world began marching to a new drum. Industry deregulation, free-trade markets and the rise of Asia and the sub-continent, for example, have all been used to explain a newfound impetus for global competition, connectivity and economic activity. In addition, disruptive technological advances—including cloud-based commerce, the Internet of Things and machine-based learning through artificial intelligence—mean that borders and geography no longer impede the transfer of information, capital, people or products. This new 'Information Age' has occurred alongside a gradual but strengthening shift in the focus of developed economies from the manufacturing and commodities sector to the information, communications and services sectors. A technology revolution in tandem with rising consumer expectations and access to global markets has contributed to shorter product life cycles and has led to the need for go-to-market speed and flexibility. In many industries, technological advances have eroded the traditional barriers to entry where high start-up costs and economies of scale no longer present severe obstacles. We have therefore seen an explosion of fast, small and nimble companies entering markets that were once the protected sanctum of industry behemoths. And, all of these organizations—old and new, large and small—scramble to keep up in a world transforming faster than most of them can possibly change.

Leaders approach change based on assumptions about how change works. Sometimes assumptions come from prominent management concepts, and sometimes they are based on experience or even just the way things have always been done in the past. For example, some schools of thought—or 'philosophies of organizational change'—cling to a logical process pivoting upon a leader's ability to conceive a new future and plan for it accordingly. Other philosophies focus on particular or distinguishing characteristics of an organization, like its 'culture'. Others still emphasize the psychological impact of change on individual organizational members. In practice, most change leaders wield numerous philosophies at once, use different approaches depending on the situation, or change their preferred approach over time. We argue that whether conscious or tacit, success depends upon understanding these distinctive but intersecting philosophies of organizational change. In the workshop of change, leaders' toolkits bulge with philosophies and their offspring theories. Philosophies describe a way of looking at organizational change: a paradigm incorporating structured assumptions, premises and beliefs presupposing the way change works in organizations.

We use the term 'philosophy of organizational change' to describe the paradigmatic set of assumptions, tacit beliefs, conscious theories and implementation approaches that govern a change agent's way of looking at the organizational world and the best approach to introducing change. In each change philosophy, hypotheses and theories about change and its nature guide problem diagnosis and the change interventions prescribed as solutions. We contend that philosophies represent the most rewarding site for studying organizational change. By categorizing, describing, examining and criticizing philosophies of change, we aim to supply readers with a comprehensive analytical toolkit.

In the classical, linear approach to organizational change, leaders rely on predictable, reducible steps to establish a new work order and routines. But under examination, conventional assumptions prove the exceptions rather than the rules. We counter that change is rarely linear, infrequently predictable and only sometimes successful. In this second edition, we respond to change's complexity and uncertainty through an interrogation of 12 organizational change philosophies. These include uni-dimensional, competing and complementary philosophies, as well as some with a mixed focus where decisions flex in the tension between change and stability. In the remainder of this chapter, we review the quest and context in which organizational change transpires. Next, we introduce the organizational change philosophies described in the forthcoming chapters and summarize how each provides a reference frame for understanding the change process, and the undeniable, though sometimes tense, link between theory and practice.

THE CHANGE QUEST

The organizational change quest has a history of prioritizing control under the stewardship of a strong leader or 'guiding coalition'. Ever popular amongst change consultants, this form of organizational change involves a series of predictable steps that can be planned and managed (Collins, 1998). However, research evidence from failed change cases reveals the limitations of a strictly one-dimensional, rational approach. Change rarely works when treated as a single, momentary disturbance that must be stabilized and controlled. In practice, change intimately entwines with continuity, allowing the simultaneous exploitation of strengths and the exploration of new opportunities. Change and continuity represent competing but complementary forces. Ambiguity encourages creativity while, at the same time, stability maintains control. So, although we present each change philosophy as an independent approach, we also acknowledge that a singular philosophy has less chance of success than a combination.

Change is a work in progress; it demands a broad-based canvas that accommodates competing voices, and adjusts to the messy ambiguities, contradictions and tensions of real life. We advocate a multi-philosophy approach because continuity depends on change as much as change depends on continuity. Both must be present for organizational growth and survival. Continuity balances change in the same way that safety defines risk. Evans and Doz (1992) counselled that most qualities of an organization have a complementary opposite. Excessive control leads to stagnation and decline while overzealous change causes disruption and crisis.

Commentary about organizational change often features observations about environmental complexity and uncertainty, as well as the need for urgent change towards more urgent change. Prescriptive advice abounds. For example, organizations have been urged to downsize, decentralize, de-bureaucratize, decouple, differentiate, empower, innovate, integrate and involve. In dramatic style, a smorgasbord of responses has been advanced to deliver organizational change: boundary-less, network, platform, virtual, clickable, hybrid, modular, horizontal, shamrock, loosely coupled, individualized, learning, knowledge-based and cellular. As the world changed, so too were organizations urged to change with it.

If the answer in the new, knowledge-driven world was to be found in swift adaptation to change, the 'old' models had to be tossed aside. Adherence to hierarchy, stability, uniformity and specialization, designed to exert authority and control over a largely uneducated workforce, all had to go. Indeed, if organizations hoped to survive and succeed in complex, high-velocity, chaotic environments, they had to make change the focus. Meanwhile, claims continued that organizations needed new ideas, paradigms and practices in order to cope with the unprecedented demands that a global, technological, knowledge economy had delivered. For example, by the late 1990s, the keywords in business literature could be summarized in seven trends: technology, globalization, competition, change, speed, complexity and paradox (Tetenbaum, 1998). In response, management theorists started to think of organizations in terms of their change capacities where faster was not just better, but critical to survival.

THE CHANGE CONTEXT

In reviewing the history of organizational change, we fast discover that it depicts a 'fuzzy, deeply ambiguous process' (Collins, 2003, p. v) with no obvious ending, and yet with no shortage of confident proclamations about its successful delivery. Consider, for example, Grundy's (1993) 'power tools for change', Kanter, Stein and Jick's (1992) 'Ten Commandments', Kotter's (1995) 'Eight Steps to Transforming Your Organization', and Hammer and Champy's (1993) 'Business Process Re-engineering'. These early but influential models wielded a formulaic approach that characterized change as a controlled and orderly affair, a simple case of 'unfreezing', 'moving' and 'refreezing'. At the centre of successful implementation, we find the 'magic' leader (Nadler and Tushman, 1989; Kotter, 1990), charismatically inspiring and galvanizing the masses through a powerful, new vision.

Too much change literature overlooks the critical flaws inherent in this perspective. First, little evidence supports the supposition that organizations are 'as amenable to control as a block of ice' (Grey, 2003). Second, rational approaches ignore the not-so-rational wild card—the human factor—treating individuals as automatons rather than active agents in the change process (Giddens, 1981). Organizational actors will not necessarily respond enthusiastically and uniformly to their leader's call to arms. With performance as the end goal, rational models tell a distorted, partial story. Senior management ignores the multiplicity of other distinctive stories unfolding around them in the organizational narrative (Buchanan, 2003). Instead of listening, the rational prescription silences dissident voices.

Although limited, the management penchant for stepwise (Collins, 1998), goal-directed change models continues unsated. Seductively simple, the labels attached (power tools, transforming, commandments, magic) imply guaranteed success if followed to the letter. In addition, stepwise models appeal to leaders by ensuring the top-down control of the change process. Management texts and business magazine 'case studies' perpetuate and legitimize the rational, leader-centred change philosophy: the magic leader principle, the focus on accountability and control and the need to eliminate contradiction, dissent and uncertainty to secure prosperity. It is for this reason that we have added a new chapter on the models philosophy with special reference to the way such models are deployed by hired, external consultants.

Other change management cases in business magazines paint a more humanistic picture. Here one sees the new twenty-first-century leader as a people-person, adopting a more participatory, inclusive style. Transformed from autocrat to democrat, the leader recognizes that organizational knowledge and expertise do not reside solely within senior management. The new leader energizes the workforce by reviving the creativity lying dormant at all levels of the organization. Influence connects with teamwork where self-focused, individualistic cultures are transformed into one of collegiality and cooperation.

The aims advocated in the popular press and in 'airport' books by high-profile former business executives are undoubtedly sincere and obviously worth pursuing. Organizational leaders should try to challenge the status quo, increase risk taking and creativity and transcend boundaries through information sharing and teamwork. Yet, the methods used to introduce the lofty changes retain a rational, analytical orthodoxy where leaders hold sovereignty by charismatic decree. A paradox lurks in the traditional mode of thinking because teamwork cannot be mandated through strategy any more than freedom can be enforced at the risk of penalties. As Eisenhardt (2000) declared two decades ago, organizations muddle through the simultaneous existence of two inconsistent states. Rational orthodoxy presupposes the importance of discipline, order and control from the top down. But, the possibility of implementing change from the bottom up without the benefit of a leader's inspiration does not enter the frame. Change management decisions appear constrained to 'either-or' choices, or a bland compromise between putative opposites such as innovation and efficiency, collaboration and competition, freedom and accountability, empowerment and leadership, and economic and social goals.

The classic model of top-down change leaves the indelible impression that organizations contour to the sturdy hands of determined and charismatic leaders. Performance arrives with increasing competitiveness through economic discipline, rigid accountability and unswerving, 'take-no-prisoners' leadership. Despite calling for employee involvement, the message dismisses complexity but triumphs control by assuming the leader's vision will canalize and animate a vast workforce. A cynical view foreshadows control by stealth as managers set performance targets rather than direction (Leana and Barry, 2000) with little tolerance for ambiguity or dissent.

However dominant and popular the logic of, or rationale for, a leader-centric approach to organizational change and development may be, it represents only one view of how to manage the troublesome change conundrum. Organizations are knotty, multi-faceted entities, populated by complex human beings, the emotional, irrational x-factor ingredient in the organizational change melting pot. Progress therefore requires combining and recombining multiple theoretical change lenses to improve integration and avoid more fragmentation (Lewin and Volberda, 1999). A commitment to a single change philosophy or theory fails to account for a non-linear, recursive and multi-level reality. As Morgan (1997, p. 350) advised, 'reality has a tendency to reveal itself in accordance with the perspectives through which it is engaged'.

Our response provides the scope to understand change from numerous angles and create a smorgasbord of tools with which to work. Since different answers lead to different philosophies of change, we need to vigilantly expose the often hidden assumptions buried in theories and the metaphors used to communicate them. Metaphors can illuminate the way organizational change works by offering abstract but accessible explanations (Palmer and Dunford, 1996; Oztel and Hinz, 2001; Wood, 2002), liberating thinking from entrenched habits, encouraging creativity with new interpretations of old events, stimulating emotional engagement and fuelling action by probing unconscious archetypes (Green and Ruhleder, 1995; Palmer and Dunford, 1996; Wood, 2002). However, metaphors translate poorly into practical guidance. Philosophies of organizational change offer superior guidance compared to metaphors because they go beyond the abstract to provide both description and prescription; theoretical explanations in concert with methods for introducing change. Philosophies should be viewed as motors of change (Van de Ven and Poole, 1995) incorporating metaphors, paradigms and theories. The following section introduces the forthcoming chapters on organizational change philosophies. We summarize our 12 philosophies, their interpretations of change and the tools and techniques each employs.

THE THEORIES PHILOSOPHIES

In Chapter 2 we explore how a philosophy's method for change reveals the inferences it holds about the best way change can be delivered. The theories philosophy advocates that the best mechanism for dealing with organizational change is to be guided by a theoretical framework. A philosophy's theories generate hypotheses and predictions about organizational change. Philosophies may generate numerous different theories, all based on similar assumptions and premises. However, without understanding philosophies, the relationship between theories becomes murky. Theories also evolve, adapt and are revised or replaced. In Chapter 2 we explore how change theories change. We begin by considering some basic questions: What is the goal of theory development in organization change? Will one single theory eventually explain all forms of change? Are theories of change subject to replacement or updating? Can two or more theories become interconnected to create a better new theory? Will there always be innumerable theories to explain change? Each question leads to long-standing and contentious philosophical arguments about the nature of theories.

The Rational Philosophy

Chapter 3 presents the rational philosophy. Sometimes referred to as a 'strategic' approach, the rational philosophy pursues an alignment between an organization's structure, its competencies and the environment (Van de Ven and Poole, 1995). As a teleological approach—because the final destination guides planning—the rational philosophy assumes that a purposeful and adaptive logic motivates organizational change (Van de Ven and Poole, 1995; Kezar, 2000). Change occurs because senior managers and other change agents deem it necessary, navigated through linear thinking and performance by objectives, with managers at the helm (Carnall, 1995; Carr, Hard and Trahant, 1996).

Early strategic choice theorists (e.g. Child, 1972; Smith and Berg, 1987) subscribed to the rational philosophy maintaining that leaders and managers wield control of their organizations. The proliferation of management 'gurus' such as Kotter (1995), Huber and Glick (1995) and Kanter et al. (1992), who each propose their own change 'holy grail', fit the rationalist mould. Leaders and managers change organizations, shaping them to a rarefied mental vision like sculptors handling supple clay. Equally, unsuccessful change implies failed leadership, even if environmental shifts or resource problems were unforeseen. When change goes well, its leaders and managers claim insight and prescience, but when change goes badly, heads need to roll.

The rational philosophy assumes that change can be introduced at any pace and on any scale deemed suitable. Leaders direct and control change towards an inexorable outcome. Approaches consistent with the rational philosophy give precedence to strategic decision making and careful planning around organizational goals. The rational philosophy commands enormous popularity for leaders seeking to impose a new direction upon an organization. However, in Chapter 3 we show how the rational philosophy and its common theories and tools overestimate the power of leaders' whims and expectations.

The Biological Philosophy

We examine the biological philosophy in Chapter 4, which leads to numerous metaphors and theories of organizational change (Witt, 2004). Appropriated from biological evolution, the philosophy refers to the adaptations experienced by species—or in this case a population of organizations—over time. The evolutionary approach to change, pioneered by Hannan and Freeman (1977) and known as population ecology, focuses on incremental change within industries rather than individual organizations. Population ecologists (McKelvey and Aldrich, 1983) take a biological view of industrial behaviour. They claim that change comes about through Darwinian-like natural selection where industries gradually evolve to match the constraints of their environmental context. Ultimately, population ecologists want to know why there are so many different kinds of organizations within an industry when the imperative for efficiency and a 'best fit' with the environment predicts that there should be a single, ideal configuration that dominates (Van de Ven and Poole, 1995).

The life-cycle model also emanates from the biological philosophy. It describes the individual life-cycle changes that individual organisms experience. However, in this case, rather than organisms within species, our interest lies with organizations within industries, and their developmental life cycle. Life-cycle theory (Kezar, 2000; Van de Ven and Poole, 1995) explains change in organizations from start-up to divestment. Birth, growth, maturity, decline and death comprise natural parts of an organization's development (Levy and Merry, 1986). As the life-cycle model compares the stages of progress in organizations to the organic processes of growth and reproduction, organizational change becomes analogous to human development. Using a life-cycle model demands a progressive view where change is relentless and inescapable, like death and taxes.

The biological philosophy can get confusing because theorists often write about organizations adapting to changing environments (Chakravarthy, 1982). While literally correct, evolutionary theory in biology treats populations or species (industries) as the unit of change rather than individual organisms (organizations). As an intuitive analogy, the biological philosophy makes use of natural suppositions about development to simplify change. The idea that organizations, and the populations of industries that contain them, grow (life cycle) and adapt (evolution) imbues a helpful sense of drama, dynamism and inevitability. However, where the analogy ends, the difficulty of translating biology into daily action begins.

The Models Philosophy

Change tends to be either disliked or avoided because it takes people out of their comfort zone, demands additional work, risks the removal of benefits and generally confounds the current state of affairs. As we explore in Chapter 5, the models philosophy, leaders often employ consultants to leverage change efforts, direct their implementation and take the blame for uncomfortable actions or failure. The chapter notes that consultants can reduce the onus for success from management and provide welcome resources to progress change, while affording a target for employee displeasure. Chapter 5 examines the nature of change interventions typically presented by consultants. The spectrum of change-management models deployed by consultants has become immense. Bespoke models abound but they all source inspiration from the kinds of models examined in this chapter. It refers to 'models' because the preferred change methods tend to import ready-made, one-size-fits-all approaches that place an exclusive emphasis on one particular concept, idea or framework. Consultants employ a models philosophy when they use the same change model with small variations for every client that employs them. The chapter introduces the context in which consultants are engaged, and how consulting models are deployed for change. It then details a series of the foundational models as a means to demonstrate their character. The chapter is different to the others in that it explores a common—perhaps the most common—but much less theoretical philosophical approach to change. The aim is not to provide an inventory of major change models provided by consultants, but rather to demonstrate how the models philosophy has been shaped by a *kind* of thinking and method that originated at the tail end of the twentieth century.

The Institutional Philosophy

Chapter 6 explores the institutional philosophy. Although it embraces some evolutionary assumptions, the institutional philosophy focuses on the way organizations change as a consequence of environmental pressures. Organizational change accompanies contextual change. Like population ecologists, institutionalists expect organizations to increase homogeneity, or become more similar, within their industrial sector over time as the shaping force of the institutional environment overpowers strategy and the competition for resources. The institutional philosophy therefore explains how similarities between organizations within some industries occur, as well as the stability of particular organizational configurations and approaches. For example, institutional advocates point to legal firms as an exemplar of institutional compliance. Most legal firms employ similar structures. We can identify some commonalities between the institutional philosophy and the biological philosophy's population ecology. However, while both prioritize adaptation to environmental pressures, the institutional philosophy explains how institutional pressures can defy organizational change attempts and buttress inertia. The pressure for change does not only emerge from the market as in population ecology, but also from other institutional bodies that regulate and intervene, including the government. Population ecology sees the environment as the shaping force for achieving best fit, while institutionalists recognize that pressures for commonality, or 'isomorphism', come from other organizations, agents or social pressures (Greenwood and Hinings, 1996).

Social change also contributes to the pressure for conformity, sometimes in ways counter-productive to organizational profitability. For example, social and environmental forces for change have proven increasingly influential (Mukherji and Mukherji, 1998). The institutional philosophy helps explain the way external pressures influence organizational structures and practices, and how an organization's ability to adapt determines its prosperity. On the other hand, the institutional philosophy downplays internal change and the power change leaders hold over their own fates.

Organizational change from an institutional perspective is less about directive strategy and success in acquiring scarce resources, and more about sensitivity to a forceful institutional context. New regulatory, financial or legal conditions compel all organizations to fit standardized forms to ensure survival (DiMaggio and Powell, 1983; 1991). Irrespective of the specific forces, change mirrors the shifting industrial landscape, and successful organizations adjust accordingly. The institutional environment coerces organizations into change, and clever strategy cannot out-manoeuvre the rules enforced by an uncompromising institutional context. But in changing with the institutional environment, organizations assume similar characteristics. Consequently, we aim in Chapter 6 to expose how organizational strategies, structures and cultures conform to external pressures (Meyer and Rowan, 2006).

The Resource Philosophy

Chapter 7 examines the resource philosophy. Where the institutional philosophy describes the industry-specific pressures encouraging organizations to conform, the resource philosophy explains deviance. For example, resource-dependence theory proposes that any given organization does not possess all the resources it needs to compete. The pursuit of resources drives change as the critical activity for survival and prosperity (Pfeffer and Salancik, 1978). Successful organizations perform best at acquiring and deploying scarce resources including money and skills, where the most valuable resources can be combined with other assets or cannot be reproduced easily (Connor, 2002).

Organizational change begins by identifying essential resources, of which only some will be available. Criticality and scarcity determine which resources constitute a priority. Resource dependency aims to expose the variables instrumental to organizational change and performance. By focusing on the type of resources needed for change, the difficult task of predicting the right level becomes less crucial. While the absence of resources might foreshadow vulnerability, the presence of resources showcases competitive advantage. An organization's competencies represent resource assets that generate new opportunities and improve performance. Resources converted into strategic capabilities determine successful change; leaders should worry less about fitting with the environment and more about dominating it. The stimulus for change arrives from within, as organizations seek the resources they require to compete and win. After all, management competence should represent the greatest of assets (Grant, 1991). As we observe in Chapter 7, however, the resource philosophy can give the false impression that change only needs the right inputs.

The Psychological Philosophy

Chapter 8 explains the psychological philosophy, where personal responses to change govern organizational success. In the applied social psychology tradition (Lewin, 1947), the psychological philosophy focuses on individual experiences as organizations attempt change. The 'human' side of change (Iacovini, 1993; Stuart, 1995) introduces links with behavioural science, human relations, human development and organizational development, all combating the mechanistic legacy of scientific management. The psychological philosophy assumes that individual employees constitute the most important unit of analyses in studying organizational change.

In Chapter 8, we highlight two prominent change theories based on psychological assumptions: change transitions, and organizational development and learning. Change transitions focus on the psychological status of organizational members. Like Kübler-Ross' (1973) stages of death and dying, from denial to acceptance, change becomes possible when traumatic psychological transitions become transparent enough to tackle (Bridges, 1980; 1992; Jick, 1990). All versions of the psychological philosophy assume that emotions are powerful change mediators, but can be managed with careful attention. Organizational development, like transitions, takes an individual perspective to change, but uses a more applied, data-driven 'action research' approach (Burke, 2002). Change managers must, first, collect the right information about the impediments to change and, second, remove them by assuaging organizational members' fears and uncertainties.

Some interpret the psychological philosophy to mean that change emerges from meaning in the workplace through deep, spiritual connections (Dehler and Welsh, 1994). Change managers must provide a spiritually nourishing environment for organizational members to alleviate anxiety and reduce the uncertainties accompanying change. Notwithstanding more extreme views, psychological change remains slow and complex because rapid change stimulates discomfort. We caution in Chapter 8 that psychological adjustment to change cannot be enforced or accelerated no matter how vigilant the change agent. As a result, the psychological philosophy clarifies resistance to change better than it prescribes a solution.

The chapter concludes by introducing a newer element of the psychological philosophy, emphasizing its cognitive dimension, which means the 'thinking' and believing aspects of psychological change. This new section examines decision-making heuristics; the cognitive rules of thumb that facilitate rapid responses to change but at the cost of inaccuracies and biases. It also discusses the nature and implications of beliefs, particularly their resistance to change including their invulnerability to rational interrogation.

The Systems Philosophy

Chapter 9 examines the systems philosophy. Encouraged by Kuhn (1974), the systems philosophy emerged from 'systems thinking'. General systems theory developed originally from viewing organizations as complex machines, later as open systems, and most recently as entities capable of self-organization (Gharajedaghi, 1999). In Chapter 9, we show how the systems philosophy looks beyond simplistic causal views of management and the constituent parts of organizations. Systems thinking developed on the basis of treating organizations holistically. Thus, organizations were seen as the sum of their parts rather than as a collection of reducible units. Systems theorists appreciate that any change instigates numerous and sometimes multiplied effects across an organization. As a consequence, successful change management must be introduced across the entire range of organizational units and sub-systems.

Systems comprise sets of objects or entities that interrelate with each other to form a whole. Examples include the physical, mental or natural (Laszlo, 1972). Change under the systems lens assumes that organizations operate rationally and in the absence of political pressures. Systemic analysis subsequently encourages 'best-practice' remedies incorporating the prescribed steps and linear solutions of the rationalist philosophy. The claim for a set of best practices commanding universal applicability may, however, underestimate powerful external technological, workforce or societal changes. Systems analyses treat organizations as interrelated parts that depend upon the whole working in tandem to function properly (Hatch, 1997). Organizational change succeeds when interventions are levelled throughout the entire system because the interrelationships between parts mean that everything is affected. Every system possesses two diverse forces: differentiation and integration. Organizational systems differentiate into specialist functions (in the human body, for example, the lungs, heart and liver), like divisions and departments for human resources, finance, operations and marketing. At the same time, coordination between the differentiated parts requires integration, through organizational features such as strategy, hierarchy, supervision, and rules, procedures and policies. Every system requires differentiation to identify its sub-parts, and integration to ensure that the system does not break down into separate elements.

The systems philosophy also gives rise to less prescriptive change theories; where planned, rational change surrenders to chaos and complexity, based on the premise that change involves an unmanageable tension between control and chaos (Druhl, Langstaff and Monson, 2001). Chaos and complexity theories from the natural sciences explain the 'chaordic' (chaos-order) change observed in organizations (Sullivan, 2004). Complexity offers a fresh perspective on change, moving from an obsession with the planned and systematic towards comfort with the messy and non-linear (Shaw, 1997; Styhre, 2002). Like several of the change philosophies we examine in this text, the further one ventures from the rational, the more troublesome prescriptive change becomes. Of course, the rational philosophy does not accommodate the messiness of real-world organizational change very well.

The Cultural Philosophy

Chapter 10 considers the cultural philosophy, which owes its emergence to anthropology where the concept of organizational culture emerged before its translation to an organizational setting (Pettigrew, 1979). The cultural philosophy prepares managers to see change as a normal response to the environment (Morgan, 1997). Most employees, including managers, construct set ways of thinking about how things should be done. As a result, imposing change means fighting entrenched sets of values and beliefs shared by organizational members. Like all the philosophies we address, culture encourages a multiplicity of interpretations leading to fragmentation, controversy and inconsistency. The most cited cultural researcher, Schein (1979; 1984; 1993; 1997), takes a psycho-dynamic view where culture reflects the most basic human assumptions and beliefs shared by organization members. Schein considers organizational members' behaviours and spoken attitudes to be the artefacts and symbolic representations of deeper unconscious assumptions.

Like the psychological philosophy, the cultural philosophy recognizes individual choice, but pays much more attention to explicit and implicit encouragement, facilitation, manipulation and coercion towards desired behaviours (Heracleous, 2001). The two philosophies take contrasting positions on the most important unit of change to manage. The psychological philosophy favours individual experiences of change whereas the cultural perspective encompasses collective experiences as well, along with the shared values that guide them.

Organizational culture change could not be more difficult. Change managers must, first, be accurate in diagnosing the values that permeate an organization (which are likely to be hidden) and, second, change them without undermining the tacit behavioural fabric holding the organization together. Unsuccessful attempts to change culture invariably lead to conflicting organizational goals and members' values, which in turn stimulate an unworkable level of competing values and goals. The greatest danger lies in changing the superficial symbols, like removing the chief executive officer's privileged car-parking space, while failing to deal with deeper values, like poor communication between hierarchical levels. The cultural philosophy assumes that change will be long and agonizing (Schein, 1985). Unlike natural cultural change, which is an ongoing reflection of incremental adjustments to the environment, imposed cultural change is internally driven. In Chapter 10, we note the power of cultural interpretations, but lament the difficulty of their implementation. Difficulty, however, defines any serious attempt at change.

The Critical Philosophy

In Chapter 11, we use the term critical philosophy to present political and postmodern theories of change. Originating from the sociological work of Marx and Hegel, political theory views change as the clash of ideologies or belief systems (Morgan, 1997). Humans generate conflict and conflict propels change during the clash of opposing political forces. When one group with a political agenda gradually gains power, they challenge the status quo towards their own interests. Conflict means that change revolves around activities such as bargaining, consciousness raising, persuasion, influence and power, and social movements (Bolman and Deal, 1991).

Organizations work as political systems governed by formal and tacit rules, and day-to-day activity necessitates 'wheeling and dealing', or finding ways to make the system work to one's advantage. As political entities, organizations comprise countless coalitions working together both overtly and secretly to secure power. Change transpires when power transfers from one coalition to another and a new combination of ideologies and values gains ascendancy. The political philosophy focuses attention on how things get done through political activity. Because coalitions compete for power and influence, conflict performs an essential, albeit unfortunate role. Change managers should cultivate robust coalitions and secure the resources that confer power, such as leadership positions and financial support. The political philosophy reveals the presence of clashing ideological forces in organizations, as well as the inescapable futility of change without power. However, the political philosophy overlooks the impetus for change from power bases external to organizations. It is dangerous to get distracted by internal political adversaries when in reality the real competition lies outside an organization.

Postmodernism introduces a second theory within the critical philosophy. Postmodern theories challenge singular or grand theories about organizational change, taking instead a socially constructed view of reality (Buchanan, 2003). The postmodern change approach finds comfort with ephemerality, fragmentation, discontinuity and chaos, but also seeks action rationally (White and Jacques, 1995). The postmodern concept accompanied the transition from industrial to post-industrial society; from manufacturing and materials to knowledge and information. Its change analysis finds words, symbols and signs in organizations divorced from direct, real-world experience (Fox, 1996). Postmodernism juxtaposes the old and new, engaged through change tactics emphasizing diffusion, empowerment, flexibility, trust and market responsiveness (Clegg, 1992).

Postmodern change takes reality as multiplicitous, fragmented and contradictory. The rational approach to change will fail because a single, unified vision defies communication. Deeply suspicious of the rational imposition of change, postmodernists, like their sibling political theorists, study power and its application closely. Power is exploitative and manipulative, and can come in many, often concealed, forms. For example, knowledge commands power, a central tenet of the 'discourse' analysis influenced by Foucault (1980). The study of discourse within organizations aims to stimulate new ways of understanding how hidden forms of power create change (Alvesson and Karreman, 2000; Hardy, Palmer and Phillips, 2000). Discursive analysis takes a textured view about the relationship between language and social phenomena (Grant, Hardy, Oswick and Putman, 2004; Clegg, Courpasson and Phillips, 2006). It recognizes that language (what is written, spoken, heard and read) creates social worlds. Furthermore, discourse analysis holds 'reality' itself as a social construction. The world appears different to everyone; there is no universal way to see organizations. For most practically minded managers, however, the postmodern philosophy ventures too far into the abstract. Relinquishing power and knowledge, while partly consistent with the psychological philosophy, remains implausible when power instantiates change. In addition, unlike the systems perspective that encourages best-practice thinking, a postmodern analysis precludes overarching theories. Since no universal 'truth' or reality exists about anything, the mere attempt to categorize postmodernism into a philosophy of change could be flawed.

The Innovation Philosophy

Change through innovation, as described in Chapter 12, can be seen as a consequence of rapid changes in globalization and technology that have forced organizations to adapt to unprecedented competition. While most organizations appreciate the importance of innovation, there remains a gap when it comes to implementing innovation in a practical, sustainable sense. As this chapter explains, according to the innovation philosophy, the long-term growth of organizations is directly tied to their continual production of innovative products and services, at the same time as they deliver their existing products and services smoothly. That is, organizations must be strategically adaptable as much as they are operationally efficient. Organizations embracing the innovation paradigm strive to be flexible, agile, intuitive, imaginative, resilient and creative in order to stimulate new ideas in the face of increasing complexity and turbulence.

A first step towards innovation-driven change involves developing a contextualized understanding of creativity by identifying the benefits of innovation for each specific work team. As there is a need for 'risk experimentation', it requires considerable nerve from leaders as they must push through failure by building momentum and speed through new learning. To theorists, innovation can be a gradual process of smaller incremental changes, rather than through one creative idea of transformational proportion. However, potential shortfalls in an organization's innovation capabilities may detract from its capacity to implement ideas rapidly and cost-effectively. In addition to outlining the process for fast prototyping new products, the chapter culminates by examining the recent popularity of user-centric innovation. Such 'design thinking' has become popular in change management efforts as it helps organizations focus on a user's experience of a new product rather than on the organization's perception of the product's functional utility. However, as with all aspects of the innovation philosophy, success delivers a significant dividend, but comes with implementation challenges, and therefore high risk.

The Dualities Philosophy

Chapter 13 details the dualities philosophy. Neither simple nor predictable, and unlikely to conform to any formula, it argues for a different way of thinking; a new sort of philosophy that captures the complexities and dynamics of organizations and connects the accumulated knowledge, skills, experience and learning of their constituents. While rationality sings to logic, without counterweight, it lulls unsuspecting managers into a scientific, clinical resolve that overrides the emotive and fluid experience of change (Badham and Garrety, 2003). As the biological philosophy reminds us, organizations live and breathe, alive in a dynamic brawl for survival and success, and continually chang*ing*, organiz*ing* and strategiz*ing*.

As the strategy-as-practice trend in strategic management proposes, managers 'do strategy', or strategize (Hendry, 2000; Johnson, Melin and Whittington, 2003; Whittington, 1996; 2003). Chandlerian (Chandler, 1962) thinking once demanded a sharp distinction between organization and strategy as two separate properties (Whittington and Melin, 2003). However intuitive dividing arrow from target seems, strategy and organization collide (Whittington and Melin, 2003), becoming a single, entangled duality. For example, introducing a change to organizing structure really constitutes a strategic change (Paroutis and Pettigrew, 2005). We brandish terms such as organizing and strategizing in a new way. As verbs, the terms embody continuous rather than static change processes. Organization and strategy transform into organizing and strategizing, where the latter two embrace dynamic change. Strategizing and organizing abandon linear, sequential thinking about change in exchange for iterative and reciprocal action (Dijksterhuis, Van den Bosch and Volberda, 2003).

The challenge lies in encouraging both change and stability. The philosophy seeks to explain how organizations manage the dynamic relationship between competing philosophies of change, all of which offer a piece of the puzzle. In Chapter 12 we introduce examples where numerous change philosophies can work together. For example, 'modular' and 'ambidextrous' theories embrace the duality philosophy where competing approaches work together, and difference, or heterogeneity, outperforms bland rationality. A dualities philosophy also sponsors 'ambidextrous' (O'Reilly and Tushman, 2004) approaches to change, where networks sit with hierarchies, horizontal integration with performance accountability, and centralized strategy making with decentralized operations (Sanchez-Runde and Pettigrew, 2003). Diversity within an enterprise enhances flexibility (Stark, 2001). Although institutional pressures

Table 1.1   *Philosophies of organizational change summary*

Philosophy	Nature of change	Strengths	Weaknesses	Management focus
Theories	Hypotheses-based	Conceptual generalizations	Abstract and inflexible	Interventions based on theoretical assumptions and predictions
Rational	Directed and planned	Emphasizes controllable aspects of change	Ignores or sidesteps external pressures	Strategy and planning
Biological	Ecological; organic and evolutionary	Explains life cycle, fitness and survival	Heavy emphasis on environment; fails to explain deliberate change	Environmental positioning; find industrial niche; progression of organization through the life cycle; growth
Models	Based on a predefined framework focusing on 'the' key to change	Linear, orderly and prescriptive application	Relies on match between the model and the organization's change problems	Stepwise application for all organizations
Institutional	Determined by institutional (industry) pressure	Reveals importance of industrial environment and pressures to conform	Lack of focus on need to find advantages against competitors	Industrial standards and benchmarks
Resource	Determined by access to resources	Shows need to acquire resources to initiate and sustain change	Assumes change cannot occur without internal resources	Acquiring and discharging resources; core competencies, particularly of management
Psychological	Embedded in minds of those affected	Highlights individual impacts and stresses of change	Can ignore systemic aspects of change in organization (e.g. structure)	Managing employee transitions and psychological adjustments to change

Philosophy	Nature of change	Strengths	Weaknesses	Management focus
Systems	Interconnected with all aspects of organization	Avoids the trap of assuming that change is contained in one organizational area	Complexities of keeping track of relationships between organizational variables	Change to all constituents and components of an organization
Cultural	Determined by entrenched values	Shows importance of collective beliefs and norms	Difficult to address directly	'Deep' rites, rituals and values
Critical	Conflict- and power-based Rejection of universal rules	Demonstrates role of power and clashing ideology Juxtaposition of old and new explains contradictions in change	Assumes all change manifests through power Can result in no approach to change at all and confusion about nature of change	Acquiring power bases Flexibility, empowerment and responsiveness
Innovation	Change represents the capacity to do new things	Link to performance is direct; encourages organizational renewal	Change needed may not revolve around products or processes	Focus on development of innovations, testing, scaling and renewing
Dualities	Dynamic, complex	Abandons the need for balance in favour of performance	Demands an understanding of all philosophies	Managing the tensions between change and continuity

drive conformity, it also stifles diversity and diminishes adaptability (Smith and Graetz, 2006). In fact, the more an organization holds historically valuable resources, the less likely it will adapt (Kraatz and Zajac, 2001). What appear as efficient strategies that copy institutional norms in fact restrict options for change (March, 1991). For example, diversity can lead to innovation while also offering greater scope for redeploying firm capabilities towards new targets (Teece, Pisano and Shuen, 2004). Table 1.1 summarizes the philosophies we present.

CONCLUSION

We opened this chapter by highlighting how short-sighted, uni-dimensional approaches to change assume everything can be controlled through direct intervention. In subsequently outlining the philosophies examined in forthcoming chapters, we maintain that all prominent change philosophies, despite strengths and weaknesses, hold unassailable assumptions and enforce rigid limitations. At one end of the spectrum, formal, rational logic articulates action and maps structure and process against strategy. Yet, the rational philosophy hides the inconsistency and ambiguity that are part and parcel of real-world organizational change. At the other end, the critical philosophy gives preference to power, but falls victim to ambiguity when faced with the Monday-morning issue of practical change. Most managers acknowledge that power creates inequality, yet fear anarchy more than disparity. Equally one-eyed, the psychological philosophy prioritizes personal experiences of change. While a proven method to bolster workplace satisfaction, channelling employees into a cohesive group all mindful of a common goal remains elusive. Occupying the middle ground, cultural theorists offer one answer, as do systems advocates, while resources, external pressures and evolutionary adaptations all vie for position in the crammed minds of change managers. Meanwhile, innovation theorists advise that the key to change is to find new ways to deliver products, while cognitive theorists suggest that products cannot be changed until beliefs are.

In addition to those theorists who occupy some form of middle ground, there are also those who want two different philosophies at once. Duality theorists, for example, propose adding to, or reconfiguring, strategic components in a modular way (Baldwin and Clark, 2000; Galunic and Eisenhardt, 2001; Schilling and Steensma, 2001; Pil and Cohen, 2006). Modular systems possess elements, or modules, that independently perform distinctive functions. As modules evolve autonomously, they do not impinge on the system's overall structure, yet maintain greater resilience during environmental flux than traditional structures (Pil and Cohen, 2006). Teams serve as a simple example of a structural 'module' that operates flexibly without the normal constraints of heavy structures. Modularity delivers flexibility when used to selectively replace hierarchical structures with looser forms, and draws upon methods such as sub-contracting, alternative work arrangements, alliances and teams. Greater heterogeneity within an organization means more options become available (Smith and Graetz, 2006). Here, change managers should accept, even encourage, the pursuit of both change and control.

As Cameron and Quinn (1988, p. 14) argued over 30 years ago, traditional models and theories of organization assume consistency and symmetry, yet studies suggest that 'disconfirmation, contradiction and nonlinearity are inherent in all organizations'. Traditional philosophies depict change as a programmatic, step-by-step process with a clear beginning, middle and end, largely choreographed by a charismatic leader. Change means establishing a new order using bold strategies, structures, systems, processes, innovation, power, culture and often fresh employees who personify the new ideology. However, a focus on re-establishing order and stability sidesteps real-world change. Most philosophies in isolation ignore the complexities as well as the contradictory nature of organizations, not to mention the diverse range of people working in them. Such a linear, simplistic approach inevitably leads to one-dimensional thinking and, as Eisenhardt pointed out (2000, p. 704), 'simplicity is elegant but often untrue'. Ambiguity and uncertainty may look unappealing, but they also feel authentic. Rather than recognizing multiple imperatives of change, philosophies tend to concentrate on one extreme at the expense of another (e.g. accountability versus freedom, leadership versus empowerment, economic versus social goals, etc.). The dilemma of change comes with the dilemma of an 'either-or world' (Davis and Lawrence, 1977). But change management, as our philosophies reveal, resists the simplicity of a binary choice.

Although this book is not designed to be a guide to change, or to offer the 'best' philosophy, it seems hard to ignore the possibility that organizational change must contend with complementary but disjoint structures (Swanson, 1991). A multi-philosophy approach recognizes the centrality of contradiction in organizations, and that it is not only possible but also desirable for two 'inconsistent states' to exist simultaneously (Eisenhardt, 2000, p. 703). We argue against concentrating on one theoretical or philosophical perspective at the expense of competing perspectives. As Hedberg, Nystrom and Starbuck (1976) argued in a seminal work on change that remains surprisingly current, a degree of ambiguity, contradiction and incoherence provides the catalyst for organizational learning, diversity and renewal. Their plea asks organizations to establish change systems that can cope with ambiguity, ambivalence and contradiction, where the tensions between continuity and change collide. For example: nurturing innovation alongside rigorous financial and operational systems; fostering empowerment through strong and supportive leadership; addressing the impact of economic realities on social goals; and balancing formalized, central controls and policies with decentralized decision making. We are not the first with the desire to understand organizational change as competing tensions that transgress a single philosophical position (Lewis, 2000).

By outlining the 12 philosophies that comprise the chapters in this text, we introduced distinctive assumptions each hold about change, its nature and best solution. We also suggest that managing change necessitates different modes of engagement and a rich understanding of context (Morgan, 1997). In Chapter 2 we provide a framework for understanding how change philosophies and theories come into existence, evolve, become marginalized and eventually die.

REFERENCES

Alvesson, Mats and D. Karreman (2000), 'Varieties of discourse: On the study of organizations through discourse analysis', *Human Relations*, **53** (9), 1125–49.

Badham, Richard and K. Garrety (2003), 'Living in the blender of change: The carnival of control in a culture of culture', *Tamara: Journal of Critical Postmodern Organization Science*, **2** (4), 22–38.

Baldwin, Charliss Y. and K. B. Clark (2000), *Design Rules: The Power of Modularity*, Cambridge, MA: MIT Press.

Bolman, Lee G. and T. E. Deal (1991), *Reframing Organizations: Artistry, Choice, and Leadership*, San Francisco, CA: Jossey-Bass.

Brandt, Eva Norrman, Ann-Christine Andersson and Sofia Kjellstrom (2019), 'The future trip: A story of transformational change', *Journal of Organizational Change Management*, **32** (7), 669–86.

Bridges, William (1980), *Transitions*, Reading, MA: Addison-Wesley.

Bridges, William (1992), *Managing Transitions: Making the Most of Change*, Reading, MA: Addison-Wesley.

Brown, Robin and Alham Abuatiq (2020), 'Resilience as a strategy to survive organizational change', *Nursing Management*, **51** (2), 16–21.

Buchanan, David A. (2003), 'Getting the story straight: Illusions and delusions in the organizational change process', *Tamara: Journal of Critical Postmodern Organization Science*, **2** (4), 7–21.

Burke, Wyatt W. (2002), *Organizational Change: Theory and Practice*, Thousand Oaks, CA: Sage.

Cameron, Esther and Mike Green (2019), *Making Sense of Change Management: A Complete Guide to the Models, Tools and Techniques of Organizational Change*, London: Kogan Page.

Cameron, Kim S. and R. E. Quinn (1988), 'Organizational paradox and transformation', in Robert E. Quinn and K. S. Cameron (eds), *Paradox and Transformation: Toward a Theory of Change in Organization and Management*, Cambridge, MA: Ballinger Publishing, pp. 1–18.

Carnall, Colin A. (1995), *Managing Change in Organizations*, 2nd edition, London: Prentice Hall.

Carr, David, K., K. J. Hard and W. J. Trahant (1996), *Managing the Change Process: A Field Book for Change Agents, Consultants, Team Leaders, and Reengineering Managers*, New York: McGraw-Hill.

Chakravarthy, Balaji S. (1982), 'Adaptation: A promising metaphor for strategic management', *Academy of Management Review*, **7** (1), 35–44.

Chandler, Alfred D., Jr. (1962), *Strategy and Structure: Chapters in the History of the American Industrial Enterprise*, Cambridge, MA: MIT Press.

Child, John (1972), 'Organizational structure, environment and performance: The role of strategic choice', *Sociology*, **6**, 1–22.

Clegg, Stewart R. (1992), 'Postmodern management?', *Journal of Organizational Change Management*, **5** (2), 31–49.

Clegg, Stewart R., D. Courpasson and N. Phillips (2006), *Power and Organizations*, London: Sage.

Collins, David (1998), *Organizational Change: Sociological Perspectives*, London: Routledge.

Collins, David (2003), 'Guest editor's introduction: Re-imagining change', *Tamara: Journal of Critical Postmodern Organization Science*, **2** (4), iv–xi.

Connor, Tom (2002), 'The resource-based view of strategy and its value to practising managers', *Strategic Change*, **11** (6), 307–16.

Davis, Stanley M. and P. R. Lawrence (1977), *Matrix*, Reading, MA: Addison-Wesley.

Dehler, G. E. and M. A. Welsh (1994), 'Spirituality and organizational transformation', *Journal of Managerial Psychology*, **9** (6), 17–26.

Dijksterhuis, Marjolijn, S., F. A. J. Van den Bosch and H. W. Volberda (2003), 'A cognitive perspective on strategizing/organizing', in Andrew M. Pettigrew, R. Whittington, L. Melin, C. Sanchez-Runde, F. A. J. Van Den Bosch, W. Ruigrok and T. Numagami (eds), *Innovative Forms of Organizing*, London: Sage.

DiMaggio, Paul J. and W. W. Powell (1983), 'The iron cage revisited: Institutional isomorphism and collective rationality in organizational fields', *American Sociological Review*, **48**, 147–60.

DiMaggio, Paul J. and W. W. Powell (eds) (1991), *The New Institutionalism in Organizational Analysis*, Chicago, IL: University of Chicago Press.

Druhl, Kai, J. Langstaff and N. Monson (2001), 'Towards a synthesis of the classical and quantum paradigms: Vedic science as a holistic approach to organizational change', *Journal of Organizational Change Management*, **14** (4), 379–407.

Eisenhardt, Kathleen M. (2000), 'Paradox, spirals, ambivalence: The new language of change and pluralism', *Academy of Management Review*, **25** (4), 703–5.

Evans, Paul A. and Y. Doz (1992), 'Dualities: A paradigm for human resource and organizational development in complex multinationals', in Vladimir N. Pucik, N. M. Tichy and C. K. Barnett (eds), *Globalizing Management: Creating and Leading the Competitive Organization*, New York: Wiley, pp. 85–106.

Evans, T. R. (2020), 'Improving evidence quality for organisational change management through open science', *Journal of Organizational Change Management*. DOI: 10.1108/JOCM-05-2019-0127.

Foucault, Michel (1980), *Power/Knowledge*, New York: Pantheon.

Fox, Charles J. (1996), 'Reinventing government as postmodern symbolic politics', *Public Administration Review*, **56** (3), 256–62.

Galunic, Charles D. I. and K. M. Eisenhardt (2001), 'Architectural innovation and modular corporate forms', *Academy of Management Journal*, **44** (6), 1229–49.

Gharajedaghi, Jamshid (1999), *Systems Thinking: Managing Chaos and Complexity: A Platform for Designing Business Architecture*, Boston, MA: Butterworth-Heinemann.

Giddens, Anthony (1981), *A Contemporary Critique of Historical Materialism*, London: Macmillan.

Grant, David, C. Hardy, C. Oswick and L. L. Putman (2004), *The Sage Handbook of Organizational Discourse*, London: Sage.

Grant, Robert M. (1991), *Contemporary Strategy Analysis: Concepts, Techniques, Applications*, Cambridge, MA: Basil Blackwell.

Green, Carolyn and K. Ruhleder (1995), 'Globalization, borderless worlds, and the tower of Babel: Metaphors gone awry', *Journal of Organizational Change Management*, **8** (4), 55–68.

Greenwood, Royston and C. R. Hinings (1996), 'Understanding radical organizational change: Bringing together the old and the new institutionalism', *Academy of Management*, **21** (4), 1022–54.

Grey, Christopher (2003), 'The fetish of change', *Tamara, Journal of Critical Postmodern Organization Science*, **2** (2), 1–19.

Grundy, Tony (1993), *Implementing Strategic Change*, London: Kogan Page.

Hammer, Michael and J. Champy (1993), *Reengineering the Corporation*, London: Nicholas Brealey.

Hannan, Michael T. and J. Freeman (1977), 'The population ecology of organizations', *American Journal of Sociology*, **82** (5), 929–64.

Hardy, Cynthia, I. Palmer and N. Phillips (2000), 'Discourse as a strategic resource', *Human Relations*, **53** (9), 1227–48.

Hatch, Mary J. (1997), *Organization Theory: Modern, Symbolic and Postmodern Perspectives*, Oxford: Oxford University Press.

Hedberg, Bo L. T., P. C. Nystrom and W. H. Starbuck (1976), 'Camping on seesaws: Prescriptions for a self designing organization', *Administrative Science Quarterly*, **21**, 41–65.

Hendry, John (2000), 'Strategic decision making: Discourse and strategy as social practice', *Journal of Management Studies*, **37** (7), 955–77.

Heracleous, Loizos (2001), 'An ethnographic study of culture in the context of organizational change', *Journal of Applied Behavioral Science*, **37** (4), 426–46.

Huber, George P. and W. H. Glick (1995), *Organizational Change and Redesign: Ideas and Insights for Improving Performance*, New York: Oxford University Press.

Iacovini, J. (1993), 'The human side of organization change', *Training and Development Journal*, **47**, 65–8.

Jick, Todd D. (1990), 'Note on the recipients of change', Boston, MA: *Harvard Business School Press*, 9-491-039.

Johnson, Gerry, L. Melin and R. Whittington (2003), 'Micro strategy and strategizing: Towards an activity-based view', *Journal of Management Studies*, **40** (1), 3–22.

Kanter, Rosabeth M., B. A. Stein and T. D. Jick (1992), *The Challenge of Organizational Change*, New York: Free Press.

Kezar, Adrianna J. (2000), *Understanding and Facilitating Change in Higher Education in the 21st Century*, Washington, DC: Jossey-Bass.

Kotter, John P. (1990), 'What leaders really do', *Harvard Business Review*, May–June, 103–11.

Kotter, John P. (1995), 'Leading change: Why transformation efforts fail', *Harvard Business Review*, May–June, 59–67.

Kraatz, Matthew S. and E. J. Zajac (2001), 'How organizational resources affect strategic change and performance in turbulent environments: Theory and evidence', *Organization Science*, **12** (5), 632–57.

Kübler-Ross, Elisabeth (1973), *On Death and Dying*, London: Tavistock Publications.

Kuhn, Alfred (1974), *The Logic of Social Systems*, San Francisco, CA: Jossey-Bass.

Laszlo, Ervin (1972), *The Systems View of the World: The Natural Philosophy of the New Developments in the Sciences*, New York: G. Braziller.

Leana, Carrie R. and B. Barry (2000), 'Stability and change as simultaneous experiences in organizational life', *Academy of Management Review*, **25** (4), 753–9.

Levy, Amir and U. Merry (1986), *Organizational Transformation: Approaches, Strategies, Theories*, New York: Praeger.

Lewin, Arie Y. and H. W. Volberda (1999), 'Prolegomena on coevolution: A framework for research on strategy and new organizational forms', *Organization Science*, **10** (5), 519–34.

Lewin, Kurt (1947), 'Frontiers in group dynamics: Concept, method and reality in social sciences: Social equilibria and social change', *Human Relations*, **1** (1), 5–41.

Lewis, Marianne W. (2000), 'Exploring paradox: Toward a more comprehensive guide', *Academy of Management Review*, **25** (4), 760–76.

March, James G. (1991), 'Exploration and exploitation in organizational learning', *Organization Science*, **2** (1), 71–87.

McKelvey, Bill and H. Aldrich (1983), 'Populations, natural selection and applied organizational science', *Administrative Science Quarterly*, **28**, 101–28.

Meyer, Heinz-Deiter and B. Rowan (2006), *The New Institutionalism in Education*, Albany, NY: SUNY Press.

Morgan, Gareth (1997), *Images of Organization*, Newbury Park, CA: Sage.

Mukherji, Ananda and J. Mukherji (1998), 'Structuring organizations for the future: Analyzing and managing change', *Management Decision*, **36** (4), 265–73.

Nadler, David A. and M. L. Tushman (1989), 'Organizational frame bending: Principles for managing reorientation', *Academy of Management Executive*, **3** (3), 194–204.

Nohria, N. and J. D. Berkley (1994), 'The virtual organization: Bureaucracy, technology, and the implosion of control', in C. Heckscher and A. Donnellon (eds), *The Post-Bureaucratic Organization: New Perspectives on Organizational Change*, Thousand Oaks, CA: Sage, pp. 108–28.

O'Reilly, Charles A. and M. L. Tushman (2004), 'The ambidextrous organization', *Harvard Business Review*, April, 74–81.

Oreg, Shaul and Yair Berson (2019), 'Leaders' impact on organizational change: Bridging theoretical and methodological chasms', *Academy of Management Annals*, **13** (1), 272–307.

Oztel, Hulya and O. Hinz (2001), 'Changing organizations with metaphors', *Learning Organization*, **8** (4), 153–8.

Palmer, Ian and R. Dunford (1996), 'Conflicting uses of metaphors: Reconceptualizing their use in the field of organizational change', *Academy of Management Review*, **21** (3), 691–717.

Paroutis, Sotiros E. and A. Pettigrew (2005), 'Studying strategizing and organizing within the multibusiness firm: Capabilities, evidence and learning', *Organization Studies*, Summer Workshop on 'Theorizing Process in Organizational Research', Santorini.

Pettigrew, Andrew M. (1979), 'On studying organizational cultures', *Administrative Science Quarterly*, **24** (4), 570–81.

Pfeffer, Jeffery and G. R. Salancik (1978), *The External Control of Organizations: A Resource Dependence Perspective*, New York: Harper and Row.

Pil, Frits K. and S. K. Cohen (2006), 'Modularity: Implications for imitation, innovation, and sustained advantage', *Academy of Management Review*, **31** (4), 995–1011.

Raeder, Sabine and Mariya V. Bokova (2019), 'Committed to change? Human resource management practices and attitudes towards organizational change', *Open Psychology*, **1** (1), 345–58.

Sanchez-Runde, C. J. and A. M. Pettigrew (2003), 'Managing dualities', in A. M. Pettigrew, R. Whittington, L. Melin, C. Sanchez-Runde, F. A. J. Van den Bosch, W. Ruigrok and T. Numagami (eds), *Innovative Forms of Organising*, London: Sage, pp. 243–50.

Schein, Edgar H. (1979), *Organizational Culture and Leadership*, San Francisco, CA: Jossey-Bass.

Schein, Edgar H. (1984), *Coming to a New Awareness of Organizational Culture*, San Francisco, CA: Jossey-Bass.

Schein, Edgar H. (1985), *Organizational Culture and Leadership: A Dynamic View*, San Francisco, CA: Jossey-Bass.

Schein, Edgar H. (1993), 'On dialogue, culture and organizational learning', *Organizational Dynamics*, **20**, 40–51.

Schein, Edgar H. (1997), *Organizational Culture and Leadership*, 3rd edition, San Francisco, CA: Jossey-Bass.

Schilling, Melissa A. and H. K. Steensma (2001), 'The use of modular organizational forms: An industry-level analysis', *Academy of Management Journal*, **44** (6), 1149–68.

Shaw, Patricia (1997), 'Intervening in the shadow: Consulting from a complexity perspective', *Journal of Organizational Change Management*, **10** (3), 235–50.

Smith, Aaron and F. Graetz (2006), 'Organizing dualities and strategizing for change', *Strategic Change*, **15**, 231–9.

Smith, Kenwyn K. and D. N. Berg (1987), *Paradoxes of Group Life: Understanding Conflict, Paralysis, and Movement in Group Dynamics*, San Francisco, CA: Jossey-Bass.

Stark, David (2001), 'Ambiguous assets for uncertain environments: Heterarchy in postsocialist firms', in Paul DiMaggio (ed.), *The Twenty-First Century Firm: Changing Economic Organization in International Perspective*, Princeton, NJ: Princeton University Press, pp. 69–104.

Stuart, Roger (1995), 'The research context and change triggers', *Personnel Review*, **24** (2), 3–88.

Styhre, Alexander (2002), 'Non-linear change in organizations: Organization change management informed', *Leadership and Organization Development Journal*, **23** (6), 343–51.

Sullivan, Terence J. (2004), 'The viability of using various system theories to describe systems of organizations', *Journal of Organizational Change Management*, **10** (3), 235–50.

Swanson, Don R. (1991), 'Complementary structures in disjoint science literatures', Paper presented at the Proceedings of the 14th Annual International *ACM/SIGIR Conference*, New York.

Teece, David J., G. Pisano and A. Shuen (2004), 'Dynamic capabilities and strategic management', in Michael L. Tushman and P. Anderson (eds), *Managing Strategic Innovation and Change*, 2nd edition, Oxford: Oxford University Press, pp. 308–32.

Tetenbaum, T. (1998), 'Shifting paradigms: From Newton to chaos', *Organizational Dynamics*, **26** (4), 21–32.

Van de Ven, Andrew H. and M. S. Poole (1995), 'Explaining development and change in organizations', *Academy of Management Review*, **20** (3), 510–40.

Waeger, Daniel and Klaus Weber (2019), 'Institutional complexity and organizational change: An open polity perspective,' *Academy of Management Review*, **44** (2), 336–59.

Weiner, Bryan J., Alecia S. Clary, Stacey L. Klaman, Kea Turner and Amir Alishahi-Tabriz (2020), 'Organizational readiness for change: What we know, what we think we know, and what we need to know', in B. Albers, A. Shlonsky and R. Mildonpp (eds), *Implementation Science 3.0*, Champaign, IL: Springer, pp. 101–44.

White, Robert F. and R. Jacques (1995), 'Operationalizing the postmodernity construct for efficient organizational change management', *Journal of Organizational Change Management*, **8** (2), 45–71.

Whittington, Richard (1996), 'Strategy as practice', *Long Range Planning*, **29** (5), 731–5.

Whittington, Richard (2003), 'The work of strategizing and organizing: For a practice perspective', *Strategic Organization*, **1** (1), 119–27.

Whittington, Richard and L. Melin (2003), 'The challenge of organizing/strategizing', in Andrew M. Pettigrew, R. Whittington, L. Melin, C. Sanchez-Runde, F. A. J. Van Den Bosch, W. Ruigrok and T. Numagami (eds), *Innovative Forms of Organizing*, London: Sage, pp. 35–48.

Witt, Ulrich (2004), 'The evolutionary perspective on organizational change and the theory of the firm', *3rd ETE workshop*, Sophia-Antipolis, 29–30 January, 1–23.

Wood, Thomaz (2002), 'Spectacular metaphors: From theatre to cinema', *Journal of Organizational Change Management*, **15** (1), 11–20.

2. The theory philosophy: 'changing theories'

INTRODUCTION

In this second edition, we introduce 12 different philosophies of change, each one a different lens for viewing paradigms, assumptions, premises, predictions, hypotheses and theories about the way organizational change works. Philosophies of change reveal the deep suppositions made about organizations and the ways change operates within and around them. In the following chapters, we examine each of the philosophies, detailing and critiquing their methods for change. Philosophies express their methods for change through inferences about the most effective way to introduce change. We use the term 'theories' as a sweeping label for these inferences (Saatsi, 2019).

The purpose of this chapter is to offer a guide to the kind of theories that lie at the heart of philosophical positions. Rather than focusing on the specific content that should direct change, this chapter revolves around a commitment to theoretical explanations and predictions for change. The theory philosophy places emphasis not only on the importance of change theories, but also on how theories change over time, whether refined, updated, expanded or replaced. In this respect, it is unlike most of the other philosophies that connect successful change to a certain approach or theory. Instead, the theory philosophy assumes that change can be explained by developing or connecting theories over time to deliver an increasingly comprehensive, overarching theory of change. As a result, the theory philosophy is less a practical approach to change than an orientation towards understanding change. However, we think it essential to describe how theories, as the fundamental building block to change philosophies, can themselves change over time. Moreover, whether tacit or overt, a change agent's perspectives and assumptions towards how to improve their philosophical approach will affect their change efforts, especially in terms of how successive change programmes are refined. For example, a practitioner might recognize that their latest programme inadequately addressed a certain aspect of the change response. A successive attempt might consequently try to connect different philosophical approaches or their constituent theories in order to fill the gap. The result tends to be a new, hybrid philosophical approach to change, like for example, the systems philosophy with a psychological philosophy supplement. At the very least, if theories aim to describe empirical observations, then a changing reality in which organizations operate should demand new theories to be developed (Shadnam, 2020).

THEORIES AND CHANGE

Theories refer to statements that express relationships among concepts (Greenwald, Pratkanis, Leippe and Baumgardner, 1986). A statement represents a theory to the extent that it offers law-like statements, or hypotheses, that make measurable predictions about change (Kuipers, 2007). Strong theories use hypotheses to present more accurate predictions with greater precision than weak theories. All philosophies possess at least one major theory. Those theories born from the same philosophy share some basic assumptions, but at some point differ on key predictions and explanations. But, they may be seen as siblings. However, the theories emanating from competing philosophies seldom agree on basic premises, although we show throughout this text where common intersections lie. We also identify how and why organizational change philosophies and their theories changed over time.

In this chapter we explore the ways in which organizational change theories can be influenced by fundamental assumptions about the nature of theoretical relations. By theoretical or 'theoretic' relations, we mean the relationships between theories from the same and from different philosophies. We draw on concepts such as reductionism, unification and paradigms, demonstrating that different perspectives can lead to different expectations about the way a change theory works. Theory development does not necessarily mean that in the end only one organizational change theory will remain with universal recognition as the pre-eminent explanation. However, if ultimate unity seems implausible, more fragmentation seems unwelcome. We propose that the most fruitful activity might be to seek more prosaic, localized relations between theories and evidence, or what has been termed pragmatic empirical theorizing (Shepherd and Suddaby, 2017). Here, new empirical observations can be used to trigger revisions to the underpinning theory in a kind of 'hypothesizing after the results are known'.

In calculating the nature of theoretic relations in organizational change, we pose some sticky questions: What is the goal of theory development in organization change? Is it: unification, where one theory explains everything about change; the replacement or updating of older theories with newer, more comprehensive theories; the establishment of interconnections between theories at sites of promising explanation; or simply developing as many different ways of explaining change as possible? Each question exposes long-standing and contentious arguments, leading to different answers. We place some structure around the questions and answers by introducing the principles of theoretic context and theoretic continuity, explained in the next section. A discussion of the key challenges and controversies in theory development follow, leading to the final section, which presents a theoretic typology; a map of approaches to theoretical 'progress' found in organizational change theory.

Our approach here focuses on theoretic relations, or the relationships between theories, as a bridge towards understanding how organizational change theories take new forms over time. Some management scholars believe that organization and change theories have seen little radical transformation over the past few decades (Davis, 2010; 2015). It has also been suggested that most theorizing has been around the edges, or has lacked innovation, and even imagination (Alvesson and Sandberg, 2013). Without getting into the debate, radical new theories of change have not taken the organizational theory world by storm over the last decade (Fiol, 2010), and certainly not since the first edition of this text. The absence of significant change might be a side effect of different perspectives about what constitutes 'theorizing' (Lounsbury and Beckman, 2015). Work can seek to both extend existing theory as well as formulate new theoretical mechanisms (Corbett, Cornelissen, Delios and Harley, 2014). Or, indeed, both at the same time. However philosophical transitions come about, theoretical change of some kind resides at the centre of future philosophical advances (Okhuysen and Bonardi, 2011). Multiple-lens and intertheory explanations are likely to become more important (Okhuysen and Bonardi, 2011). Generational transitions in organizational leadership and research might accompany significant shifts in theoretical focus too. To paraphrase a controversial proposition, perhaps organizational change theory advances one funeral at a time (Azoulay, Fons-Rosen and Graff Zivin, 2019).

THEORETIC RELATIONS: THEORETIC CONTEXT AND THEORETIC CONTINUITY

In examining theoretic relations—the relationships between theories—we utilize the principles of theoretic context and theoretic continuity. Theoretic context refers to the level at which a theory operates: either at a single analytical level (intra-level) or at multiple levels (interlevel). For example, an intra-level theory explains a change aspect at a single level of analysis, such as the organizational level. However, some change theories take an interlevel perspective using multiple levels of analysis, such as organizational behaviour *and* individual psychology. Theoretic context demonstrates that the more levels of analysis, the more complicated the theory. But, the more levels of analysis a theory relates to, the greater its explanatory power.

Theoretic continuity refers to how a new theory relates to existing theories. Little or no continuity between two theories trying to explain the same aspect of change means that the new theory will replace outright an existing theory with little or no overlap between the two. For example, as we will discuss in Chapter 4, within the biological philosophy, the punctuated equilibrium theory sought to replace the evolutionary theory of change. Both occurred at the same theoretical context—an intra-level context—but with little continuity between the two, as each employed different assumptions about how organizational change comes about. Low continuity between theories leads to revolutionary theory change. The less continuity between two theories, the more radical the outcome. In contrast, a high level of continuity means that a new theory may build upon, or correct the deficiencies of, an existing theory. High continuity between theories leads to incremental theory change. For example, in Chapter 6 we observe that 'new institutionalism' builds upon early institutionalism. A high correspondence or continuity between the two exists.

To summarize, context specifies the level at which a theory operates. Higher-level theories deal with more complex variables because they try to explain change across different analytical levels: the individual, group, organizational and industrial levels of change. Lower-level theories involve less complexity and fewer variables, tackling a single change phenomenon. For example, postmodern theory interrogates change at every level, while organizational development focuses on the individual psychological experience of change. Continuity describes the relationship between theories explaining the same change phenomenon. Intra-level describes the relations between theories at the same level. Interlevel theory describes the relations between theories at multiple levels. The philosophical debate underpinning context concerns reductionism/unification, while paradigm incommensurability reflects continuity. Both are explored next.

THE PARADIGM PROBLEM

A paradigm may be understood as the established or commonly accepted perspective of a discipline. Kuhn (1970) thought that although paradigms define and restrict the activity of disciplines, they flex to accommodate changing data. He argued that research suppresses novelty by attempting 'to force nature into the conceptual boxes supplied by professional education' (p. 5). However, a shift in shared assumptions occurs when problems and anomalies begin to emerge which a paradigm's theories cannot resolve. A challenge to existing tradition of theoretical doctrine eventually leads to its subversion.

Kuhn labelled paradigmatic shifts 'scientific revolutions'. A theoretical paradigm, like the life-cycle approach to change, holds sway for a period while researchers try to make sense of all the available evidence through the lens of that paradigm. However, over time the weight of evidence suggests some gaps exist. If the flaws become too great, the paradigm collapses in favour of a competing paradigm waiting in the wings, and a revolution takes place.

According to Kuhn, paradigms supply their own answers. For example, if a paradigm insists that organizations should be viewed as organisms, then the answers it will find about change will draw on life-cycle notions of birth, growth, maturity, decline and death. Kuhn even claimed that rival paradigms cannot share their meanings due to incommensurability. Competing paradigms—and in our case change philosophies—suffer from fatal incompatibilities.

The incommensurability thesis predicts that the content of competing paradigms (and theories) cannot be compared due to the absence of common ground (Sankey, 1997). Every paradigm employs a unique language and labelling system that cannot be translated (Feyerabend, 1981). Even though two rival change philosophies might use the same terms, they each hold different connotations, both obviously and subtly. In the same way that love commands a unique meaning to each partner in a couple, the incommensurability thesis holds that concepts cannot be transferred from one paradigm, or change theory, to another.

The diametric approach denies the existence of paradigms altogether. Paradigm incommensurability deserves outright dismissal in the study of organizations (Wilmott, 1993). Westwood and Clegg (2003) not only rejected the possibility of competing paradigms, but evaluated the entire incommensurability debate to be misplaced and redundant. At best, incommensurability draws upon differential values and beliefs, perhaps leading to troublesome but surmountable vocabulary translations. At worst, incommensurability engineers an illusion and encourages the spurious view that paradigms cannot co-exist or coalesce. Some management theorists believe that all organizational theories function in pre-paradigmatic states, unready to escalate into a scientific form (McKelvey, 1999).

A multi-paradigm (or multi-philosophy) approach to change management would need to either clearly account for, or reject, incommensurability (Hassard, 1988). For example, the presence and utilization of several paradigms might provide some advantages (Burrell, 1999), including numerous avenues for theoretical exploration. Numerous theories to explain the same form of change could prove helpful.

On the other hand, theoretical diversity and paradigm plurality could undermine the study of change. After all, how can any field claim legitimacy if it generates a multiplicity of competing theories (Westwood and Clegg, 2003)? Surely this only increases the confusion around change and provides no guidance to managers. For example, Pfeffer (1993) argued that organizational studies generate numerous paradigms which encourage fragmentation and discourage progress. Scientific status becomes compromised without a coherent and consensual paradigm and associated theories.

One solution imposes a dominant paradigm. For example, no fan of 'paradigm proliferation', Donaldson (1995) argued for concentration around theories of consensus. He remarked that the goal of theoretical unification should be held by all persons of good 'scientific conscience'. One theory describing organizational change will prevail because it has proven correct. As this text exemplifies, however, no single change paradigm, philosophy or theory enjoys a consensus. We think it unlikely to occur soon, either.

Incommensurability demands locating the 'right' paradigm for change management. If, however, theorists have overstated the importance of paradigms, or incommensurability does not exist at all, then no barrier obstructs theory integration or interconnection. A better theory arrives by bolting different change interpretations together.

Serious implications arise from the two views on paradigms. For the former, change theorists would be best advised to work on single, promising paradigms until they achieve consensus or succumb to a revolutionary replacement. For the latter, anything goes, including bolstering one theory with strands from others, although this might become challenging in the event that innumerable competing theories offer explanations. The degree to which change knowledge can be unified remains contentious.

THE REDUCTIONISM–UNIFICATION PROBLEM

What analytical level best explains change? And, should change be explained at all levels by a single philosophy or theory? For example, must a theory account for individual, group, organizational and industrial change? Moreover, can higher-level, complex theories be reduced to lower-level, basic theories?

The most fundamental theoretic relationship explains higher-level phenomena through lower-level phenomena (McCauley, 1998). The lower the level of theoretic reduction, the more powerful the theory. Consider, for example, the psychological philosophy's (Chapter 8) change theory 'organizational development', which explains change at the organizational level by reducing it to individual psychology. But individual psychology remains complex, so a theory attempting even greater levels of reduction would reveal the elements of individual psychological responses to change. In turn, psychology reduces to elements such as fear and uncertainty, which would also require theoretical explanations. The sub-disciplines of organizational theory formed over time as each reduced area became a unit of analysis in its own right. Equally, some scholars ventured in the other direction by theorizing about more complex phenomena such as industrial or social change.

The methodological approach employed to differentiate between analytical levels also affects the nature of reduction. Different methodologies employ characteristic tools, approaches and standards, resulting in theories at different explanatory levels. For example, psychologists studying change use survey instruments whereas sociologists use ethnographic observation. Even though both may be interested in the same aspect of change, their approaches automatically determine the analytical level at which their theories will operate. The level of the theory, whether high or low, reflects the target of analyses where measurements and generalizations occur (Klein, Dansereau and Hall, 1994; Rousseau, 1985). The level defines the properties of a theory's construct and the relationships between the constructs (Klein et al., 1994).

Some social scientists argue that complex systems like organizations cannot be fully explained by their components alone. Yet, reductionism holds a prominent place in organizational change methods as researchers attempt to strip away higher-level ideas in order to identify more basic commonalities. Reductionists assume that despite the diversity of organizations and their change circumstances, all change looks the same when examined at its lowest level. To understand why reductionism remains popular, we need to revisit some important historical developments.

By the early part of the twentieth century, empiricism, also known as logical positivism, had established a foothold first in Europe and then in the United States. Its proponents advocated an observational approach to research based on logic, where theories were derived from careful analysis of a phenomenon. The logical positivists pursued unity of knowledge through reductionism. Their idea of unity demanded that more complex phenomena be explained or validated by less complex phenomena. Big concepts reduce to a string of small concepts (Carnap, 1934). For change, reductionists maintain that we need to drill down deeper and deeper.

The debate about reductionism remains lively. The opposing view of bottom-up theory development, or emergentism (Wilson, 2001), counters the legitimacy of reductionist approaches. Change phenomena interconnect, but not necessarily in the mechanical ways that reductionism presumes. As the complexity theory lobby insists (see Chapter 9), the whole exceeds the sum of its parts. At the very least, they contend, the whole is different to the sum of its parts. However, a major problem lies in identifying what the whole consists of. After all, where does an organizational change theory start and stop? For example, individuals can also belong to multiple groups within an organization, muddying the analysis (Drazin, Glynn and Kazanjian, 1999) and making it difficult to attribute perceptions and behaviour to specific groups. Moreover, the levels themselves may be variable and subject to influence and change. Independent individuals may drift together to form groups allied to common views or causes (Dansereau, Yammarino and Kohles, 1999). Similar examples of organizational effects from individual activity may be seen (Waldman and Yammarino, 1999). Establishing connections remains less problematic than making complete reductions.

DYNAMIC AND MULTI-LEVEL THEORIES

Change theories describe a dynamic and complex phenomenon. For this reason, some change concepts like the life-cycle model appeal readily to intuition. However, organizations defy general classification, their unique properties encouraging competing change philosophies to form. As reductionism shows, the more levels of explanation a theory offers, the more complex it must become. Multi-level theories present compelling solutions because they incorporate previously unrelated explanations.

Klein, Tosi and Cannella (1999) considered the benefits of multi-level theory development. They defined multi-level theories as those spanning numerous levels of organizational behaviour and performance, describing combinations of individuals, dyads, teams, businesses, corporations and industries. Multi-level theories bridge the micro–macro divide by integrating the micro focus on individuals and groups with the macro focus on organizations and industries, providing a richer, more comprehensive portrait of organizational life: 'Thus, multi-level theory building fosters much needed synthesis and synergy within ... connect the dots, making explicit the links between constructs previously unlinked within the organizational literature' (Klein et al., 1999, p. 243). Integration assumes that different change theories can intersect or seamlessly meld. For example, individuals may be described psychologically, organizations from a social perspective and industries in economic terms. Researchers labour towards a common framework that unites these disciplinary interpretations under one overarching theoretical roof. Reductionists see theory unification as inevitable, just a matter of time and knowledge. But it means overcoming a number of substantial barriers (Klein et al., 1999; Yammarino and Dansereau, 2009).

First, multi-level theories inevitably traverse disciplines, invoking parent disciplines such as psychology, anthropology, political science or economics. But in the end, one philosophical or disciplinary tradition tends to adopt the parent role. Second, the agendas, interests, values and preferences of researchers present contradictions and tensions. As we argue throughout this text, each change philosophy demands a novel methodological and conceptual attitude towards research. In the same way that someone learning another language translates and thinks in their indigenous language, change theorists and practitioners cling to their comfortable worldviews. Forging transitions between two theories from different philosophies demands practice and energy. Third, the chasm between theoretical complexity and practical oversimplification can sometimes seem unbreachable. A good multi-level theory must subtly explain sophisticated relationships yet still present lucid and succinct practical guidance. A powerful multi-level change theory should be capable of saying something useful about industries *and* individuals using only a handful of principles. Fourth, researchers can be discouraged by a lack of peer appreciation as multi-level change theories cannot please any one philosophical faction. Finally, multi-level change research suffers from the collection and analysis complications of multi-level data, which are notoriously difficult to bring together.

IRREDUCIBILITY

While less contention surrounds attempts at making connections between levels, one view holds that trying to unify philosophies and theories wastes time (Kitcher, 1999). Organizations cannot be depicted as theory hierarchies emanating from basic, general principles that can reduce higher-level theories. Some forms of knowledge, like the social sciences, do not convert into collections of axiomatic laws. Devising a comprehensive change theory fully explaining all of its nuances necessitates inventorying every possible kind of change. This might eventually be possible, but it might also demand an even more complex repository of every possible kind of human response to organizational circumstances.

Another argument against change theory unity proposes that some branches of knowledge employ concepts that cannot be reduced. Consider, for example, the cultural philosophy (Chapter 10), which treats organizations as cultures precisely because cultures can be more easily understood. However, organizations are not *literally* cultures. When researchers dissect parts of organizations, they hope to reveal insights about the whole. For those committed to anti-unity, organizations represent the only genuine analytical unit.

A final argument suggests that while reductions can occur from higher-level to lower-level theories, the derivation would not necessarily prove explanatory. For example, some change theorists believe that although useful, the psychological change philosophy (Chapter 8) cannot explain organizational change. Just because organizations constitute individuals, explaining individual change does not equal explaining organizational change. Besides, what if organizations thwart intelligible explanations (Dupré, 1993)? Perhaps the explosion of change philosophies exposes a disorderly organizational world where knowledge cannot be pieced together into a grand, unified synthesis. The absence of a unified change theory may not reflect intellectual or methodological limitations. Rather, the disunity of change knowledge mirrors the disunity of the organizational world.

The most extreme kind of anti-unification rejects the use of a single philosophical or paradigmatic approach to examine change. New hypotheses should not have to be consistent with accepted theories. Feyerabend (1975), for example, maintained that hypotheses contradicting well-established theories lead to new kinds of evidence. And, if a few contradictory hypotheses look helpful, then lots of them must be even better. Thus, Feyerabend considered theory proliferation advantageous. Moreover, if we want more theories, then we do not want unity because a uniform approach to change curtails theoretical free agency. Lots of different change philosophies auger well for the future. Amidst all these different approaches, somehow, someone will, sooner or later, stumble across something pivotal.

Perhaps organizations adhere to complementary but disjointed structures (Swanson, 1991). Complementary refers to the relationship between two separate theories, which when combined, yield new insights that had previously been overlooked. Disjointed, however, implies that the theories cannot be integrated or unified. Complementary but disjointed philosophies or theories contain important new inferences about change, but do so through interconnections rather than unifications. The most fruitful activity might be to seek more prosaic, localized relations between philosophies (Wylie, 2000).

Whether all change theories will eventually be consumed or replaced by a single, unified theory goes to the heart of assumptions about theory itself and the nature of the way knowledge can be determined. Organizations might look different when viewed through a critical (Chapter 11) compared to a rational (Chapter 3) lens, but often the differences that come through the tint prove useful to understanding change. Just because change is complex does not mean that it cannot be better understood. However, rather than an orderly march towards theory unification, we think that the path will be bumpy. Progress in understanding change means coming to terms with the lessons from numerous philosophies and their messy interconnections. In the following section we show how different views on context and continuity can reveal a change theory's underpinning assumptions.

A TYPOLOGY OF INTERTHEORETIC PERSPECTIVES

On the basis of intertheoretic context and intertheoretic continuity, the typology in Figure 2.1 can be constructed. It depicts four categories of theoretic relations, or four different kinds of fundamental assumptions about the way theories can develop and relate to each other.

Theoretic continuity			
		Low	High
Theoretic context	Intra-level theory (same level theory replacement over time)	*Theoretic revolution* • New theory eliminates the old theory • Paradigmatic change • E.g. linear relationships replaced by non-linear complex systems Major assumption: paradigmatic incommensurability means that different theories compete to explain a given phenomenon at the same level, but do not interact Discontinuous at the same level	*Theoretic evolution* • New theory updates or corrects old theory • Increasing comprehensiveness of theories over time • Recent theories are used as useful guidelines, but eventually get replaced or rendered obsolete • E.g. Maslow's Hierarchy slowly subsumed by more sophisticated theories of motivation Major assumption: eventual unity of knowledge within theoretical level occurs as the best theory increases its comprehensiveness Continuous at the same level
	Interlevel theory (different level theories at the same time)	*Theoretic pluralism* • Multiple and disparate explanations of phenomena • Inter-disciplinary excursions are heuristic approaches to discovery • E.g. psychology and sociology offer different explanations of the same organizational phenomena Major assumption: theoretical connections are at best loose heuristics There are numerous useful theories for every phenomenon Discontinuous and at different levels	*Theoretic connections* • Different theoretic perspectives intersect irrespective of the levels • Possible theoretic interconnection but constrained within disciplinary boundaries • E.g. social-psychological explanations of organizational phenomena Major assumption: connections can be made between levels and represent intersections Reduction and unification can occur but it will not necessarily lead to the elimination of higher-level theories Continuous at different levels

Figure 2.1　　　*Intertheoretic alternatives*

Theoretic Pluralism

The bottom-left quadrant of Figure 2.1 represents theoretical development
with low continuity and low context, and assumes that a new theory offers
little connection to its predecessor. New theories do not update, correct or
enhance existing theories. Rather, they replace, subvert and/or compete.
Moreover, theories cannot be expected to bridge contexts or analytical levels.
No relationship can exist between theories operating at different levels,
like a change theory that focuses on social factors and one that emphasizes
psychological variables. Adopting theoretic pluralism means assuming the
presence of a complex, heterogeneous world that requires a complex, heterogeneous description. And, both might just be irreducible. Theories exist alone
with no connections to others and cannot be broken down into smaller parts.
Proponents of theories with 'pluralistic' assumptions argue that human factors
in change make it too difficult to conceive a single and generalizable theory
of change. Pluralists predict that more rather than fewer theories will arrive
over time because multiple and disparate explanations of change make theory
proliferation inevitable. For example, pluralists draw from diverse sources in
a form of bricolage rather than incremental evolutions or outright replacements
of theory (Boxenbaum and Rouleau, 2011). They can also advocate conceptual
blending (Cornelissen and Durand, 2012) where theoretical explanations can
be melded together.

At best, theories work as heuristics; rules of thumb to discovery and understanding. A theory accompanies every useful angle on change. Theoretical
development occurs at multiple levels concomitantly, but can do no more than
offer unconnected explanations of the same change phenomenon. Little continuity between alternative theories makes them incommensurate.

Theoretic pluralism means that no one best way to secure knowledge about
change exists. To some, acknowledging such a limitation undermines scientific inquiry as a privileged form of knowledge (White and Jacques, 1995).
Pluralists think that we all see organizational change quite differently and that
we are all correct. For example, in describing the divide between rationalism
and pluralism, Jones and Bohm (2004, p. 1) commented that the difference
'is not something which the managerialists fail to see while the critics see
it clearly ... deluded by the strange suggestion that they might actually be
talking about the same thing'. In brief, we all see organization differently.
Change can be studied from innumerable perspectives, all of which legitimately help. Organizational change cannot be summarized under a single
homogeneous perspective, but instead should be viewed in terms of dynamic
interdependence, encoded with layers and embedded with sub-discourses
(Westwood and Clegg, 2003). Any change theory that describes the dynamic,
multiple discourse inherent in the world needs fluidity. An example may be

found with Lewis and Grimes (1999), who argued for multiple paradigms in studying organizations. However, critics claim that pluralism falls into the trap of relativism, where any explanation can be made legitimate without a mechanism for determining whether some are better explanations than others (Reed, 1999). Despite the intuitive appeal that all change theories offer something useful, their contributions vary considerably. While we agree that different theories may be essential in explaining all levels of change, we do not agree that they can never connect.

Theoretic Connections

Theoretic connections assume that intersections can be found between adjacent theories. Reductions and unifications can occur, but will at most only deliver the partial replacement of previous theories. Complex systems possess relationships and interactions between interconnected parts. Novel connections reveal new insights and make familiar phenomena look different. Theories connect at different levels by accommodating each other through local integration (around a common problem or phenomenon). Sometimes locally integrated theories become known as interfield theories because they show relationships between theories in different fields (Østreng, 2006), like a social-psychological theory of change.

Theories from different organizational change philosophies become connected in one of three ways. First, 'heuristic dependence' shows where the theories and/or methods of one philosophy may be used to guide the generation of new hypotheses in another. For example, political theories can make psychological predictions. Second, 'confirmational dependence' occurs where the methods and/or data from one field confirms hypotheses in another field. For example, through different methods, both institutional theory and resource dependency theory conclude that industrial composition affects organizational change. Correspondence suggests that both philosophies might be on to something important about the way organizational change works. Third, 'methodological integration' arises when methods cohere to assess common hypotheses and data. For example, discourse analysis in postmodern theories emerged in response to the perceived failure of conventional approaches.

Theoretic Revolution

The third quadrant, theoretic revolution, proposes that theories get exchanged wholesale at the same analytical level. New replaces old outright because the former offers superior predictions and explanations than the latter. However, the new theory becomes incompatible—or incommensurate—with the old explanation because it employs different assumptions or paradigms. Although well worn, the arguments surrounding paradigms continue unreconciled in organization studies. If incommensurability exists between organizational change philosophies, in terms of language, research methods and analytical tenets, then we should be observing an explosion of change theories. The theoretic revolution mindset also presumes that there are innumerable as yet unconceived theories potentially waiting in the wings to replace inferior existing theories (Rowbottom, 2019). In contrast, the evolutionary replacement of theories reflects paradigm commensurability, described next as theoretic evolution.

Theoretic Evolution

Under theoretic evolution, the best theories get better, becoming more comprehensive through incremental and evolutionary updating, correction and consolidation. One common evolutionary approach involves attempting to replicate important findings from earlier studies. Despite its intuitive appeal, replication in organizational science occurs infrequently (Tsang and Kwan, 1999). Nevertheless, evolutionary assumptions spring up commonly within change philosophies that work within a single analytical level. A theory evolves over time, becomes more comprehensive, makes more predictions and generates greater insight. For example, institutional theory gave rise to new versions over time, which added to rather than replaced the original version.

CONCLUSION

This chapter outlined the theories philosophy, which advocates that organizational change should be guided by theoretical architecture. It subsequently provided a structure for understanding how change theories change. We introduced several assumptions which influence theoretical relations including reductionism, unification and paradigms. Different perspectives on each can lead to different expectations about the way a change theory will develop, and what role it will play in explaining and prescribing change interventions. Theoretical unification is an illusion for some and merely troublesome in practice for others (Clegg, 1990). Also, most change scholars and practitioners like borrowing from a variety of philosophies, and few do so indiscriminately (Watson, 1997). Rather than concentrating on one theoretical or philosophical perspective at the expense of the rest, we argue that the nexus between multiple philosophical perspectives presents the best opportunities. Different lenses lead to a richer understanding of change situations and previously overlooked approaches (Lewis, 2000; Morgan, 1997). A multi-philosophy approach recognizes tension in organizations, and that 'inconsistent states' exist simultaneously (Eisenhardt, 2000). Theories do not have to become more unified in order to make a valuable contribution to change knowledge. In fact, instead of holistic theory unification where all change philosophies become subsumed by a single, overarching philosophy, the most fruitful approach seeks localized relations between philosophies. Interventions conforming to a single change philosophy suffer from inflexibility. It is also possible that we need to reconsider the conditions for theory revisions and entertain hybrid definitions of 'progress', such as accounting for more interplay between the accumulation of information and predictive explanation (Goebel, 2019); that is, avoiding a trade-off between knowledge and understanding.

REFERENCES

Alvesson, M. and J. Sandberg (2013), 'Has management studies lost its way? Ideas for more imaginative and innovative research', *Journal of Management Studies*, **50**, 128–52.

Azoulay, P., C. Fons-Rosen and J. S. Graff Zivin (2019), 'Does science advance one funeral at a time?', *American Economic Review*, **109** (8), 2889–920.

Boxenbaum, E. and L. Rouleau (2011), 'New knowledge products as bricolage: Metaphors and scripts in organizational theory', *Academy of Management Review*, **36**, 272–96.

Burrell, Gibson (1999), 'Normal science, paradigms, metaphors, discourses and genealogies of analysis', in Stewart R. Clegg and C. Hardy (eds), *Studying Organization: Theory and Method*, London: Sage, pp. 388–404.

Carnap, Rudolf (1934), *The Unity of Science*, trans. M. Black, London: Kegan Paul.

Clegg, Stewart R. (1990), *Modern Organizations: Organization Studies in the Postmodern World*, London: Sage.

Corbett, Andrew, J. Cornelissen, A. Delios and B. Harley (2014), 'Variety, novelty, and perceptions of scholarship in research on management and organizations: An appeal for ambidextrous scholarship', *Journal of Management Studies*, **51**, 3–18.

Cornelissen, J. and R. Durand (2012), 'More than just novelty: Conceptual blending and causality', *Academy of Management Review*, **37**, 152–4.

Dansereau, Fred, F. J. Yammarino and J. Kohles (1999), 'Multiple levels of analysis from a longitudinal perspective: Some implications for theory building', *Academy of Management Review*, **24** (2), 346–57.

Davis, G. F. (2010), 'Do theories of organizations progress?', *Organizational Research Methods*, **13**, 690–709.

Davis, G. F. (2015), 'Celebrating organization theory: The after-party', *Journal of Management Studies*, **52**, 309–19.

Donaldson, Lex (1995), *American Anti-Management Theories of Organization: A Critique of Paradigm Proliferation*, New York: Cambridge University Press.

Drazin, Robert, M. A. Glynn and R. K. Kazanjian (1999), 'Multilevel theorising about creativity in organizations: A sensemaking perspective', *Academy of Management Review*, **24** (2), 286–307.

Dupré, John (1993), *The Disorder of Things: Metaphysical Foundations of the Disunity of Science*, Cambridge, MA: Harvard University Press.

Eisenhardt, Kathleen M. (2000), 'Paradox, spirals, ambivalence: The new language of change and pluralism', *Academy of Management Review*, **25** (4), 703–5.

Feyerabend, Paul (1975), 'How to defend society against science', *Radical Philosophy*, **11** (1), 3–9.

Feyerabend, Paul (1981), *Realism, Rationalism and Scientific Method: Philosophical Papers*, Cambridge: Cambridge University Press.

Fiol, C. M. (2010), 'Acting as if we were new', *Journal of Management Inquiry*, **19**, 85–8.

Goebel, C. (2019), 'A hybrid account of scientific progress: Finding middle ground between the epistemic and the noetic accounts', *Kriterion*, **33** (3), 1–16.

Greenwald, Anthony G., A. R. Pratkanis, M. R. Leippe and M. H. Baumgardner (1986), 'Under what conditions does theory obstruct research progress?', *Psychological Review*, **93** (2), 216–29.

Hassard, John (1988), 'Overcoming hermeticism in organization theory: An alternative to paradigm incommensurability', *Human Relations*, **41** (3), 247–59.

Jones, Campbell and S. Bohm (2004), 'Handle with care', *Ephemera*, **4** (1), 1–6.

Kitcher, Philip (1999), 'Unification as a regulative ideal', *Perspectives on Science*, **7** (3), 337–48.

Klein, Katherine J., F. Dansereau and R. J. Hall (1994), 'Level issues in theory development, data collection, and analysis', *Academy of Management Review*, **19** (2), 195–229.

Klein, Katherine J., H. Tosi and A. A. Cannella (1999), 'Multilevel theory building: Benefits, barriers, and new developments', *Academy of Management Review*, **24** (2), 243–8.

Kuhn, Thomas S. (1970), *The Structure of Scientific Revolutions*, 2nd edition, Chicago, IL: University of Chicago Press.

Kuipers, Theo A. F. (2007), 'Laws, theories, and research programs', in Theo A. F. Kuipers (ed.), *Handbook of the Philosophy of Science: General Philosophy of Science – Focal Issues*, Amsterdam: Elsevier, pp. 1–95.

Lewis, Marianne W. (2000), 'Exploring paradox: Toward a more comprehensive guide', *Academy of Management Review*, **25** (4), 760–76.

Lewis, Marianne W. and A. I. Grimes (1999), 'Metatriangulation: Building theory from multiple paradigms', *Academy of Management Review*, **24** (4), 672–90.

Lounsbury, M. and C. M. Beckman (2015), 'Celebrating organization theory', *Journal of Management Studies*, **52**, 288–308.

McCauley, Robert N. (1998), 'Levels of explanation and cognitive architectures', in William Bechtel and G. Graham (eds), *A Companion to Cognitive Science*, Oxford: Blackwell, pp. 611–24.

McKelvey, Bill (1999), 'Toward a Campbellian realist organization science', in Donald T. Campbell, J. A. C. Baum and B. McKelvey (eds), *Variations in Organization Science: In Honor of Donald T. Campbell*, Thousand Oaks, CA: Sage, pp. 383–411.

Morgan, G. (1997), *Images of Organization*, Thousand Oaks, CA: Sage.

Okhuysen, G. and J.-P. Bonardi (2011), 'Editors comments: The challenges of building theory by combining lenses', *Academy of Management Review*, **36**, 6–11.

Østreng, W. (2006), *Science without Boundaries: Interdisciplinarity in Science and Politics*. Lanham: Rowman and Littlefield.

Pfeffer, Jeffrey (1993), 'Barriers to the advance of organizational science: Paradigm development as a dependent variable', *Academy of Management Review*, **18** (4), 599–620.

Reed, Michael (1999), 'Organization theorizing: A historically contested terrain', in Stewart R. Clegg and C. Hardy (eds), *Studying Organization: Theory and Method*, London: Sage, pp. 25–50.

Rousseau, Denise M. (1985), 'Issues of level in organizational research: Multilevel and cross-level perspectives', in Larry L. Cummings and B. M. Staw (eds), *Research in Organizational Behavior*, Greenwich, CT: JAI Press.

Rowbottom, D. P. (2019), 'Extending the argument from unconceived alternatives: Observations, models, predictions, explanations, methods, instruments, experiments, and values', *Synthese*, **196** (10), 3947–59.

Saatsi, J. (2019), 'What is theoretical progress of science?', *Synthese*, **196** (2), 611–63.

Sankey, Howard (1997), 'Incommensurability: The current state of play', *Theoria*, **12** (3), 425–45.

Shadnam, M. (2020), 'New theories and organization research: From the eyes of change', *Journal of Organizational Change Management*, https://doi.org/10.1108/JOCM-07-2019-0209.

Shepherd, D. A. and R. Suddaby (2017), 'Theory building: A review and integration', *Journal of Management Review*, **43**, 59–86.

Swanson, Don R. (1991), 'Complementary structures in disjoint science literatures', Paper presented at the Proceedings of the 14th Annual International ACM/SIGIR Conference, New York.

Tsang, Eric W. K. and K. M. Kwan (1999), 'Replication and theory development in organizational science: A critical realist perspective', *Academy of Management Review*, **24** (4), 759–80.

Waldman, David A. and F. J. Yammarino (1999), 'CEO charismatic leadership: Levels of management and levels of analysis effects', *Academy of Management Review*, **24**, 266–85.

Watson, Tony J. (1997), 'Theorizing managerial work: A pragmatic pluralist approach to interdisciplinary research', *British Journal of Management*, **8** (1), 3–8.

Westwood, Robert I. and S. Clegg (2003), 'The discourse of organization studies: Dissensus, politics, and paradigms', in Robert I. Westwood and S. Clegg (eds), *Debating Organization*, Oxford: Blackwell.

White, Robert F. and R. Jacques (1995), 'Operationalizing the postmodernity construct for efficient organizational change management', *Journal of Organizational Change Management*, **8** (2), 45–71.

Wilmott, Hugh (1993), 'Breaking the paradigm mentality', *Organization Studies*, **14** (5), 681–719.

Wilson, Robert A. (2001), 'Philosophy', in Robert A. Wilson and F. C. Keil (eds), *The MIT Encyclopedia of the Cognitive Sciences*, Cambridge, MA: MIT Press.

Wylie, Alison (2000), 'Questions of evidence, legitimacy, and the (dis)unity of science', *American Antiquity*, **65** (2), 227–37.

Yammarino, Francis J. and F. Dansereau (2009), 'A new kind of organizational behaviour', in Francis J. Yammarino and F. Dansereau (eds), *Multi-Level Issues in Organizational Behavior and Leadership*, Champaign, IL: Wolfram Media, pp. 13–60.

3. The rational philosophy: 'changing plans'

INTRODUCTION

The impetus for change may be obvious or subtle, arriving in forms as varied as strategy failure, technological innovation, financial necessity, market variation, competitive pressure and political activity. The cause provides a context from which responses can be formulated. Change methods also reflect indirect and arbitrary factors such as the quality and strength of leadership, the time factor, resource availability, access to technical knowledge and existing systems. However, knowing what to change does not avert change failure. In fact, most leaders introduce change programmes with a clear appreciation for the problem, a strong commitment to its resolution, and a definitive path for intervention. Yet, the research suggests that more often than not, something still goes wrong. In this chapter we introduce the most prominent approach to change, the rational philosophy. At the centre of the rational philosophy is the presumption that strategy—and strategic theories—should drive change initiatives.

At the most basic level, change means altering or modifying something; a procedure, a policy, a capability or something simpler, and substituting an alternative in its place. Managing change requires a systematic approach that requires both organizational and individual involvement, and where formulating the change method falls to organizational leaders as the chief strategists (Adcroft, Willis and Hurst, 2008). There can be no separating change and strategy; their link is intractable and inevitable.

Determining which method of change to adopt presents an organization with a kind of multiple schizophrenia, like reading Machiavelli for the first time. Does one accept the ostensibly republican sentiment found in *The Discourses*, or should one adopt the counsel given to absolute rulers in *The Prince*? Each appears to contradict the other. In reality, Machiavelli gives the impression that he really did not mind how society achieved government so long as the result was a strong, capable, integrated whole underpinned by firm leadership. He advised that achieving change requires an assessment of the context, considering what worked in similar circumstances, and what failed. A modern

Machiavelli might acknowledge that while different organizations pursue different goals, the methods employed are immaterial provided the desired result arrives forcefully. Machiavelli's vision of effective change sidestepped political ideals and regulation. He emphasized management practicalities. What, he would have asked, will work under the available conditions? So too with organizational change; leaders must look at their organization's capabilities, consider what has worked before in other organizations and, ultimately, proceed towards their goals with vigour.

Machiavelli practised the rational change philosophy, viewing performance and success as a function of correct strategy. Jones' (2002, p. 325) advice exemplifies the rational philosophy: 'To be most effective, any type of restructuring must be clearly and explicitly aligned with a firm's business-level strategy in order to maximize the efficient and effective allocation of resources in pursuit of competitive advantage.' This chapter describes and analyses the rational change philosophy, a pre-eminent approach widely popular with researchers and practitioners that situates organizational leaders and leadership ability as the authority on change (Rosenbaum, More and Steane, 2018). We deconstruct its core assumptions and prescriptions for change before examining its strengths and weaknesses.

RATIONAL STRATEGY ASSUMPTIONS

From a rational philosophy perspective, the impetus for change holds less importance than the need for a coherent framework in which to manage the response. We do not suggest that rationalists think cause unimportant, just that the reaction should materialize through a change process. Confronted by a deteriorating bottom line, a loss of business, a change in technology or one of a hundred other possibilities, rationalists confront problems that previously seemed too difficult or too entrenched. Unfortunately, many organizations get bogged down in the minutia of how to come to grips with the need for change. Not until later, when the desperate scramble for organizational survival becomes all-consuming, do leaders begin the change process. By then, despite frantic and aggressive efforts, too little can be accomplished.

We label the most common philosophy governing change the 'rational' philosophy, although it may also be known as 'strategic change'. Despite the ubiquity with which the term gets thrown around, Chaharbaghi and Willis (1998) unearthed 54 different yet frequently wielded definitions of strategy. One influential definition depicts strategic change as a difference in the form, quality or state over time in an organization's alignment with its external environment (Van de Ven and Poole, 1995). Yet most change leaders scarcely have time for definitions when it comes to strategy. Strategy feels like great art in that we know it when we see it. The rational philosophy assumes that the final destination desired shapes change attempts in the same way that the top of a mountain defines the end of a climb. A rationalist approach requires an organization and its leaders to apply both logic and honesty to define a current position and then to determine precisely where it would like to be at the end of the change process. The difference between the two positions then dictates the requirements for change. While an oversimplification, the gap method characterizes rational change because the inspiration for action focuses on bridging the difference between the current and desired state. It has to do with decisions about the deployment of scarce resources within the boundaries of environmental circumstances in order to achieve objectives (Rajagopalan and Spreitzer, 1997). Planned organizational change should generate positive change in work performance (Robertson, Roberts and Porras, 1993).

Sometimes called teleological theories because the final destination represents its guiding logic, or planned change, the rational philosophy assumes that organizations behave with purposeful, adaptive proactivity (Kezar, 2000; Van de Ven and Poole, 1995). Change occurs because senior managers and other change agents deem it necessary, proceeding in a rational and linear fashion with leaders as the pivotal instigators and arbiters (Carnall, 1995; Carr, Hard and Trahant, 1996). Although now incorporating different leadership styles, the notion of leadership as a crucial determining factor in the implementation of planned organizational change remains underpinned by theoretical assumptions about the centrality of strategic change (Magsaysay and Hechanova, 2017).

So-called strategic choice theorists (e.g. Child, 1972; Smith and Berg, 1987) belong to the rational philosophy and maintain that managers wield the ultimate control of their organizations. Leaders introduce various processes, structures and products until they either reveal the most successful recipe or catastrophe strikes. Change management 'gurus' who profited during the boom years of the 1990s, such as Kotter (1995), Huber and Glick (1995) and Kanter, Stein and Jick (1992), and who each propose their own staged model of change interventions, employ a rational philosophy. They hold in common the view that successful change lies firmly in the hands of leaders, all of whom can benefit by introducing the steps advocated. Conversely, unsuccessful change must be due to managerial or leadership inadequacy. Advocates of strategic, teleological change approaches are now attempting to reconcile the need for flexibility and iterative leadership decision processes with early theory on prescriptive, predetermined change.

EARLY INSPIRATIONS

Change from a rational philosophy takes a managerial, interventionist approach. It emphasizes the manipulation of organizational parts by strategically aware leaders in response to environmental circumstances. In this respect, the rational approach has its earliest expression in military literature. Written in the sixth century BC, Sun Tzu's (1963) exposition of strategic insight remains popular today, available in at least a dozen forms edited specially for the contemporary leader, executive or business-person. Similarly, Von Clausewitz's (1976) principles of war, written shortly after Napoleon's campaigns, formed the basis of modern military strategy. Both books concentrate on careful competitor (enemy) analysis, strategy formulation and disciplined execution.

The term 'strategy' may be traced to military origins, originally used to reinforce the importance of imposing unfavourable fighting conditions upon an enemy. From its military legacy the rationalist mentality inherited a central place for the notion of an enemy, or in the case of organizations, competitors. Other military analogies flavour the rational philosophy as well, from its aggressive, combat-infused language to the tough, bend-to-will directives of leaders.

Early management theorists picked up on the notions of strategic positioning and began to write about organizations as rational systems, where an efficient transformation of inputs to outputs was the key priority (Scott, 1987). Around the turn of the twentieth century, Frederick Winslow Taylor started to flesh out the rational philosophy as he grappled with efficiency through 'scientific management'. Although his focus was on a systematic approach to the management of organizational activity, based largely on specialization, Taylor also pioneered a kind of management thinking where logic and rationality held precedence. To Taylor, all management could be optimized, almost perfected, with only the correct information and appropriate analysis. Later, Weber's theory of bureaucracy provided intellectual weight to the rational philosophy. Efficiency could be achieved through a fixed division of tasks, hierarchical supervision and detailed rules and regulations. The role of strategy had yet to be formalized but both Taylor and Weber paved the way for thinking about organizations as closed systems under the full control of powerful leaders. Such thinking remains obvious in organizational leaders today whose use of the rational philosophy uncovers a certainty about the cause and effect relations between strategic decisions and performance consequences.

When change emanates from the rational philosophy, it presumes the sequential, planned pursuit of optimal solutions to clear and well-understood problems (Ansoff, 1965; Mintzberg, 1990). Rational change managers believe that they optimize their organization's performance by finding the fit between a vision and the environment. In this respect, the rational philosophy relies on a conventional interpretation of strategy in that it reflects an alignment between organizational objectives, internal capabilities and environmental opportunities. Almost any change or strategy textbook will describe the strategic approach from vision to evaluation. One conventional model advocated by Okumus (2003) describes 11 discrete steps of organizational change from strategy development to outcomes. Repetitive sequences of goal formulation, implementation, evaluation and modification always feature as stalwarts.

Most rational models elaborate upon one of the first systematic approaches to change introduced by Lewin (1947). For him, the process of change required three steps beginning with an 'unfreezing' of current circumstances, followed by the change and then a final step of 'refreezing'. Numerous other stepwise systems enjoy popularity, exemplified by the eight-part process devised by Kotter (1995). Rosenbaum et al. (2018) identified 13 popular theories of planned organizational change, concluding that rationalist organizational change research has developed rather than revolutionized this original teleological approach. Most of these change initiatives give the strategy process a prominent place where variations on analysis, visioning and objective setting, environmental scans, strategy formulation and evaluation represent key activities.

Another influential conceptualization of the rational philosophy was provided by Robbins (1983). His seminal text on organizational theory (2007), described a model of planned organizational change. While Robbins concentrated on how to go about the change process, other models (Burke and Litwin, 1992) depict which organizational and external variables are subject to change. While unfair to suggest that these models do not attempt to accommodate the complexities of organizational change, they do present it in a rational fashion. Change can be controlled because everything in an organization should be subservient to the will, vision and action of executive leaders. Yet, the emerging reality is that, to a greater extent, middle-level managers and supervisors determine how change emerges (Van der Voet, 2014).

ASSESSING THE RATIONAL PHILOSOPHY

The rational change method offers a definitive solution by laying a prescriptive, logical process upon a confusing, complex problem. Its advantage comes from confidence. By presenting change as a linear phenomenon, resolution seems no further away than vision, analysis and implementation. Rational models follow a set pattern that resonates intuitively, but also enjoys an unparalleled, and sometimes blindly optimistic popularity. According to fashionable assumption, rational change produces the greatest impact in larger organizations that work through hierarchical management systems, and which require transformational change rather than subtle, progressive shifts. However, the evidence would suggest that change in an organization occurs through a series of lower team level and concurrent ongoing processes (Pollack and Pollack, 2015). The rationalist approach can, however, also lead to disaster unless change agents understand that no matter how logical, future action can rarely be clearly defined and calculated in advance. However, it does seem good advice to plan change.

An inability to determine the need for change until forced upon the organization surely represents a fundamental flaw in any change management approach. Insufficient time to plan, or the need to undertake planning on the run, presents a recipe for confusion in an approach that counts on causal certainty. As a result, limited planning and analyses undermine strategic change more than most other change methods. In fact, while organizations may benefit from clear direction, the evidence demonstrates that change can be instigated by innumerable forces, many of which operate externally.

Beneath the strategic change route lies a mass of information. Many large, corporate organizations choose this path and have even publicly detailed their actions in a direct step-by-step format, claiming success at least to some degree. Although a significant number might be correct in declaring their success, for others, success really only appears fleetingly. While the pattern for obtaining strategic change appeals to a prescriptive logic, many organizations move rapidly from prescriptive to rigid and unyielding. Excluding the neat, stepwise, transaction-based models declared by consulting authors as one-stop solutions, strategic change should not be immutably unwavering before it has even begun. Although rational, strategic change incorporates transparent and well-defined individual steps, where action within them depends upon organizational type, management leadership, urgency of change and type of change required, not to mention resource issues supporting change such as finance and staff. The dawning reality for change leaders is that stepwise strategies are not an easy approach after all, and require the ability to work individually with multiple stakeholders at different points in the process (Pollack and Pollack, 2015). Most importantly, undergoing the strategic route exposes organizations to failure through poor leadership. A dangerously common problem, chief executive officers (CEOs) or change management teams can push in the wrong direction or without the support of the corporate elite or a critical mass of general staff. Enthusiasm for change can cool sharply if obstacles appear early in the change process, and if not handled expeditiously. Once failure becomes accepted as the normal consequence of change, upholding the trend seems inevitable. In addition, the potential for open rebellion to the change process (as we discuss in Chapters 8 and 11) remains embedded in all methods. This aligns with growing calls for rationalist approaches towards organizational change to adopt an ethical, utilitarian leadership approach, rather than a dictatorial stance (Burnes, Hughes and By, 2018).

A striking and appealing feature of the rational philosophy resides with its assurance that mapping out change can be done in advance. For change agents seeking control in uncertain contexts, the rational philosophy offers a compelling and risk-averse framework. Providing each step in the change process can be clearly formulated prior to attempting any intervention, and if important members of staff offer galvanizing support, change can be introduced with some measure of confidence (ill-founded or not). We will not argue that the strategic change path alone ensures a greater degree of success than other modes of change, but its importance to organizational change management remains prominent.

LEVELS, MAPS AND STEPS

Rational philosophical approaches seldom differentiate between levels of change. Change occurs throughout an organization, from the largest departments to the smallest business units, although little consideration goes to the individual experience of change. Nor does the rational philosophy say much about the environment. For the most part, strategic change considers the external environment to be an unmanageable, objectively determined, unassailable entity that cannot be influenced by organizational activity. This is clear by the focus on individual actions and the lack of comparative research concerning how different organizational leaders deal with the same external factors (Kuipers et al., 2014). Better to combat environmental pressures with careful strategic responses, the best of which reveal themselves after sufficient analysis. Further, watchful consideration should be given to organizational capabilities and deficiencies as well as those of competitors.

The assumed demarcation between an organization and its environment leads to a contradiction. Rationalist change strands organizations, isolating them from the environment. Yet, organizations remain subject to environmental influences. Strategic change gets bogged down in complexity because it demands the control of both an organization and the environment in which it operates (Adcroft et al., 2008). Strategy therefore involves correct assessments of overt organizational features like structure and finance, along with intangible characteristics such as culture and knowledge. These operate within the fluid and uncertain landscape of competitors, suppliers, customers and shareholders, as well as broader changes in the economic, political, technological and social environment. The rational approach to change wagers that divergent and unknowable environmental forces present opportunities for those leaders who choose the correct strategy from the innumerable alternatives. No problem cannot be navigated by an energized strategist who knows how to read the internal and environmental signs, and react accordingly.

To understand strategic change, a leader must understand the underlying pattern for change, which requires a procession through defined steps. While consistent in basic content, the steps vary somewhat from organization to organization, but all commonly begin by assessing current operations, determine an accepted vision of how the organization might best operate in the future and then chart a series of tactics and activities to achieve and measure that vision.

Like some economists and politicians, rationalists can fall into the trap of seeing the world as black or white. But, extremes rarely if ever exist in the muddy world of organizational change, where innumerable shades of grey make choosing strategy a far more nuanced and uncertain process than the rationalist model implies. As a consequence, no organization can realistically expect to transform from its starting point to its desired vision without adapting its policies and change methods along the way. A plan for change will likely fail along the way, but acceptance of this realism should not prevent a change plan from being formulated. Ironically, strategic change should account for the time when reality drifts from the words on paper. Although not quite at this level of contingency planning yet, there does appear to be greater recognition that stepwise approaches need to account for some degree of unpredictability. The growing number of data analysis and service information organizations suggest that swifter strategic decision making and contingency responses are gaining more prominence (Kitsios and Kamariotou, 2017). Yet, inbuilt mechanisms for dealing with unexpected events or unsatisfactory progress do not combine seamlessly with the rationalist penchant for certainty.

As we noted earlier, most books on strategic change recommend a systematic framework, usually through some kind of methodical step process. Two comments need to be made at this point. First, frameworks do help in change attempts, and second, slavishly following a framework will almost certainly result in failure, either in part or in whole. We do not suggest that strategic change frameworks should be avoided, but we do observe that reality necessitates modifications and amendments along the way. The rational philosophy relies too heavily on getting the change strategy right at the outset.

All organizations work with constant change taking place, albeit minor, and unlikely to be of strategic importance. Often daily change goes almost unnoticed by management. It transpires in small organizational areas where progressive, knowledgeable and frequently bright individuals find some way of either reducing their workload without affecting results or improving procedures so that the entire operation becomes marginally more effective. Machiavelli might even think of these individuals as minor visionaries. In fact, such individuals often forge the basis for strategic change success. Early approaches suffered from a lack of interest in people, as a result overlooking individual contributions and underestimating the impact of personal responses to change. The former represents an underutilized resource for innovation, while the latter foreshadows the dangerous potential for resistance. Again, contemporary discussions of planned change are, if not championing, acknowledging the role of staff support in organizational change (King, Hopkins and Cornish, 2018).

How this is aligns with the prominence placed on chief strategists in leadership steering the ship from a rationalist philosophy still remains open to debate.

LEADERSHIP AND RATIONAL CHANGE

Strategic change theorists advocate that the key to a successful change effort lies not just with the vision of organization leaders, but also with their preparedness to actively direct the change effort. Leaders as implementers of change introduce new advantages and disadvantages, although the magnitude of organizational change provides a mitigating factor. For example, sometimes a change programme presages a complete and obvious revolution in business model and organizational structure. In this case, the CEO's involvement in heralding the change, advising staff of its direction and form, and nominating the key players in the change project serves as a powerful catalyst. Indeed, evidence suggests that staff expect a change leader to possess strategic and technical insight, execution competencies, social awareness, character and resilience (Magsaysay and Hechanova, 2017). Once initiated, leaders can take a more comfortable back seat and only appear or intervene when circumstances dictate.

There are three primary disadvantages associated with organizational leaders heading the change process. First, in the event of a structural obstacle, or an argument, either ideological or between senior staff, then no one exists to whom objective appeals can be made. For leaders who imagine their views to be sovereign, the absence of independent change advice might seem unproblematic. Other leaders resolve the issue of impartiality through the use of consultants, although cynical commentators might suspect that the resulting reports reflect the instructions of leaders anyway.

Second, if the CEO becomes involved in the day-to-day change process then his or her normal, operational work will likely suffer. Third, and most important, the appearance of the CEO in the driver's seat of change conveys the impression, whether true or false, that change imposes the exclusive will of the leader through autocratic dictatorship. Recognition of this concern is growing, evidenced by the stated need to develop stepwise strategies using both an executive top-down approach and an employee-driven bottom-up approach (Busby, 2017).

The rational philosophy implicitly assumes that change bears the mark of organizational leaders. Leaders hold responsibility and therefore invest their reputations in success. Furthermore, the success of change pivots on a leader's ability to personally embody the transformation. As a result, an immense prescriptive literature has emerged recommending traits, characteristics and practices of great leaders. The research evidence depicts a murkier picture with far greater ambiguity about which features exemplify outstanding personal leadership. However, it does universally commend leaders who make a personal commitment to change. In fact, transformational leadership methods, where leaders charismatically proclaim the importance of change, have been positively associated with followers' change commitment (Herold, Fedor, Caldwell and Yi, 2008). While the evidence reinforces the effect of transformational leaders in successful—and particularly radical—change, it also illustrates that change works better when subordinates become involved in the process (Appelbaum, Berke, Taylor and Vazquez, 2008). No doubt good advice includes avoiding the impression of a change imposition. As Burnes et al. (2018) suggested, organizational change leadership may be best approached by trying to do the most amount of good for the most amount of people. Perhaps the best counsel follows the dictates of Machiavelli (2003 [1531], ch. 25), and ensures that leaders retain 'the shadow of ancient forms', regardless of the degree of change being sought, for, as Machiavelli observed, 'the general mass of men are satisfied with appearances' rather than reality.

If change foreshadows a complete and obvious revolution in organizational structure, then the active involvement of leaders cannot be escaped. Be warned though, as the evidence from detailed cases shows that change, more often than not, encounters vigorous resistance. Not every worker believes in Plato's concept of just rulers who rule by moral virtue. We should keep in mind that all change activities result in winners and losers. As a result, time should be invested to identify who in the organization will stand to benefit from the changes and who will suffer from them. Understanding the winners and losers allows a leader to take appropriate steps to bring those who may benefit onside at the start of the process, and to take actions to moderate against severe effects upon those who will be adversely affected by the change. Precautions around resistance and change failure reflect less a case of 'know thine enemy' and more a need to avoid making enemies in the first place, particularly within the same organization. Accordingly, perceptions of leadership communication and employee resistance to change have become a focal issue from a rationalistic perspective, with evidence supporting the importance of two-way communication (Canning and Found, 2015).

The initial development of a change plan remains the one essential action leaders must control. At the heart of strategic change plans beats the mission, goals, objectives and strategies of the organization. It may seem a fruitless exercise determining or reconsidering a strategic plan, but doing so has strong advantages. It focuses the entire organization on current circumstances and often reinforces the imperative to change. The essence of correctly determining a mission, goals and vision lies in the honesty with which leaders undertake the task. If leaders cannot correctly identify the starting point for change, then the gap between where the task begins and the required outcome begins flawed. And, it must be said, honesty does not always figure prominently in the task. Strategic plans frequently evolve in an ad hoc manner, and may reflect individual or sectional perspectives rather than organizational needs. Even a sound strategic plan needs to be confirmed if for no other reason than to establish the starting point for future or potential changes.

RATIONAL CONNECTIONS

With a robust set of strategic choices in place encompassing a mission and vision, as well as objectives, strategies and tactics, the next task involves facing organizational culture. Although we venture deeply into the cultural philosophy in Chapter 10, the rational philosophy connects because it seeks to change culture in a linear and strategic way. Cultures emerge over years making it the most intractable element in any change strategy. But in many cases, poor change outcomes can be traced to ignoring cultural problems and obstacles. Managers face constraints imposed by organizational history, particularly because resistance to change accompanies tradition. Younger organizations tend to find significant shifts more plausible than their older counterparts, for which modest, incremental changes appear difficult enough (Kelly and Amburgey, 1991).

Staff members basically happy with an organization's culture tend to stay, while those unhappy tend to depart. Over time, organizational culture unceremoniously transforms into a set of values and beliefs to which everyone ostensibly subscribes. And while it may not be a tissue of lies, it can be a fragile safety net, because frequently only specific aspects of organizational culture gain acceptance where they conform to personal needs or wishes.

We highlight culture in this chapter because its change requires far more than a plan and commitment. It requires an elemental reason sufficient to inspire both executives and staff to voluntarily remove themselves from their comfort zones in order to embrace novel beliefs and behaviours. Since culture can present a hurdle to innovation, or even an impassable obstruction, rational strategic change methods can face an immediate roadblock. The rationalist response to plan for cultural renewal subsequently hits another problem as strategy demands a transparent analysis of current culture in order to provide a gap against the desired culture. Yet, although it may be easy to describe an intended culture, an accurate diagnosis of the present state means peering deep into a cloaked, covert phenomenon. Rational models of strategic change need unambiguous and transparent targets to function best. Changing a system or a policy can be tackled directly, but employees' cavernous and elusive cultural responses could not be more difficult to pin down.

While the culture of an organization relates to 'how things are done', the concepts of beliefs, ideals, values and behaviour can differ markedly within an organization. On the surface, organizational culture transcends, or should transcend, the beliefs of any given individual. However, culture research suggests that individuals may not even be aware of their own values and beliefs until faced with change, and sometimes even not then. Unfortunately, the evidence shows that being forced through such a process stimulates resistance. Some leaders react by adopting the Machiavellian concept of assigning a crucial and key role to agents. Perhaps some truth can be found in Machiavelli's dictum that, '[Princes] should delegate to others the enactment of unpopular measures and keep in their own hands the means of winning favours' (2003 [1531], ch. 19).

Even for Machiavelli, the sublimation of private good for public good necessitates a compromise between people and elites, or to translate to the modern world, between management and workers. Many organizations, however, take the Machiavellian approach a step further and almost deliberately ferment conflict between various parties to effect some change. The twin Machiavellian concepts of conflict and consensus figure prominently as tools of strategic change managers, although whether valid or not depends upon the capability, not to mention the deviousness, of the change manager. We explore some of these ideas in depth in Chapter 11 on the critical philosophy. For the present, we note a vulnerability in the rational model without constant interventions along the way, more consistent with political approaches to change. For real-world managers, change and power cannot be divorced, even though they scarcely get a mention. Our position remains that a multi-philosophy approach will always prove superior as long as the underpinning assumptions, as well as strengths and weaknesses of each approach, remain uppermost in mind.

BEHAVIOURAL STRATEGY

Although strategic change emphasizes the technical issues associated with analyses and choice, when a close look is taken at senior managers' ideologies, rational and objective strategic solutions appear to be contested territory (Diefenbach, 2007). Part of the problem lies with the layers of complexity. For example, behaviour appears to be more superficial than beliefs, but while it might be accepted that beliefs underlie behaviour, a lag between the two can be observed. Moreover, ideals may not, and indeed frequently do not, match behaviour. Equally, a difference between beliefs and values can be revealed between how members would like to believe the organization actually operates and the way it actually operates. A complex web of cultural variables drives a marked difference between beliefs, ideals, values and behaviour.

A further problem related to culture can appear in the strategic change process. Having diagnosed the existing culture, the new culture's features can be specified. Fraught with danger, deciding on a future culture before undertaking the development of the new organizational vision, goals and objectives may lead to conflict or ruin. Culture inscribes values upon an organization's imagination rather than its day-to-day reality. New inscriptions demand fresh ink supplied by a lofty new vision. Strategic direction represents a powerful form of cultural change.

If an organization's leaders seriously want change, they can do worse than spend time talking to staff who have previously endured a change process. In so doing, leaders tend to be confronted with claims of 'corporate drivel'; 'the latest fad'; 'it's a plan to make us work harder with nothing in it for us'; or 'another case of management not knowing the difference between talk and reality'. While apparently derogatory to management, such observations highlight the seemingly ad hoc way change leaders rationalize and communicate the change management plan.

Most rational change models, like that of Kotter (1995), note that selling a change initiative starts with collective urgency and the need for a plan. Every employee must be convinced that his or her future flexes upon the plan's successful implementation. Unfortunately, many change leaders enact Sun Tzu's (1963) aphorism to, 'Let your plans be dark and as impenetrable as night, and when you move, fall like a thunderbolt', rather than his counsel that, 'Strategy without tactics is the slowest route to victory. Tactics without strategy is the noise before defeat.' In some cases, relinquishing the advantage of taking the competition by surprise ensures that you do not take your own organization by surprise.

CONSOLIDATING THE RATIONAL PHILOSOPHY

Adopting strategic change appeals to logic and has accumulated a significant list of converts, particularly for large-scale transformational change. Rational approaches, however, offer no guarantees in the murky, perplexing world of organizational change. We noted numerous pitfalls, including the tendency to rigidly impose predetermined changes. Nonetheless, the provenance of the rational philosophy holds sound, comprising a series of methodical steps that transform an organization from its current existence to a visionary position; from 'where we are to where we want to be'. The steps need not be constrictive, but do generally follow basic guidelines.

First, before any consideration of what change will take place, a supporting case to all staff incites urgency about the need for change. Without a plausible, fundamental and perhaps even desperate reason, no change process will secure the essential endorsement of staff. Indeed, research has demonstrated that when leaders are able to justify the need for change, resistance from staff is reduced (Canning and Found, 2015). Change without an accepted reason might result in change, but will be accompanied by deep-rooted, often unspoken opposition. And, with opposition, any change may not last. Also recognize our use of the term 'plausible'. In the real world, the reason or necessity for change must be accepted as valid. The degree of truthfulness underlying that validity may be one of degree. We do not suggest that organizations lie about the need for change, but rather that the world operates neither in black nor white, but in shades of grey. After all, many successful organizations and governments employ public relations 'spin doctors' to produce a more acceptable way of defining the change imperative.

Second, no lasting change can begin without acceptance or direction from an organization's leadership. The rational approach advocates for leaders to be recognized as initiators and supporters of change. However, once the change process becomes recognized, the process should be openly run by an agent, or senior staff member, leaving the leader free to adjudicate, intervene and refocus when necessary. This raises questions about the best way for a leader to canvas information from their staff.

Third, identifying the winners and losers in a change programme helps to anticipate pockets of support and resistance. No other variable predicts a response to change as well as an overt personal gain or loss. Action to bring winners into the change process early must be undertaken while ensuring that potential losers do not become the rallying point for opposition. Leaders acknowledging this must consider their communication with staff, providing enough justification to gain buy-in and support, and without alienating those likely to lose from the conceived plan.

Fourth, change programmes seldom progress unless leaders honestly determine where the organization currently dwells; the starting place for change. Typically, the review of an existing strategic plan, the development of a new plan or an analysis of significant existing processes play a role. Rational change proponents argue that a true assessment of organizational direction demands a view towards the road ahead.

Fifth, any successful change process requires an accurate assessment of organizational culture. Not the perceived culture, but the measured culture. Belief and reality may be the same, but more often than not the two diverge. Successfully 'measuring' the reality of organizational culture is not a task well suited to senior leadership, so how change strategists draw from the available organizational resources becomes critical. Most classic commentary on strategy assumes that leaders play the instrumental role in organizational renewal, but tend to be light on specifics (Barr, Stimpert and Huff, 1992). To make matters more complicated, how leaders deploy the linear thinking involved in a rational philosophy depends on the assumptions they make about causality, which in turn hinges upon their unique, individual beliefs.

RATIONAL OPTIMISM

But one should not be too pessimistic. Many leaders and change management teams get to the stage of converting an unhappy or unsupportive staff to the need for change, correctly determining their current situation, and making a realistic stab at their existing culture. Having successfully met and pinned to the floor the first major hurdles of the change process, the victorious team now faces the new task of determining what the future vision should be.

Future direction depends largely upon the reason the change process initially started; whether from organizational failure, technological innovation, financial necessity, market variation, competitive pressures, political activity or simply a change in business strategy. With the base cause recognized, change leaders can begin to specify a direction. At a primal level, the cause probably relates to resource utilization and its impact on the bottom line. We note here a connection to the resource philosophy examined in Chapter 7. The availability of critical resources enforces severe constraints upon the strategic options an organization may choose from, and yet this obvious reality does not feature in the rational process.

Despite turbulence in the wider business environment and the need for organizations to accommodate, stability remains a core requirement in strategic management (Baden-Fuller and Volberda, 1997). A solid foundation gives change a head start. An anomaly lies in the rational philosophy's treatment of change and the way its content stands separate to its process. Imagine that change possesses both spatial and temporal properties (Baden-Fuller and Volberda, 1997). The former reflects the location of change within an organization and indicates change content, whereas the latter concerns speed of execution. However we conceptualize these elements of change, they should be viewed as inseparable, rather than independent and linear as the rational philosophy implies. The rational philosophy tends to overlook the fact that change infrequently starts from a point of organizational stability. In fact, change managers both seek to shift an organization from chaos to control, as well as the reverse, as exemplified in the innovation and dualities philosophies (Chapters 12 and 13).

STRATEGY-AS-PRACTICE

Notwithstanding the rational philosophy's presentation of change as a clearly determined process envisioned at the outset, plenty of case study evidence shows that organizational change exhibits emergent properties (Ciborra, 1996). Ironically, change programmes change. Leaders and commentators tend to offer neat and systematic reconstructions after the event, implying a careful calculation behind every move. In counterpoint, detailed empirical studies depict a lot of muddling and messiness. A rational presentation of change might be clean and neat, but few managers and employees experience change as anything but fuzzy. Original plans seldom come to fruition. While plans can go wrong and unanticipated issues can arise in the environment, disconnections between strategic planning and strategic thinking appear inevitable (Graetz, 2002). Further, with the entry of 'big data' and the ability to rapidly analyse changing internal and external trends, the demands for flexible organizational change strategy have never been higher (Constantiou and Kallinikos, 2015). In addition, the need for organizational change in the first place demonstrates a failure of organizational planning and strategy (Head, 2006).

The proper response, according to a rational philosophy, means proceeding with even more strategic change. A growing acknowledgement that change programmes tend to be emergent and require spontaneous and ongoing responses has propelled the 'strategy-as-practice' movement. The practice perspective focuses on how leaders go about strategizing, rather than on the strategies that organizations come up with (Whittington, 1996). An advantage of the approach is that it gives insight into the practical methods of strategy making, how these methods are utilized and the specific role of those in charge of strategy development (Vaara and Whittington, 2012). As a result, it reveals the importance of viewing strategy as something that leaders do, as well as how they do it; a position that shifts away from the conventional perspective that strategy is something an organization possesses (Dahl, Kock and Lundgren-Henriksson, 2016). More recent evidence suggests that a strategy-as-practice approach can accelerate strategic decision making (Netz, Svensson and Brundin, 2019), as well as be applied successfully in small firms as well as large (Kearney, Harrington and Kelliher, 2019).

In rational change, leaders and managers assume a prodigious task. On the one hand, as Okumus (2003, p. 879) explained, the complexity of strategy implementation precludes prescriptive linear models, but change managers nevertheless should 'place themselves in a position where they can make informed judgments about the process of strategy implementation, rather than following ready-made solutions'. Okumus further recommended that managers, 'employ a holistic approach to viewing the formulation and implementation of strategy, and then evaluate how the implementation factors interact with each other and how they impact on the process'.

No matter how well planned, how strongly agreed by the majority of staff, how well led or how important the change plan, someone or some group of individuals within, or occasionally outside, the organization will attempt to derail it. This may occur because an individual or group feel that the proposed change plan will adversely affect them, because they misunderstand the requirements of the plan, because they genuinely lack the capability to readily accept change or because they believe the plan to be flawed. When faced with change not everyone reacts with the same rationality supposedly driving the change process. Equally, the evidence bears out the complex, multi-dimensional relationship between employee-perceived justice and resistance to change (Georgalis, Samaratunge, Kimberley and Lu, 2015). Almost all books and articles on strategic change will acknowledge the prospect of possible obstruction from some element of the workforce. Most will provide sensible suggestions for improvement, but it remains problematic to plan for resistance while employing a rational mindset.

The strategic change model within the rationalist philosophy does not perform equally well for all organizations, levels of change or contexts (Rosenbaum, More and Steane, 2017). However, for substantive change across a large organization, the strategic model offers a powerful organizing framework. Given committed leadership together with a clear impetus for change, we conclude that the rational philosophy's concepts offer a useful, if too rigid, initial guide. Organizations are not rational actors in the change process. Their fate is not exclusively determined by a leader's ability to make correct analyses and to formulate appropriate plans to meet predetermined objectives.

CONCLUSION

The rational philosophy implies that change works in a one-dimensional way. However, change occurs at different levels, and with varying magnitudes and directions. This is most evident when examining the progression of different departments through a 'change plan' in the same organization. Moreover, while not an immutable force, the external environment cannot always be mitigated with clever tactics. Organizations contribute to and interact with their environments in a way that makes choices about responses far more ambiguous and complex than the rational philosophy suggests. In some cases, change managers find that more analysis leads to more complexity as the subtle idiosyncrasies of various possibilities become apparent. Another obvious oversight of the rational philosophy accompanies its treatment of management decision making; a 'black-box' that produces the correct outputs when the correct inputs are computed. The development of organizational change leadership research has demonstrated that decision making is just the start, and a leader's ability to gain support is emerging to a point of equal, if not greater, importance than predetermined change plans. As we will explore in later chapters, change managers' approaches to decision making depend on a range of variables including the availability of resources, personal psychological states, political pressures and the legacies of historical choices.

We note many positives about the rational philosophy, but like many change approaches we shall be dealing with in this text, it suffers from limitations. Researchers like Pettigrew (1985) have argued for decades that a narrow focus makes organizational change perilous. In the case of the rational philosophy, organizations tend to be separated from their socio-historical circumstances (Clark, 2000). The evidence from meticulous studies demonstrates that organizational change functions in a messy and non-linear manner as a consequence of environmental turbulence and historical baggage, not to mention the 'human factor'. Neither can we ignore the fact that the majority of change programmes follow the rational philosophy, but only a third succeed. Despite the wisdom of conducting environmental analyses and establishing clear goals, the future often runs contrary to expectations based on linear trends (Grint, 1998). Rationalist organizational change theorists appear to be grappling with this schism, and thorough reflection on the original works of planned organizational change management theorists may offer more complete understandings of teleological change (Rosenbaum et al., 2018). Perhaps as Van der Waldt (2004, p. 135) commented, the 'challenge today is not so much to plan for change, but to learn to live with it, anticipate it and to capitalise on it'.

REFERENCES

Adcroft, Andy, R. Willis and J. Hurst (2008), 'A new model for managing change: The holistic view', *Journal of Business Strategy*, **29** (1), 40–50.

Ansoff, Igor H. (1965), *Corporate Strategy*, New York: McGraw-Hill.

Appelbaum, Steven H., J. Berke, J. Taylor and J. A. Vazquez (2008), 'The role of leadership during large scale organizational transitions: Lessons from six empirical studies', *Journal of American Academy of Business*, **13** (1), 16–24.

Baden-Fuller, Charles and H. W. Volberda (1997), 'Strategic renewal: How large complex organizations prepare for the future', *International Studies of Management and Organization*, **27** (2), 95–120.

Barr, Pamela S., J. L. Stimpert and A. S. Huff (1992), 'Cognitive change, strategic action and organizational renewal', *Strategic Management Journal*, **13**, 15–36.

Burke, Warner W. and G. H. Litwin (1992), 'A causal model of organizational performance and change', *Journal of Management*, **18** (3), 523–45.

Burnes, Bernard, M. Hughes and R. T. By (2018), 'Reimagining organisational change leadership', *Leadership*, **14** (2), 141–58.

Busby, N. (2017), *The Shape of Change: A Guide to Planning, Implementing and Embedding Organisational Change*, London: Taylor and Francis.

Canning, J. and P. Found (2015), 'Resistance in organisational change', *International Journal of Quality and Service Sciences*, **7** (2/3), 274–95.

Carnall, Colin A. (1995), *Managing Change in Organizations*, 2nd edition, London: Prentice Hall.

Carr, David K., K. J. Hard and W. J. Trahant (1996), *Managing the Change Process: A Field Book for Change Agents, Consultants, Team Leaders, and Reengineering Managers*, New York: McGraw-Hill.

Chaharbaghi, Kazem and R. Willis (1998), 'Strategy: The missing link between continuous revolution and constant evolution', *International Journal of Operations and Production Management*, **18** (9/10), 1017–27.

Child, John (1972), 'Organizational structure, environment and performance: The role of strategic choice', *Sociology*, **6**, 1–22.

Ciborra, Claudio U. (1996), 'The platform organization: Recombining strategies, structures, and surprises', *Organization Science*, **7** (2), 103–18.

Clark, Peter (2000), *Organisations in Action: Competition between Contexts*, London: Routledge.

Constantiou, I. D. and J, Kallinikos (2015), 'New games, new rules: Big data and the changing context of strategy', *Journal of Information Technology*, **30** (1), 44–57.

Dahl, Johanna, Sören Kock and Eva-Lena Lundgren-Henriksson (2016), 'Conceptualizing coopetition strategy as practice: A multilevel interpretative framework', *International Studies of Management and Organization*, **46** (2–3), 94–109.

Diefenbach, Thomas (2007), 'The managerialistic ideology of organisational change management', *Journal of Organizational Change Management*, **20** (1), 126–44.

Georgalis, Joanna, R. Samaratunge, N. Kimberley and Y. Lu (2015), 'Change process characteristics and resistance to organisational change: The role of employee perceptions of justice', *Australian Journal of Management*, **40** (1), 89–113.

Graetz, Fiona (2002), 'Strategic thinking versus strategic planning: Towards understanding the complementarities', *Management Decision*, **40** (5/6), 456–62.

Grint, Keith (1998), 'Determining the indeterminacies of change leadership', *Management Decision*, **36** (8), 503–8.

Head, Thomas C. (2006), 'Strategic organization development: A failure of true organization development', *Organization Development Journal*, **24** (4), 21–8.

Herold, David M., D. B. Fedor, S. Caldwell and L. Yi (2008), 'The effects of transformational and change leadership on employees' commitment to a change: A multilevel study', *Journal of Applied Psychology*, **93** (2), 346–57.

Huber, George P. and W. H. Glick (eds) (1995), *Organisational Change and Redesign: Ideas and Insights for Improving Performance*, New York: Oxford University Press.

Jones, Marc T. (2002), 'Globalization and organizational restructuring: A strategic perspective', *Thunderbird International Business Review*, **44** (3), 325–51.

Kanter, Rosabeth M., B. A. Stein and T. D. Jick (1992), *The Challenge of Organisational Change*, New York: Free Press.

Kearney, Arthur, Denis Harrington and Felicity Kelliher (2019), 'Strategizing in the micro firm: A "strategy as practice" framework', *Industry and Higher Education*, **33** (1), 6–17.

Kelly, Dawn and T. Amburgey (1991), 'Organizational inertia and momentum: A dynamic model of strategic change', *Academy of Management Journal*, **34** (3), 591–612.

Kezar, Adrianna J. (2000), *Understanding and Facilitating Change in Higher Education in the 21st Century*, Washington, DC: Jossey-Bass.

King, S., M. Hopkins and N. Cornish (2018), 'Can models of organizational change help to understand "success" and "failure" in community sentences? Applying Kotter's model of organizational change to an Integrated Offender Management case study', *Criminology and Criminal Justice*, **18** (3), 273–90.

Kitsios, F. and M. Kamariotou (2017), 'Strategic IT alignment: Business performance during financial crisis', in N. Tsouni and A. Vlachvei (eds), *Advances in Applied Economic Research*, Cham: Springer, pp. 503–25.

Kotter, John P. (1995), 'Leading change: Why transformation efforts fail', *Harvard Business Review*, **73** (2), 59–67.

Kuipers, Ben S., M. Higgs, W. Kickert, L. Tummers, J. Grandia and J. Van der Voet (2014), 'The management of change in public organizations: A literature review', *Public Administration*, **92** (1), 1–20.

Lewin, Kurt (1947), 'Frontier in group dynamics: Concepts, method, and reality in social equilibria and social change', *Human Relations*, **1**, 3–41.

Machiavelli, Niccolo (2003 [1531]), *The Discourses*, trans. Leslie J. Walker, revisions Brian Richardson, London: Penguin.

Magsaysay, Jowett F. and M. R. M. Hechanova (2017), 'Building an implicit change leadership theory', *Leadership and Organization Development Journal*, **8** (6), 834–48.

Mintzberg, Henry (1990), 'The design school: Reconsidering the basic premises of strategic management', *Strategic Management Journal*, **6**, 257–72.

Netz, Joakim, Martin Svensson and Ethel Brundin (2019), 'Business disruptions and affective reactions: A strategy-as-practice perspective on fast strategic decision making', *Long Range Planning*, https://doi.org/10.1016/j.lrp.2019.101910.

Okumus, Fevzi (2003), 'A framework to implement strategies in organizations', *Management Decision*, **41** (9), 871–82.

Pettigrew, Andrew (1985), *The Awakening Giant: Continuity and Change in ICI*, Oxford: Blackwell.

Pollack, Julien and R. Pollack (2015), 'Using Kotter's eight stage process to manage an organisational change program: Presentation and practice', *Systemic Practice and Action Research*, **28** (1), 51–66.

Rajagopalan, Nandini and G. Spreitzer (1997), 'Toward a theory of strategic change: A multi-lens perspective and integrative framework', *Academy of Management Review*, **22** (1), 48–79.

Robbins, Stephen P. (1983), *Organizational Theory, the Structure and Design of Organizations*, Englewood Cliffs, NJ: Prentice Hall.

Robbins, Stephen P. (2007), *Organizational Theory, the Structure and Design of Organizations*, 3rd edition, Englewood Cliffs, NJ: Prentice Hall.

Robertson, Peter J., D. R. Roberts and J. I. Porras (1993), 'Dynamics of planned organizational change: Assessing empirical support for a theoretical model', *Academy of Management Journal*, **36** (3), 619–34.

Rosenbaum, David, E. More and P. Steane (2017), 'A longitudinal qualitative case study of change in nonprofits: Suggesting a new approach to the management of change', *Journal of Management and Organization*, **23** (1), 74–91.

Rosenbaum, David, E. More and P. Steane (2018), 'Planned organisational change management', *Journal of Organizational Change Management*, **31** (2), 286–303.

Scott, Richard W. (1987), *Organizations: Rational, Natural and Open Systems*, 2nd edition, Englewood Cliffs, NJ: Prentice Hall.

Smith, Kenwyn K. and D. N. Berg (1987), *Paradoxes of Group Life: Understanding Conflict, Paralysis, and Movement in Group Dynamics*, San Francisco, CA: Jossey-Bass.

Sun Tzu (1963), *The Art of War*, translated by Samuel B. Griffith, Oxford: Oxford University Press.

Vaara, E. and R. Whittington (2012), 'Strategy-as-practice: Taking social practices seriously', *Academy of Management Annals*, **6** (1), 285–336.

Van de Ven, Andrew H. and M. S. Poole (1995), 'Explaining development and change in organizations', *Academy of Management Review*, **20**, 510–40.

Van der Voet, Joris (2014), 'The effectiveness and specificity of change management in a public organization: Transformational leadership and a bureaucratic organizational structure', *European Management Journal*, **32** (3), 373–82.

Van der Waldt, De la Rey (2004), 'Towards corporate communication excellence in a changing environment', *Problems and Perspectives in Management*, **3**, 135–43.

Von Clausewitz, Carl (1976), *On War*, Princeton, NJ: Princeton University Press.

Whittington, R. (1996), 'Strategy as practice', *Long Range Planning*, **29** (5), 731–5.

4. The biological philosophy: 'changing organisms'

INTRODUCTION

The earliest organizational change philosophies found inspiration in metaphors and analogies appropriated from the natural world. Indeed, the change management literature bursts with references to various kinds of creatures and organisms, from 'cash cows' to spider's webs. For the most part, the acquisition of biological concepts yields excellent returns in understanding how change works. After all, nature provides all the environmental components analogous to those faced by organizations and industries. Individual organizations compete with others in a battle for resources where prosperity and growth roughly equate to survival and reproduction. Industries and sectors compete with each other for the same capital, customers and resources, like species fighting to adapt in a deadly world of predators and starvation. Even the individual life cycle of an organism, from birth, development, maturity, decline and inevitable death, matches organizational experience. Revealing the character of the cycle anticipates the main challenges at each stage of progress.

The biological philosophy suggests that organizations, industries and sectors 'live' and endure vulnerabilities like any fragile, mortal organism. In fact, the idea that organizations suffer the merciless vagaries of a competitive arena and must fight for their very survival stimulated the most intuitive change philosophy ever devised. We shall see that the biological philosophy birthed two major theories. First, the life-cycle model maps the developmental progress of individual organizations; and second, the Darwinian concept of evolution by natural selection describes the process of environmental adaptation and change. From these theories, the biological metaphor of an 'ecosystems' approach to organizational change, originally proposed by Moore (1993), has experienced a resurgence as technological forces have increased the importance of networks and cooperation (Demil, Lecocq and Warnier, 2018).

This chapter first explores the life-cycle offshoot of the biological philosophy, which uses the developmental progress of organizations to structure and explain the natural evolution of change. Life-cycle models treat change as endemic, but linked to a stage of development, from start-up to divestment.

Birth, growth, ageing and death represent natural and inexorable parts of an organization's experience. From a change management viewpoint, common challenges accompany each stage. The good news is that the staged challenges transpire universally, and can therefore be anticipated. The bad news is that knowing what kind of problem to anticipate does not necessarily make the right change any easier to introduce. Next, we comment on the use of living organisms as a metaphor for understanding change. We then tackle the life-cycle model of organizational change before moving on to organizational ecology, which applies a Darwinian framework in explaining change, before commenting on ecosystems. Finally, we introduce the punctuated equilibrium model as a way of understanding revolutionary change within a biological philosophy.

LIVING METAPHORS

Biological systems metaphors can offer particularly helpful insights and conceptualizations about how organizations, sectors and industries change (Witt, 2004). For example, the growth in popularity of applying biological design to better understand change in organizations—or what has been termed biomimetics—suggests that such abstract metaphors can provide insight (Tamayo and Vargas, 2019). While biological concepts provide generally useful approximations of change as an adaptive process for any given organization, the absence of an explanatory change mechanism limits the power to description. For example, the idea that organizations must adapt and evolve to their environments helpfully expresses what literally occurs, but the terms adaptation and evolution really act only as similes for change. We already know that organizations have to change either in response to competitive forces or through deliberate, cooperative initiatives. More elusive is a theory that explains the causal forces that precipitate change and the likely outcomes that it will produce. In response, models of Darwinian evolution have gained traction, as we consider later in this chapter.

Darwinian evolution provides a theory explaining how species experience adaptations. When applied to the equivalent of species in the organizational world—industries—a new model of change emerged under the principle of biological population ecology, later becoming organizational ecology. Organizational ecologists think that Darwinian-like selection occurs when industries gradually evolve to match the constraints of their environmental context. As one of its major goals in understanding change, ecologists seek to explain why there are so many different kinds of organizations within a population, when the biological reality suggests that there should be a best configuration.

Organisms all turn out much the same, patterned through DNA that evolved in response to environmental selection pressures. But organizations do come in different shapes, sizes and flavours, although research from organizational ecology studies demonstrates that strong environmental pressures impel organizations to assume certain compositions for success. Perhaps most noteworthy, ecologists conclude that competition forces the continual adaptation of an industry, where the fluid and versatile command the best chance of survival and prosperity. This is contrasted with a Darwinian ecosystems approach that highlights the benefits of symbiotic evolutionary organizational change and innovation.

We note a typical confusion in using the right unit of change in biological models. Technically speaking, the term evolution properly concerns the adaptations an industry (species) makes, whereas the life-cycle metaphor refers to organizational development. The popular idea of 'survival of the fittest' is often applied to an individual organization, but technically correct Darwinian 'survival of best fit', applies to species and therefore industries. Unsurprisingly, change commentators regularly write about organizations adapting to their environments, which makes practical sense, but nevertheless presents a misleading application of a Darwinian perspective.

THE LIFE-CYCLE CHANGE MODEL

For at least 50 years the life-cycle model has enjoyed a place in change management thinking (Haire, 1959). Its central tenet remains unchanged; organizational progress follows a regular sequence where each stage exhibits universal but characteristic features. Life-cycle theory seeks to explain change in organizations from start-up to divestment by suggesting common responses (Kezar, 2000; Van de Ven and Poole, 1995). Birth, growth, maturity, decline and death should be viewed as natural parts of an organization's development (Levy and Merry, 1986). Since all organizations encounter the same challenges, they also share the best change responses.

The life-cycle model figures prominently in change management, underpinned by a formidable historical literature. It also migrated into the strategy and product management arena, as a way of classifying and anticipating change over time. Under the life-cycle metaphor, time is an inward measure reflecting an organization's developmental rather than actual age. In addition, the cycles of age correspond to stages, each characterized by accumulated experiences. Like with any organism, periods of growth and maturity precede inevitable decline and death. Life-cycle models assume that every organizational stage features a common set of problems. In change management, this way of thinking offers some key advantages. For example, new market entrants face some generic challenges, like the need to gain an immediate slice of market share in order to survive. Conversely, organizations with mature market positions encounter similar obstacles in defending their market shares. For instance, organizations at the same life-cycle stage tend to employ the same business models (Jabłoński and Jabłoński, 2016). This signals the most typical use of life-cycle concepts, that of describing the product development issues an organization must grapple with.

It is a far more complex and troublesome proposition to describe an organization's entire operation through the life-cycle model. Moreover, the model inexorably leads to the same tautological end point that all organizations needing significant change have entered decline and the prospect of imminent death without responding with decisive action. Since from a life-cycle viewpoint rebirth offers the only way forward, every organization confronts the same need to institute renewal. In most cases, organizational leaders and employees do not require the assistance of the life-cycle model to recognize that they need renewal. Most of the time, the need for change could not be more blindingly obvious. The real problem is what to change to, and how to go about doing it.

Life-cycle approaches make assumptions about the generic problems that arise during each stage. Change management models using the life-cycle approach as a vehicle tend to apply change rules and programmes to stages as guidelines for action. Every organization within the same life-cycle stage shares key problems related to their specific point of development. For example, there should be consistent and endemic issues for each stage around structure, strategy, processes, culture, human resources and governance. The first premise of the life-cycle model holds that a natural sequence or rhythm governs the challenges presented to organizations. Equally, these predictable issues must have elicited a standard set of responses by organizations successful in navigating their way through to the next stage.

Despite their intuitive appeal, while organizations may wrestle with generic problems at certain stages in their life cycles, prescribed life-cycle change responses can be too generic. Consider the predicament of an organization that has moved from maturity to decline. Some common problems undoubtedly impede success, often including a tired and inefficient bureaucracy, products and services that no longer command market leadership, diminishing standards of customer service and even general dissatisfaction and apathy across the organization. Organizational leaders, stakeholders and employees can readily agree to the existence of such obstacles. Reaching a consensus about the best response remains more elusive, however. In addition, no obvious set of best practices for change has emerged from life-cycle studies. The absence of uniform and specific guidance makes converting common developmental problems into practical change solutions problematic. In fact, most of the organizational change research suggests that situational factors dominate change responses and that life-cycle problems may not be as universal as popularly assumed. Life-cycle issues may vary depending upon industry, sector, organization, products, technology, resources and employees.

Life-cycle and developmental approaches diverge from evolutionary change models. The former focus on growth and the prospect of death without rebirth and renewal, while the latter emphasize constant adaptation and change, which successfully employed, mitigate against the certainty of decline and failure. Life-cycle models also contradict other philosophies and theories presented in this text including, most notably, the institutional philosophy and contingency theory. Both bring to the fore another potential limitation of the life-cycle view: considerable evidence positions other situational variables as more important in shaping the change needs of an organization, such as industry nature and level of competition. Environmental pressures can moderate and potentially diminish the relevance of life-cycle stages, or even change their timing significantly. As we shall discuss shortly, evolutionary models more adeptly accommodate contextual forces, even if they do not offer much specific advice about how to intercede.

The Organizational Life Cycle

Analogous to genetic and environmental variations between individual organisms, organizations possess their own indigenous structures and circumstances. Just as organisms need the basic resources for survival and growth, organizations require access to the financial and human resources they need to feed themselves and to grow. But organizations are not literally organisms of course, so life-cycle models present less precise explanations than physiological growth stages. As a result, we cannot expect more than a broad depiction of cycle stages. Since the transition between stages and the time spent within each stage can vary immensely, life-cycle models assume that the stages drive change management responses. However, life-cycle models with more stages have emerged adding greater detail and texture to the general stages (Lester, Parnell and Carraher, 2003).

The organizational life-cycle approach reaches deeply into historical management literature with researchers and commentators offering models depicting stages of organizational development from birth to death. The earliest (Chandler, 1962; Greiner, 1972; Galbraith, 1982; Churchill and Lewis, 1983; Quinn and Cameron, 1983; Miller and Friesen, 1980; 1984) tend to show the cycle in terms of discrete parts of a linear and inescapable process. For example, Chandler's (1962) seminal five-stage model of birth, growth, maturity, revival and decline established an early benchmark. Most commentators followed Chandler in suggesting that organizations display characteristic structures at each stage as a common response to their developmental position and the market implications of those stages. This thinking has developed to consider the nuances of life cycles specific to professions, such as Lawrence, Zhang and Heineke's (2016) iterative life cycle of validation, diffusion, commodification and innovation in energy and environmental design consulting.

A representative definition of the organizational life cycle provided by Jones (2004) emphasizes the sequence of growth and development through which all organizations must pass. This focal position reveals why there might be commonality to each stage. For example, most growing organizations need to adjust around their labour force and production methods in order to capitalize on early success. Similarly, when faced with decline, the same organizations make further adjustments around new competitive advantages, greater efficiencies and improved value creation. To understand the change interventions advocated by life-cycle theorists, we must examine each stage in turn.

Life-Cycle Stages

Birth reflects the start-up period of an enterprise, including its initial forays into the marketplace and its attempts to secure viability. Unsurprisingly, this stage features the great struggles that accompany a transition from infancy to establishment. Change management commentators rarely say much about the birth process in the life cycle, as change interventions usually target existing organizations entering decline. An early life-cycle model proposed by Greiner (1972) presented five stages of organizational development. Greiner suggested that particular crises accompany each stage. He named his first the 'leadership crisis', as the start-up stage pivots upon the direction articulated by an organization's founders. Greiner also proposed that this early leadership has to provide a creative strategy in order to generate a business without an initial base from which to begin.

Growth transpires when an organization has managed to forge a place in the market by developing some distinctive competencies around its first products or services. The change literature emphasizes structure at this point in the life cycle. A successful strategy was set in motion by organizational leaders in the first stage, and now with growth comes the need to restructure. Functionally based structures dominate recommendations and lead to middle managers overseeing operational performance and allowing the leadership some time to consider strategic matters. Usually this stage marks the seeds of bureaucracy complete with formalized positions, procedures and policies around work. Since the major problem seems like an absence of standardized ways of doing things, the natural response means introducing new layers of authority responsible for devising and maintaining new systems. Typical demands include increasing sales, ensuring reliable production or delivery, capitalizing on increased demand and managing fluctuating cash flow (Dodge and Robbins,

1992). Many of these imperatives devolve to the hands of new employees under a formal organizational structure. Greiner's crisis at this stage revolves around autonomy as leaders relinquish their operational responsibilities to the new structures. However, the new direction is also critical to growth.

Maturity inevitably succeeds growth as product performance declines, the market reaches saturation, inefficiencies grow and innovation becomes more time-consuming and expensive. Ironically, the solution to the problems of growth becomes the biggest problem in the maturity stage. With bureaucracy comes inefficiency and redundancy. Change managers therefore focus their efforts on the structures and systems that now seem overly complex and con-voluted. A revision of accountabilities ensues, which sometimes means the introduction of new performance measures and other times means that some employees lose their jobs. Greiner believes this stage to be a crisis of control, as power must be delegated to the roles that can implement the necessary changes. Bureaucracy leads to a constriction of power around central roles even though they may not necessarily be best placed to make informed change.

Revival comes with a successful response to maturity. In practice, organiza-tions have diversified by introducing new products or services while consoli-dating their structures. The most common next response involves introducing product-based structures so that specialized departments can manage the nuances of a more complex and often heterogeneous market. At the same time, change managers launch sophisticated strategic planning and control mecha-nisms designed to squeeze every bit of value they can out of the products and resources available. Greiner (1972) thought that the revival challenge pivots around staff and the need for more effective collaboration. In order to mount a revival, change leaders must mobilize the organization towards a common objective, clearing the strategic path from long-standing detritus. Rigid plan-ning and control make a comeback.

Decline represents the final stage where an organization wrestles with the problems that threaten its very survival. The life-cycle model depicts the decline stage as an irreversible position where the prospects of a revival have passed or cannot be brought about in time. Greiner considered this unknown territory for good reason. Change managers become most active during the decline stage but their efforts may be in vain, often coming too late.

Life-Cycle Limitations

We suggest that the life-cycle model provides a helpful, rudimentary road map for change managers to anticipate the macro problems they will likely encounter with growth, and the normal responses to changed market condi-tions (Hanks, Watson, Jansen and Chandler, 1993; Beverland and Lockshin, 2001; Wagner, 2011). Some progress has been made towards specifying the variables that might help describe the challenges and changes associated with each stage, yet the vulnerability of organizations at the early stages continues to dominate life-cycle studies (Abatecola, 2013). Pundziene, Kundrotas and Lydeka (2006), for example, compared organizations' life cycles with a consolidated list of 11 features: age, size, growth rate, number of employees, change in the number of employees, structure, centralization, formalization, composition of top management, reward system and strategy. Other authors suggest leadership, diversity and complexity as well. Using a range of common descriptive features helps change managers conceptualize the impact of important variables at each particular life-cycle stage. The life-cycle model becomes two dimensional in that choices can be made on the basis of the stage as well as specific internal attributes. In theory, the dimensions can be combined into a prescriptive matrix providing a change intervention for each combination of stage and organizational configuration. While conceptually interesting, selecting a change intervention becomes impossibly complex when all 11 features are mapped against each stage. Perhaps the best lessons from the life-cycle model accompany expectations that early stages will need different changes than later stages, and that the best specific intervention at a given stage remains contingent upon organizational and environmental variables.

The life-cycle model makes best use of the logic that organizations possess a differential capacity to meet environmental demands and generate new competitive advantages according to their developmental stage. Nevertheless, the life-cycle model does view entropy—the inability to avoid chaos, disintegration and death—as fundamental. Many change managers and organizational leaders would disagree with this premise on the basis that survival and prosperity depends upon cycles of rejuvenation. An interesting side effect of the wide-ranging commentary on organizational life cycles comes with its application to new domains within organizations. For example, the life-cycle concept has been employed to help understand organizational learning (Arthur and Huntley, 2005; Tam and Gray, 2016) and status within organizations (Washington and Zajac, 2005).

ORGANIZATIONAL ECOLOGY AND ECOSYSTEMS

Another change theory emerging from the biological philosophy is organizational ecology. The approach aligns with the life-cycle model in that it tries to explain the way organizations grow and transform, as well as succeed and fail. At the centre of organizational ecology lies research findings that contradict conventional wisdoms about what governs success and failure in change, some of which relate to the importance of competition (Hannan, Polos and Carroll, 2007). Most theories of change management claim that influencing an organization hinges upon finding the right intervention. In fact, some theories imply that change comes easily with the correct approach. But research in organizational ecology suggests the opposite. After all, if change were straightforward and organizations pliable, then failure would not be so common. According to ecologists, the reality remains that inertia prevails; a consequence of the bureaucratic structures and systems introduced to propel organizations through growth. However, by the time organizations reach maturity, the once essential systems and structures have converted into obstacles to further growth. The ecological viewpoint offers a different perspective where the study of change should not be limited to individual organizations. A better analysis, organizational ecologists claim, begins by acknowledging that the environment for any given organization also comprises a range of other organizations, many of which act as competitors. Thus, the central way of thinking about change mirrors biological evolution. Change occurs at the species level, and in this case constitutes the entire population of organizations. Thinking from this perspective leads to some unconventional propositions.

The biological driver underpinning organizational ecology encourages more appreciation of what might be seen as mortality and reproduction. If organizations constitute part of a larger population or species of organizations, then studying the activities of the prosperous minority seems inadequate. Ecologists seek to understand why the majority failed. But even this presents a complex set of problems to resolve. In fact, most start-up businesses fail before they even get noticed. Despite countless hours of application, development, resource acquisition and planning, most organizations go from inception to extinction. New species struggle desperately to gain a foothold in the organizational kingdom. Organizational ecologists claim that as few as 10 per cent of new hopefuls in some industries make it to the point of production and activity. If these estimates hold across numerous industries, then it is worthwhile investigating why one organization in an industry fails to get past the starting line while another can win the race for market share. Organizational ecologists are the archaeologists of the change management world. They dig up the fossils of dead companies and tell us why they were poorly adapted for survival. The answers serve as lessons about how organizations need to respond to their environments, and in particular, their competition.

In the article that kick-started the organizational ecology position, Hannan and Freeman (1977) proposed a theory they named 'density dependence'. Like the biological notion they appropriated, density dependence hypothesizes that the growth and death of a given organization depends on the total number of organizations in the population. Accordingly, population density has two effects, first through a process Hannan and Freeman described as legitimation, and second, through competition.

The process of legitimation channels organizations towards specific, accepted and standardized ways of doing things. It functions in much the same way as institutional theories (see Chapter 6) where organizations copy each other as a response to common industrial pressures. Legitimation encourages more organizations to be founded while restricting the numbers that fail. Success comes easier with a formula. In contrast, competition arrives as more organizations compete for the same finite resources, including capital and customers, resulting in fewer new organizations and more that go out of business. For example, Bennett's ecological study of British charities (2016) found that resource competition between charitable organizations was more important to survival than other factors such as initial investment size, employee size or charitable cause.

Change managers should be interested in the population density of an industry because the theory makes some important predictions about when legitimation and competition rise. Early in an organization's life, legitimation bolsters success by providing structures and approaches that can be readily duplicated. However, as time goes on, competition increases and the legitimation effect begins to erode. Eventually, as an industry enters maturity, the remaining organizations reap the greatest benefits of legitimation, having staved off the competition and consolidated their market positions. Change becomes most significant in the dangerous middle ground between industrial growth and fierce competition. Growth makes staying in the industry compelling, but competition makes gaining market leadership cutthroat. Therefore, organizations must focus on both capacity *and* effectiveness when fierce competition threatens survival (Yu, 2016). Organizational ecology also suggests that institutional norms help organizations navigate this time and secure a solid position in order to enjoy the rewards that a mature and less competitive industry can afford. On the other hand, the theory predicts that constant change and progress remain critical.

The Red Queen

Consider the wrinkle on competition ecologists call the 'Red Queen' hypothesis (Barnett and Hansen, 1996). Borrowing its name from Lewis Carroll's *Through the Looking Glass*, the sequel to *Alice's Adventures in Wonderland*, in which the central character Alice encounters the Red Queen who appears to be running but fails to move. The analogy describes the situation facing organizations successfully adapted to their environments but which suddenly encounter additional competition. Successful adaptation for one organization leads to worsening conditions for the others, which in turn must adapt in order to survive. Of course, if they do adapt, the conditions for survival pivot again, making adaptation and change an escalating situation where an organization, like the Red Queen, has to adapt more and more just to stay in the same spot. Success can also work against an organization. The 'speed' at which an organization has to run is determined by the density of innovators within an ecosystem, with highly innovative ecosystems demanding even greater innovation or imitation just to keep up (Oldham, 2018). The resulting vicious circle of competitive pressure means that constant change is essential just to keep up.

The lessons from the Red Queen reinforce the role of change managers. For example, the theory predicts that those organizations with a history of surviving competitive environments have learned to adapt fluidly to change. These organizations continue to innovate and outperform any competitors who prosper on the basis of shorter-term advantages such as technology or geographic market opportunities. In fact, the evidence from organizational ecology research indicates that change drives long-term success, which in turn comes with surviving highly competitive, ruthless environments where innovation triumphs. For organizations seeking a global presence, the only option would seem unremitting change.

To make matters even more complicated, ecologists suggest another twist on life-cycle interpretations. Where start-up companies appear vulnerable because of their age, ecologists think the problem really comes down to size. Because change is so difficult to successfully and consistently introduce, many companies have great difficulty growing. They struggle to shed the now intractable structures and strategies that were once critical to gaining a foothold. An enduring change paradox arrives whereupon great risk accompanies changes to core organizational elements, but without change, failure becomes inescapable. While organizational change must be endemic for survival, its practice signals danger because the benefits it reaps may never have the chance to overcome the disruptions it causes. Ecologists think that 'best practices' undermine successful change for most organizations because the same strategies will not work universally.

The idea of organizational change best practice has come from the few organizations that have changed most easily. Instead, some of the most useful lessons about change rarely get told because they concern those organizations constantly fighting to survive. The challenge of managing change from an ecological perspective is most clear in the complexity of Amankwah-Amoah's (2016) process model of organizational failure, which inventories a seemingly never-ending cascade of potential problem stages and domains for misfortune.

ECOSYSTEMS

Given that organizational ecology focuses on populations of organizations, it also leads to some hard lessons about the way industries operate. While most change philosophies and their theories concentrate on the behaviours of individual organizations, ecologists examine the broader field of players within an industry. As a result, ecologists claim that the driving force behind industrial change is not individual firm adaptation, but the replacement of key industry players. Ecological 'cascades' stemming from the failure of one organization in a system can lead to multiple organizations dying, critical ecological tipping points and lasting system change (Garnett, Mollan and Bentley, 2015). Dying companies shape an industry rather than the surviving, adapting ones. Ecologists suggest that change managers suffer from an obsession with organizational change success stories at the expense of learning from the important reasons most change programmes fail.

If population ecology guides change by focusing on the competition, survival and failure of organizations, an ecosystems approach to change focuses on *cooperation* between stakeholders in an environment. Moore's (1993) conceptualization of an economic ecosystem of stakeholders that interact to generate innovation and change flourished with the emergence of the silicon revolution (Demil et al., 2018). Integral to viewing change from an ecosystem's perspective is the assumption that organizations are not only dependent on each other, but symbiotic. That is, the evolution of two or more organizations is inextricably linked as each has a role in the ecosystem, which, if unfulfilled, has consequences for the survival of the entire ecosystem.

To use the biological terms, symbiotic relationships involve different 'species' of organizations from different roles, industries or sectors, cooperating to share knowledge, experience and resources. Extending the biological metaphor of an ecosystems approach to change, economic ecosystems also go through evolutionary life cycles (Lu, Rong, You and Shi, 2014). The stage of the ecosystem will have consequences for what kinds of different organizations are needed within the ecosystem for it to survive and prosper. Veile, Kiel, Müller and Voigt (2019) captured why an ecosystems approach is valuable to change managers in the modern business environment: 'The importance of partnerships and networks is constantly increasing and has become a vital source of competitiveness' (p. 18). The key takeaway for organizational change is that improved competitiveness can be fostered and developed through collaboration, as opposed to learning from the failure of others, or even facilitating it.

DARWIN, EVOLUTION AND NATURAL SELECTION

The architects of evolutionary theory, Charles Darwin and Alfred Russel Wallace, could scarcely have imagined the effect their theories would have on biology, let alone organization theory. In fact, infamously, Darwin and Wallace's theory was met with only a lacklustre response in the first instance, their presentation to the Linnean Society in 1858 barely making a ripple. The president of the Society noted in his annual report that the scientific year had yielded little worthy of particular mention, and nothing that would 'confer a lasting and important service on mankind' (Jones, 1999, p. xxix). A century and a half later the Darwinian concept of evolution by natural selection helps to explain how organizations change within industrial populations. In this final section we hope to clarify some of the ambiguities associated with the biological philosophy that emanate from its connection to Darwinian evolution. In particular, by explaining the actual process of evolution and its analogous processes in industries, we aim to provide a platform from which further biological metaphors can be explored.

Natural selection may be defined as 'the differential survival and reproduction of different genetic forms' (Wilson, 1998, p. 51). Evolution guides the development of species acting as a kind of 'genetic churn' of individuals within populations over successive generations (Mayr, 2002). Darwin's evolution through natural selection explains that individuals within a population best suited to their environments have the greatest probability of survival and reproduction. Given that many of these attributes are predetermined by genes, those inheriting advantages slowly form an over-representative contribution to a population.

In Darwinian evolutionary theory, variations or mutations in DNA give individual organisms novel characteristics. Since this is a process of chance, the majority of genetic mutations do not help and fail to offer a survival or reproductive advantage. However, periodically mutations prove useful and provide a competitive procreation advantage, enabling a disproportionate overcontribution to the gene pool. If the mutation continues to prove advantageous, the genetic line slowly becomes more dominant until it replaces the previous one.

A strict overlay of the evolution metaphor to an organizational context suggests that occasionally one organization in a population or species of organizations (an industry) does something unique that gives it a competitive advantage in reproduction (growth or market share). If the metaphor were held directly, this unique advantage would not have come about by design, but in practice it could of course have been intended. Over time, the new practice, structure or product delivering the competitive advantage gets shared amongst the remainder of the industry (species) through takeovers and copying, thereby explaining how industrial change encourages commonality; the industrial equivalent of species change. If the biological metaphor were translated exactly, theorists would discuss how industries adapt and evolve, while organizations become selected for success (propagation) because their attributes confer to them an advantage in the environment worthy of copying.

Progress and Direction

The notion of intentionality is worth considering in light of the role change managers seek to play. Natural selection works on necessity, rewarding those organisms that possess genetic characteristics that happen to lead to greater reproductive success within their specific ecological niche. Unlike organizational leaders or change managers, natural selection cannot think ahead; no intelligent force guides a species towards a predetermined end state. Natural selection occurs randomly wherein the replication of genes during reproduction creates genetic mutations, a tiny proportion of which provide a new physical advantage upon an individual given their particular environmental circumstances. The mutation that created the first opposable thumb, for instance, clearly delivered an advantage to its recipient. Evolution is not linear, progressive or smart. However, change leaders can be. Many successful organizations enjoy growth and a disproportionate market share because they have been smarter than their competitors. On the other hand, more like in biological evolution, some organizations hit upon a world-beating practice through circumstance, luck or a combination of other contingent factors. A third evolutionary option, termed co-evolution, is also worth noting. Co-evolution suggests that there can be an interdependency between an organization's evolution and that of its environment (Porter, 2006). Co-evolution therefore shifts the focus of organizational change to the relationship between internal and external developmental alignment (Breslin, 2016). By implication, change leaders should concern themselves with both micro- (organizational capabilities) and macro-level (environmental change) evolution, in the context of reciprocity between the two (Abatecola, 2014).

To biologists, evolution has no aim. The few random mutations proving beneficial to a species return better reproduction rates. Over time, this process delivers a species better adapted to its ecological niche. A sort of path of least resistance unwinds that has nothing necessarily to do with increasing complexity or progressiveness. But to change managers, it does not really matter how the practices came about that deliver competitive advantage, or who started them first, the important issue concerns implementation and further innovation. Change theorists have no need to adhere to a strict formulation of evolution. In order to best represent organizational and industrial change, two additional theoretical models allied to the biological philosophy have emerged. First, complexity theory accounts for unpredictable but innovative phenomena through structural patterns. We explore this theory in Chapter 9 on the systems philosophy. Second, appropriated from the boundaries of biology, the punctuated equilibrium model adeptly explains how industrial change can come about rapidly as well as through incremental adaptation.

Although evolutionary theorists generally agree that natural selection transpires incrementally on species, quite obviously industries can undergo significant change rapidly. In an attempt to express this possibility, organization theorists picked up on the punctuated equilibrium theory of evolution developed by Gould and Eldridge (1977). The theory predicts that species can experience radical change in a comparatively short period. Translated into an organizational position, the punctuated equilibrium model suggests that change can be revolutionary as well as evolutionary (Meyer, Goes and Brooks, 1993). Change researchers use the model to conceptualize how industries can experience immense restructuring and upheaval in between lengthy periods of relative stability (Anderson and Tushman, 1990; Kimberly and Miles, 1980). Massive industrial transformations can be stimulated by unusual accelerations through the normal life-cycle stages (Kimberly and Miles, 1980), or from acute change in structure, strategy or technology (Laughlin, 1991; Miller and Friesen, 1984; Miles and Snow, 1978; Tushman and Romanelli, 1985). Change can be unpredictable as well as uncontrollable.

CONCLUSION

The idea that organizations and industries progress through common life cycles and collectively adapt via competition and collaboration represent productive metaphors within the biological philosophy. It helps that we relate intuitively to organisms, and conceptualizing organizations in this way proves helpful for consolidating the complex world of change into some understandable principles. However, the biological philosophy labours when organizations and industries depart from the way nature works.

The life-cycle model views organizational change in terms of progress through stages of natural development. The life-cycle approach assumes that change proceeds progressively, sequentially and predictably in an unstoppable hierarchical fashion. Offering vague but prescriptive advice, the life cycle's basic premise holds that stages determine the best change management intervention, although sometimes organizations can move from one stage to the next due to poor environmental fit (Baird and Meshoulam, 1988).

Where the life-cycle model has waned, biological evolution as applied through organizational ecology and ecosystems has gained some ground. Change managers should pay close attention to the lessons organizational ecology offers concerning density of competition and its impact on adaptation. Environment plays a pivotal role in determining the nature of change organizations require in order to obtain competitive advantage (Hu, 2017). It is apparent that understanding symbiotic relationships that offer access to new knowledge, resources and experience will be important to practitioners looking to a biological philosophy for guidance.

Despite the intuitive appeal of biological metaphors, their application tends to overlook the most troublesome part of change: its implementation. What to change will be an easier question to answer than how to change. Yet, this would be expected given the mutual exclusivity between organizational strategy and organizational ecology (Hu, 2017). We repeat a theme common to this text. Irrespective of a theory's elegance, organizational change is less linear and clean than disjointed and messy. Charles Darwin never approved of the use of his theories to human affairs. In Steve Jones' update of Darwin's revolutionary book, *The Origin of Species*, he claimed that his own book 'has nothing on the various attempts, more or less infantile, to apply Darwinism to Civilization' (Jones, 1999, p. xxix). Accounting for human intentionality adds a level of complexity difficult to model with any metaphor than adheres to immutable laws. In organizational change, the exceptions should command our interest as acutely as the rules.

REFERENCES

Abatecola, Gianpaolo (2013), 'Survival or failure within the organisational life cycle: What lessons for managers?', *Journal of General Management*, **38** (4), 23–38.

Abatecola, Gianpaolo (2014), 'Research in organizational evolution: What comes next?', *European Management Journal*, **32** (3), 434–43.

Amankwah-Amoah, Joseph (2016), 'An integrative process model of organisational failure', *Journal of Business Research*, **69** (9), 3388–97.

Anderson, P. and M. Tushman (1990), 'Technological discontinuities and dominant designs: A cyclical model of technological change', *Administrative Science Quarterly*, **35** (4), 604–33.

Arthur, Jeffrey B. and C. L. Huntley (2005), 'Ramping up the organizational learning curve: Assessing the impact of deliberate learning on organizational performance under gainsharing', *Academy of Management Journal*, **48** (6), 1159–70.

Baird, Lloyd and I. Meshoulam (1988), 'Managing two fits of strategic human resource management', *Academy of Management Review*, **13** (1), 116–28.

Barnett, William P. and M. T. Hansen (1996), 'The red queen in organizational evolution', *Strategic Management Journal*, **17**, 139–57.

Bennett, Roger (2016), 'Factors contributing to the early failure of small new charity start-ups', *Journal of Small Business and Enterprise Development*, **23** (2), 333–48.

Beverland, Michael B. and L. S. Lockshin (2001), 'Organizational life cycles in small New Zealand wineries', *Journal of Small Business Management*, **39** (4), 354–62.

Breslin, Dermot (2016), 'What evolves in organizational co-evolution?', *Journal of Management and Governance*, **20** (1), 45–67.

Chandler, Alfred D., Jr. (1962), *Strategy and Structure*, Cambridge, MA: MIT Press.

Churchill, Neil C. and V. L. Lewis (1983), 'The five stages of small business growth', *Harvard Business Review*, **61** (3), 30–50.

Demil, B., X. Lecocq and V. Warnier (2018), 'Business model thinking, business ecosystems and platforms: The new perspective on the environment of the organization', *M@n@gement*, **21** (4), 1213–28.

Dodge, Robert H. and J. E. Robbins (1992), 'An empirical investigation of the organizational life cycle model for small business development and survival', *Journal of Small Business Management*, January, 28–37.

Galbraith, Jay (1982), 'The stages of growth', *Journal of Business Strategy*, **3** (1), 70–9.

Garnett, Philip, S. Mollan and R. A. Bentley (2015), 'Complexity in history: Modelling the organisational demography of the British banking sector', *Business History*, **57** (1), 182–202.

Gould, Stephen J. and N. Eldridge (1977), 'Punctuated equilibria: The tempo and model of evolution reconsidered', *Paleobiology*, **3**, 115–51.

Greiner, Larry E. (1972), 'Evolution and revolution as organizations grow', *Harvard Business Review*, **76** (3), 55–67.

Haire, Mason (ed.) (1959), *Modern Organization Theory*, New York: Wiley.

Hanks, Steven H., C. J. Watson, E. Jansen and G. N. Chandler (1993), 'Tightening the life-cycle construct: A taxonomic study of growth stage configurations in high-technology organizations', *Entrepreneurship: Theory and Practice*, **18** (2), 5–29.

Hannan, Michael T. and J. Freeman (1977), 'The population ecology of organizations', *American Journal of Sociology*, **82**, 929–64.

Hannan, Michael T., L. Polos and G. R. Carroll (2007), *Logics of Organization Theory: Audiences, Code, and Ecologies*, Princeton, NJ: Princeton University Press.

Hu, Yixin (2017), 'Strategy and ecology: A synthesis and research agenda', *International Journal of Organizational Analysis*, **25** (3), 456–67.

Jabłoński, Adam and M. Jabłoński (2016), 'Research on business models in their life cycle', *Sustainability*, **8** (5), 430.

Jones, Gareth R. (2004), *Organizational Theory, Design, and Change: Text and Cases*, Upper Saddle River, NJ: Pearson Education International.

Jones, Steve (1999), *Almost Like a Whale: The Origin of Species Updated*, London: Doubleday.

Kezar, Adrianna J. (2000), *Understanding and Facilitating Change in Higher Education in the 21st Century*, Washington, DC: Jossey-Bass.

Kimberly, John and R. H. Miles (1980), *The Organizational Life-cycle*, San Francisco, CA: Jossey-Bass.

Laughlin, Richard C. (1991), 'Environmental disturbances and organizational transitions and transformations: Some alternative models', *Organization Studies*, **12** (2), 209–32.

Lawrence, Benjamin, J. J. Zhang and J. Heineke (2016), 'A life-cycle perspective of professionalism in services', *Journal of Operations Management*, **42**, 25–38.

Lester, Donald L., J. A. Parnell and S. Carraher (2003), 'Organization life cycle: A five-stage empirical scale', *International Journal of Organizational Analysis*, **11** (4), 339–54.

Levy, Amir and U. Merry (1986), *Organizational Transformation: Approaches, Strategies, Theories*, New York: Praeger.

Lu, Chao, K. Rong, J. You and Y. Shi (2014), 'Business ecosystem and stakeholders' role transformation: Evidence from Chinese emerging electric vehicle industry', *Expert Systems with Applications*, **41** (10), 4579–95.

Mayr, Ernst (2002), *What Evolution Is*, London: Phoenix.

Meyer, Alan D., J. B. Goes and G. R. Brooks (1993), 'Organizations reacting to hyperturbulence', in George P. Huber and W. H. Glick (eds), *Organizational Change and Redesign: Ideas and Insights for Improving Performance*, New York: Oxford University Press, pp. 66–111.

Miles, Raymond E. and C. C. Snow (1978), *Organizational Strategy, Structure, and Process*, New York: McGraw-Hill.

Miller, Danny and P. H. Friesen (1980), 'Momentum and revolution in organizational adaptation', *Academy of Management Journal*, **23** (4), 591–614.

Miller, Danny and P. H. Friesen (1984), 'A longitudinal study of the corporate life cycle', *Management Science*, **30** (10), 1161–83.

Moore, James F. (1993), 'Predators and prey: A new ecology of competition', *Harvard Business Review*, **71** (3), 75–86.

Oldham, Matthew (2018), 'How fast to run in the Red Queen race?', *Intelligent Systems in Accounting, Finance and Management*, **25** (1), 28–43.

Porter, Terry B. (2006), 'Coevolution as a research framework for organizations and the natural environment', *Organization and Environment*, **19** (4), 479–504.

Pundziene, Asta, V. Kundrotas and Z. Lydeka (2006), 'Management challenges in rapidly growing Lithuanian enterprises', *Baltic Journal of Management*, **1** (1), 34–48.

Quinn, Robert E. and K. Cameron (1983), 'Organizational life cycles and shifting criteria of effectiveness: Some preliminary evidence', *Management Science*, **29** (1), 33–51.

Tam, Steven and D. E. Gray (2016), 'Organisational learning and the organisational life cycle', *European Journal of Training and Development,* **40** (1), 2–20.

Tamayo, Unai and G. Vargas (2019), 'Biomimetic economy: Human ecological-economic systems emulating natural ecological systems', *Social Responsibility Journal*, **15** (6), 772–85.

Tushman, Michael L. and E. Romanelli (1985), 'Organization evolution: A metamorphosis model of convergence and reorientation', in Larry L. Cummings and B. M. Staw (eds), *Research in Organizational Behaviour*, Greenwich, CT: JAI Press, pp. 171–222.

Van de Ven, Andrew H. and M. S. Poole (1995), 'Explaining development and change in organizations', *Academy of Management Review*, **20** (3), 510–40.

Veile, Johannes W., D. Kiel, J. M. Müller and K. Voigt (2019), 'Ecosystem 4.0: A supply chain perspective on business model innovation', *Proceedings of the XXX International Society for Professional Innovation Management Innovation Conference, Florence, Italy*, pp. 16–19.

Wagner, Stephan M. (2011), 'Supplier development and the relationship life-cycle', *International Journal of Production Economics*, **129** (2), 277–83.

Washington, Marvin and E. J. Zajac (2005), 'Status evolution and competition: Theory and evidence', *Academy of Management Journal*, **48** (2), 282–96.

Wilson, Edward O. (1998), *Consilience: The Unity of Knowledge*, London: Little, Brown and Company.

Witt, Ulrich (2004), 'The evolutionary perspective on organizational change and the theory of the firm', 3rd ETE Workshop, Sophia-Antipolis, 29–30 January, 1–23.

Yu, Zhiyuan (2016), 'The effects of resources, political opportunities and organisational ecology on the growth trajectories of AIDS NGOs in China', *VOLUNTAS: International Journal of Voluntary and Nonprofit Organizations*, **27** (5), 2252–73.

5. The models philosophy: 'changing consultants'

INTRODUCTION

At some stage, almost all organizations must face the need for change, whether due to external factors such as increasing competition or decreasing market share, or internal factors such as new technologies or processes. To achieve change most organizations utilize a formal strategy both to achieve success and to minimize any negative effects. The primary consideration underlying most basic questions relevant to change relates to economic factors. For example, will the change help promote the organization internally or against its competitors, or will it produce savings, increase productivity, employ more people or improve its product range? In essence, is the change fundamentally and economically worthwhile or necessary? This chapter introduces the models philosophy, which advocates predetermined, one-size-fits-all, stepwise, linear frameworks for introducing change that are 'guaranteed' to deliver on the standard list of outcomes almost all change agents seek.

Organizations will always need the intellectual agility to react to problems and there is inherently a constant need to invest in capabilities to promote or restore stability. The degree of risk involved in seeking to alter the existing methodology working within an organization needs to be understood. Risk must be measured against the holistic wellbeing of the organization. Change leaders must consider the effect on the drivers of growth, the complexity of the proposed change, the appropriateness of the timing for the change, the potential social, economic and technological repercussions inherent in the change, and the psychological effect on the staff. To successfully achieve change, organizations need to create an approach to achieve that change. Any approach needs to determine how best to implement change, how to mitigate its effect upon staff and how to measure its effectiveness.

As a generalization, change is almost universally disliked, as we shall explore in detail in Chapter 11, the critical philosophy. Change takes people out of their accustomed comfort zones and invariably precedes the need for additional effort, the potential for displacement or the removal of benefits, as well as everything from aggravation to confrontation. As a natural consequence, leaders and other senior staff frequently employ consultants to be the bearers of what might be considered by employees as bad news. Consultants, in this regard, are highly useful because they take the onus off management and provide welcome resources to progress change, while affording a target for employees' anger or annoyance. In the event of failure, they also provide a convenient scapegoat for management. This chapter examines the nature of change interventions typically presented by consultants. It refers to 'models' because the preferred change methods tend to import ready-made, one-size-fits-all approaches that place an exclusive emphasis on one particular concept, idea or framework. Consultants employ a models philosophy when they use the same change approach for every client that employs them. Naturally, delivering variations on the same model for every client is the most economically advantageous structure that a change consultant can use, so it is also the default approach. In the forthcoming sections, we first present the context in which consultants are engaged, and how consulting models are deployed for change, before outlining some of the most common models as a means to demonstrate their character. This chapter is a little different to the others in that it explores a common, but much less theoretical philosophical approach. Our aim is not to provide an inventory of recent change models wielded by consultants, but rather to demonstrate *how* the models philosophy has been shaped by a *kind* of thinking and method that originated at the tail end of the twentieth century.

THE CHANGE REALITY

Change introduces a critical moment in the life cycle of an organization. This is especially true if the organization decides to utilize external consultants in an endeavour to investigate what is, in effect, a coal-face problem. It risks declaring an unspoken suggestion to staff that management has lost a degree of faith in their combined ability to solve internal problems or to secure sufficient improvements in existing systems to satisfy the needs of management. For management, it is a reminder that staff should never be demeaned or lost to a misplaced sense of management's moral, intellectual or economic superiority. However, overcoming the resistance of entrenched cultures, or the need to acquire new skills, may make the selection of consultants to oversee the change process almost inevitable.

If the decision to employ a consultant is made, then the most difficult question for management relates to the selection of who. Does it really matter what change model is adopted to drive change? Some models are more effective under certain circumstances and some are more suited to specific organizations. Further, models can be based on one primary fulcrum for change, like the individual employee, technologies, systems, policies or culture. In fact, not only do consultants tend to use a simplified version of a favourite philosophy to guide their change models, they can also mix and match.

As organizations begin to work with consultants, they tend to establish a formal change methodology to ensure that the negative effects of change can be minimized. The well-matched selection of change model to organization can result in a successful outcome, while conversely, a poor match can not only invalidate the change process, but also may cause irreparable harm. Selection of a consultant is not and should not be straightforward. It should be premised upon considerations such as the type and size of the organization seeking the change, its leadership structure, the degree of change being sought and whether the change is being pursued by management or is being imposed by the board or external stakeholders. It is easy to understand that a bureaucracy will have a different mindset to a manufacturing company, a large organization to a small one, and a privately owned organization to one that has to satisfy both a board of directors and a number of shareholders.

Once a decision has been made to seek assistance via the use of consultants, questions relating to the selection of both the consultant and the model the proposed consultant may use to progress the change arise. The multitude of reasons for seeking change within an organization have been noted and discussed throughout this book. Nonetheless, it is useful to reiterate some of the more basic considerations surrounding change management. This is because the change philosophy an organization prefers will influence the selection of consultant. Conversely, the selection of consultant will dictate which method of change philosophy is to be utilized. This is not to suggest that every consultant or group of consultants will employ predetermined models, but most consulting firms already have their own bespoke models and will naturally gravitate towards them.

Selection of a consultant or change philosophy may simply depend upon such basic factors as whether a particular consultant has been utilized in the past or whether the change leader has familiarity with a particular change model. It may depend upon the degree of change required, whether one or several problems need to be considered, the degree of rigidity within the system or the primary basis upon which the need for change is formulated. Almost inevitably, the bigger consultants become the prime movers of change particularly when the change to be delivered is substantial. It is worth remembering that consultants are not always creators or originators; often they simply seek aggregation.

There are numerous philosophies of change, and each one has the potential to underpin a suite of change models. While many are successful under certain circumstances, those successes may be mitigated under less fortunate circumstances. Many philosophies retain some utility under any conditions, but it is almost inevitable that many change models will ultimately become captive to the entropic laws of decay, and will diminish in relevance as the organizational world transforms. Most change and transition models display some similarities. An understanding of the differing models tends to show that elements of many models might be more usefully combined to form new models that better fit an organization.

The aim of this chapter is to propose and examine a selection of modern change models, and to suggest some of their benefits and deficits. It is best to bear in mind, however, that change management models are frequently contradictory in nature and evidence of success may well be confined to the unique circumstances of organizations. Next, we begin with some older but well-entrenched models that remain influential as the philosophical foundations to newer models.

LEWIN'S UNFREEZING

Of all the change models, Kurt Lewin's is probably in itself the least complex, although it does permeate the underlying structure of several other models. Lewin was a follower of the classical school of thinking regarding organizational change. He argued that for most organizations, stability was the norm, and that for change to occur there would be a need to either reduce the forces underlying that stability, or conversely, increase the forces for change. To that end he proposed a change model emphasizing change as a journey rather than a single step, and one requiring both time and leadership. Though Lewin developed his model in the 1940s, it retains some validity today. Lewin's philosophy involves three basic steps, or what he termed unfreezing, changing and refreezing. The process requires the removal of the existing system, the development of a new way of working and, finally, cementing the revised approach as the norm.

It might be argued that Lewin's model has certain loose similarities with Hegel's 'concrete, abstract, absolute' model, which in turn was based upon Johann Fichte's, triadic idea 'thesis–antithesis–synthesis', as a formula for the explanation of change. Thesis, antithesis, synthesis is a progression of three ideas or propositions wherein the first idea is followed by a second idea that negates the first, and the conflict between the first and second ideas is resolved by a third idea (Schnitker and Emmons, 2013). Lewin's philosophy appears to have adopted the thought that the 'thesis' explains the existing process that needs to be unfrozen, the 'antithesis' represents the development of the new idea that comes about as a result of the change, while the 'synthesis' is the acceptance and then refreezing of the new idea.

Unfreezing

Unfreezing relates to the existing system. It reminds all stakeholders of the existing status quo and how that existing system is hindering or failing the organization in some way. In this process, it is necessary to both identify the existing arrangement and to show clearly why current ways of strategy, processes or organizational structures need to be changed. Involving all applicable organizational members in this process is essential. The logic underlying the change must be well documented and understood. Once the need for change is understood and accepted by staff, the greater will be their motivation to accept the change. The primary aim of unfreezing is to break the psychological attachment to the past.

Changing

Changing represents the new values, attitudes and processes, and the method by which they are to be implemented. This can be a difficult time as staff and other stakeholders need to unlearn the old and embrace the new. The stage requires strong communication and education, as well as reinforcement of the reason for the change, and the benefits that will accrue from acceptance of the new norm.

Refreezing

The final activity under the Lewin model is refreezing. Lewin also refers to it as model freezing. Once the new norms of behaviour surrounding the replacement structure and processes have been established, it becomes essential to cement them into the organization's culture. The process requires the endorsement of all organizational members, including unions and management. Lewin accepts that the transition from one step to the next may be time-consuming and that the time spent by any single individual in any one stage may vary.

Benefits of Lewin's Model

In its simplistic form, Lewin's model has numerous attractions. Identify the problem, have everyone appreciate the problem, identify a new paradigm to replace the old problem, and solidify that into place. If practice follows theory, Lewin's philosophy may be one of the most effective organizational change models available, and one of the easiest to implement. The model becomes most effective when the change required is straightforward, relatively simple to explain and easy to implement. It also has greater prospects for success when positive rewards move individuals out of their comfort zones and reinforce key, desired behaviours. Because of the necessity to analyse all aspects of change, hidden mistakes can be readily spotted. Its major benefit lies with implementing in-depth analysis rather than in dealing with minor or ongoing change.

Disadvantages of Lewin's Model

Although logical in concept, and undoubtedly goal- and plan-orientated, a number of complications may arise. If, for example, change is required not because of an existing problem but because changes in technology require a completely new process, Lewin's unfreezing stage may be compromised. It is, after all, difficult to unfreeze something that did not previously exist. The unfreezing process itself may be time-consuming and difficult to achieve. In addition, the need to marshal all organizational members and stakeholders at each stage of the change process is paramount. There is no guarantee that once started the process can effectively continue without the complete and wholehearted backing of those who control the process. In consequence, the entire change process has to be carefully executed. Members who too readily accept the new process may be oblivious to the feelings and attitudes of those still transitioning, which in turn might cause resistance or a total lack of enthusiasm. Consequently, failure here may result in members reverting to previous, more comfortable ways of thinking. An understanding of the emotional concerns of members could, arguably, also be lacking. A final common criticism of Lewin is that his model fails to understand that most organizations need to change constantly, which means that refreezing will inevitably become the beginning of the next cycle seeking to unfreeze again.

BRIDGES' TRANSITION MODEL

In his classic book, Bridges (1991) created the transition model, which focuses on what he called transitions, rather than change. Though only subtle in difference, the distinction is important in order to understand the evolution of the models philosophy. We shall see this evolution in bold when we delve into the psychological philosophy in Chapter 8. According to Bridges, change 'happens' to people, desired or not. Because change often occurs quickly, it affords individual organizational members little say in the matter, typically resulting in discomfort and resistance. Transitions, on the other hand, reflect what occurs in individuals' minds as they slowly experience the impact of change. It precedes the physical end state of the transformation and is measurable in both the psychological disposition of an organizational member as well as in their behaviour. Bridges emphasized the importance of understanding transitions as a key for organizations to succeed in making changes stick.

Bridges' model has some similarities to Lewin's unfreezing approach. Both have three stages to be undertaken before change can be accepted. Lewin's model, however, requires deliberate direction from above, while Bridges' model is more facilitative, requiring managers to assist individuals in progressing through the change. The focus for Bridges lies with the psychological changes that underpin major organizational change and particularly on those that impact an individual's transition through the change. Bridges' model insists that individuals progress through three transitions in order to realize change. They are: ending, losing and letting go; the neutral zone; and the new beginning. According to Bridges, individuals will experience each stage at their own pace, some quickly and some more slowly. As a result, for the collective organization, all phases will end up overlapping.

Ending, Losing and Letting Go

This first stage of transition involves identifying what will be lost in the change process and accepting that loss. At this stage, confusion, anxiety and resentment appear. Individuals face losing that with which they are familiar and comfortable. Actual loss of job security may occur as well as the perceived loss of values, status or other benefits. Low morale and motivation are common and resistance towards the change tends to peak. Bridges suggested that individuals can experience a range of heightened emotions before they will accept that something is ending and something new is taking its place. In many ways it has overtones of Elizabeth Kübler-Ross' grief model, which we explore shortly.

The Neutral Zone

The neutral zone comprises the second stage of transition. The second stage marks the ending of the old system and the beginning of acceptance and adoption of the change; the bridge between the old and the new. Some organizational members may still be mourning the loss of the familiar while others may be welcoming the new approach. During the neutral zone, old patterns of behaviour are extinguished while new patterns gradually take their place. Direction and support will be needed from leaders, enhanced by some quick wins if possible. All change seeks a seamless transition from concept to practice. However, the speed of transition is moderated by the degree to which individuals accept the change; a process that calls for an indeterminant neutral zone wherein the changes can be accommodated.

The New Beginning

The new beginning signals the period of final acceptance, and if it resolves smoothly can be a time of energy and initiative. Assuming a successful transition through the neutral zone, individuals now commit, psychologically and practically, to the new reality. There can be no new beginning, however, unless organizational members have found some closure to the neutral zone period, and the uncertainty and disquiet it brings. At the new beginning stage, organizational members often take on new roles, and with them a renewed understanding of their purpose. For some, the opportunity to slip back into the previous stage remains strong; returning to the neutral zone is necessary for these individuals.

Benefits of Bridges' Model

The most important advantage of Bridges' model is that it requires the involvement of every individual involved in the change process. Involvement inspires bonding and fosters loyalty to each other and to the organization as a whole. The model also has a 'self-help' nature to it, which permits management and staff to work closely together. Indeed, by accounting for individual emotions and views, the model recommends numerous ways in which the individual may proceed through the transition stage. Yet, in terms of its contribution to the models philosophy, Bridges' model has proven both prescient and resilient because of the neutral zone. During the neutral zone period, organizations do not press change, but rather allow individuals time to proceed through the grieving process and to adapt and accept the change. Bridges' model clings to optimism, however, assuming that eventually everyone will travel through the neutral zone to a favourable conclusion. Completed successfully, everyone will be on board with the change and for the most part will be totally enthused about the opportunities presented. The opportunity to progress from a situational change to a psychological transition seems to be the key.

Disadvantages of Bridges' Model

Perhaps the biggest disadvantage of Bridges' model is that it does not constitute a structured framework that allows an organization to manage change from beginning to end within a designated timeframe. There appear to be few tangible, actionable steps and no conditions impeding progress from one step to the next; the model does not offer a step-by-step mechanism for implementing change. Furthermore, the model's main advantage—the limitless time within the neutral zone—may also be a debilitating disadvantage. The delay between ending the old process and initiating the new process relies upon the slowest transitions, which tend to be found with the most disgruntled and disaffected organizational members. Bridges acknowledged the resulting frustration from change leaders when most organizational members have reached a new beginning, but remain obstructed by a minority still mired in the neutral zone. Dealing with emotional reactions to change requires understanding and patience. People rarely behave as the models predict. In fact, conflict between individuals, between managers, and between managers and employees, can derail the grieving process and replace it with a power struggle. If enough people refuse to accept change then no amount of transitional time will produce the required effect. According to Bridges, a specified change management plan must be visible to all organizational members that accounts for both the change and the consequent transition.

KOTTER'S EIGHT-STEP CHANGE MODEL

When Kotter (1995) introduced his influential eight-step change model, he also set into motion a new era in the models philosophy as it popularized consulting-style interventions. Kotter clearly appreciated Lewin's model but suggested that it was limited by a lack of specificity. In response, Kotter centred his model on organizational processes, arguing that processes constitute the way things are done. He therefore reasoned that if organizational leaders could change processes, they could also change the foundational ways that their organizations operated. Yet, Kotter recognized that change can never be a quick and simple process. Consequently, he proposed that eight key steps must be completed in order for change to be truly endorsed and accepted: 1: create a sense of urgency; 2: form a powerful coalition; 3: create a vision for change; 4: communicate the vision; 5: remove obstacles; 6: create short-term wins; 7: build on the change; and 8: institutionalize the new approach.

Step 1: Create a Sense of Urgency

Kotter began with the premise that organizational members must understand the need for change, which would then create a sense of urgency to band together and take immediate action. To aid the sense of urgency, problems, issues and potential solutions need to be discussed openly with all concerned. Kotter indicated that for change to be successful at least 75 per cent of a company's management needed to 'buy in' to the change. Given the level of buy-in necessary, Kotter argued that the initial stage should not be rushed and should concentrate on the need for change rather than on the change itself. He further claimed that most change failures are attributable to insufficient investment in the first urgency step.

Step 2: Form a Powerful Coalition

To avoid the belief that change is being imposed by one leader or manager, Kotter suggested that an organization must build and present a coalition encompassing individuals with a variety of skills, and representing all activities and areas. He assumed that change coalitions have a synergistic effect that maximizes effectiveness, spreading the word to all areas of the organization and permitting useful delegation. In addition, a good coalition builds trust, fosters creativity and promotes the sense of ownership of the change process.

Step 3: Create a Vision for Change

According to Kotter the creation of a vision creates both an understanding of the overall aim and the method by which change will proceed. To be effective it needs to be simple in concept, inspirational and easily communicable. A strategy for achieving the vision must be developed.

Step 4: Communicate the Vision

Having developed the vision, the next step involves continuously communicating it to all organizational members in order to garner feedback. The need for feedback is absolutely paramount particularly with those individuals most closely connected to the change. Use of the coalition provides the opportunity for the widespread dissemination of the change vision.

Step 5: Remove Obstacles

Almost invariably there will be obstacles to the change, whether they be individuals, traditions, legislation, competitive pressures or alternative ideas. All must be identified and overcome quickly and decisively. The step may require a degree of risk taking, especially if it affects other systems and structures.

Step 6: Create Short-Term Wins

Kotter emphasized the importance of fostering motivation to continue on the path towards activation of the vision for change. Deliberate or manufactured short-term wins are beneficial as they can demonstrate the benefits of the proposed change. Recognizing and rewarding individuals becomes essential during the sixth step.

Step 7: Build on the Change

Consolidating any improvement becomes a key function during the penultimate step, as it avoids complacency and allows for the process to be reinvigorated. Constantly challenging existing systems and seeking continuous improvement should be normalized.

Step 8: Institutionalize the New Approach

The final step has strong similarities to Lewin's refreezing stage in that it is important to celebrate and reward the new behaviours and successes. Continuing attention must be directed towards ensuring that the change has become, and will remain, part of the organization's culture. Kotter claimed that only near the end of the change cycle will culture and change coalesce.

Benefits of Kotter's Model

Kotter's model has depth with its eight steps providing clear guidance together with suitable steps for employee communication. Though an easy model to apply, it has several degrees of added complexity compared to Lewin's three stages. Nonetheless, it can be argued that if all steps are followed through correctly, the chances of success for the change initiative will be improved, especially since the process focuses on the preparation and acceptance of change rather than the actual change. The model also displays unmistakable similarities with a suite of other approaches that emphasize the creation of a clear vision, excellent communication, the creation of short-term wins and the celebration of successes. Kotter's model can be distinguished by its priority on identifying obstacles and taking tangible steps to overcome them. The early steps in Kotter's model are the most productive: creating a sense of urgency and building a vision of change via a united group of individuals. Accordingly, the first two steps provide the motivation for continuance.

Disadvantages of Kotter's Model

The primary disadvantage of Kotter's model is its rigidity. He insisted that every step must be followed without exception, and even if undertaken correctly, change may take an inordinate amount of time to accomplish. Ignoring any step may cause the entire initiative to fail. Identified obstacles can be difficult to overcome particularly if they involve disruption or amendments to other systems, opposition from key individuals or the limitations of existing legislation or workplace laws. Even after change has been implemented, it is important to ensure that backsliding does not occur. Kotter accepted the possibly that up to 70 per cent of change initiatives will fail as a result of inadequate preparation, or the failure to follow all eight steps precisely. While the early stages of Kotter's model tend to be more attractive to change leaders, the latter stages can easily end up being delegated. While the model fits well into classical hierarchical organizations, it does have the disadvantage of being seen as top-down with limited opportunities for true participation by everyone. With feedback constrained, frustration, and even grief, may emerge. If, as Kotter stated, 75 per cent of an organization's management need to 'buy in' to the change, then that still leaves up to 25 per cent who may actively oppose or simply ignore the change.

MCKINSEY 7 S FRAMEWORK

The foundations for the 7 S model came out of work conducted in the late 1970s, initially by Tom Roberts, then a consultant with McKinsey & Company. Roberts was later joined by another McKinsey consultant, Robert Waterman, and along with academics Tony Athos and Richard Pascale, developed what became known as the 7 S framework. Originally outlined in a journal article authored by Waterman, Peters and Phillips (1980), the model became a major part of the platform onto which Peters and Waterman (1982) launched their influential book *In Search of Excellence*. The framework remains in use today, and has been developed and modified countless times. We include it here because the framework exemplifies the typical composition of consulting approaches upon which the model philosophy relies.

Peters and Waterman's concern focused primarily on how organizations were organized and managed. They started by identifying seven internal elements of an organization that should be aligned and mutually reinforcing. Consequently, if change becomes necessary, the model would show an organization how to determine what elements of the business need to be realigned to again achieve harmony. In a sense, alignment represents the 7 S version of (re)freezing. The model categorized the seven elements as either hard or soft. In their writings, Peters and Waterman emphasized that the most important aspects of an organization reside not in the hard technical aspects of the organization, but rather in the soft cultural aspects. Aspects classified as hard relate primarily to those influenced by management. They are: strategy; structure; and systems. By contrast, the elements considered soft may be considered within the bounds of culture. They are: shared values; skills; style; and staff.

Strategy

Strategy refers to how the organization operates and how, by clearly communicating what its objectives and goals are, it maintains an advantage over its competitors. Strategy also determines an organization's ability to manage its resources.

Structure

As the name implies, this element considers how the organization is constructed, how its chain of command operates, and how all sections within the organization interrelate, report and operate.

Systems

Systems cover the formal processes and procedures including information technology, operated by the organization.

Shared Values

The standards, norms and behaviour expected and often promulgated within the organization make up the shared values. It is around these shared values that the culture of the organization becomes scaffolded. When represented visually as a circle of six categories, Peters and Waterman placed shared values at the centre, demonstrating that values are central to all elements of the model.

Skills

The expertise accumulated and developed by all levels of staff and management determine the skills level within an organization. Skills help determine the level of achievement that the organization can accomplish. It is often the lack of skills or the need to alter or improve that skill level that creates the need for change.

Style

Style represents the way in which management leads the organization, which in turn reflects on the culture within the organization, and thus on its productivity.

Staff

The basis for any organization's effectiveness lies in the capabilities of its staff. Consideration here is with its training, knowledge, skills and behaviour.

Benefits of the McKinsey 7 S Framework

Although the model was initially intended to guide organizational effectiveness in the broadest sense, its effectiveness as a tool for determining how a given strategy may be implemented should not be underestimated. Because the 7 S presents a holistic model, it allows leaders to consider potential changes in advance by looking at how that change affects every element of the organization. As a result, management has a lens through which to identify those elements that need to be amended in order to restore equilibrium, or to enact a change successfully. Moreover, the model allows both an immediate analytical checklist and an effective and useful tool in decision making during change implementation. And, by displaying weaknesses and highlighting areas requiring attention, the 7 S model provides a sound basis for processing change.

The 7 S model—and the innumerable models like it that have subsequently been developed—has proven most effective when assessing internal business, providing a comprehensive framework for analysing the potential impact of changing elements, and providing a useful strategy for determining and reaching the required organizational state. It provides assurance that all elements of an organization are aligned with its vision, objectives and strategy. Like Lewin's change model, the 7 S framework has the potential to be most useful when contemplating change at the macro level, and with large-scale organizations.

Disadvantages of the McKinsey 7 S Framework

While for most Western-style organizations McKinsey can be a value-driven model, this may not be so certain in some cultural contexts. For example, it may be less useful as an international model. Sufficient empirical evidence to validate the model is also lacking. Failure to ensure alignment in any of the seven Ss may also affect reliability. Indeed, one of its potential disadvantages is created by its own internal capability. Because seven different factors are considered, their very interrelationship makes for complexity, which is amplified by the qualitative variables in the model that make adequate measurement difficult. A further disadvantage of the 7 S model lies with its inability to consider how the external environment can impact upon change. In addition, the model operates in a static mode and lacks the flexibility to accurately measure any component, let alone how they all interrelate. Implementation of the model may also be time-consuming and highly complex. While of greater use in a smaller establishment, larger organizations may find impediments to providing sufficient dedicated staff to oversee all aspects of the change procedure at once.

NUDGE THEORY

Nudge theory was introduced by Thaler and Sunstein (2008). Based upon the emerging disciplines of behavioural economics and social psychology, its central premise holds that human brains have built-in cognitive biases that affect rational decisions. Although to date most 'nudges' have been aimed at public policy, the consulting world has taken to it with enthusiasm for application to change management. The theory represents an important inclusion here as it presaged a new kind of change model placing greater emphasis on the link between psychology and behaviour.

Nudge theory requires management to understand how people think, make decisions and behave, and then 'nudge' them via behavioural guidance towards new objectives. By steering organizational members into improving their thinking and decision making, managing change becomes more flexible and positive. Standard people management practices, including rewards systems, leadership development and promotion, all serve to steer behaviour one way or another. Nudge theory relies mainly on three specific characteristics: first, the nudge should not be economic in nature; second, it should help people choose useful behaviours; and third, it should occur voluntarily.

In a similar manner to Kotter and other change systems, the nudge change model has nominated steps. They are: 1: define the change; 2: consider the change from the employees' point of view; 3: use evidence to demonstrate to the employee the best option; 4: present the change as a choice; 5: listen to feedback; 6: limit obstacles; and 7: maintain momentum with short-term wins.

Step 1: Define the Change

For many the reasons for change may not be immediately obvious or its benefits worthwhile. Consequently, the proposed change needs to be clearly spelt out so that all organizational members understand the problem and the requirement for action.

Step 2: Consider the Change from the Employees' Point of View

Everyone involved in the change needs to feel part of the process. Participation avoids the belief that the change is being imposed. Failure to consider the employees' point of view may reinforce negativity towards the change and thus lead to resistance or underperformance. By noting and accepting the feelings, opinions and knowledge of individuals, resistance to change can be minimized. Initial criticism should be welcomed and individuals should be encouraged to participate in the change process.

Step 3: Use Evidence to Demonstrate to the Employee the Best Option

Because nudge theory begins with the assumption that people's hardwired biases can undermine rational decision making, leaders need to show that change will be in the interests of both the organization and its members. Thaler and Sunstein advised nudging people to make certain choices by influencing their situational or social beliefs. As a result, organizational members should voluntarily choose behaviours that satisfy both their own needs and those of the organization. The aim is to nudge against unfavourable biases and towards the decisions suggested by change leaders.

Step 4: Present the Change as a Choice

An essential principle of nudge theory maintains that the individual must retain freedom of choice; nudges cannot therefore involve coercion, and must remain transparent. However, as long as it does not prohibit any other options, a nudge can seek to modify existing unhelpful biases towards a selection determined by management.

Step 5: Listen to Feedback

Feedback provides an expression of current beliefs, information on how well the change is being accepted, and importantly, provides an understanding of the psychological status of organizational members, and thus the opportunity for further and future nudges.

Step 6: Limit Obstacles

Resistance to change may occur at any time during the change process. It may appear in the form of catastrophizing the change, operational resistance, deliberate sabotage, cultural misconception, lack of top or senior management involvement or inadequate middle-management support. It may also be limited by ineffective communication with employees, especially as a consequence of providing insufficient or vague information about the intended change.

Step 7: Maintain Momentum with Short-Term Wins

Like most change models, nudge theory attempts to maximize the potential for short-term wins. This improves employees' morale, generates momentum and helps confirm the efficacy of the change. It further helps those committed to change to remain motivated, while sidelining and placating cynics.

Recognizing and rewarding individual contributions plays an important role too.

Advantages of Nudge Theory

Nudge theory can be effective, despite its potential subtlety, as a model for change management that helps organizations understand how their members think, make decisions and behave. Such understanding allows the identification and subsequent modification of unhelpful influences, and helps place individuals in positive environments. By assisting employees to understand the importance of the change, while providing them with the opportunity to help choose the solution, nudges offer the motivation to see change through. It thus provides a bond between leaders and followers. If undertaken successfully, a nudge may influence choice and behaviour without taking away an individual's power to choose. Nudges can be cheap to implement while providing significant payoff. The theory eliminates coercive actions within the organization, and by influencing people's decision making can minimize opposition to change. The step-by-step approach provides a continual opportunity to influence behaviour towards the organizational requirements for change. Once initiated they may continually exert influence on behaviour.

Disadvantages of Nudge Theory

A major disadvantage of nudge theory is its paternalistic nature, focusing on perceived vulnerabilities in people's psychological behaviour; it thereby does little to promote autonomy and empowerment. In this respect, nudges are reminiscent of Plato's argument that philosophers should be the rulers of the republic as they alone possess the needed level of knowledge. After all, it may be that many people prefer to behave in what they believe is a rational way. In addition, no guarantee ensures that the originators of the nudge are free from cognitive bias, or that they know precisely how an individual may think or what it is that the individual really wants. Because actions ultimately reside with individuals, nudges may end up being unpredictable. Nudge theory—like other change approaches emanating from the models philosophy—can diminish or overlook the ethical ramifications that arise from its use. If applied inappropriately, some nudges become manipulations. It may not always be clear whether the benefit is to the organization rather than the individual. Additionally, nudges may be accidentally introduced and thus produce an unwelcome or unwanted result.

ADKAR MODEL

The genesis for the ADKAR model came from the work of Hiatt (2006), who analysed the change management programmes of a multitude of organizations and reached a view about the common elements in successful attempts. Hiatt argued that while it was the senior management who was ultimately responsible for change, their role was to be objective and not prescriptive. They were to be responsible to facilitate and enable change; to interpret rather than impose. Most importantly, enabling change should be managed with the individuals undertaking that change. As a result, ADKAR introduced a different emphasis for change models and, inevitably, for the role that consultants played within organizations as change agents.

ADKAR focuses on the individuals behind the change rather than on the change itself. Hiatt proposed that organizations do not change, but rather it is the people within the organizations who change, which in turn transforms the organization for which they work. Differing from many change models, ADKAR assumes that major change reflects the cumulative effect of individual, minor changes. The implication is that all involved individuals must support and willingly accept the change if it is to be successful, and in the process of so doing must personally change. ADKAR emphasizes the need for individuals to change and accept new ideas before an organization can improve its performance.

Just as Bridges' transitions model draws on the psychological philosophy (Chapter 8), ADKAR employs some of the ideas embedded in cognitive approaches to change (which we consider in detail as a strand within the psychological model in Chapter 8). ADKAR maintains that the cognitive (thinking) changes that need to occur within the minds of those affected by the change tend to be overlooked. In response, Hiatt proposed a methodology comprising five sequential actions or individual steps related to the ultimate goal. The steps are: 1: awareness—of the need and requirement for change; 2: desire—to bring about change as a participant; 3: knowledge—and ability to bring about the change; 4: ability—to utilize the knowledge gained in practice; and 5: reinforcement—to ensure everyone sticks to the new process.

Step 1: Awareness

Identifying the need for change and raising the awareness of that need to all organizational members arises as a common thread in change management models. Heightening awareness allows both managers and employees to accept the change or give reasons for their opposition. It also allows leaders to identify the areas in which employees remain unmotivated. Discussion with all organizational members is critical, especially with those initially unconvinced of the need for change in the first place.

Step 2: Desire

An awareness of the need for change does not mean that it will be automatically accepted. Criticism or ennui may still prevail even after leaders have described the necessity for change. Hiatt recommended additional work with those individuals still dissatisfied to ensure that they understand the negative consequences of inaction. If required, appeals to their emotional or logical nature may be necessary.

Step 3: Knowledge

Knowledge relies on the successful completion of the first two steps. Organizational members need to be committed for the change to flourish, which requires everyone involved to understand the practical aspects of the change. In short, everyone involved in the change must have the knowledge to enact the change in a practical sense. Translating understanding to practical knowledge will likely demand additional training.

Step 4: Ability

Providing that sufficient additional training has been completed, organizational members should be well placed to deliver change through their practical performance. There remains, however, a frequent divergence between theory and practice, and for a time, many individuals may need constant support during the initial phases of the change. Further and more extensive training and mentoring may need to be introduced.

Step 5: Reinforcement

Just as with other change management models, the ADKAR steps recognize the need to ensure that organizational members do not revert to old habits or previous processes, even subconsciously. Check systems can be employed to ensure that the new methodologies are maintained and sustained throughout a transition period. Additional time in implementing the change process will be required, along with the reinforcement of financial or other benefits for those involved.

Advantages of the ADKAR Model

The ADKAR model offers a bottom-up, structured, yet flexible approach to organizational change. It differs from other change models in that its emphasis is on individual change and outcomes rather than on process and tasks. Its focus on outcomes allows for easy transition and adaption of any change into the structure and culture of an organization. The model permits measurement throughout of how the change is progressing, allowing problems to be more easily recognized and rectified. Of all the change methods, the ADKAR model places far greater priority on how change ultimately relies on the people involved, thus suggesting that failure to change may not be the result of a poor change model, but rather because insufficient emphasis has been given to securing change within individuals.

Hiatt advised that the model would be particularly insightful in tackling dysfunctional change processes because it provides the opportunity to identify and evaluate what, if any, element is missing, whether it be awareness, desire, knowledge, ability or poor reinforcement. Dysfunctional change may also arise due to a small number of individuals who either do not see the need for change, or through lack of knowledge or skill are unable to function at the required level. ADKAR's primary benefit may be in deploying incremental change rather than in wholesale reorganization. Its weighting on people rather than on the more technical or business aspects of the organization provide the opportunity for a high success rate. ADKAR is similar to Kotter's model in that both methods tend to focus on the people within an organization rather than on the organization itself.

Disadvantages of the ADKAR Model

Although the model accepts that all appropriate steps discussed need to be implemented before continuation, it does offer the prospect of delay or uncertainty if some steps are completed inadequately. Attempts to move on without achieving success in all the preceding steps may cause resentment in some staff, particularly since the model places limited value on the emotional aspects of how change affects individuals. One advantage of the ADKAR model is that it works best with incremental change. As a consequence, it may be at a disadvantage when an organization requires macro-level or a wider level step-change, or when more complex and sophisticated change is warranted.

The ADKAR model requires that a specified series of steps needs to be followed in order for the change to be successful. A linear progression implies a process-led approach rather than the stated purpose of emphasizing an approach based on individual change. In turn, a more holistic programme management approach may need to be superimposed over the model to ensure that all required steps are formulated and undertaken thoroughly. Because the model is premised on change and outcomes rather than on process and tasks, it may not align favourably with hierarchical organizations that prefer a top-down approach to change management wherein the role of leadership looms large.

KÜBLER-ROSS FIVE-STAGE (GRIEF) MODEL

Although arguably difficult to categorize Kübler-Ross' (1969) five-stage (grief) theory as a formal change model, it exemplifies a style of intervention that maintains popularity amongst consultants, the legacy of the staged approach readily found in many current offerings. The reason revolves around its ability to work in harmony with other change models by providing a rationale for the emotional and psychological impact upon individuals working through the process of change.

The Kübler-Ross model documents the psychological changes dying patients undergo. The five-stage model, also known as the grief model or stage theory, maintains that while there is no specific pattern in an individual's emotional response, dying people generally progress through five stages of grieving: denial, anger, bargaining, depression and, finally, acceptance. These stages are not unique to death and may be applicable in any personal trauma including changes in the workplace. As a result, the stages can provide an insight into how individuals react to the impact of change. Several change models such as Lewin's unfreezing model and Kotter's eight-step change model, for example, were designed to help decide how change can be planned, while Kübler-Ross' model focuses on how the effect of that change on organizational members can be better understood and managed. Undertaking the process of change produces powerful emotions in individuals and Kübler-Ross' five stages of grief show how to deal with the sense of loss and uncertainty that change generates. Kübler-Ross was never of the belief that the stages must follow a linear pattern. She recognized that reactions may well differ. Nonetheless, as a model or framework, it retains popularity as a set of convenient signposts for understanding the feelings that may be encountered during the process of change.

Step 1: Denial

The initial denial stage occurs immediately after the trauma occurs; in the change process denial can arise when change is first seriously mooted. Once an organizational member enters denial, they become unable or unwilling to accept the inevitability of change, or even its reality. Under a denial mindset, the need for change—however real—seems unacceptable, leading to its resistance and rejection. From a psychological viewpoint, anxiety and fear of a new working reality drive an active opposition to the change. Unless confronted and managed, work productivity may decrease while sick or stress leave escalates.

Step 2: Anger

Once change has been initiated, denial can transform into anger, particularly if the change has a personal bearing on the way in which an individual works or has worked. In the first instance, a person's anger targets a scapegoat or someone to blame like a leader or supervisor. At the same time, leadership at this stage becomes critical as leaders must face up to the resistance and channel it in a positive way.

Step 3: Bargaining

In death, the bargaining process may be undertaken with God or reflect a person's metaphysical worldview. During change, however, compromise emerges as the bargaining tool; an attempt to avoid what is perceived as the worst-case scenario, or if that is not possible, to delay the inevitable.

Step 4: Depression

Depression arises when a person recognizes that change is certain and that its arrival will bring with it a new and, assumed to be, unfavourable reality. Although accepted, there often remains an emotional attachment to the pre-change era.

Step 5: Acceptance

The final stage of the Kübler-Ross model is acceptance. Ultimately, people begin to accept the change and to gain a measure of objectivity about, and resignation to, the changed situation. Acceptance allows for a measure of peace and even invigoration.

Advantages of the Kübler-Ross Five-Stage (Grief) Model

It should be remembered that Kübler-Ross' model was devised in order to help both those dying, and their families to cope with death and the subsequent bereavement. The application to change management has been a late but impactful arrival. Prior to Kübler-Ross, denial and suppression of feelings regarding death—and later change—were, at best, matters of the second order.

Although presented in an order, Kübler-Ross' stages should not be seen as perfectly linear or immutable. For example, individuals can travel back and forth within the stages or may remain in one stage for some time. In this regard, the model's approach was echoed by Lewin who also accepted that the period of transition from one stage to the next may not always be swift or clear. In addition, the stages originally outlined have evolved somewhat over the years and were never meant to pigeonhole all emotional reactions to change. Consequently, while they may be tempered or amended by the individual undergoing change, they do provide a clearly understood set of possible, even likely, reactions. Their explication provides change leaders with an understanding and an interpretation of the emotional reactions that might arise in organizational members.

Disadvantages of the Kübler-Ross Five-Stage (Grief) Model

While the five-stage model holds importance as a seminal theory, it remains a theoretical model, and if applied too rigidly can risk damage to the change management process. Just as there can be no set timetable for grieving over death, neither can we expect to pinpoint a timetable for grieving over change. Indeed, because grieving constitutes a personal psychological and emotional response, the expectation that all individuals should progress through nominated stages of grieving, and in a set order and set timeframe, can be harmful to those who grieve in a different manner. The stages should therefore be considered descriptive rather than prescriptive, with the nominated stages not necessarily providing a complete list of all emotions like, for example, shock, despair and guilt.

The model also fails to seriously account for loss and how individuals might effectively cope with it, fails to provide suitable identification of those at high risk, and fails to provide adequate resolution of the various problems incurred within each stage of the model. The sequential stages of grief are poorly defined and fail to fit logically together as they combine both emotional stages with cognitive ones. Acceptance of the model may raise undue expectations about the course that grief should take. These limitations have infused a whole generation of contemporary change models that commit to linear steps that depict an idealized process.

ROGERS' INNOVATION DIFFUSION THEORY

Rogers' (1962; 1995; 2003; 2004; Rogers and Shoemaker, 1971) diffusion of innovations has enjoyed a long life, emblazoned by periodic updates and new-found generations of consultants. Applied to an organizational change context, the theory reveals why some people are more willing to accept change than others. The model remains salient because it provides a deeper understanding of an aspect of change that will always be relevant: how and when those on the receiving end of possible change go about deciding to adopt it.

Rogers argued that when faced with new technology, an innovation or a change, individuals experience an adoption process during which they gather information, test the technology/change and then consider whether it offers sufficient improvement to warrant the investment of time and energy required (Rogers, 1995). Based on his research, Rogers maintained that leaders and managers can identify the type of individual adoption reactions to change by using five different categories: innovators; early adopters; early majority; late majority; and laggards. Collectively, the five categories constitute the diffusion of innovations theory. By understanding the nature of the categories, and the likely traits of organizational members who fit within them, change managers can best determine how to respond, and even how to deal with resistance.

Because innovation, or in our case change diffusion, is a process wherein innovation spreads among a group of people over a period of time, every individual determines the speed and progress of their own adoption and acceptance. In order to explain the adoption of the innovation/change process, Rogers proposed that individuals initially undertake a decision process involving five steps: knowledge; persuasion; decision; implementation; and confirmation. Typically, these steps follow in sequential order. As an individual undergoes the adoption process they are influenced by four external elements: the innovation itself; the communication channels through which the innovation is spread; the amount of time involved in the change; and the social network jointly working on the introduction of the change. Taken to its logical conclusion, the evaluative decision-making process will inform the individual of the need for the innovation/change, and will invest them with an emotional and psychological commitment to its successful adoption. At some stage, Rogers suggested, there will be a point when critical mass is achieved and the majority of people will adopt the changes.

Step 1: Knowledge

Step 1 requires that change managers indicate the reasons for the change, suggest how it will occur and who will be involved. It is the initial exposure of a new change idea, but the recipients lack complete information about the change.

Step 2: Persuasion

Leaders in the second step will seek to persuade individuals to accept change by informing them of more detailed information. At the same time, organizational members who are interested in the innovation will themselves seek further details. Attitudes, both favourable and unfavourable, to the change begin to be formed.

Step 3: Decision

After analysing all available data and possibly implementing a pilot trial of the new processes formed by the change, an individual may decide to adopt or reject it. Often, they will mentally apply the change to their present situation before deciding whether to adopt, or whether to seek additional information or evidence.

Step 4: Implementation

By step 4, the change has been implemented on a more established basis, and the driving ideas and innovations behind it are put into use. Individuals, however, adopt the innovations and change ideas at varying rates.

Step 5: Confirmation

Finally, the individuals responsible for, and affected by, the change evaluate the results of the decision made by management and confirm adoption.

Characteristics of the Innovators/Adopters

With most change, success is heavily dependent on the decisions of all members of the system. As a result, change is more likely to succeed if people believe that it yields greater validity and advantage than its predecessor, or in the case of organizations, the status quo. The speed with which an organization can enact change will be determined by the length of time required for a critical mass of its members to adopt the innovation. Change consultants can employ Rogers' adoption theory to understand individual adoption types and to respond accordingly.

Innovators

Innovators are the implementers of change; an organization's change agents. They view their innovations as exciting and self-evidently attractive. They tend to feel comfortable with change and like the idea of being a change agent. The speed with which innovators implement change has ramifications for the subsequent decisions of the remaining potential adopters.

Early adopters

Early adopters rely on the data provided by the innovators. If the data confirm the reliability of the changes proposed, then they will be encouraged to adopt the change. Because this group is judicious in its decision making, it will frequently become the area where most opinion leaders live. They see themselves as role models.

Early majority

Many of those involved in change are indifferent to detailed information about the proposed change. They tend to be pragmatic and prefer proven applications. Consequently, they trust the decisions made by the opinion leaders. If the opinion leaders favour the change then many of the remainder—and especially those seeking conformity—are willing to adopt the change. At this point the likelihood of success becomes almost assured.

Late majority

In a domino effect, the majority of those who are still sceptical about the innovation gradually follow suit, whether out of necessity or belief, as they accept the perceived benefits of the change. They are usually a little more conservative but will respond to peer pressure.

Laggards

Most of those who remain unconvinced of the need for change are committed traditionalists or are isolated in their beliefs. They may be suspicious of the change or sincerely believe that it will affect them in a negative manner, and thus wish to retain the status quo. Consequently, it takes much longer than average for laggards to accept the change.

Innovation Characteristics

Of course, not all change successfully comes into effect. Rogers explained that the potential for change failure can be attenuated by identifying five distinct innovation characteristics that affect adoption: observability; relative advantage; compatibility; trialability; and complexity.

Observability

Observability relates to the extent to which the innovation will be visible to everyone, allowing potential adopters the opportunity to physically view the potential or actual results of the change.

Relative advantage
This characteristic considers to what extent the change may be considered an improvement on the existing process. It allows consideration of all the financial, social, emotional and psychological advantages or disadvantages of the change compared with the existing system.

Compatibility
Consideration here is given to the degree to which the innovation remains consistent with existing values, needs, ideas and technologies. It also considers the ease with which a change might be incorporated into an individual's workplace.

Trialability
Trialability relates to the extent to which a limited trial to test and modify the change might be utilized. A trial allows any potential adopter to test the innovation with minimal resource investment.

Complexity
Complexity refers to the difficulty associated with understanding or utilizing the change.

Advantages of Rogers' Change Theory

One of the main advantages of Rogers' work is that he has constantly expanded and reworked his theory's underlying framework while expanding it in several directions. Unlike many other change models, Rogers' theory remains dynamic and its use in many enterprises and industries suggests that the adoption and diffusion of change and innovation provides a solid and replicable approach. By appreciating the mechanisms of diffusion, an organization retains a sound basis for determining what methods are most successful in encouraging the spread of a desired change. Acknowledging the role of opinion leaders in the process allows diffusion theory to be seen as both a powerful and unique tool in effecting change. There remains a requirement though, for capable supporting infrastructure to underpin the pattern of diffusion.

The theory also offers an alternate perspective to mainstream change models as it focuses on how innovation or change is spread throughout an organization, while at the same time noting the characteristics to be considered when initially considering innovative change. As technology advances, diffusion processes may be expected to occur more rapidly and this may aid in the transition of change.

Disadvantages of Rogers' Change Theory

Since change may originate within an industry, such as for example education or health, rather than within a single organization, concern may justifiably be expressed over the role of the mass media and its ability to spread knowledge or a point of view to a large audience rapidly and in a manner that may be considered biased at best and manipulative at worst. Articles and commentary by opinion leaders or internet influencers may affect adoption as well. In a similar vein, the ultimate users of an innovation or change, like teachers in education or nurses in health, are frequently distinct from the instigators. With innovations continually evolving, later adopters may consider an innovation somewhat differently to that of early adopters.

Rogers' theory identifies five distinct innovation characteristics which he recommended might be considered when initially considering change. Two of these, observability and trialability, are readily measured, however, the three remaining characteristics, relative advantage, compatibility and complexity, are less easily measurable. Perhaps a minor disadvantage to Rogers' theory is that it might usefully have incorporated a sixth step—that of non-adopter.

MODEL COMPLICATIONS

Consultants will inevitably argue that change continues at an intense rate. This is especially true in organizations where strategies, structures, competition, values and expectations of stakeholders relentlessly evolve. Change does not happen in isolation. It requires leadership and a willingness on the part of organizational members to become involved. While neither organizations nor individuals within those organizations experience change in any consistent or uniform way, the process of change can usually be both observed and analysed. Management on its own cannot implement change; individual organizational members need to be involved and empowered in order to be integral to the change process. And, it must always be remembered that allowing or initiating change is not necessarily the same as implementing change successfully.

Before embarking on change, leaders must take into consideration the size and type of organization involved, the degree of change being sought, the motivation for the change, and the potential impact on all involved in the change. If then a decision is made to initiate change, and to do so with the help of a consultant or consultants, consideration of the change model to be employed will become of vital concern. Many powerful and predictive models of change exist in literature, and an even greater number of bespoke models have been developed by both major and minor consulting firms. Each offers putative insights into ways to direct and initiate change in an organization. Models must, however, be utilized with care. Many are contradictory or supported by minimal evidence, while others are underpinned by unchallenged hypotheses. Some are simply one-dimensional in aspect or ignore complexities, while others underestimate the practical requirements within differing organizations. There is no right or wrong method for change. Each has its own peculiarities; its own strengths and weaknesses. In practice it might be that no change model fully, and in all respects, explains and deciphers the organizational change puzzle. Although not discussed, the interaction and interdependency between client and consultant is also of obvious importance.

CONCLUSION

Organizations must, under law, be aware of the duty of care they owe to employees. A duty of care means that leaders are required to mitigate the worst impacts of organizational change, which in turn requires them to understand how people think and react to change in the workplace. Understanding such social realities is crucial in organizational change. One such model that considers the way in which individuals go through a psychological process during change has been expressed by Kübler-Ross. The approach to change began through research about the way in which terminally ill patients react to the prospect of death, but quickly segued into organizational change where its legacy can be seen in a myriad of linear, psycho-dynamic models. Similarly, Bridges' transition model seeks to understand an individual's emotional reaction to change, though the model itself deals with change at a more micro level and fails to promote a structured framework that allows for change within a designated timeframe. Nonetheless, it is a useful and practical change model, but may be best employed in conjunction with other change management tools. To a lesser extent, other change models like nudge theory and Rogers' adoption theory consider to some extent the psychological and emotional impact on the individual.

Lewin's three-step change model offers a rational goal- and plan-orientated approach that also has left a lasting imprint on consulting interventions. In contrast to Kübler-Ross, it limits the degree to which it considers personal feelings, attitudes or experience that might affect change. If a large-scale change is required, both the Kotter and McKinsey models appear to be most useful. Kotter's work, based on his own research, remains popular because of its straightforward and usable format. While Kotter does incorporate to a limited extent both emotional and situational components in his model, it might be usefully enhanced with the addition of a complementary model such as ADKAR or Rogers' adoption theory, both of which would anchor into organizational culture. Both the Kotter and the Rogers models have been in the past successfully employed in changing large organizations.

The 7 S McKinsey model considers the seven organizational factors Peters and Waterman claimed could be diagnosed in order to separate excellent businesses from others. The model exemplifies the consulting mindset given the combination of a top-down model for large-scale change, and a component-based and modular diagnostic framework. However, if leadership has a definitive idea on what change they require, then the ADKAR model, or something like it, becomes the tool of choice. Its emphasis on individual change and outcomes rather than on process and tasks differentiates it from more systems-led change models like the 7 S framework. Some middle ground might be located in the kinds of change models that have arisen with reference to the foundational ideas incorporated into the adoption approach. In general, when someone is confronted with a change, they can progress through an adoption decision process during which they gather information, test the change ideas and then consider whether it offers a sufficient improvement to warrant the investment of time and energy that is required to add it to their repertoire of skills.

The spectrum of change management models deployed by consultants has become immense. Bespoke models abound but they all sourced inspiration from the kinds of models examined in this chapter. These reviewed approaches to various forms of change collectively inspired the models philosophy. Of course, there remain innumerable other, highly specific models that consultants use to drive certain kinds of change, including those focusing on innovation, technology, horizons, digital transitions, teams, leadership and capabilities. While not the purview of this chapter or this book to consider each one, we would note that most draw upon aspects of the models philosophy to structure their change analyses and recommendations.

REFERENCES

Bridges, W. (1991), *Managing Transitions: Making the Most of Change*, Reading, MA: Addison-Wesley.

Hiatt, Jeff (2006), *ADKAR: A Model for Change in Business, Government, and Our Community*, Loveland, CO: Prosci Learning Center Publications.

Kotter, John P. (1995), *Leading Change*, Boston, MA: Harvard Business School Press.

Kübler-Ross, E. (1969), *On Death and Dying*, New York: Macmillan.

Peters, Thomas and Robert Waterman (1982), *In Search of Excellence: Lessons from America's Best-Run Companies*, New York: Harper and Row.

Rogers, Everett M. (1962), *Diffusion of Innovations*, 1st edition, New York: Free Press of Glencoe.

Rogers, Everett M. (1995), *Diffusion of Innovations*, 4th edition, New York: Free Press.

Rogers, Everett M. (2003), *Diffusion of Innovations*, 5th edition, New York: Free Press of Glencoe.

Rogers, Everett M. (2004), 'A prospective and retrospective look at the diffusion model', *Journal of Health Communication*, **9** (1), 13–19.

Rogers, Everett M. and F. Shoemaker (1971), *Communication of Innovations: A Cross-Cultural Approach*, New York: Free Press of Glencoe.

Schnitker, Sarah A. and Robert A. Emmons (2013), 'Hegel's thesis–antithesis–synthesis model', in A. L. C. Runehov and L. Oviedo (eds), *Encyclopedia of Sciences and Religions*, Berlin: Springer, pp. 1807–14.

Thaler, Richard H. and Cass R. Sunstein (2008), *Nudge: Improving Decisions about Health, Wealth, and Happiness*, New Haven, CT: Yale University Press.

Waterman, Robert, Thomas J. Peters and Julien R. Phillips (1980), 'Structure is not organization', *Business Horizons*, **23** (3), 14–26.

6. The institutional philosophy: 'changing conformity'

INTRODUCTION

In this chapter we introduce the institutional philosophy and consider why it has made such a significant impact on organizational change theory. We ask, what insights can we gain about the process of organizational change through institutional theory? Institutional theory represents 'the dominant approach' to understanding organizations (Greenwood, Oliver, Lawrence and Meyer, 2017; Vogel, 2012). It allows us to study how and why organizations behave in particular ways, and what consequences accompany these behaviours. Institutional theory provides a popular and powerful explanation for both individual and organizational change (Alvesson and Spicer, 2019; Dacin, Goodstein and Scott, 2002). Where biological models assume evolutionary adaptations drive change in order to give organizations novel competitive advantages, institutional theories suggest that the pressure for conformity impels organizations to change towards the norm.

This chapter aims to explore significant transitions and developments in institutional theory and examine the central ideas, questions and concerns that have stimulated debate and shaped the philosophy's nature and direction. Through our exploration of key institutional debates, we firstly illuminate the way in which institutions evolve, adapt and respond to various social, political and environmental pressures in their struggle for survival, and a progressive move to a social judgements approach. Second, we illustrate how the interplay between different institutional processes and field-level complexity can work to assuage the prospect of a bureaucratic 'iron cage', and act as a powerful force for institutional change. The next section introduces the varieties of institutionalism. We subsequently explore 'new' institutionalism, followed by a section injecting identity, power and culture into the mix. The chapter concludes by reviewing institutional entrepreneurship as a force for innovation and change through disruptions to institutional norms.

CONCEPTS OF INSTITUTION

The very words 'institution' and 'institutionalism' suggest strength, endurance and stability; a combination of processes, systems and structures that have withstood the test of time and become deeply embedded in organizational norms and values. This image strengthened as the new institutionalism perspective gained momentum in the late 1970s through the influential writings of Meyer and Rowan (1977), Zucker (1977), DiMaggio and Powell (1983) and Scott (1983). The proponents of 'new' institutionalism viewed organizations as captives of their *institutional contexts* (Meyer and Rowan, 1977; Zucker, 1977; Scott, 1983), comprising the 'rules, norms, and ideologies of the wider society' (Meyer and Rowan, 1983, p. 184). Institutionalism and institutionalized practices came to represent an organization's response to its institutional environment with the focus on conformity, legitimation and the role of shared meaning. Institutional theory assumed a role as 'a theory of stability' (Demers, 2007, p. 35). Zucker (1983, p. 5) underscored the notion of institutional perpetuity when she argued that, 'institutionalization is rooted in—not conformity engendered by sanctions (whether positive or negative) … but conformity rooted in the taken-for-granted aspects of everyday life … what is appropriate and, fundamentally, meaningful behaviour'. The institutional philosophy's core premise holds that organizations change when they need to in order to better fit their environments.

Zucker's (1983) explanation of institutional perpetuity foreshadowed a nexus between institutionalism and culture, the latter examined in Chapter 10. This connection also persisted in Selznick's (1957) early work, where the theme of institutionalization 'as a process of instilling values' emerged (cited in Aldrich and Ruef, 2006, p. 39). Berger and Luckmann (1967) expanded on the same theme, describing institutionalization as a process of creating reality wherein organizational actors create an external, objectified reality that others internalize. Much later, Barley and Tolbert (1997) argued that the key difference between traditional theories of organization and neoinstitutional theories can be pinpointed to the latter's interest in the impact of cultural influences on decision making and formal structures. From an institutional viewpoint, organizations and organizational members are 'suspended in a web' of values, norms, rules, beliefs and taken-for-granted assumptions, which prescribe the way the world operates. This collection of cultural ascriptions provide 'blueprints for organizing by specifying the forms and procedures an organization of a particular type should adopt if it is to be seen as a member-in-good-standing of its class' (Barley and Tolbert, 1997, pp. 93–4). Institutionalists therefore interpret institutions as amalgams of historical practices and understandings that enforce conditions upon action (Barley and Tolbert, 1997). Organizational change aligns with changes to the dominant ways in which groups of institutions work. Pressure from an institutional group arrives through tacit and explicit expectations, which propel organizational change towards conformity, and therefore legitimacy.

SITUATED AND SOCIOLOGICAL

Early work by so-called Chicago School sociologists (e.g. Hughes, 1942) studying institutions and institutional behaviour first encouraged the 'historically situated' perspective on organizational change. The Chicagoans claimed that institutions become captive to ideologies 'championed' by dominant coalitions in society that confer institutional legitimacy. Changes to the dominant ideology lead to a crisis of legitimacy. In order to maintain conformity and approval, change cascades throughout an organization (Barley, 2017). The early position advocated by the Chicago School sociologists now corresponds to the more recent institutional philosophy branch known as new or neoinstitutionalism (Barley, 2017).

The differences between 'old' and 'new' institutionalism represent a significant transition in change theory development. In addition to concerns relating to power and evolving informal structures, old institutionalism focused on influence, coalitions and competing values (DiMaggio and Powell, 1983; 1991). New institutionalism, however, emphasizes legitimacy, the embeddedness of organizational fields, and the centrality of classification, routines, scripts and schema (Greenwood and Hinings, 1996). Other institutional analysts, reflecting institutional theory's sociological foundations, view institutions as 'distinct social systems' concerned with the influence of family, religion, economy, government and education (Aldrich and Ruef, 2006). These theorists took inspiration from the sociological approaches which emerged in the 1950s and 1960s based on Weber's concept of bureaucracy, and his interest in social structures such as power, domination, authority and legitimacy (Lounsbury and Ventresca, 2003). Empirical studies, grounded in the early sociological approach, explored 'the interplay of interests, intentional choices, and broader political dynamics' (Lounsbury and Ventresca, 2003, pp. 459–60); organizations were viewed as sites for understanding how power always remains situated in broader social structures. We venture further into power and change in Chapter 11 on the critical philosophy.

Given such a complex pedigree, pinning down precise definitions of 'institution' and 'organizational institutionalism' remains troublesome (Greenwood, Oliver, Lawrence and Meyer, 2017). Precise definitions do not account for the many faces of institutional theory (Aldrich and Ruef, 2006). In the first edition of his influential book, *Institutions and Organizations*, Scott, for example, wryly noted that new meanings for 'institution' had amassed 'much like barnacles on a ship's hull' (1995, p. xiv). Later, he presciently advised that the best way to approach institutional theory is to appreciate that 'there is not one but several variants', some clear and explicit, and others more abstract and complex (Scott, 2008). Meaning and intention remain elusive in many accounts. Institutionalism and institutionalization have inspired conceptual diversity along with ambiguity. As a result, institutional theory has come at the cost of a troubled, complex and controversial adolescence (Alvesson and Spicer, 2019).

Institutional theorists do generally agree on two fronts (Heugens and Lander, 2009). First, they have little time for 'atomistic accounts' of social processes as these depict an 'undersocialized' view of organizational behaviour. Ignoring the impact of social forces on organizational action represents a critical error because organizations, 'inhabited' by people communicating and working with each other, perform as members of social networks (Hallett and Ventresca, 2006; Demers, 2007). Second, institutionalists tend to agree that organizational action occurs in response to *exogenous*, or external, forces. The environment not only generates contingencies and disturbances to which organizations must adapt, it also delivers a socially constructed context that canalizes the process of organizational decision making (Heugens and Lander, 2009).

EXPLANATORY DISPUTES

A central quarrel dividing institutionalists concerns the structure versus agency debate (Heugens and Lander, 2009), otherwise known as the paradox of embedded agency. The paradox of embedded agency asks, 'How can actors change institutions if their actions, intentions, and rationality are all conditioned by the very institution they wish to change?' (Holm, 1995, p. 398). The question revolves around whether organizational behaviour represents a product of macro-social forces or of organizational agency. Whereas biological theorists regard social forces as more significant, strategic theorists claim agency as paramount. Within the institutionalist debate, structuralists believe that over time populations of organizations become increasingly isomorphic, or similar; collectively incorporating 'templates' and patterns that ensure legitimacy. On the other hand, agency theorists argue that organizations experience 'differing degrees of discretion' while responding to institutional pressures. To agency theorists, increased institutionalization can stimulate deviance in the form of innovation and institutional entrepreneurship (Heugens and Lander, 2009). This can be exacerbated under different conditions of institutional complexity where an organization is subject to multiple, and potentially conflicting, isomorphic pressures to retain legitimacy (Raynard, 2016). Under such conditions, new organizational hybrid forms may emerge as logics from different institutions become connected (Pache and Santos, 2010).

A further heated debate surrounds the impact of isomorphic conformity on performance (Heugens and Lander, 2009; Greenwood et al., 2017; Boxenbaum and Jonsson, 2017). While nearly all theorists agree that conformity brings about more positive social evaluations, controversy exists around the pro-conformance argument that organizations pursue conformity in order to be perceived as acceptable and appropriate (legitimation), rather than to improve performance. The pro-performance argument suggests that organizations favour templates that lead to benefits beyond social condonement (Heugens and Lander, 2009). Practitioners may have trouble with such a dichotomy. After all, why would an organization change if not to improve performance? Conformists think that the answer has more to do with the power of environmental pressures and less to do with a weakness in strategic choice. Implying that change comes about through one or the other may be misleading anyway. Critically, creating a pretence of conformity with emerging institutional pressures whilst maintaining 'business as usual' can lead to severe legitimacy challenges (Hensel and Guérard, 2019).

The structure versus agency debate highlights a key limitation in new/neoinstitutionalism (DiMaggio and Powell, 1983). Its fixation on homogeneity (similarity), at the expense of organizational agency, promotes an excessively narrow view of organizational change (Dacin et al., 2002; Demers, 2007). For example, agency theorists disagree with the behavioural determinism of structuralism. Social structures can also be sources of deviance, innovation and change (Heugens and Lander, 2009; Washington and Ventresca, 2004). Performance and conformity may not be mutually exclusive. In fact, Barley and Tolbert (1997) highlighted the interplay between action and structure through a model where institutionalization works as a 'structuration' process. They pointed out that early institutionalists like Giddens (1976; 1979; 1984) referred to an inherent duality within institutions where structures emerge from, as well as influence, actions. A circuitous and reciprocal relationship between structure and agency makes separating the two impossible. However, on the upside, seeing organizational composition and strategic intentions as mutually dependent and reinforcing seems like a more plausible vision of change. Accordingly, organizations are enacted through scripts that are reflected in recurrent activities and patterns of interaction that are shaped by context and expectations about particular settings at the micro-foundational level (Barley and Tolbert, 1997; Gray, Purdy and Ansari, 2015). The increasing attention paid to how micro-level behaviours amass to macro-level social structures represents a significant turn in new institutionalism (Bitektine and Haack, 2015).

NEW INSTITUTIONALISM

The seminal works of Meyer and Rowan (1977) and DiMaggio and Powell (1983) captured the context and ethos of the emerging 'new' institutionalism. Their research and writings reflected on Weber's (1968) rationalized formal structures and rules that brought legitimacy and power through bureaucratization. In his epic work, *The Protestant Ethic and the Spirit of Capitalism*, Weber (1930) expressed serious concerns about the irreversible power and traction of bureaucracy as a means of control. He worried that people would be forever imprisoned in an 'iron cage' of rationalist order (Weber, 1952; 1968; DiMaggio and Powell, 1983). Drawing from Weber's work, Meyer and Rowan (1977) focused their attention on the rationalization and diffusion of formal bureaucracies in a changing, modern world (Greenwood et al., 2017). Organizational structures evolved as reflections of rationalized institutional rules diffused throughout organizations (Meyer and Rowan, 1977, p. 340). Once set in place, structures provide legitimacy, resources, stability and improved prospects for survival (Meyer and Rowan, 1977; Greenwood et al., 2017).

In turn, DiMaggio and Powell (1983), revisiting Weber's 'iron cage', argued that the engine of organizational rationalization had shifted. In the second half of the twentieth century, the state and the professions assumed charge of the rationalist agenda. Consequently, the impetus for structural change came from the desire to make organizations more similar, or homogeneous, rather than more efficient and competitive. DiMaggio and Powell referred to the emergence of 'an organizational field', which they defined as 'those organizations that, in the aggregate, constitute a recognized area of institutional life: key suppliers, resource and product consumers, regulatory agencies, and other organizations that produce similar services or products' (p. 148). Organizational fields provide a useful frame of reference because they highlight those firms competing or networking (interacting) in the 'field', as well as the 'totality' of key players within the field (p. 148). However, an organizational field needs to be institutionally defined in order to provide instructive information.

Defining an organizational field—a process known as 'structuration'—comprises four parts (DiMaggio and Powell, 1983): firstly, an increase in the level of interaction among organizations in the field; secondly, the rise of sharply defined interorganizational structures and patterns of coalition; thirdly, an increase in the volume of information handled within an organizational field; and fourthly, the development of 'mutual awareness' among organizational field players that they share a 'common enterprise' (DiMaggio and Powell, 1983, p. 148). This leads us to the broad definition of a field as 'relational spaces that provide an organisation with the opportunity to involve itself with other actors' (Wooten and Hoffman, 2017, p. 64). As first identified by Giddens (1979, 1984), structuration represents a series of evolving processes; changes that are ongoing and recursive, combining both the symbolic and the material components of organizing and structuring.

ISOMORPHISM

The term 'isomorphism' describes the process of homogenization that organizations undergo as they gain acceptance, legitimacy and power within an organizational field (DiMaggio and Powell, 1983). Isomorphism refers to the constraining process that forces an organization to resemble others facing the same environmental conditions (DiMaggio and Powell, 1983). Three 'mechanisms' determine how isomorphism spreads through organizations: coercive, mimetic and normative (DiMaggio and Powell, 1983). *Coercive* isomorphism occurs where other influential, powerful organizations, including governments, exert pressure for change through both formal and informal means. Dependent organizations comply in order to avoid sanctions. Compliance pressures may be in the form of explicit rules or laws designed to ensure both conformity and social acceptance. *Mimetic* isomorphism occurs where uncertainty forces an imitation of 'model' organizations. Less powerful, dependent organizations covet the success and legitimacy of others in the organizational field and attempt to copy their structures, practices and outputs. *Normative* isomorphic changes occur primarily through the influence of professionalization and represent the collective struggle of employees to continually define their approach to work (DiMaggio and Powell, 1991).

To gain acceptance and legitimacy, organizations feel compelled to recognize and respect social obligations and conform to society's system of beliefs, norms and values (Greenwood et al., 2017). Institutional isomorphism forcefully suggests that organizational success and survival do not depend simply on being more efficient or more competitive. Instead, successful change accompanies conformity to institutional norms and the attainment of social legitimacy. As DiMaggio and Powell (1983) explained: 'Organizations compete not just for resources and customers, but for political power and institutional legitimacy, for social as well as economic fitness' (p. 150). On this basis, institutional isomorphism helps make sense of the politics and ceremony that underpin organizational change and behaviour. From a micro-foundational perspective, suppressing factors may exist that support isomorphism, as those who voice opinions that challenge the legitimate behaviours of the time face negative repercussions (e.g. industrial exclusion), and conformity provides positive gain (e.g. financial investment) (Bitektine and Haack, 2015).

In the 1990s, the pendulum shifted away from the factors driving *homogeneity* in organizational forms and practices, to questioning how organizations acquire, manage and use *legitimacy*. Perhaps more importantly, the new wave of thinking focused on how organizations adapt and change (DiMaggio and Powell, 1983; Greenwood et al., 2017). While the shift in focus may be attributed in part to the realization that organizations and their environments are not homogeneous, there was also growing interest in the neglected role that power and agency play in shaping institutional practices and configurations (Greenwood et al., 2017; Deephouse and Suchman, 2008).

Legitimacy gained in status because it explains an organization's prospects of survival. But it also acts as a kind of legal currency, excusing and validating the actions of influential leaders. Meyer and Rowan (1977) argued that legitimacy results from assumptions about 'rational effectiveness', 'legal mandates' and collectively valued purposes, means and goals. They stressed how legitimacy functions as a barrier between an organization and external pressures, thus making it difficult for organizational actors to question existing organizational forms and practices, or raise the possibility that alternative courses of action might have a more compelling claim as the 'legitimate' option (Meyer and Rowan, 1977; Deephouse and Suchman, 2008).

Scott (1995) claimed that, 'Legitimacy is not a commodity to be possessed or exchanged but a condition reflecting cultural alignment, normative support, or consonance with relevant rules of laws' (p. 45). For Scott, legitimacy represents an anchor-point that constrains, constructs and empowers organizational actors. Consequently, how organizations acquire, manage and use *legitimacy* depends on powerful actors who dictate the rules and norms, 'manage' values and align organizational change to bring about a new culture (DiMaggio and Powell, 1983). Considered from a social judgement perspective, the organization able to articulate its opinion on what legitimate behaviour constitutes, is also better able to dictate the direction of change. Power and culture have become critical ingredients in the perspective institutional theory now takes.

SHAPING INSTITUTIONAL IDENTITY THROUGH POWER AND CULTURE

The relationship between power and institutionalism recurs throughout the institutional literature. Institutions survive when they successfully exercise power by influencing the behaviours, beliefs and opportunities of individuals, groups, organizations and societies (Lawrence and Buchanan, 2017). Recent studies have transferred interest from isomorphism to the roles of conflict, politics and agency in organizational fields (Lawrence and Buchanan, 2017). Culture also plays a pivotal role in the power–institution dynamic. For example, Lounsbury and Ventresca (2003) argued that new structuralism challenges the highly rational, instrumental twentieth-century conception of social structure by introducing cultural forces and meanings. The connection to meaning systems emanates from Bourdieu (1984), who laboured to explain why social inequality persists without resistance. His answer returns to the way unequal social relations maintain strength through cultural resources, practices and institutional functions. Power permeates through cultural rules and meaning systems, making inequality seem natural or inevitable (Lounsbury and Ventresca, 2003). However, power and culture have not figured prominently in the literature despite the relationship between institutional processes and elite interests (Greenwood et al., 2017; Haack and Sieweke, 2018).

Scott (1995) brought order to the different conceptions of institutional analysis by establishing three defining institutional 'pillars'. He put the case for an 'omnibus' conception of institutions as a composite of 'regulative, normative, and cultural-cognitive elements' that provide stability and meaning to social life (2001, p. 48; 2003, p. 880). Scott (2003) characterized the three elements as 'pillars' of institutions, arguing that each aligns with different motives and logics in order to secure legitimacy. The *regulative* pillar focuses on establishing rules, and monitoring and sanctioning activities, both formal and informal. Central ingredients include force, fear and expedience tempered by rules. The regulative element of institutional life reflects the power and influence of leadership interests in meting out reward and punishment according to their code of conduct. The *normative* pillar introduces an evaluative, prescriptive and obligatory dimension, stressing prescribed norms and roles, and setting the standards for appropriate behaviour. The *cultural-cognitive* pillar concerns how an organization's shared values and beliefs construct and interpret social reality, as well as guide behaviour. Taken-for-granted beliefs and shared values, rather than rules or normative expectations, form the basis for social order (Scott, 2003). Within the elements of the cultural-cognitive pillar we see not only the impact of organizational culture on the institutional framework, but also how the social construct of culture depends upon who pulls the strings.

While these pillars may be analysed separately, Scott recognized that they co-exist. He strongly argued, however, that the cultural-cognitive pillar reflects the deepest foundations of institutional forms where norms and rules rest (Scott, 2004). The connection between culture and cognition underscores the role of positional power in determining cultural precedent. The cultural-cognitive intersection frames the rules of the game, guiding the form and function of the regulative and normative pillars. Powerful organizational actors 'script' an organization's identity, mediating how organizations interpret and respond to institutional expectations (Greenwood et al., 2017). The concept of identity has a long history in institutional theorizing (Glynn, 2008). Over 50 years ago, Selznick (1957) claimed that institutionalization in the form of infused value produces distinctive organizational identities. Indeed, maintaining a distinctive identity remains integral to organizational survival and prosperity. As organizational identity fuses with culture, a link between culture, power and legitimacy forms, reflecting accepted practices, routines, organizing forms, language and the way members interact.

POWER AND POLITICS

The lack of interest about power and institutions that existed throughout the 1980s has since been addressed (Lawrence and Buchanan, 2017). Research shows that power shapes how organizations operate, as well as their relationship to other organizations. Lawrence and Buchanan (2017) demonstrated that the relationship between power and institutions, or the concept of 'organizational politics', has three dimensions reflecting an interrelationship between institutional control, institutional agency and institutional resistance. Firstly, institutional control explains how institutions impact on the behaviour and beliefs of individual and organizational actors. It focuses on adherence to institutional rules and norms. Institutional control reflects the influence of 'systemic' forms of power, and the use of discipline and domination as instruments of institutional control. Understanding systemic forms of power from an institutional perspective brings into focus the power of formal or legal bodies as well as the actors operating within these structures.

Secondly, institutional agency refers to individual and group action that creates, transforms and disrupts institutions. It emphasizes the influence and role organizational members effect upon the configuration of their institutions. Institutional agency refers to 'episodic' forms of power where self-interested agents engage in 'discrete, strategic acts of mobilization' (Lawrence and Buchanan, 2017, p. 480), often exemplified in studies of production and workforce management. Institutional agency resurrected a central premise of 'old' institutionalism, and has gained added significance through institutional entrepreneurship (Lawrence and Buchanan, 2017; Hardy and Maguire, 2017), which highlights the role of 'relational' and 'discursive' strategies in bringing about institutional change (Garud, Jain and Kumaraswamy, 2002; Lawrence and Suddaby, 2006; Suddaby and Greenwood, 2005). We examine institutional entrepreneurship in the next section of this chapter.

Thirdly, institutional resistance describes how organizational actors try to impose limits on institutional agency and control (Lawrence and Buchanan, 2017). Resistance underscores the relationship between the three dimensions. For Lawrence, power operates as a 'relational' phenomenon whereby one actor's beliefs and behaviours are subject to influence by another actor or system. Consequently, enduring structures, practices, rules, beliefs and norms all affect organizational behaviour and change. While systemic power underpins institutions, this would not be possible without input and socialization from knowing and unknowing groups, both advantaged and disadvantaged, who serve to maintain social and organizational institutions (Lawrence and

Buchanan, 2017). While the leadership elite set the cultural agenda, the rank and file maintain and embed the systems and structures. For change to transpire, entrenched structures, norms, rules and practices must be brought to the surface, challenged and replaced. Criticism remains that institutional theory is only concerned with institutional processes, rather than institutional processes *as part of* societal domination, oppression and resistance (Willmott, 2015). Therefore, the lack of criticality in institutional change can be viewed as a limitation by some (Munir, 2015).

INSTITUTIONAL ENTREPRENEURSHIP

Within the institutional philosophy, institutional entrepreneurship and organizational change have become synonymous. As a result, the central tenet of institutional change from the late 1990s moved towards new practices, with institutional entrepreneurship evolving as a flourishing 'cottage industry' in the early 2000s (Greenwood et al., 2017, p. 19). This movement brought the role of change agents firmly to centre stage. Organizations became less important than their members in the change process (Greenwood et al., 2017). Institutional entrepreneurship refers to the 'activities of actors who have an interest in particular institutional arrangements and who leverage resources to create new institutions or to transform existing ones' (Maguire, Hardy and Lawrence, 2004, p. 657). Institutional entrepreneurs are the actors responsible for instigating change when periods of institutional change present themselves (Bitektine and Haack, 2015; Hardy and Maguire, 2017). The activities undertaken by entrepreneurs to create, maintain or disrupt the institutional order are typically referred to as institutional work (Lawrence, Suddaby and Leca, 2011).

Organization theorists tend to view change as problematic because large institutions present sites of enduring stability and order. Institutional entrepreneurs are interest-driven, aware and calculative (Greenwood and Suddaby, 2006). Entrepreneurial awareness, or openness to alternatives, depends on an individual's 'embeddedness', or their relative satisfaction with their position, their 'alignment' with the status quo, and the 'richness' of resources at their disposal (Greenwood and Suddaby, 2006; Hardy and Maguire, 2017). With all these in place, an individual would be predisposed to question existing institutional norms and practices. However, while 'low' or 'peripheral' embeddedness and high 'interest dissatisfaction' serve as individual motivators for change (Sherer, 2017), it does not provide the context that initiates a drive for change (Greenwood and Suddaby, 2006).

Some evidence suggests that 'latent contradictions', or 'gaps' within organizational fields, may act as an impetus for entrepreneurial action by destabilizing existing practices. Seo and Creed (2002) identified four contradictions:

gaps between existing performance levels as a result of existing rules and opportunities in the marketplace (the 'efficiency' contradiction); powerlessness to respond either proactively or effectively to external changes because of entrenched patterns of behaviour (the 'non-adaptability' contradiction); inconsistencies in shared values within an organizational field (the 'interinstitutional incompatibility' contradiction); and conflicts of interest and tension between those in favour and those operating on the margins (the 'misaligned interests' contradiction). The four contradictions offer two insights. Firstly, they highlight the capacity for internal (or endogenous) factors to precipitate institutional change without the need for external (or exogenous) forces. Secondly, they infer that change most likely occurs when organizational actors feel disenfranchised and marginalized, or when conflict erupts as a result of inconsistencies in shared beliefs and values.

Studies have confirmed that institutional entrepreneurs can play a critical role in reshaping organizational fields, and in creating new industries, practices, identities and structures (Hardy and Maguire, 2017; Micelotta, Lounsbury and Greenwood, 2017). In their seminal study of the big five accounting firms, Greenwood and Suddaby (2006), for example, concluded that institutional entrepreneurs were instrumental in establishing a new multi-divisional form of organizing. In addition, Greenwood, Suddaby and Hinings (2002) noted the significant role professional associations play in driving and legitimating change within a highly institutionalized work context (accounting firms). Garud et al. (2002) described the 'institutional entrepreneurship' of Sun Microsystems as the primary sponsor of Java Internet technology. Sun Microsystems subverted existing taken-for-granted practices, creating new technological standards and rules of competitive engagement in the software industry. Such new rules, 'forged through conflict', resulted in further tensions within the software industry, thus ensuring 'further struggle and ongoing institutional change' (Dacin et al., 2002, p. 47).

Interorganizational collaboration also acts as an entrepreneurial force for change and innovation. Lawrence, Hardy and Phillips (2002) defined institutions 'as relatively widely diffused practices, technologies, or rules that have become entrenched in the sense that it is costly to choose other practices, technologies, or rules' (p. 282). Higher levels of *involvement* (form of relationships between participating organizations) and *embeddedness* (the extent to which collaboration is 'enmeshed in organizational relationships') lead to new practices, technologies and rules in the form of 'proto-institutions' (pp. 283, 285, 286). 'Proto-institutions' represent institutions 'in the making', with the potential to become fully developed. Institutional entrepreneurship need not be confined to 'powerful actors' such as government organizations or professional associations. Through interorganizational collaborations, smaller, less powerful organizations have the means to overcome size or resource limitations and initiate change.

CONCLUSION

The long-standing image of institutions has been gilded in a frame of permanence, stability and conformity. From this perspective, the environment strongly influences and constrains organizational fields (Demers, 2007). A focus on institutional isomorphism, and the importance of maintaining a standard landscape to ensure acceptance and survival, has been usurped by studies claiming that agents, power, conflict and culture represent the more powerful sources of deviance, entrepreneurship and innovation (Heugens and Lander, 2009). Where the traditional institutional script held that organizations were at the mercy of external factors over which they had little control, evidence has tipped the balance towards internal factors independently capable of triggering change (Gray et al., 2015). Seo and Creed's (2002) 'latent contradictions' highlight the potential of political conflict, clashing ideologies and value inconsistencies as internal forces for change. We agree that the role of culture and power in change demand full explanations (Willmott, 2015). Chapter 10 on the cultural philosophy, and Chapter 11 on the critical philosophy, add to the inclinations expressed here. In terms of the institutional philosophy, we conclude that the dynamics of institutional change involve far more than a reflexive 'survival' response to exogenous forces. Change from an institutional perspective also encompasses the intersection between actions (practices and structures), rhetoric, meanings and actors (Micelotta et al., 2017; Zilber, 2002).

We used Scott's three pillars to emphasize a shift in focus to internal socio-political factors and the tension between stability and change. While the regulative, normative and cultural-cognitive pillars provide the basis for meaning, order and stability, their very existence points to a dynamic interplay of institutional factors. Organizational rules, norms and values come about through complex, inseparable mechanisms. Institutional thinking encourages an appreciation of multiple modes of change. We must consider external and internal factors. While decision makers can mould culture through power, we also need to acknowledge how other institutional actors direct the action, define meanings and appoint other actors (the 'institutional mechanics') to monitor and maintain the rules of the game. Institutional work is as much about maintaining institutions as it is about disrupting them (Lawrence et al., 2011). With such complexity and dynamism, however, nothing can be certain. As institutional entrepreneurship illustrates, influential elites can be challenged. The currency of existing standards and practices falls open to scrutiny and question, and existing structures and practices can be dismantled or altered via evolutionary or revolutionary practices (Micelotta et al., 2017). As a consequence, the composition of the three institutional pillars may be transformed. We reconsider some of the complexity themes noted in the institutional philosophy when we examine the systems philosophy in Chapter 9.

Our discussion pointed to the influence of culture and organizational power in shaping the nature and form of organizational fields. We again caution about the dangers of relying on only one change philosophy when considering organizational change interventions. Unfortunately, while the institutional philosophy offers a realistic and textured explanation for organizational change, it fails to provide much practical guidance. Consideration of how day-to-day behaviour can influence institutions is insightful (Smets, Morris and Greenwood, 2012), but translating the complex contextual interrelationships between institutional logics, field dynamics and micro-level behaviours into a one-size-fits-all stepwise system would seem ridiculous. Perhaps the best that a change practitioner could hope for is a better appreciation for the nuances of the environment and the impact of socio-cultural forces. Those responsible for organizational change might also consider the extent that they need to accommodate competing institutional pressures to remain legitimate to stakeholders (Pache and Santos, 2010). Factors such as culture, power, language and identity have affected the philosophical development of institutional theory. Managing the change process means accounting for mediating variables. One such variable comes in the form of resource availability, which we examine in Chapter 7.

REFERENCES

Aldrich, Howard E. and M. Ruef (2006), *Organizations Evolving*, 2nd edition, London: Sage.

Alvesson, Mats and A. Spicer (2019), 'Neo-institutional theory and organization studies: A mid-life crisis?', *Organization Studies*, **40** (2), 199–218.

Barley, Stephen R. (2017), 'Coalface institutionalism', in Royston Greenwood, C. Oliver, T. B. Lawrence and R. Meyer (eds), *The Sage Handbook of Organizational Institutionalism*, 2nd edition, Thousand Oaks, CA: Sage, pp. 338–64.

Barley, Stephen R. and P. S. Tolbert (1997), 'Institutionalization and structuration: Studying the links between action and institution', *Organization Studies*, **18** (1), 93–117.

Berger, Peter L. and T. Luckmann (1967), *The Social Construction of Reality: A Treatise in the Sociology of Knowledge*, New York: Anchor Books.

Bitektine, Alex and P. Haack (2015), 'The "macro" and the "micro" of legitimacy: Toward a multilevel theory of the legitimacy process', *Academy of Management Review*, **40** (1), 49–75.

Bourdieu, P. (1984), *Distinction: A Social Critique of the Judgement of Taste*, Boston, MA: Harvard University Press.

Boxenbaum, Eva and S. Jonsson (2017), 'Isomorphism, diffusion and decoupling: Concept evolution and theoretical challenges', in: Royston Greenwood, C. Oliver,

T. B. Lawrence and R. Meyer (eds), *The Sage Handbook of Organizational Institutionalism*, 2nd edition, Thousand Oaks, CA: Sage, pp. 77–101.

Dacin, Tina M., J. Goodstein and W. R. Scott (2002), 'Institutional theory and institutional change: Introduction to the special research forum', *Academy of Management Journal*, **45** (1), 45–57.

Deephouse, D. and M. Suchman (2008), 'Legitimacy in organizational institutionalism', in R. Greenwood, C. Oliver, K. Sahlin-Andersson and R. Suddaby (eds), *Handbook of Organizational Institutionalism*, London: Sage, pp. 49–77.

Demers, Christiane (2007), *Organizational Change Theories: A Synthesis*, Thousand Oaks, CA: Sage.

DiMaggio, Paul J. and W. W. Powell (1983), 'The iron cage revisited: Institutional isomorphism and collective rationality in organizational fields', *American Sociological Review*, **48** (2), 147–60.

DiMaggio, Paul J. and W. W. Powell (1991), 'Introduction', in P. J. DiMaggio and W. W. Powell (eds), *The New Institutionalism in Organizational Analysis*, Chicago, IL: University of Chicago Press, pp. 1–38.

Garud, Raghu, S. Jain and A. Kumaraswamy (2002), 'Institutional entrepreneurship in the sponsorship of common technological standards: The case of Sun Microsystems and Java', *Academy of Management Journal*, **45** (1), 196–214.

Giddens, Anthony (1976), *New Rules of Sociological Method*, London: Hutchinson.

Giddens, Anthony (1979), *Central Problems in Social Theory*, Berkeley, CA: University of California Press.

Giddens, Anthony (1984), *The Constitution of Society*, Berkeley, CA: University of California Press.

Glynn, M. A. (2008), 'Beyond constraint: How institutions enable identities', in R. Greenwood, C. Oliver, K. Sahlin-Andersson and R. Suddaby (eds), *Handbook of Organizational Institutionalism*, London: Sage, pp. 414–30.

Gray, Barbara, J. M. Purdy and S. Ansari (2015), 'From interactions to institutions: Microprocesses of framing and mechanisms for the structuring of institutional fields', *Academy of Management Review*, **40** (1), 115–43.

Greenwood, Royston and C. R. Hinings (1996), 'Understanding radical organizational change: Bringing together the old and the new institutionalism', *Academy of Management*, **21** (4), 1022–54.

Greenwood, Royston and R. Suddaby (2006), 'Institutional entrepreneurship in mature fields: The big five accounting firms', *Academy of Management Journal*, **49** (1), 27–48.

Greenwood, Royston, R. Suddaby and C. R. Hinings (2002), 'Theorizing change: The role of professional associations in the transformation of institutionalized fields', *Academy of Management*, **45** (1), 58–80.

Greenwood, Royston, C. Oliver, T. B. Lawrence and R. E. Meyer (2017), 'Introduction: Into the fourth decade', in Royston Greenwood, C. Oliver, T. B. Lawrence and R. Meyer (eds), *The Sage Handbook of Organizational Institutionalism*, 2nd edition, Thousand Oaks, CA: Sage, pp. 1–24.

Haack, Patrick and J. Sieweke (2018), 'The legitimacy of inequality: Integrating the perspectives of system justification and social judgment', *Journal of Management Studies*, **55** (3), 486–516.

Hallett, Tim and M. J. Ventresca (2006), 'How institutions form: Loose coupling as mechanism in Gouldner's *Patterns of Industrial Bureaucracy*', *American Behavioral Scientist*, **49** (7), 908–24.

Hardy, Cynthia and S. Maguire (2017), 'Institutional entrepreneurship and change in fields', in R. Greenwood, C. Oliver, T. B. Lawrence and R. E. Meyer (eds), *The Sage Handbook of Organizational Institutionalism*, 2nd edition, Thousand Oaks, CA: Sage, pp. 261–281.

Hensel, Przemysław G. and S. Guérard (2019), 'The institutional consequences of decoupling exposure', *Strategic Organization*, https://doi.org/10.1177/1476127019831023.

Heugens, Pursey P. M. A. R. and M. W. Lander (2009), 'Structure! Agency! (And other quarrels): A meta-analysis of institutional theories of organization', *Academy of Management Journal*, **52** (1), 61–85.

Holm, Petter (1995), 'The dynamics of institutionalization: Transformation processes in Norwegian fisheries', *Administrative Science Quarterly*, **40** (3), 398–422.

Hughes, E. C. (1942), 'The study of institutions', *SF*, **20** (3), 307–10.

Lawrence, Thomas B. and S. Buchanan (2017), 'Power, institutions and organizations', in R. Greenwood, C. Oliver, T. B. Lawrence and R. E. Meyer (eds), *The Sage Handbook of Organizational Institutionalism*, 2nd edition, Thousand Oaks, CA: Sage, pp. 477–506.

Lawrence, T. B. and R. Suddaby (2006), 'Institutions and institutional work', in S. Clegg, C. Hardy, T. Lawrence and W. Nord (eds), *Sage Handbook of Organization Studies*, 2nd edition, London: Sage, pp. 215–54.

Lawrence, Thomas B., C. Hardy and N. Phillips (2002), 'Institutional effects of inter-organizational collaboration: The emergence of proto-institutions', *Academy of Management Journal*, **45** (1), 281–90.

Lawrence, Thomas, R. Suddaby and B. Leca (2011), 'Institutional work: Refocusing institutional studies of organization', *Journal of Management Inquiry*, **20** (1), 52–8.

Lounsbury, M. and M. Ventresca (2003), 'The new structuralism in organizational theory', *Organization*, **10** (3), 457–80.

Maguire, S., C. Hardy and T. B. Lawrence (2004), 'Institutional entrepreneurship in emerging fields: HIV/AIDS treatment advocacy in Canada', *Academy of Management Journal*, **47** (5), 657–79.

Meyer, John W. and B. Rowan (1977), 'Institutionalized organizations: Formal structure as myth and ceremony', *American Journal of Sociology*, **83** (2), 340–63.

Meyer, John W. and B. Rowan (1983), 'The structure of educational organization', in John W. Meyer and W. R. Scott (eds), *Organizational Environments: Ritual and Rationality*, Beverly Hills, CA: Sage, pp. 179–97.

Micelotta, Evelyn, M. Lounsbury and R. Greenwood (2017), 'Pathways of institutional change: An integrative review and research agenda', *Journal of Management*, **43** (6), 1885–910.

Munir, Kamal A. (2015), 'A loss of power in institutional theory', *Journal of Management Inquiry*, **24** (1), 90–2.

Pache, Anne-Claire and F. Santos (2010), 'When worlds collide: The internal dynamics of organizational responses to conflicting institutional demands', *Academy of Management Review*, **35** (3), 455–76.

Raynard, Mia (2016), 'Deconstructing complexity: Configurations of institutional complexity and structural hybridity', *Strategic Organization*, **14** (4), 310–35.

Scott, R. (1983), 'The organization of societal sector', in J. W. Meyer and W. R. Scott (eds), *Organizational Environments: Ritual and Rationality*, Newbury Park, CA: Sage, pp. 129–53.

Scott, W. Richard (1995), *Institutions and Organizations*, 1st edition, Thousand Oaks, CA: Sage.

Scott, W. Richard (2001), *Institutions and Organizations*, 2nd edition, Thousand Oaks, CA: Sage.

Scott, W. Richard (2003), 'Institutional carriers: Reviewing modes of transporting ideas over time and space and considering their consequences', *Industrial and Corporate Change*, **12** (4), 879–94.

Scott, W. Richard (2004), 'Reflections on a half century of organizational sociology', *Annual Review of Sociology*, **30**, 1–21.

Scott, W. Richard (2008), 'Approaching adulthood: The maturing of institutional theory', *Theory and Society*, **37** (5), 427–42.

Selznick, P. (1957), *Leadership in Administration*, New York: Harper and Row.

Seo, Myeong G. and W. E. D. Creed (2002), 'Institutional contradictions, praxis and institutional change', *Academy of Management Review*, **27** (2), 222–47.

Sherer, Peter D. (2017), 'When is it time to stop doing the same old thing? How institutional and organizational entrepreneurs changed Major League Baseball', *Journal of Business Venturing*, **32** (4), 355–70.

Smets, Michael, T. Morris and R. Greenwood (2012), 'From practice to field: A multilevel model of practice-driven institutional change', *Academy of Management Journal*, **55** (4), 877–904.

Suddaby, R. and R. Greenwood (2005), 'Rhetorical strategies of legitimacy', *Administrative Science Quarterly*, **50** (1), 35–67.

Vogel, Rick (2012), 'The visible colleges of management and organization studies: A bibliometric analysis of academic journals', *Organization Studies*, **33** (8), 1015–43.

Washington, M. and M. J. Ventresca (2004), 'How organizations change: The role of institutional support mechanisms in the incorporation of higher education visibility strategies, 1874–1995', *Organization Science*, **15** (1), 82–97.

Weber, M. (1930), *The Protestant Ethic and the Spirit of Capitalism.* New York: Allen and Unwin.

Weber, M. (1952), 'The essentials of bureaucratic organization: An ideal-type construction', *Reader in Bureaucracy*, **19**, 19–21.

Weber, M. (1968), *On Charisma and Institution Building*, Vol. 322, Chicago, IL: University of Chicago Press.

Willmott, Hugh (2015), 'Why institutional theory cannot be critical', *Journal of Management Inquiry*, **24** (1), 105–11.

Wooten, Melissa and A. J. Hoffman (2017), 'Organizational fields: Past, present and future', in R. Greenwood, C. Oliver, T. Lawrence and R. Meyer (eds), *The Sage Handbook of Organizational Institutionalism*, Thousand Oaks, CA: Sage, pp. 55–76.

Zilber, Tammar B. (2002), 'Institutionalization as an interplay between actions, meanings, and actors: The case of a rape crisis centre in Israel', *Academy of Management Journal*, **45** (1), 234–54.

Zucker, L. G. (1977), 'The role of institutionalization in cultural persistence', *American Sociological Review*, **42** (5), 726–43.

Zucker, L. G. (1983), 'Organizations as institutions', *Research in the Sociology of Organizations*, **2** (1), 1–47.

7. The resource philosophy: 'changing opportunities'

INTRODUCTION

The resource philosophy originates with the assumption that an organization's ability to acquire and leverage valuable resources will determine its ongoing competitive success and survival. Change from a resource perspective depends not only upon how an organization's resources coalesce and evolve, but also on the way in which they are reconfigured and redeployed over time; a position supported by a respectable body of evidence. For example, a meta-analytic review of evidence from 29,561 organizations published in 125 research articles concluded that the possession and utilization of critical resources predicts organizational performance (Crook, Ketchen, Jr., Combs and Todd, 2008). This chapter begins by defining and exploring what constitutes resources and a resource-based perspective. It considers how the resource perspective evolved and its place in change management. Whilst an organization must acquire and build strategically valuable resources and capabilities, whether these result in value creation or competitive advantage ultimately relies on how the resources are deployed. The way in which an organization structures, bundles and leverages its resources will impact profoundly upon their effectiveness. Hence the importance of a focused, strategic approach to resource management if they are to create value and provide novel opportunities for organizational change and development (Pisano, 2017).

We examine the resource-based view (RBV) of the firm and its contribution to the resource philosophy. The acquisition and deployment of resources occupies a central place in organizational change management, often via strategy. Earlier theories, such as Porter's (1980) competitive forces model, focused on the dictates of external market forces and industry players in determining a firm's competitive strategy and resource acquisition. In contrast, firm-level factors represent the primary concern of the resource-based view. The focus thus shifted dramatically from the external environment to an organization's internal dynamics, how it chooses what capabilities to invest in, how it goes about using its resources, and how it explains the success of 'open' innovation strategies that share valuable resources with other organizations. While this has led some to argue that firms should concentrate on their internal rather than external environments (Das and Teng, 2000), the evidence strongly indicates that a thorough understanding of environmental conditions and contingencies remains critical to developing and maintaining a firm's capabilities.

In the subsequent section, we discuss the developments and extensions appended to the RBV to extend its relevance to strategic decision making for change. Resource dependence theory, for example, recommends adopting a two-way, open systems perspective, particularly in the context of complex, rapidly changing and hyper-competitive environments. The theory encourages the identification of relationships organizations can form to secure critical resources for competitive advantage (Malatesta and Smith, 2014). We highlight the distinctions between resources and capabilities and consider the role of dynamic capabilities, such as absorptive capacity. In addition, we reveal an important connection between managing resources and contingency theory via an emphasis on studying the external environment. The final section on resource dependence highlights the impact of environments on organizations, and of organizations on environments (Pfeffer and Salancik, 1978). Finally, we draw together some of the key concepts of dynamic capabilities and contingency theory.

RESOURCE PERSPECTIVE

Resources shape an organization's prosperity and even survival. As a result, change managers face the challenge of coordinating and deploying resources to ensure they yield optimum efficiency and impact. At its most simplistic, resource theory begins with the assumption that knowledge about resources, their abundance, scarcity and ownership, contributes to effective strategic decision making and allows an organization to build a solid, sustainable base (Barney, 2001a; Priem and Butler, 2001). Analysing 'economic units' in terms of the resources they possess enjoys a long history in economics, but has tended to focus on production factors such as labour, capital and land (Wernerfelt, 1984). However, the work of early resource theory proponents, Wernerfelt (1984) and Rumelt (1984), demonstrated that an organization's resources come in many guises and can impact significantly upon decision making. Eisenhardt and Martin (2000), for example, described three key types of resources: physical (e.g. specialized equipment, geographic location), human (e.g. expertise in a particular field), and organizational assets (e.g. leadership, culture, superior customer services), that can be implemented as part of a range of value-creating strategies. Similarly, Rumelt (1984) observed that firms are characterized by bundles of linked and idiosyncratic resources, or what he called 'resource conversion activities'. The concept of conversion reinforces the importance of the change manager who assumes custodianship of resources and the responsibility for using them to create value. Resourcing involves creating assets in the form of people, time, money, knowledge or skills. But these assets need conversion into substantive benefits and outcomes through relationships, trust and careful authority, which facilitate interaction among organizational members to enact change (Feldman, 2004).

Sirmon, Hitt and Ireland (2007, p. 273) described resource management as the 'comprehensive process of structuring the firm's resources to build capabilities', then leveraging these to create and maintain value for all stakeholders. As this definition implies, creating value requires more than just possessing critical resources. Rather, value creation depends on how a firm accumulates, combines and exploits its resources. The management of resources—how effectively they are structured, bundled and leveraged—governs competitive advantage (Sirmon et al., 2007). The concept of structuring introduces a link to 'structuration' theory, which focuses on the way rules and resources create social systems (Giddens, 1984). Accordingly, operations management—the management science concentrating on maximizing efficiency—has become a key area in understanding how to best integrate resources for competitive advantage (Hitt, Xu and Carnes, 2016). In the case of change, the combination of rules and resources creates systems and structures that restrain behaviour. In response, change managers face the task of breaking the cycle.

Highlighting the link between resource management and value creation, Wernerfelt (1984) claimed that 'resources and products are two sides of the same coin' (p. 171). But, as Dierickx and Cool (1989) noted, change managers can fail to understand that the right bundle of assets in the first place establishes the decisive opportunity for value creation. Sometimes organizational systems for deploying resources can be overrated, particularly when it is the resources themselves that confer value. Knott (2003, p. 929) expressed similar sentiments arguing that 'superior organizational routines can be a source of value if and only if there is an isolating mechanism preventing their diffusion throughout industry'. The employment of unique resources can be more easily copied than their original acquisition unless they receive protection from an isolating mechanism. Isolating mechanisms influence business strategy because they defend and stabilize competitive positions (Rumelt, 1984). Resources therefore play a central role in strategic change. As Teece, Pisano and Shuen (1997) argued, understanding how firms succeed in realizing sustainable competitive advantage represents a key issue in strategy and organizational change.

RESOURCES AND COMPETITION

The importance of resources in strategy making and change has led researchers to devote considerable attention to how they influence competitiveness through their structure, function and characteristics. Another side effect has been the emergence of numerous different resource-based theories (Feldman, 2004). The chief theories include the political economy model, power-dependence model, and resource dependence theory. All three suggest that organizations depend upon the external environment for their resources. These theories represent an 'inside-out', open systems perspective in which the management of external dependencies is viewed as critical. The RBV and its offshoot, the dynamic capabilities approach, emerged later. While the earlier theories viewed resources as dependent on the external environment, the RBV accentuated internal organizational dynamics; how a firm goes about *using* its resources (Feldman, 2004; Das and Teng, 2000).

During the 1980s, Porter's competitive forces model represented the 'dominant paradigm' for strategic decision making (Teece et al., 1997, p. 510). Founded on the 'structure–conduct–performance' triumvirate, change managers focused their efforts on the action organizations can take to defend their positions against competitive forces, including new rivals and substitute products, and the power of suppliers and buyers. The competitive forces orientation encourages managers to think about change from a defensive viewpoint. Change helps bolster an organization's advantages by protecting them from identified competitive forces.

Similarly, the strategic conflict model, an approach from game theory also popular during the 1980s, held that competitive advantage was achieved by keeping competitors guessing through novel tactics (Teece et al., 1997). 'Competitive forces' or 'conflict' perspectives have their focus on how external market forces dictate the terms of strategy and reflect economic theory (Black and Boal, 1994; Barney, 2001b). The problem with economic theory is that it does not look at change from an organizational perspective (Rumelt, 1984). Instead, it prioritizes industry structure as a means of assessing the industry's 'rent earning potential' in relation to exit and entry barriers (Black and Boal, 1994, p. 131), where rent means a return in excess of a resource owner's opportunity costs (Mahoney and Pandian, 1997, p. 205). As a result, an economist would recommend change when an organization fails to make more profit from its resources than could be returned from their use elsewhere. As an addition to an economic worldview, the RBV assumes that models of competition should allow for strategic choices to be made in response to environmental interactions (Fahy, 2000). For the change manager taking a more rounded approach, economic returns through competitive advantage come with 'capturing entrepreneurial rents stemming from fundamental *firm-level* efficiency advantages' (Teece et al., 1997, p. 510). The focus on firm-level factors marks a clear shift away from the 'positioning' perspective of earlier models such as Porter's competitive forces, and their primary focus on industry or market factors (Connor, 2002).

ORGANIZATIONAL ECONOMICS

With the growing interest in organizational economics (OE) and heightened attention placed upon the impact of technological and organizational change as key factors in strategy making, approaches arguing for firm-level efficiency and effectiveness have provoked considerable debate (Combs and Ketchen, 1999; Teece et al., 1997). OE asserts that a firm's primary concern is to structure its activities to maximize performance (Combs and Ketchen, 1999). Organizational boundaries are permeable, emphasizing a structural contingency approach, where adapting structures and processes, and responding swiftly to uncertainty in the economic and social environments, leads to competitive advantage (Blackmur, 1997).

While OE seeks to structure an organization's activities efficiently to ensure optimum performance at minimal cost, the RBV aims to extend an organization's unique bundle of resources and capabilities (Combs and Ketchen, 1999). OE wants more power from the same engine, while the RBV wants a bigger engine. For example, Teece, Pisano and Shuen (2004, p. 313) argued that 'if control over scarce resources is the source of economic profits, then it follows that such issues as skill acquisition, the management of knowledge and know-how, and learning become fundamental strategic issues'. Those organizations excelling in the global economy demonstrate responsiveness, innovation and a capacity for the quick redeployment of competencies. Control of scarce resources generates the primary source of economic profits, but change managers should not neglect how the control of resources can be used to attenuate organizational weaknesses (Sirmon, Hitt, Arregle and Campbell, 2010).

The lesson for change management can be seen in the nexus between the resource-based perspective and OE. While they comprise distinctive characteristics and origins, they also take complementary standpoints. Taken together, the two approaches provide greater insight into change decision making. For example, successful change involves coordinating and redeploying both internal and external competencies; a two-way, open systems, inside-out/outside-in lens. Studies have confirmed that the interplay of this duality can be seen in the success or failure of new product commercialization (Thornton, Henneberg, Leischnig and Naudé, 2019). Institutional theory therefore underscores the importance of studying an organization's external environment given that the utility and value of resources will inevitably change as 'the relationships among participants in the field change' (Feldman, 2004, p. 295).

Another view proposes that theories in the field of strategic management can be reduced to governance-based theories (agency theory, transaction-cost economics and property-rights theory), and competence-based theories (RBV, evolutionary economics and dynamic capabilities) (Williamson, 1999).

Change can either go down a path of governance and relationships, or competence and performance. However, top-performing organizations excel in both competence and governance (Makadok, 2003). Governance theories explain the existence and boundaries of economic institutions and relationships, while competence-based theories explain the emergence and sustainability of economic rents. We note again the interconnection between the resource- or capabilities-based perspectives and rational economic theory, which endeavours to minimize governance costs while maximizing performance (Combs and Ketchen, 1999).

RESOURCE-BASED VIEW

The term 'resource-based view' of the firm was first introduced by Wernerfelt (1984, p. 173) who defined resources as 'those assets that are tied semi-permanently to the firm'. But it was Barney's (1991) seminal article that presented the most detailed and formal definition of the RBV. According to Barney, resources that will yield a sustained competitive advantage must meet four criteria. They must be: (1) economically valuable, (2) rare and therefore difficult for competitors to access or obtain, (3) difficult to imitate and (4) non-substitutable. Collectively, resources meeting these criteria may be seen as 'heterogeneous', 'sticky' and immobile in that they would be too costly to move from one firm to another (Teece et al., 1997). Heterogeneity of firm resources and capabilities represents a 'cornerstone' of resource-based theory (Helfat and Peteraf, 2003; Miller, 2019; Peteraf, 1993), and explains performance differences among relatively close rivals (Hoopes, Madsen and Walker, 2003). The heterogeneous, sticky nature of resources has added fuel to the argument that firms should concentrate on their internal rather than external environments (Das and Teng, 2000, p. 32). While debatable (see, for example Teece et al., 2004), the RBV does at least demonstrate that firms create some of their own resources (Feldman, 2004). The challenge for change managers lies in harnessing the insight and ability to evaluate their organizations, not just in terms of visible capabilities, but also in terms of *invisible* assets and core capabilities (Schoemaker, 1992, p. 75). This requires an understanding that intangible or invisible assets are not limited to what the organization actually owns, but also includes factors that resonate *outside* the organization (such as reputation and good relations with suppliers). In some service-based businesses, for example, 'goodwill' could represent a major intangible asset coming from features such as brand name, good contacts or company image (Johnson and Scholes, 2002). The potential scope and scale of intangible assets further highlights the imperative to consider both internal and external factors. It is, however, easy to overlook the importance of invisible or intangible assets as a resource-building capability. As Connor (2002, p. 307) explained, 'It is the acumen and experience of managers and their ability to create unique advantages in the marketplace which are difficult, if not impossible, for other firms to emulate or compete away, which lay the foundations for value creation and sustained competitive advantage.'

As our earlier discussion indicated, the RBV originated from economic theory (Barney, 2001b; Feldman, 2004). Economics assumes that a firm's resources and capabilities are 'elastic' in supply. In contrast, the RBV holds that enduring competitive advantage depends on exploiting rare and valuable resources that are 'inelastic' in supply (Wernerfelt, 1984; Barney, 1991; 2001b; Ray, Barney and Muhanna, 2004). 'Elastic' means that an increase in demand for a particular resource will trigger a price increase without affecting the availability of the resource. The RBV, however, predicts that resources and capabilities can take several years to come to fruition, and therefore must be seen as 'inelastic' in supply (Barney, 2001b; Ray et al., 2004). In the short term at least, firms are 'stuck with what they have and may have to live with what they lack' (Teece et al., 1997, p. 514). A challenge the RBV has had to confront is the recent tendency for organizations to adopt open strategies that freely provide competitors access to critical resources. To reconcile this with a RBV of firms, open strategies are successful when providing access to one resource, increasing the value of a bundle of valuable resources the firm possesses, like a Trojan horse strategy (Alexy, West, Klapper and Reitzig, 2018). Providing access to a resource that provides competitive advantage can actually create dependencies on the firm providing it, often seen in the computer and technology sectors to the immense benefit of the owners.

RESOURCE-BASED VIEW AND EVOLUTION

Through economics, the RBV intersects with biological models of change. Evolutionary economics, for example, studies the impact of three key processes: variation, selection and retention (Barney, 2001b). Traditionally the 'growth' of the firm was considered in terms of 'economic growth' or 'economic development' (Penrose, 1997). Another approach from biology applies the 'life-cycle' perspective, where an organization comes into existence, grows in size, reaches maturity and ultimately declines. Evolutionary economics argues that over a period of time, industry followers will adopt the behaviours of industry leaders through a process of adaptation in order to become one of the 'fittest' (Knott, 2003; Nelson and Winter, 1982; Hannan and Freeman, 1977).

One prominent evolutionary framework adopts 'routines' as the basic unit of analysis, based on the assumption that organizations deploy *varying* routines in conducting their day-to-day business (Nelson and Winter, 1982). Routines establish 'sustained performance differences' across firms (Knott,

2003, p. 930). Operating in a competitive marketplace, an organization tests its routines, selecting and retaining those which prove to be the most efficient and effective in generating competitive advantage, and discarding or replacing those that prove ineffective (Barney, 2001b). The willingness to develop new capabilities often comes down to a decision between relevance to an organization's current routines and economic cost to identify new potential routines that are 'strategically interesting' and economically feasible (Pisano, 2017, p. 751).

Firm heterogeneity reflects the *variety* of business routines within a single organization, and a firm's resources and capabilities lead to 'superior' routines (Knott, 2003), which are selected and deployed to gain competitive advantage. Fitness and prosperity come from a variety of unique and effective routines. The type of market (e.g. bottom of the pyramid) will also determine what is an effective routine that enables business to be conducted (Schuster and Holtbrügge, 2014). From this perspective, *organizing* and *strategizing* are evolving, dynamic components of routines. While the conventional image of routines in the organizational context implies predictability and stasis, an evolutionary perspective focuses on routines as process, restructuring and reforming to capture and maximize individual, organizational and environmental-level changes (Feldman, 2000). Consequently, routines not only link the RBV to the rational philosophy through strategy, and the biological philosophy through evolutionary thinking, but also to the systems philosophy considered in Chapter 9.

Institutional theory and the RBV also overlap. While the former emphasizes the institutional environment and the latter holds a task focus, they both share the view that change managers' actions will be constrained by numerous external environmental pressures. Success and survival depend on an organization's ability to respond to these external demands and expectations. In addition, both theories find motivation in the need for stability, predictability and legitimacy (Oliver, 1991). However, the two perspectives clearly diverge in the way they respond to these challenges. From an institutional perspective, survival and legitimacy depend upon conformity to accepted institutional norms and beliefs, the result of which is institutional isomorphism.

While institutional theory relies on compliance, resource-based theory in contrast favours an opportunistic, rule-breaking approach, actively inviting non-compliance. Survival and legitimacy from a resource perspective depend upon an ability to respond swiftly and decisively to environmental fluctuations and uncertainties. The RBV approach to change depends on 'the strategic capability of the firm' rather than on trying to ensure a 'perfect environmental fit' (Connor, 2002, p. 308). The resource-based choice therefore aims to actively challenge and confront external exigencies. Furthermore, power and control play a central role in exploiting external pressures and acquiring critical resources (Pfeffer and Salancik, 1978). Batuev and Robinson (2019) confronted the relationship between power, resource dependency and isomorphism using the example of climbing as an Olympic sporting event. Change in the International Federation of Sport Climbing represented non-compliance with the traditions of the sport, and isomorphism with other federations in the pursuit of resources afforded by Olympic inclusion, which necessarily meant ceding control to the International Olympic Committee. We explore these issues further in the forthcoming section on resource dependence theory.

RESOURCES AND DYNAMIC CAPABILITIES

While the RBV offers an influential framework for understanding how enduring competitive advantage can be generated, numerous uncertainties and criticisms linger, particularly in the context of complex and turbulent environments (Kraaijenbrink, Spender and Groen, 2010). The RBV has been branded vague, tautological and empirically deficient (Teece et al., 1997; Eisenhardt and Martin, 2000; Priem and Butler, 2001; Makadok, 2001; Connor, 2002). One argument claims that operating in turbulent, hyper-competitive and 'high-velocity' environments means dealing with 'discontinuous' change; sudden, unpredictable change requiring a swift and resolute response. Organizations must therefore juggle multiple external contingencies, which can only be successfully countered with a 'dynamic capabilities' approach. Reactions of this nature reflect an organization's ability to align and 'stretch' its resources and competencies to not only cope with, but also take advantage of, imposed conditions. Going beyond the adaptability of an organization, dynamic capabilities also address the consequences of strategic choices, whether in the form of deepening existing capabilities, broadening organizational capabilities, or investing in general-purpose or market-specific capabilities for competitive advantage (Pisano, 2017). Dynamic capabilities therefore extend the relevance of the RBV as a practical management tool for generating competitive advantage while operating in difficult and unpredictable environments (Teece et al., 1997; Eisenhardt and Martin, 2000; Makadok, 2001; Helfat and Peteraf, 2003; Connor, 2002; Sirmon et al., 2007).

Some commentators prefer to use 'resources' as a blanket term for both resources and capabilities (e.g. Barney, 1991; Peteraf, 1993; Fahy, 2000; Ray et al., 2004), while others demarcate clearly between the two (Amit and Schoemaker, 1993; Teece et al., 1997; Eisenhardt and Martin, 2000; Makadok, 2001). Makadok (2001, p. 387), for example, when distinguishing between resources and capabilities, referred to 'resource picking' and 'capability building' as the processes by which managers create 'economic rents'. Resources are observable, though not necessarily tangible, assets that can be valued and traded. Examples include brands, patents, real estate and licences

(Makadok, 2001). In contrast, a capability cannot be observed because it is a 'firm-specific', non-transferable resource embedded in organizational processes. Furthermore, capabilities bolster the performance of a firm's resources, and will not generate economic returns if the firm does not possess the requisite resources. Where resources can be bought, capabilities must be built (Teece et al., 1997). An example of a dynamic capability is 'absorptive capacity', which reflects how well an organization obtains and applies external information to foster competitive advantage (Flatten, Adams and Brettel, 2015).

A different view was adopted by Helfat and Peteraf (2003, p. 998), who advocated that resource-based theory 'as a whole' needs to be viewed in 'dynamic terms'. Given that it takes some time to acquire key resources and develop unique capabilities in order to generate competitive advantage (or disadvantage), Helfat and Peteraf put the case for a 'capability lifecycle', a 'foundational framework' (p. 1008) to assist in understanding how capabilities evolve over time and thereby ensure a robust, dynamic RBV. Their capability life cycle comprises three initial stages: founding, development and maturity, with the scope to branch into one or more of six additional stages, known as the six Rs of capability transformation. These are retirement, retrenchment, renewal, replication, redeployment and recombination. By understanding the *evolution* of resources and capabilities, the 'dynamic' form of RBV can be used to address problems or questions regarding competitive advantage over time. Resources and capabilities are therefore mutually dependent on enacting growth and development. For resources to yield long-term value, they need to be underpinned by dynamic capabilities that are continually reviewed and reinvigorated.

SYSTEMIC DYNAMISM

It could be argued that prominent scholars writing on the RBV and dynamic capabilities have instinctively assumed a holistic, dynamic approach to resource-based theory. For example, both Makadok (2001) and Eisenhardt and Martin (2000) described dynamic capabilities as processes 'embedded' in firms, taking a particular interest in how they evolve. Eisenhardt and Martin's definition of dynamic capabilities confirms the prevailing view of systemic dynamism with capabilities constantly changing, evolving and reconfiguring. They defined dynamic capabilities as the 'organizational and strategic routines by which firms achieve new resource configurations as markets emerge, collide, split, evolve, and die' (p. 1107). All this depends ultimately on a firm's capacity to acquire critical resources, easily jeopardized when at the mercy of harsh external market conditions, government and regulatory pressures, resource scarcity, and aggressive competition for these resources.

Based on their empirical study, Eisenhardt and Martin (2000) identified 'commonalities', or 'best-practice' skills and processes across high-performing firms, suggesting that dynamic capabilities have 'greater equifinality, homogeneity and substitutability' (p. 1106) than can be inferred from conventional RBV thinking. Dynamic capabilities may be necessary, but not sufficient, conditions for the achievement of competitive advantage. In fact, the value of dynamic capabilities to long-term competitive advantage stems from the ability to choose and create resource configurations rather than in the capabilities themselves (Pisano, 2017). In addition, the most effective patterns of dynamic capabilities vary depending on the level of environmental dynamism in the firm market. In relatively stable environments, dynamic capabilities resemble routines; traditional, analytical processes reliant upon existing knowledge to produce predictable outcomes. However, in complex, volatile environments, dynamic capabilities assume markedly different characteristics. They become 'simple, experiential, unstable processes' dependent on creative new knowledge (Eisenhardt and Martin, 2000, p. 1106). Uncertainty around capabilities exist within both supply-side dominant markets and demand-side dominant markets (Pisano, 2017). By evolving characteristics that reflect the dynamics of the market in which they are operating, dynamic capabilities serve to reshape and expand conventional RBV thinking.

'High-velocity' markets also act as a 'boundary condition' for the RBV (Eisenhardt and Martin, 2000). In such volatile markets, competitive advantage becomes uncertain and unpredictable, and a firm's dynamic capabilities come under threat. In addition, there is also the complication of changing consumer behaviour, as the development of a capability previously perceived as valuable may offer no competitive advantage by the time the organization possesses it (Pisano, 2017). Confronted with high uncertainty and volatility, the RBV of the firm as a bundle of assets is undermined by the imperative to continually add, recombine or drop resources. The RBV advocates leveraging bundled resources to achieve competitive advantage. However, successful strategy in high-velocity markets creates novel advantages through timing and flexibly structured organizing.

The strategic logic revolves around opportunity, and the ability to change determines whether an organization can make it in a high-velocity market (Eisenhardt and Martin, 2000). These sentiments introduce a contingency logic into the resource-based perspective. Wielding dynamic capabilities to generate opportunities means negotiating situational factors as a method of change. If we accept the argument that environmental awareness and understanding are essential prerequisites to managing a firm's resources, it makes sense that contingency theory should be integrated into our understanding of the RBV (Sirmon et al., 2007).

CONTINGENCY THEORY

Contingency theory assumes that organizational performance reflects the fit between two or more factors, such as an organization's environment, use of technology, strategy, structure, systems, style or culture (Pfeffer, 1982). However, variables such as inertia, inflexibility, resource immobility and industry pressure make the fit between factors difficult to predict. Contingency theory advocates suggest that over the long term, change managers in competitive markets must adjust their practices and their organizations' configurations to meet efficiency demands (Alder, 1992; McLoughlin and Clark, 1988). For example, the ability to create innovative products has a significant impact on business performance in dynamic markets with emerging niches, whereas business process innovations improve performance in highly competitive, stable markets (Prajogo, 2016). However, the search for best fit is limited by the impossibility of modelling all the contingent variables, and the difficulty of predicting their connections and causal relations.

The advantage in adopting a contingency approach lies with its explanations for organizational change from a behavioural viewpoint. Change managers should make decisions that account for specific circumstances, focusing on those most relevant, and intervening with the most appropriate actions. As Peteraf, Di Stefano and Verona (2013) concluded, 'Regardless of the level of market dynamism or the nature of dynamic capabilities, dynamic capabilities may enable firms to attain a sustainable competitive advantage in certain conditional cases' (p. 1407). That is, how competitive advantage is derived from dynamic capabilities may be formulated by the market, manager experience, timing and a host of other difficult-to-predict contingencies. The best actions to initiate change come back to two words: 'It depends'. In fact, the best course of action must always be situational, matched to circumstances. The focus of management in organizational change should be on achieving alignment and 'good fits' to ensure stability and capture opportunity.

Resource dependence theory and contingency theory share a number of fundamental assumptions regarding the role of environmental uncertainty and dependencies (Hillman and Dalziel, 2003). We discuss the link between resource theory and contingency theory further in the following section on resource dependence.

RESOURCE DEPENDENCE

One way of looking at resource dependency is to recognize that dependence on resources increases uncertainty for an organization. It therefore becomes most useful when analysing environmental opportunities and threats. Resource dependence theory maintains that responsiveness to fluctuating, uncertain and sometimes conflicting external demands and expectations reveals the importance of contingency models. Organizational choice, therefore, will be constrained by both internal and external pressures (Pfeffer and Salancik, 1978; Oliver, 1991). In addition, the institutional environment (governments, regulatory structures, professions, laws) can exert pressure to comply, and impede an organization's access to resources if it tries to avoid or subvert established institutional norms and expectations. Consequently, power and influence are integral to survival from a resource dependence perspective (Oliver, 1991). Being able to exert sufficient power and influence over environmental and institutional factors enables an organization to reduce uncertainty and control critical resources, which can mean the difference between success and failure. Possessing quality resources that are valuable, rare, inimitable and non-substitutable will also help to reduce the dependency between organizations and external contingencies. The right resources decrease uncertainty and lower transaction costs, thereby bolstering an organization's prospects for long-term competitiveness (Pfeffer and Salancik, 1978; Williamson, 1984; Hillman and Dalziel, 2003).

Resource dependency theory operates best under change conditions where competitive processes have caused resource scarcities. It shows how organizations seek to innovate through the acquisition of new resources (Sherer and Lee, 2002). As this suggests, resource dependency focuses squarely on innovation and change, seeking out new opportunities to ensure ownership of valuable and scarce resources that provide a distinctive edge over competitors. As a result, interorganizational relationships (e.g. mergers, alliances, sub-contracting) to secure resources have become a chief concern of resource dependency scholars (Malatesta and Smith, 2014). Indeed, meta-analytic evidence supports the hypothesized relationship between securing resources through interorganizational relationships to improve autonomy and legitimacy, and ultimately organizational performance (Drees and Heugens, 2013). Resource dependence highlights the importance of adopting a dynamic capabilities approach that is sensitive and responsive enough to capitalize on external market contingencies. Moreover, McCann (2004) suggested that organizations need to develop 'adaptive capacity' by incorporating a contingency approach. As organizational environments continue to evolve, adaptive capacity—the unique mix of concepts, skills, capabilities and technologies residing in the organization—must also evolve in order to successfully coordinate 'relationships' with different environments (McCann, 2004, p. 49). Accordingly, a resource dependency approach to relationship building can be advantageous to managers working in non-profit organizations, who struggle to secure resources (Doyle, Kelly and O'Donohoe, 2016). Resource dependency places the ability to initiate rapid change at the centre of adaptive capacity.

CRITICAL CONTINGENCIES

We noted earlier the criticisms levelled at the RBV, which among other things has been accused of deficiencies, contradictions and ambiguities. Some have even suggested that these problems have rendered the RBV implausible (Fahy, 2000; Priem and Butler, 2001). For example, RBV logic concludes that being able to measure a resource makes it less likely to be a source of sustained competitive advantage because it might be more easily duplicated (Lado, Boyd, Wright and Kroll, 2006). In addition, RBV relies on a kind of paradoxical and circular reasoning where competitive advantages create value, but also emanate from resources possessing value. Lado et al. (2006) countered such criticisms, suggesting that this represents a narrow and 'traditional view of science which asserts that paradox is counter to scientific inquiry' (p. 117). In having to deal with the challenges and complexities of structuring and leveraging bundles of linked and idiosyncratic resources, the RBV has the capacity to encourage a 'complicated understanding' (p. 116) of change theorizing. Paradox impels us to question taken-for-granted assumptions concerning 'reality, truth and knowledge' (p. 118). In fact, the more severe criticisms display a practical, rational choice bias, in claiming that the RBV offers too little prescriptive advice for change managers.

The conjunction of resource dependence theory and the concept of dynamic capabilities provides the breakaway lever from traditional economic orthodoxy within the RBV, and offers a lens to understanding paradox. Traditional economic thinking focused on achieving and maintaining a stable, steady state in which acquiring unique, valuable and hard-to-copy resources delivers the competitive antidote. In contrast, resource dependence theory and dynamic capabilities together encourage deviance from the status quo. They demonstrate that if organizations are to survive and succeed in complex, uncertain and often hostile environments, they must embrace contradiction and conflict and challenge deep assumptions about firm performance and competitive advantage (Lado et al., 2006, p. 124). Drawing on these within a contingency theory framework enables the integration of the kind of problematic environmental contingencies that other philosophies of change struggle to reconcile (Sirmon et al., 2007).

CONCLUSION

A major contribution of the resource philosophy is its firm-level focus. Foss (1997, p. 347), for example, asserted that the overall objective that 'informs' the resource-based perspective 'is to account for the creation, maintenance and renewal of competitive advantage in terms of the characteristics and dynamics of the internal resources of firms'. The value of the resource-based model accompanies its ability to explain enduring differences in firm performance that cannot be explained by differences in the external industry environment (Peteraf, 1993). Within this domain, the RBV of the firm, dynamic capabilities, and resource dependency theory have been successful in contributing to understanding organizational change (Crook et al., 2008; Hillman, Withers and Collins, 2009; Miller, 2019).

The resource philosophy borrows from the systems and biological philosophies by presenting the firm as a system of resources and capabilities that coalesce, evolve and reconfigure over time. When firms are seen as a web of interconnecting resources and capabilities, change managers enjoy a better opportunity to develop 'leveraging strategies' that enable them to align firm capabilities against the prevailing market and environmental context to create value (Lado et al., 2006). Moreover, from an open systems perspective, resource management primarily aims to understand both 'the effect of environments on organizations and the effect of organizations on environments' (Pfeffer and Salancik, 1978, p. 11).

While firms seek to acquire resources and develop rare, inimitable and non-substitutable capabilities, possession alone does not guarantee competitive success. On the contrary, the resource philosophy demonstrates unequivocally that competitive advantage lies in how resources are managed and manipulated, to the extent that resources can be freely given away if they increase the value of a bundle of other resources. To create value and build sustainable competitive advantage, a firm needs to enact an effective resource management process which will identify and implement the processes and capabilities needed to acquire, build, combine and leverage resources. In other words, while each part is individually important, the whole is greater than the sum of its parts; synergies or value creation come from synchronizing the individual components (Sirmon et al., 2007). Change, therefore, from a resource-based perspective, continues in an evolving process in which organizations acquire, utilize, develop and reconfigure their resources. A firm can 'bundle' its assets in unique and potent ways in order to bring about change (Connor, 2002).

We also noted that the 'acumen and experience' of managers plays a pivotal role in enabling a firm to create 'unique advantages' in the marketplace, and thereby build enduring competitive advantage. For example, the non-tangible capability to not only take knowledge from the environment, but then apply it to commercial ends, is critical to competitive advantage. Resource dependence theory illustrates that resource scarcity and a hostile environment may stymie a firm's best intentions, rendering it incapable of acquiring the resource and skill capabilities critical for bringing about change. Despite this, understanding resource dependence can assist in challenging accepted, 'conforming' institutional practices that may be embedded in an organization's culture, management style, organizing structures and processes. As Pfeffer and Salancik noted (1978, p. 18), a firm's environmental constraints are not 'predestined and irreversible'. They expounded the role of a change manager as 'an advocator, an active manipulator of constraints and of the social settings in which the organization is embedded' (p. 19). Resource dependence theory encourages a 'dynamic capabilities approach' that recognizes organizations must be sensitive to, as well as manage, a myriad of external contingencies within the context of complex and constantly shifting environmental conditions (Peteraf et al., 2013).

Rather than seeking acceptance through conformity and legitimacy, a resource dependence perspective, combined with a dynamic capabilities focus, actively seeks out new opportunities wherein the focus is on 'when, where and how often' to innovate and change (Eisenhardt and Martin, 2000, p. 1111), as well as what to change (Pisano, 2017). A resource dependence–dynamic capabilities nexus can therefore assist firms to proactively develop strategies to engage and respond to their environments either independently or in partnership with other stakeholders. Drawing on these approaches within a contingency framework encourages firm adaptation and responsiveness to changing external exigencies. In addition, a contingency perspective, which tends to emphasize alignment and 'good fits' to ensure efficiency, stability and control, provides a counter-foil to the rule-breaking, conflict-inducing focus of the resource dependence and dynamic capabilities partnership.

REFERENCES

Alder, Paul S. (1992), *Technology and the Future of Work*, New York: Oxford University Press.

Alexy, Oliver, J. West, H. Klapper and M. Reitzig (2018), 'Surrendering control to gain advantage: Reconciling openness and the resource-based view of the firm', *Strategic Management Journal*, **39** (6), 1704–27.

Amit, Raphael and P. J. H. Schoemaker (1993), 'Strategic assets and organizational rent', *Strategic Management Journal*, **14** (1), 33–46.

Barney, Jay B. (1991), 'Firm resources and sustained competitive advantage', *Journal of Management*, **17** (1), 99–120.

Barney, Jay B. (2001a), 'Is the resource-based "view" a useful perspective for strategic management research? Yes', *Academy of Management Review*, **26** (1), 41–56.

Barney, Jay B. (2001b), 'Resource-based theories of competitive advantage: A ten-year retrospective on the resource-based view', *Journal of Management*, **27** (6), 643–50.

Batuev, Mikhail and L. Robinson (2019), 'Organizational evolution and the Olympic Games: The case of sport climbing', *Sport in Society*, **22** (10), 1674–90.

Black, Janice A. and K. B. Boal (1994), 'Strategic resources: Traits, configurations and paths to sustainable competitive advantage', *Strategic Management Journal*, **15** (Special Issue), 131–48.

Blackmur, Douglas (1997), 'Determinants of organisational size: BHP and vertical integration 1885–1915', *Journal of the Australian and New Zealand Academy of Management*, **3** (1), 15–29.

Combs, James G. and D. J. Ketchen, Jr. (1999), 'Explaining interfirm cooperation and performance: Toward a reconciliation of predictions from the resource-based view and organizational economics', *Strategic Management Journal*, **20** (9), 867–88.

Connor, Tom (2002), 'The resource-based view of strategy and its value to practising managers', *Strategic Change*, **11** (6), 307–16.

Crook, Russell, D. J. Ketchen, Jr., J. G. Combs and S. Y. Todd (2008), 'Strategic resources and performance: A meta-analysis', *Strategic Management Journal*, **29** (11), 1141–54.

Das, T. K. and B. S. Teng (2000), 'A resource-based theory of strategic alliances', *Journal of Management*, **26** (1), 31–61.

Dierickx, Ingemar and K. Cool (1989), 'Asset stock accumulation and sustainability of competitive advantage', *Management Science*, **35** (12), 1504–11.

Doyle, Gerardine, R. Kelly and S. O'Donohoe (2016), 'Resource dependence as a mechanism for survival: The case of the Mater Misericordiae University Hospital', *VOLUNTAS: International Journal of Voluntary and Nonprofit Organizations*, **27** (4), 1871–93.

Drees, Johannes M. and P. P. Heugens (2013), 'Synthesizing and extending resource dependence theory: A meta-analysis', *Journal of Management*, **39** (6), 1666–98.

Eisenhardt, K. M. and J. A. Martin (2000), 'Dynamic capabilities: What are they?', *Strategic Management Journal*, **21** (10–11), 1105–21.

Fahy, J. (2000), 'The resource-based view of the firm: Some stumbling-blocks on the road to understanding sustainable competitive advantage', *Journal of European Industrial Training*, **24** (2/3/4), 94–104.

Fahy, J. (2002), 'A resource-based analysis of sustainable competitive advantage in a global environment', *International Business Review*, **11** (1), 57–77.

Feldman, Martha S. (2000), 'Organizational routines as a source of continuous change', *Organization Science*, **11** (6), 611–29.

Feldman, Martha S. (2004), 'Resources in emerging structures and processes of change', *Organization Science*, **15** (3), 295–309.

Flatten, Tessa, D. Adams and M. Brettel (2015), 'Fostering absorptive capacity through leadership: A cross-cultural analysis', *Journal of World Business*, **50** (3), 519–34.

Foss, Nicolai J. (ed.) (1997), *Resources, Firms and Strategies: A Reader in the Resource-Based Perspective*, Oxford: Oxford University Press.

Giddens, A. (1984), *The Constitution of Society*, Berkeley, CA: University of California Press.

Hannan, Michael T. and J. Freeman (1977), 'The population ecology of organizations', *American Journal of Sociology*, **82** (5), 929–84.

Helfat, Constance E. and M. A. Peteraf (2003), 'The dynamic resource-based view: Capability lifecycles', *Strategic Management Journal*, **24** (10), 997–1010.

Hillman, Amy J. and T. Dalziel (2003), 'Board of directors and firm performance: Integrating agency and resource dependence perspectives', *Academy of Management Review*, **28** (3), 383–96.

Hillman, Amy J., M. C. Withers and B. Collins (2009), 'Resource dependence theory: A review', *Journal of Management*, **35** (6), 1404–27.

Hitt, Michael A., K. Xu and C. M. Carnes (2016), 'Resource based theory in operations management research', *Journal of Operations Management*, **41**, 77–94.

Hoopes, David G., T. L. Madsen and G. Walker (2003), 'Guest editors' introduction to the special issue: Why is there a resource-based view? Toward a theory of competitive heterogeneity', *Strategic Management Journal*, **24** (10), 889–902.

Johnson, Gerry and K. Scholes (2002), *Exploring Corporate Strategy*, 6th edition, Harlow: Prentice Hall.

Knott, Anne M. (2003), 'The organizational routines factor market paradox', *Strategic Management Journal*, **24** (10), 929–43.

Kraaijenbrink, Jeroen, J. C. Spender and A. J. Groen (2010), 'The resource-based view: A review and assessment of its critiques', *Journal of Management*, **36** (1), 349–72.

Lado, Augustine A., N. G. Boyd, P. Wright and M. Kroll (2006), 'Paradox and theorizing within the resource-based view', *Academy of Management Review*, **31** (1), 115–31.

Mahoney, Joseph T. and J. R. Pandian (1997), 'The resource-based view within the conversation of strategic management', in Nicolai J. Foss (ed.), *Resources, Firms and Strategies: A Reader in the Resource-Based Perspective*, Oxford: Oxford University Press, pp. 204–31.

Makadok, Richard (2001), 'Towards a synthesis of resource-based and dynamic capability views of rent creation', *Strategic Management Journal*, **22** (5), 387–402.

Makadok, Richard (2003), 'Doing the right thing and knowing the right thing to do: Why the whole is greater than the sum of the parts', *Strategic Management Journal*, **24** (10), 1043–55.

Malatesta, Deanna and C. R. Smith (2014), 'Lessons from resource dependence theory for contemporary public and nonprofit management', *Public Administration Review*, **74** (1), 14–25.

McCann, Joseph (2004), 'Organizational effectiveness: Changing concepts for changing environments', *Human Resource Planning*, **27** (1), 42–50.

McLoughlin, Ian and J. Clark (1988), *Technological Change at Work*, Buckingham: Open University Press.

Miller, Douglas (2019), 'The resource-based view of the firm', *Oxford Research Encyclopedia of Business and Management*, DOI: 10.1093/acrefore/9780190224851.013.4.

Nelson, Richard R. and S. G. Winter (1982), *An Evolutionary Theory of Economic Change*, Cambridge, MA: Harvard University Press.

Oliver, Christine (1991), 'Strategic responses to institutional processes', *Academy of Management Review*, **16** (1), 145–79.

Penrose, E. (1997), 'The theory of the growth of the firm', in N. J. Foss (ed.), *Resources, Firms, and Strategies: A Reader in the Resource-Based Perspective*, Oxford: Oxford University Press, pp. 27–39.

Peteraf, Margaret A. (1993), 'The cornerstones of competitive advantage: A resource-based view', *Strategic Management Journal*, **14** (3), 179–91.

Peteraf, Margaret A., G. Di Stefano and G. Verona (2013), 'The elephant in the room of dynamic capabilities: Bringing two diverging conversations together', *Strategic Management Journal*, **34** (12), 1389–410.

Pfeffer, Jeffrey (1982), *Organizations and Organizations Theory*, Boston, MA: Pitman.

Pfeffer, Jeffrey and G. R. Salancik (1978), *The External Control of Organizations: A Resource-Dependence Perspective*, New York: Harper and Row.

Pisano, Gary P. (2017), 'Toward a prescriptive theory of dynamic capabilities: Connecting strategic choice, learning, and competition', *Industrial and Corporate Change*, **26** (5), 747–62.

Porter, Michael E. (1980), *Competitive Strategy*, New York: Free Press.

Prajogo, Daniel I. (2016), 'The strategic fit between innovation strategies and business environment in delivering business performance', *International Journal of
Production Economics*, **171**, 241–9.

Priem, Richard L. and J. E. Butler (2001), 'Is the resource-based "view" a useful perspective for strategic management research?', *Academy of Management Review*, **26**
(1), 22–40.

Ray, Gautam, J. B. Barney and W. A. Muhanna (2004), 'Capabilities, business processes, and competitive advantage: Choosing the dependent variable in empirical
tests of the resource-based view', *Strategic Management Journal*, **25**, 23–37.

Rumelt, R. P. (1984), 'Towards a strategic theory of the firm', *Competitive Strategic
Management*, **26** (3), 556–70.

Schoemaker, Paul J. H. (1992), 'How to link strategic vision to core capabilities', *Sloan
Management Review*, Fall, 67–81.

Schuster, Tassilo and D. Holtbrügge (2014), 'Resource dependency, innovative
strategies, and firm performance in BOP markets', *Journal of Product Innovation
Management*, **31**, 43–59.

Sherer, Peter D. and K. Lee (2002), 'Institutional change in large law firms: A resource
dependency and institutional perspective', *Academy of Management Journal*, **45** (1),
102–19.

Sirmon, David G., M. A. Hitt and R. D. Ireland (2007), 'Managing firm resources in
dynamic environments to create value: Looking inside the black box', *Academy of
Management Review*, **32** (1), 273–92.

Sirmon, David G., M. A. Hitt, J. L. Arregle and J. T. Campbell (2010), 'The dynamic
interplay of capability strengths and weaknesses: Investigating the bases of tempo-
rary competitive advantage', *Strategic Management Journal*, **31** (13), 1386–409.

Teece, David J., G. Pisano and A. Shuen (1997), 'Dynamic capabilities and strategic
management', *Strategic Management Journal*, **18** (7), 509–33.

Teece, David J., G. Pisano and A. Shuen (2004), 'Knowledge and competence as
strategic assets', in Michael L. Tushman and P. Anderson (eds), *Managing Strategic
Innovation and Change: A Collection of Readings*, 2nd edition, Oxford: Oxford
University Press, pp. 308–32.

Thornton, Sabrina C., S. C. Henneberg, A. Leischnig and P. Naudé (2019), 'It's in the
mix: How firms configure resource mobilization for new product success', *Journal
of Product Innovation Management*, **36** (4), 513–31.

Wernerfelt, B. (1984), 'A resource-based view of the firm', *Strategic Management
Journal*, **5** (2), 171–80.

Williamson, Oliver E. (1984), 'Corporate governance', *Yale Law Journal*, **93**,
1197–229.

Williamson, Oliver E. (1999), 'Strategy research: Governance and competence perspectives', *Strategic Management Journal*, **20** (12), 1087–108.

8. The psychological philosophy: 'changing minds'

INTRODUCTION

Change management philosophies tend to ignore how individuals respond to change. The psychological philosophy of organizational change treats the impact of change as complex, powerful and potentially severe. People become accustomed to performing tasks in certain ways that make them feel comfortable and proficient. Changing tasks or priorities undermines their sense of mastery and replaces it with fears about inadequate performance, escalating workloads, ridicule and termination. The psychological philosophy assumes that resistance represents the first instinct towards change.

While the rational and cultural philosophies acknowledge both change acceptance and change avoidance, they do not consider the psychology of traumatic change. Consider Kübler-Ross' (1969) five-stage model we introduced in Chapter 5, describing how people come to terms with serious loss: denial, anger, bargaining, depression and acceptance. Although an oversimplification of change responses, particularly when traumatic, the stages exemplify the dynamic nature of change psychology. For example, initially an employee foresees no need for any change at all, or believes that the proposed changes will never be implemented. Once change becomes inevitable, an employee directs their dissatisfaction towards management over the trauma and discomfort caused. Next, through bargaining, the employee hopes that a compromise can be found abbreviating the full change programme. Depression follows after implementation as the employee questions whether the change was worth the sacrifice. Eventually, acceptance arrives to make the best of the change. Bridges (1995) similarly described three stages in the transition process: endings, the neutral zone and new beginnings. A detailed analysis of each stage helps diagnose employees' stress and health.

In the following section, we examine psychological responses to change with particular interest in resistance and empowerment. Next, we further explore the philosophy, then comment on several common practices used to help organizational members accommodate change, where organizational spirituality provides an extreme interpretation of a change adjustment practice.

More conservatively, we consider the popular psychological approach known as organizational development (OD) as well as its offspring, organizational learning (OL). We end the chapter by introducing a newer element of the psychological philosophy, which emphasizes its cognitive dimension; that is, the 'thinking' and believing aspects of psychological change. This section examines decision-making heuristics; cognitive rules of thumb that facilitate rapid responses to change but at the cost of introducing inaccuracies and biases. It also discusses the nature and implications of beliefs, particularly their resistance to change and their immunity to rational interrogation.

'SOFT' INTERVENTIONS

Counterpoint to the 'hard' interventions proposed by advocates of strategic, systemic and structural change-based philosophies, social and organizational psychologists take softer, more textured positions. Psychological analysts recommend techniques that reveal how managers and employees respond to change, which in turn guides how to handle the accompanying stress, conflict and emotional trauma. The psychological philosophy may be differentiated from other philosophies by its interest in the personal impact of change. It steadfastly focuses on the most fundamental building blocks of an organization: its people. If you can change the people in an organization, then it stands to reason that you are changing the entire organization. In contrast, the systems philosophy emphasizes the macro-change impact where organizations represent the key 'unit of change'.

The key motif throughout the psychological philosophy is to minimize the trauma and discomfort associated with organizational change. Accordingly, the philosophy encourages employee involvement and empowerment in organizational decisions. Employee involvement activities can either promote or undermine the trust necessary to ensure success in navigating change. Employees can be cynical. If involvement and communication is exploited to overcome resistance, employees will resist change. As a result, the psychological philosophy cautions that decision makers have to act on the feedback and recommendations of employees. The line between consultation and democracy blurs. Organizations cannot function as democracies, yet if the consultation process does nothing but communicate an inexorable change, employees disengage and refuse to cooperate. Even those employees who accept the change may feel disenfranchised and powerless. The key issues for employees revolve around a loss of status, attachment, meaning, opportunity, identity and control. In fact, fear of loss drives resistance to change. It is for this reason that change managers are encouraged to view employee resistance to change instead as employee readiness to change (Choi and Ruona, 2011). Employee readiness to change shifts the conversation; employee hesitancy to change is natural, rather than being dismissed as stubborn resistance.

RESPONSES TO ORGANIZATIONAL CHANGE

Most change management attempts encounter some type of resistance. Explanations for resistance abound, ranging from unfavourable politics and the misapplication of power, to cultural change and lack of trust. For change leaders, overcoming resistance is a prerequisite to success in implementation. However, different philosophical approaches to change advocate diverse, and sometimes contradictory, solutions. Some philosophies approach the acceptance and rejection of change separately, as if they have no connection to each other. Rational and systems philosophies, for example, view resistance as any structural, cultural, systemic or strategic barrier that impedes either introduced or externally pressured change. Psychological approaches, in contrast, see change in all of its forms as something that naturally draws a complex response. In the psychological philosophy, the acceptance or rejection of change may be conceptualized as a continuum that stretches from commitment to resistance. Commitment and resistance do not occur separately. They may be better understood as polar extremes of a single issue: responses to change. As Dent and Goldberg (1999) argued, a strong case can be made for retiring the phrase 'resistance to change'. In fact, adopting other terms, such as readiness to change, may fundamentally affect how change agents treat employees (Choi and Ruona, 2011).

Advocates of the psychological philosophy argue that change stimulates unhelpful responses such as uncertainty, lack of tolerance, differences of opinion concerning the need for change, and threatened self-importance. Fear and anxiety thread through as inescapable themes; organizational members fear change because they associate it with some form of personal trauma. Employees may fear loss of status or privilege, become anxious in the face of the unknown, or simply lack trust in the change plan (Gray, 2002). For example, in an evaluation of nine organizations implementing change programmes, Bovey and Hede (2001) found a heavy emotional component in resistance, amplified by sometimes irrational ideas about the impact of change. They also noted a high correlation between irrational thinking and behaviours such as blaming, avoidance and feelings of powerlessness. Resistance to change equally applies to middle management as their resistance can challenge the dialogue between executives and the rank and file (Raelin and Cataldo, 2011).

Common psychological solutions for overcoming negative but intuitive responses to change include empowerment, participation, education, facilitation and negotiation (Friedman, 2004), some of which we will explore later in this chapter. Organizational psychologists believe that organizations do not resist change. Rather, people resist change. Organizational members therefore need to be guided through a process of psychological transition in order to accommodate the change. Equally, managerial perceptions of employee resistance can dictate what strategies are applied to guide change (Bringselius, 2014). If we accept resistance as natural and intuitive, change programmes need to incorporate methods for ameliorating fear.

Sometimes resistance might be legitimate and advantageous because it delays or obstructs a poorly conceived change project (De Val and Fuentes, 2003). However, most of the time resistance proves counter-productive, manifesting actively (where change is aggressively challenged) and passively (where change is indirectly undermined). Apathy exists somewhere between resistance and acceptance. Understanding why employees respond to change with ambivalence can be useful to change agents. Cynical humour, for example, characterizes many change responses (Piderit, 2000). Equally, change acceptance can be strong, and according to psychologists, is associated with workplace communication, challenge, training and development, and collaboration and teamwork. Empowerment enhances commitment to change, occupying a privileged position in the psychological philosophy's change toolkit.

EMPOWERMENT

To change managers favouring a rationalist philosophy, empowerment merely decorates structural delegation with a fancy name. Empowerment for the rationalist represents a solution to resistance. The real aim, however, remains improved financial performance and better customer relations as a result of higher levels of employee satisfaction. In rationalist empowerment programmes, morale and equitability deliver a means to an end; the real aim is greater productivity, customer satisfaction and lower costs. Resistance to change impedes progress and undermines competitive advantage. Rationalists attempt to neutralize resistance within bureaucratic structures, typically taking the form of decentralization and team-based organizing forms. Rationalists prefer 'hard', formal management solutions. But in the psychological philosophy, empowerment stands for more than offering decision-making involvement to employees.

Change psychologists counter that empowerment does not mean chasing strategic objectives. Instead it aims to foster community, contribute to society and help organizational members to feel better about their work. Authentic empowerment recognizes that organizational members possess vast quantities of knowledge and motivation. Empowerment less strives to give power away and more assumes that employees already have it. Converting existing power into change action comes by creating ownership and capability using cooperative goal setting and positive reinforcement. The involvement associated with empowerment lends itself to increased employee commitment, which offers a beneficial tool for change managers to wield (Joo and Shim, 2010). The psychological alternative gently sidesteps the rigid, formal structures that increase resistance. In fact, the structural delegation of power falls secondary to open communication and cooperative goal setting, where commitment and involvement take priority. Other common strategies involve role modelling, OL and positive encouragement to offset stress or anxiety, and to persuade individuals of their capability and worth (Bokeno, 2003). Change leaders need to counteract feelings of powerlessness because they present the major impediments to performance. Psychologists think that genuine empowerment may occur with or without the structural delegation of power.

Research demonstrates that psychological-style empowerment enhances workplace creativity (Smith and Rupp, 2003). Better organizational outcomes come through greater sensitivity to the negative psychological and emotional experiences that employees endure when they feel powerless. It helps if change managers provide a demonstration of their sincerity when introducing empowerment, such as through a commitment to OD techniques. As we shall see later, danger lurks if either employees or managers (or both) interpret psychological techniques to be intangible, inauthentic or insubstantial.

Despite the intuitive and popular appeal of empowerment, the technique has proven troublesome to implement. For example, employees may not want to be empowered if it leads to more work, responsibility and risk (Foegen, 1999). Some employees do not want the 'power' to make decisions if it means accepting accountability for the outcomes. Kirkman, Jones and Shapiro's (2000) research concluded that employee resistance accompanies perceived unfairness, increased workloads, unclear role definitions, uncertain managerial support and the absence of team backing. Further, the extent to which change managers can empower employees through environmental change is limited by the psychological resources employees use to cope with change (Kirrane, Lennon, O'Connor and Fu, 2017). Even if empowerment helps manage psychological adjustments to current and future change, it can still be undermined by a lack of trust. Some employees assume that empowerment programmes will attempt to disguise control by putting a 'human' face on it. However, psychologists maintain that the potential outcomes from successful empowerment, including its ability to predict attitudes towards organizational change programmes, commend the risk (Lamm and Gordon, 2010). We therefore need to explore which empowerment practices lead to autonomy, variety, challenge, informality, personal initiative, emotional attachment, feelings of value and passion.

ADJUSTMENTS TO CHANGE

The psychological philosophy encourages employees to develop their own capacities, learn independently and advocate for their own wants. With or without formal empowerment, when employees develop a sense of self-determination their responses to change become more positive (Fenwick, 2003). While each change programme with sympathies towards the psychological philosophy has its own nuances, the common ingredients revolve around sharing knowledge and decision making, being adaptable and flexible, and acknowledging the contributions of all team members. Resistance to change should diminish as employees take ownership of decisions in an inside-out, or bottom-up, approach to change management. After all, if employees drive change, success seems more likely.

Learning and development can also occur during regular duties where change has not necessarily been actively sought. For example, job enrichment and job rotation programmes may encourage employees to engage in novel ways leading to higher levels of satisfaction. Furthermore, such development programmes can show employees where change should be targeted. The challenge here lies with balancing functional skill acquisition with experiential development styles (Lau, Lee and Chung, 2019).

Another common psychological approach involves coaching and mentoring. Coaching in organizations refers to training, guidance and feedback about specific tasks and performance. The coach in an organizational change context provides a special form of advice about personal improvement and behaviour in order to better align employees with the type of change desired by upper management (Rosha and Lace, 2016). Joyce (1998) suggested that a coach acts as a combination of counsellor, advisor, mentor, cheerleader and best friend. However, a common problem with coaching programmes is the potential vagueness surrounding what constitutes a good result, and then being able to measure it (Rosha and Lace, 2016). Similar to a coach, a mentor can be from within or outside the workplace, their role to provide experienced guidance through emotional support and tutoring. Sometimes emotional ties exist between mentor and protégé.

Reviewing previous recommendations, Gormley and van Nieuwerburgh (2014) suggested that building a coaching culture requires positioning coaching as an integral organizational component where senior leadership promote examples of leaders being coached as well as coaching themselves. Coaching and mentoring relationships generate some tricky questions. What if a coach provides poor advice to a manager, particularly if that manager commands an instrumental role in organizational change? Can and should a coach be a counsellor and friend? What are the professional and personal boundaries in this relationship, and who is accountable? In addition, the process of coaching and mentoring demands intense resourcing of a magnitude impractical for a large group of employees.

If coaches and mentors only work for change managers, then the conventional challenges with resistance come back into play. Psychologists might respond that coaches and mentors help change managers anticipate employee responses to change. Goleman, Boyatzis and Mckee (2002), for instance, suggested that successful change leaders learn how to manage the emotions of their staff through emotional intelligence. Emotional intelligence can be acquired through the development of four broad competencies and capabilities: self-awareness, self-management, social awareness and relationship management. Other organizational psychologists make the more extreme claim that change managers need to create an environment in which employees can explore their spiritual sides.

ORGANIZATIONAL SPIRITUALITY

Although nebulous, spirituality in the workplace has attracted both organizational researchers and management practitioners (Benefiel, 2003a; King and Crowther, 2004; Dean, Fornaciari and McGee, 2003). Part of the interest stems from an inclusive scope, incorporating religious, personal, social, value, identity and existential elements (Burack, 1999; Freshman, 1999; Krishnakumar and Neck, 2002). Moreover, both anecdotal and empirical reports suggest that organizational spirituality can generate honesty, trust, creativity, morale, satisfaction, fulfilment, commitment and even financial performance (Ashmos and Duchon, 2000; Benefiel, 2003b; Dehler and Welsh, 1994). Equally, employees with higher perceived organizational spirituality are less likely to engage in organizational misbehaviour (Weitz, Vardi and Setter, 2012). Our interest surrounds claims that spirituality influences organizational change through personal psychology (Heaton, Schmidt-Wilk and Travis, 2004). Since the approach enjoys a strong alignment with the psychological philosophy, we think it worth exploring organizational spirituality from a change management perspective.

The deeply personal concept of organizational spirituality has led to a proliferation of interpretations. The term has been variously defined in relation to religious principles, existential questioning, non-religious transcendental concepts, mystical experiences, and a human drive for unity and connection (Burack, 1999; Freshman, 1999; Krishnakumar and Neck, 2002). Despite the diversity, a common psychological thread places emphasis on individuals as the most important parts of organizations. Change transitions should support individual spiritual development (Cunha, Rego and D'Oliveira, 2006; Heaton et al., 2004). Notwithstanding religious and metaphysical interpretations, the spiritual approach to change concerns questions about the meaning of work as a life pursuit (Krishnakumar and Neck, 2002). Spirituality therefore inextricably connects with an individual's search for meaning about their life, their work and their organization (Naylor, Willimon and Osterberg, 1996). To Schmidt-Wilk, Heaton and Steingard (2000), organizational spirituality prioritizes the personal inner experience of interconnectedness with fellow employees and the organization. In doing so, employees purportedly gain improved quality of life and meaning in their occupation, while employers gain more reflective, hopeful and creative employees (Karakas, 2010). For the change manager, nothing trumps the collection of values, ethics, principles and personal qualities that can be expressed through organizational policies and behaviours. Spirituality provides a values and principles 'bridge' between organizations and employees. According to advocates, spiritual growth results, marked by maturity and enhancement of both inner virtues and their outward expression (Schmidt-Wilk et al., 2000; Porth, McCall and Bausch, 1999).

Critics counter that organizational spirituality barely constitutes more than an extreme fad, and a particularly vague one at that. Specifically, Karakas (2010) highlighted proselytism, incompatible business philosophies, the potential for employee manipulation, and a lack of perceived legitimacy as challenges to operationalizing organizational spirituality. While the ideas of spirituality, personal growth and values sound nice, their potential as agents of change remains unclear. We suspect that few practising change leaders could imagine a more intangible path to change than through an attempt to bolster spirituality. On the other hand, as we have noted, research evidence does suggest that employees who feel that their principles are respected, and their personal growth supported, report greater satisfaction and perform more productively. However, the literature offers little advice in terms of organizational action towards greater spirituality. Devendhiran and Wesley (2017) proposed that change leaders can learn from organizations embracing spirituality, like Google, and implement ideas such as providing spaces for spirituality, corporate-based mindfulness training and developing internal support groups. As a result, change leaders who acknowledge the importance of managing responses to change take the more balanced approach advocated by the OD movement.

ORGANIZATIONAL DEVELOPMENT

As a psychological approach to change, OD explores the human side of change responses. Its inspiration emerged as a legacy of humanistic psychology (Maslow, 1968; Rogers, 1972; Ellis, 1973), which placed enormous importance on individual and subjective experience. In a change context, OD converges on the values, intentions and perceptions of employees, whose personal experiences of change need to be positively managed. But since organizations struggle—by nature of their structures—to accommodate employees' psychological growth, creating the right conditions for change requires leaders to intervene directly (Beckhard, 1969). It is a challenge made all the more difficult with the transition from development via instruction to unstructured collective experience and learning (Lau et al., 2019).

Influenced by its humanistic background, OD emphasizes the value of employees as a tremendous resource for learning, development and productivity. However, in order to reach their potential, employees must be placed in working environments that encourage self-determination, creativity and the opportunity for flexible responses to change. Flexibility also involves exposure to new experiences that offer challenges and personal growth. The change manager must integrate the developmental needs of employees with the strategic objectives of the organization. OD practitioners believe that this challenge should include programmes that enable employees to uncover their potential. Psychologically fulfilled employees create and adapt to change better than those who remain unfulfilled (Cummings and Worley, 2008).

OD comprises an applied form of behavioural science in that it expressly concerns change. It tries to create working environments that meet employees' needs, support interpersonal relationships, promote satisfaction and fulfilment and bolster commitment (French, Bell and Zawacki, 2005). However, achieving integration between employee development and organizational performance tends to be problematic. OD practitioners assume that the way organizations manage and structure operations is incompatible with the healthy fulfilment of employees' potential. For example, hierarchies and centralization undermine personal expression. Employees wrestle to gain satisfaction through self-determination when bound by rigid policies and formal rules. In fact, according to OD, organizational structure precludes the full, personal development of employees. After all, organizations give preference to rational objectives over human needs. Emotions seem counter-productive; organizations offer little time for personal adjustments to change, and little interest in the opinions of non decision makers. To OD advocates, this combination destroys trust, responsibility, creativity and ultimately overall performance. Organizations need to become as flexible as the individuals they employ. In practice, however, this means that change leaders must find ways to introduce open, trusting and collaborative structures (Cummings and Worley, 2008).

Like many philosophies we have addressed, OD recommends simultaneous and widespread organizational change. In this respect, the OD perspective maintains some consistency with the systems philosophy. Most OD interventions include strategy, structures and systems or processes as areas of activity. Again, like the systems philosophy, OD seeks to establish an alignment between all organizational functions. However, OD uniquely uses human intervention as the vehicle for introducing change. Through an ongoing, and often escalating series of processes involving diagnosis, planning, implementation and evaluation, change agents serve as the catalysts for change. The change agent may or may not be a regular leader as OD places a high regard on the objectivity of outsiders. Unlike other forms of change agency, like those associated with the rational philosophy, the OD agent does not dictate or direct change. They instead act as a facilitator to help organizational members solve their own problems. 'Action research' becomes the change intervention.

ACTION-BASED CHANGE

For action research to be successful, organizational members must get involved in the process of change. Participation involves experimentation with new ways of thinking and acting, and learning from change facilitators and colleagues. OD assumes that participation leads to contribution, which in turn brings about learning as new approaches and insights find voice through debate. Change agents also help organizational members to reflect upon past practices in the context of future decisions. Commonly, OD agents introduce data collection and analyses methods to help understand employees' perspectives. Interviews, focus groups, open discussions and questionnaires all form part of the OD change agent's toolkit. Results from data collection and consultations get shared with employees and leaders as part of the reflection process.

While instrumental to OD, action research tends to be impractical. Organizations cannot rely on the constant interventions (or cost) of consultants. Change agents therefore develop new practices and structures designed to permanently support job enrichment, teamwork, employee involvement and communication. In some cases, the supporting mechanisms take a tangible form, such as new structures and policies. Many others systemically spread across large parts of the organization and involve cultural change, with learning and feedback loops. For example, research by Bunker, Alban and Lewicki (2004) reported several promising areas for OD work, including virtual teams, conflict resolution, work group effectiveness, social network analysis, trust and intractable conflict. Of course, all organizations work differently, and will use the same techniques in different ways (Patchett, 2005; Teo and Crawford, 2005). For critics of OD, the admission that all organizations operate idiosyncratically undermines, perhaps fatally, all psychological approaches to change. While overdramatic, OD does not offer generic prescriptions for change, having less in common with the systems philosophy and more in common with the contingency approach of the resource philosophy.

In the end, despite all the complexities of change and its introduction, all philosophies pursue the same aims. Organizational leaders face an obligation to achieve better performance and want to maximize the impact of limited resources. The psychological philosophy and OD are not exceptions. Convincing leaders to invest in transformative employee development rather than systemic development that has more easily measurable productivity benefits may present a challenge (Lau et al., 2019). But, OD commits to the premise that change must emanate from a critical mass of engaged employees. Better performance comes with interested, valued and empowered employees.

Most change practitioners find their inspiration from rational and systems philosophies. As a result, OD has failed to gain strong favour with managers. OD problematically sidesteps the conventional importance of top-down strategy in response to competitive market conditions (Bradford and Burke, 2004; Greiner and Cummings, 2004). Instead, OD turns inward to face the psychological processes that stand in the way of social cooperation and personal growth. In a management world where environmental turbulence and the need for rapid change carry weight, OD has been criticized for failing to bridge the gap between theory and practice (Bunker et al., 2004). The gap has also been exacerbated by the growth and diversity of OD (Greiner and Cummings, 2004), as the vast range of recommended tools and techniques makes implementation confusing. Few senior leaders find comfort with a change approach that does not directly combat the financial, strategic, market positioning and competition issues that occupy the majority of their attention. Coaching, team building and facilitation sessions as stalwart OD techniques (Church, Waclawski and Berr, 2002), may be seen as soft options to leaders who have to answer to boards about margins and growth. Nevertheless, some change leaders selectively adopt OD ideas, particularly where a high-performance workforce must be capable of learning and adapting.

ORGANIZATIONAL LEARNING

OL marries the developmental side of OD with the cognitive side of the culture philosophy and a smattering of critical theory, to create a psychological approach that emphasizes knowledge. For OL proponents, navigating the complex undercurrents of organizational change demands a learning map comprising 'texts', or rules, symbols, language, artefacts, routines and leadership styles. Change means challenging established ways of behaving (Huber, 1991), and transpires when employees make sense of organizations, important issues, activities and events, and then adapt accordingly. At this point, it can be said that a 'learning organization' exists (Lau et al., 2019).

OL and OD make comfortable bedfellows because they both feature open communication and collaboration (Argyris and Schon, 1996), aiming for common enquiry, where organizational members recognize, question and replace existing practices and behaviours (Boreham and Morgan, 2004). First, however, leaders must create an environment where employees feel they can question and learn from errors (Bligh, Kohles and Yan, 2018). Coming to terms with OL means understanding employees' responses to change (Holmqvist, 2009). OL concentrates on responses to change that emerge when exposing and challenging convention.

The OD component of OL encourages the idea that employees interpret their experiences and share them. Collectively, the voices of employees represent a knowledge repository from which change leaders learn. For example, knowledge management practices, such as knowledge exchange through prescribed social interaction and codification of knowledge in documents, supports successful organizational change (Imran, Rehman, Aslam and Bilal, 2016). In addition, boundaries cross over and 'communities of practice' assemble to interrogate new ideas. Emergent communities of practice collect and distribute knowledge (Wenger, 1998). Most important, practice communities provide a common interpretive context allowing employees to derive meaning about their work activities. Open dialogue marks the essence of OL (Boreham and Morgan, 2004). The dialogue process shapes meanings and experiences into a shared 'schema' or frame of reference. Through common schema, OL helps to reveal how common knowledge guides behaviour through rules (Norman, 1988). An organizational schema evolves as individual experiences converge into shared behaviours; the cognitive content that makes up organizational culture. According to Wenger (2000), communities of practice driven by social learning systems transform knowledge into practice. Social capital builds cumulatively through the transfer and diffusion of shared experiences, in time becoming the connective glue between employees (Van Buren III and Leana, 2000).

For knowledge-intensive organizations, innovation, growth and productivity gains rely upon sharing and combining information (Wenger, 2000). You, Kim and Lim (2017) argued that human resource professionals are particularly well suited to function as change agents by understanding employee scepticism towards learning-based change. Unfortunately, large organizations lumber rather than sprint towards communities of practice. Research by Boreham and Morgan (2004) showed that collective learning depends upon the integration of individual learning experiences into the organizational schema. While contentious, transfer may also be achieved through other forms of organizing that duplicate communities of practice.

One side of the debate argues that flexible forms of organizing, characterized by fluid and permeable structures and boundaries, can enhance learning. Networks and teams constructed around mobile workers increase the possibility of innovative knowledge combinations (Tempest and Starkey, 2004). Projects become the repository of a network of shared individual knowledge and expertise, where fresh insights trump obstructing schema. The less sanguine view proposes that organizational longevity depends on the shared learning experiences of permanently fixed employees. Mobile workforces do not foster collective learning relationships powered by identification with a stable community.

To any change agent sympathetic to the psychological philosophy, a rational, top-down approach will fail. Instead, change must emerge from the ground up through collaboration and a willing desire for improvement. Yet, not every employee has a desire to improve soft skills, such as emotional intelligence, which moderate OL and may vary between employees (Pradhan, Jena and Singh, 2017). While intuitive, OD rarely appeals to change agents who prefer more tangible methods not reliant on the goodwill and cooperation of large numbers of employees. OL takes a step in the rational direction by connecting with the cultural philosophy through the concept of organizational schema. OL, further to its counterpart OD, champions the psychological cause by combining hearts and minds. From here we can take another step by examining the position taken by cognitive psychologists who recommend leveraging or reprogramming the innate decision-making heuristics, or 'rules of thumb', people use when faced with complex change.

THE COGNITIVE DIMENSION

According to cognitive psychologists, encouraging employees to explore workplace satisfaction may not be helpful in bringing about change. In studies on decision making, individuals tend not to choose options that maximize their happiness. For example, while people covet freedom, too much choice can delay and disrupt decision making (Hsee and Hastie, 2005) because it introduces an emotional dimension.

Classical economics-based change approaches such as agency theory presuppose that people will make decisions that reflect their best interests. Change in the short term will be unlikely to serve the interests of most employees because it requires them to perform and behave in unfamiliar ways. While forward-thinking employees might observe that in the longer term, change could be important to save their jobs, few employees will benefit from change while change managers enjoy the prospects of advancement; a position held by the critical philosophy, outlined in Chapter 11. Accordingly, cost–benefit analyses offer poor explanations for decision making. In fact, as a generalization, people might be bad at making decisions in their own best interests. This is reflected in the rapidly expanding interest in heuristics and decision making within organizational contexts (Loock and Hinnen, 2015).

According to Hsee and Hastie (2005), people fail to choose optimally because they either do not accurately predict the consequences of the choices they are pressed to make, or because they ignore their own predictions when they come to choose. Sometimes decisions go wrong for both reasons. Optimal choices require decision makers to form accurate predictions about the impacts and consequences of the options available to them. Research indicates that individuals exercise a set of intuitive decision-making strategies ranging from an emphasis on emotional responses to an over-reliance on experience. Systematic biases in predictions appear to be important to understanding the nature of change responses. For example, when employees perceive procedural injustice during organizational change (e.g. being overlooked) due to a leader's biases, commitment to change is reduced (Lee, Sharif, Scandura and Kim, 2017).

Impact biases refer to individuals' tendencies to overestimate the effect of an emotional event while overlooking the contextual circumstances (Wilson and Gilbert, 2005; Wilson, Wheatley, Meyers, Gilbert and Axsom, 2000). For example, the euphoria of a work promotion can get swallowed up in the aftermath of added responsibilities, higher workloads and more stress. Similarly, despite the sense of belonging that communities of practice inspire, their impact may be short-lived. The warm glow of belonging wears off.

In one revealing study, American college football fans overestimated the pleasure they would receive in the days following a victory because they did not predict the other events during those days that impinged upon their pleasure (Wilson et al., 2000). Returning to work on Monday morning, for example, had a nasty habit of undermining the joy of victory on the weekend. However, when fans were asked to consider the other factors that might impact upon their futures, they made more accurate predictions (Dunn, Wilson and Gilbert, 2003). People also tend to rationalize events that do not turn out as planned or desired. As a result, despite a significant loss or failure associated with an emotionally charged event, individuals bounce back more resiliently than they had predicted. After all, there is always the next game, next season, next job and next change programme. In organizational change, many employees imagine a worse outcome than actually transpires. Resistance might be overinflated by negative expectations. Equally, the changes that employees do champion through communities of practice might lead to greater satisfaction than originally anticipated.

Prediction biases accompany skewed emotional arousal states (Van Boven and Loewenstein, 2003). Current states get projected into future imagined states, which reinforces why change programmes need to focus on a new vision. One study, for example, confirmed the social potential to underestimate a fear of embarrassment (Van Boven, Loewenstein and Dunning, 2005). Participants in the study consistently overestimated the willingness of others to engage in embarrassing public performances (miming and dancing) in exchange for money. Prediction biases might explain why managers so frequently underestimate how difficult change will be, and how willing employees will be to engage positively.

Distinction biases occur in predictions made during different modes of evaluation as well as emotional states. For example, people evaluate options differently before and after the decision (Hsee and Zhang, 2004). Before the decision, a comparison between alternatives occurs, such as between different proposed changes. However, after the decision the actual experience remains confined to only one change approach. Employees might become preoccupied with the difference between the actual change and no change at all. Worse, the comparison will tend to overlook what might have occurred if change had been avoided for a lengthy period. Romanticizing the past prior to change seems easier than contemplating the impact of a failure to change at all. Since change programmes stimulate turbulence and trauma, they inspire a retrospective amnesia where the ugly truth about the consequences of no change fades quickly.

How past decisions worked out also affects the accuracy of future predictions. Memory introduces a systematic bias disproportionately skewed in the direction of events that involved high emotional levels (Karney and Coombs, 2000). For example, Kahneman, Fredrickson, Schreiber and Redelmeier (1993) showed that higher levels of pain are remembered more favourably when they have a less unpleasant ending. Employees shy away from future change when previous experiences ended badly, but equally will accept change more readily if the last programme worked out well in the end.

Memory also plays a role in biases where assumptions about what makes people happy operate as decision-making heuristics, or rules of thumb. The intuitive presumption that more choices are better than fewer appears misleading. In fact, the evidence suggests that more options can lead to worse experiences (Iyengar and Lepper, 2000), a subtle psychological axiom that strengthens the rationalist agenda. Choice heuristics might also help to explain when OD interventions will fail. Debating the problems and having a voice does not go far enough. The process has to narrow the vast range of change options to a clear decision; a process more efficient through senior management. The problem of options in decision making also explains why simplification heuristics, such as satisficing, that rely on finding the first acceptable, compromise solution, can outperform rational thinking under certain conditions (Artinger, Petersen, Gigerenzer and Weibler, 2015).

DECISION MAKING, REASONING AND CHANGE

Decision-making problems do not merely come with poor predictions, but also with failures to act in accordance with predictions when made accurately. Rather than choosing what they predict will lead to greater happiness, people may select the option that offers the greatest immediate appeal or that fits previous experience (Kivetz and Simonson, 2002). Impulsivity reflects a failure to predict long-term experience accurately, such as the decision to avoid the dentist despite a mild toothache. The avoidance of minor changes can grow into a serious problem.

Rule-based decisions ostensibly appear rational. For instance, in experiments, when faced with a choice between two free products, consumers are more likely to choose the more expensive item even if they predict that it will give them less satisfaction than the cheaper item (Arkes and Blumer, 1985). The 'psychology of sunk cost' materializes in change programmes going badly, but not abandoned. When heavy investments in time and resources have been involved, sunk cost thinking can lead change leaders to persist with poor decisions. Worryingly, evidence consistently suggests that experience does not mitigate against this bias (Roth, Robbert and Straus, 2015).

Of all the variables affecting predictions, the most obvious psychologists refer to is medium-maximization, when individuals resolve to focus on something other than the target outcome. For example, people work harder and longer to maximize their status and wealth without making any actual improvements to their happiness (Layard, 2005). Similarly, change agents may end up working with greater dedication and intensity in the wrong areas. For example, changing structure may be readily implemented but will not resolve deeper issues like cultural problems.

The evidence demonstrates a systematic tendency for people to make sub-optimal decisions. For our purposes in this chapter, cognitive biases help to reveal the complexities of psychological models of organizational change. It is worth noting that there are circumstances where fast heuristic-based decisions can outperform rational thinking, such as when a manager is experienced, time is constrained and uncertainty abounds (Artinger et al., 2015). However, not only is it difficult to access and understand psychological responses to change, good decisions can never be guaranteed even with the best of intentions.

BELIEFS AND PSYCHOLOGICAL CHANGE

The role and influence of personal beliefs is central to the psychological philosophy of change. Beliefs provide explanations about the world and its contents, or a way of approaching the world in a consistent and functional way. Beliefs lay a scaffold in our minds to which we can mortar our experiences into a shape that makes sense. Patterns emerge, allowing us to make predictions, act swiftly and generally avoid sensory paralysis by prioritizing those stimuli that have proven worthy of our previous attention. Like a series of partially overlapping Venn diagrams, ideas and concepts make up beliefs, and beliefs assemble to produce more global belief sets that heavily influence what we see as legitimate or important to change, or conversely, what kind of change should be resisted. As a side effect, well-established beliefs assuage anxiety, relieve uncertainty and moderate indecision. In a world of limitless choices and unknowns, beliefs add confidence. Security comes from the sense of certitude that a faith in them affords. As a result, organizations seeking change that confronts or contradicts those held deeply by members will likely fail.

From security, structure arrives, as socially shared belief sets form the basis for both explicit law as well as the myriad of informal, tacitly assumed behavioural norms that permeate organizations (Sperber, 1997; 2006). Social order accompanies common beliefs, whether in a micro version through small groups or through the macro interactions of entire organizations. Some beliefs play critical roles in guiding behaviour, often reflected in the universal principles of all successful social configurations, like placing value on the safety of organizational members and respecting the ownership of property.

Some beliefs did probably emerge through the random confluence of culture and mind, more chance or historical legacy than useful social or personal mental model. Amongst these beliefs we can find examples that seem to rely on irrational assumptions or factual inaccuracies. Cognitive scientists like Atran (2002a; 2002b) ask whether such beliefs might even be mental illusions of sorts, the unintended side effects of other cognitive functions. Whether some beliefs arrived by accident or through social conditioning, it is clear that organizational members use certain beliefs to understand their working worlds and the socio-cultural indoctrination they demand (Duveen, 2002). According to cognitive theorists, some of the most significant personal and social beliefs arrived as accompaniments to minds that 'like' to hold certain kinds of ideas, and where some of these fell into well-worn cultural and social grooves making their ongoing presence consistently useful. Just as Norenzayan et al. (2016) concluded about religious concepts and practices, it is plausible that some organizational beliefs flourish because they were culturally prioritized for their pro-social impacts.

UNDERSTANDING BELIEFS AND CHANGE

Beliefs help us understand the world by providing an explanatory framework (Halligan, 2007). Collectively they sort out the wheat from the chaff, and give us a basis for making decisions and acting (Connors and Halligan, 2015). As neuroscientist Damasio (2000) demonstrated, based on his ground-breaking work connecting thinking and emotions, beliefs also allow us to turn inwards, giving structure to identity, and feedback on the assumptions we make about ourselves. Emotions also moderate beliefs and the behaviours they instantiate. For example, positive emotional states like excitement encourage people to take more risks and display more confidence than their beliefs would typically support (Kuhnen and Knutson, 2011). Conversely, negative emotions such as fear lead to anxiety and conservatism.

Given the natural drift to hold positive emotional states, the mind also conveniently modifies and updates our beliefs in order to maintain an upbeat emotional condition. To do so, however, requires that any contradictory information acquired during previous experiences be ignored. We are all guilty of it, whether displacing the memories of guilt and regret that accompanied the last failed change attempt, or allowing the satisfaction of a recent trivial change to ignore the problems of an imminent major one. Curiously, the drive to confabulate—hold false beliefs that are incorrect but held as true despite irrefutable evidence—comes with confronting ease. According to brain studies, thinking about confabulated beliefs feels more pleasant, leading to an emotional bias in favour of the beliefs under reflection (Turnbull, Berry and Evans, 2004). As a result, leaders and managers cannot necessarily dislodge certain beliefs held by organizational members, even when they are bordering on absurd.

Not only do we both attenuate and amplify our beliefs to fit with pleasant emotions, we avoid uncomfortable emotions by avoiding evidence that can compromise our most strident beliefs. Anthropologist Chaves (2010) recorded the cases, for example, of a tribal rainmaker who refused to dance for rain during the dry season, and a practising but agnostic minister. Other case examples can be readily found in organizations because we all form our beliefs asymmetrically (Sharot et al., 2012). That means the bad news gets distorted, discounted or disowned, while the good news gets magnified, glorified and exaggerated. Worse, it is often organizational leaders who fall most deeply into this cognitive trap. Research shows that organizational belief asymmetry leads to a range of troubling social impacts like financial bubbles and crashes.

Beliefs perform a tremendously influential function in either accelerating or obstructing organizational change. From them flow personal identity, social belonging, interpersonal relationships and a gamut of values, attitudes, assumptions and behaviours. For example, research demonstrates that belief-driven social attitudes can be used to predict behaviour (Kraus, 1995). The implication is that beliefs locate the targets against which we allocate and assess happiness and satisfaction in our working experiences. However, we should distinguish beliefs from items of knowledge and from the content of memory. Beliefs overlay upon knowledge and memories, like a tint from coloured goggles, adding value and pertinence to neutral information. These values come in the form of attitudinal interpretations and evaluations.

FEATURES OF BELIEFS

In this chapter we take more of an interest in beliefs for what they do more than how they can be defined, especially since their cognitive foundations and impact have received only modest attention (Bell and Halligan, 2013).

Nevertheless, some relatively uncontentious features of beliefs are warranted to help inform the forthcoming conversation. As a foundational premise, beliefs can be understood as pre-existing notions (Halligan, 2007). However, because beliefs are inextricably woven into personal convictions, they work differently in cognition compared with other kinds of information or knowledge that remain value-neutral until a belief is activated in order to interpret them. Of course, this process transpires seamlessly so that the assignment of value to information occurs unconsciously and automatically. More technically speaking, beliefs can be expressed or captured as propositions endorsed with heavy bias. Furthermore, beliefs comprise cognitive, affective and behavioural components extending well beyond an abstract value or statement of preferences, and possess greater durability than opinions (Irwin, 2009).

Evidence or critical reflection is rendered unnecessary for the strongest form of beliefs, as we have already reached the conclusion that they are right and correct. Although typologies of belief types can lead to some general categories, there is no way to identify a 'standard' belief format, flavour or style without gross oversimplification. On the other hand, when focusing on what beliefs do, it becomes transparent that they act as a kind of cognitive operating system by sorting, coding, organizing and processing inputs, and delivering in response, intuitive inferences and reflective judgements about their relevance and value (Smith, 2016).

By implication, the scope of what beliefs do in constructing mental commitments to ideas and concepts means that they have to operate both consciously and unconsciously. At times beliefs occupy our deepest contemplations, but mostly they remain automatic, shielded from awareness, and so engrained that we do not even realize that judgements are being made. We might be able to reflect on some of our beliefs but the whole picture remains forever unavailable. We can never examine our own beliefs or any others with objectivity, understand their entire composition, or identify some so deeply buried that their origins emerged from an undetectable collection of natural inclinations, hardwired intuitions and tacit social programming. These covert features make their management during organizational change even more troublesome.

DEFINING BELIEFS

At a more micro level, some psychologists have tried to nail down beliefs by focusing on specific elements, typically expressed in the form of 'isms' common to personality assessments, like authoritarianism (Jost, Glaser, Kruglanski and Sulloway, 2003). Personality and beliefs seem undeniably interconnected, and together are demonstrable precipitants to action (Saucier, 2000). At this point, however, psychologists work principally with 'isms' and 'ists' because they can be quantified through descriptive terms such as communist, fundamentalist, democratic or autocratic (Saucier, 2013). No doubt certain belief sets can be better understood by reducing them to well-defined references, opinions, ideas, concepts, principles, views or convictions. It turns out, for example, that 'isms' help expose ideologies within belief sets particularly well, at times even leading to common demographic and motivational features common in people advocating certain strong positions (Milfont, Milojev, Greaves and Sibley, 2015).

Differentiating between multitudes of colloquially interchangeable terms remains a challenge. What is the difference between terms such as values, attitudes, worldviews, ideologies, opinions and convictions? For the theorist embracing the psychological philosophy, the answer emerges from a cognitive lens. Here, beliefs can be understood as a cognitive position—a way of thinking—where certain concepts receive acceptance and commitment, under some circumstances to a point of faith; they are right and true, sovereign over evidence and impervious to critique. Despite the surfeit of terms available, they all refer to aspects and elements of a larger belief commitment that offers some shortcuts about what is right, true, good or important amidst tremendous uncertainty.

The big challenge to change makers comes into play when consciously acknowledged beliefs escalate, effectively operating as self-governing, untouchable cognitive ecosystems, invulnerable to critical examination and resistant to change. That certain beliefs resile from change has been recorded in psychological studies for some time. For example, 35 years ago Abelson (1986) concluded that our beliefs are firewalled by at least two kinds of cognitive failures. First, even in the face of compelling evidence, disconfirmed beliefs loiter in the mind. Just as worrying, second, when presented with flimsy evidence, we are vulnerable to being easily convinced by charismatic leaders—a pretty face, a sympathetic disposition, a smooth line, an emotional appeal, a personally relevant example or a heroic narrative. To add to the cognitive drama, we find it relatively effortless to find reasons for what we believe and how we act, but experience far more trouble in not doing what reason and evidence clearly show that we should. As we noted in an earlier section, such 'cognitive biases' play a formative role in underpinning the beliefs that organizational members hold dear.

Instrumental, daily-automated, routinized beliefs go on in the background of life, from how to make a photocopy to where to find the office coffee. Their importance seems undisputable, but prosaic beliefs would hardly need organizational change efforts mandating our compliance and directing meaning. One relevant theory suggests that our cognitive 'distance' from a belief affects its susceptibility to testing and verification (Abelson, 1986). For example, routine, micro beliefs about the best browser to use, or how to dial an external line, can be easily subjected to feedback. Trial and error leads to better choices about what works. In contrast, more distal beliefs—typically more abstract and wider in scope—tend to be experienced remotely, or removed from immediate feedback. Distal beliefs therefore sit above the mundane but defy interrogation from irrefutable tangible feedback. Leaders will have a tough time if they want to challenge deeply held beliefs about co-workers, work practices, bureaucracy and even the authenticity of leaders.

INDIVIDUAL CHANGE BELIEFS

A further complication has to do with the specific collections of beliefs that any individual holds. Studies show that each of us wields a completely unique cluster of beliefs, even compared with people we think share the same beliefs, such as those within the same organizational work group or social sphere. The problem seems to be that a good chunk of our cognitive processes go on behind the scenes, unconscious, and as a result, inaccessible to our deliberations (Atran, 2002a). Three critical implications arise.

First, what we think about our own beliefs cannot be trusted because their foundations reside beneath our conscious awareness. Second, faith in beliefs may involve a blurred concoction of intuitive and reflective thoughts. Inevitably we think about only the visible iceberg's tip of our most tenacious beliefs, which goes some way to explaining why faith in them provides a successful and practical shortcut. A third implication from the unconscious processing underpinning many significant beliefs is that we cannot function without them, and there is no such thing as a belief vacuum. Combined, the three implications reveal the psychological philosophy's greatest strength and weakness. Regarding the former, it decisively exposes what it is about organizational change that makes it so difficult. Regarding the latter, it suggests that organizational change might even be impossible.

BRINGING ABOUT BELIEF CHANGE

Although strong beliefs tend to be unique to the individual, it appears as though they still have something in common. How we access our minds—through conscious self-awareness and reflection—affects the character of the kinds of beliefs that take occupancy. To make the messy melange work, an illusion of continuity helps to smooth out our perceptual processing and ensure a seamless experience of consciousness. Perceptual continuity shuffles our vast sensory inputs into an understandable stream, a little like how a sequence of 24 single frames can be played back to back every second to create a motion picture. In a roughly analogous way, we experience an illusion of continuity when it comes to strong beliefs. According to cognitive theorists (Smith, 2016), the metaphor refers to the way we automatically project our central beliefs upon other people, especially when we interact with them. Our assumption maintains the illusion that we share the same deep beliefs. The illusion is helpful in organizations because it facilitates communication for the most part, at least under conditions where the assumption holds, or reflects some authentic shared ground, in the process allowing tacit presumptions to do some heavy lifting. It all goes wrong, of course, when the illusion is in fact revealed as an illusion. Such disjuncture helps to explain why some behaviour strikes us as incomprehensible and shocking, especially when it involves extreme action.

Shattering the illusion means a sudden, and often forceful realization of a powerful misalignment in deep, guiding beliefs between individuals. Extreme behaviours are underpinned by what psychologists call 'extreme overvalued beliefs' (Rahman, Resnick and Harry, 2016). Suicide bombing and terrorism offer confronting examples, but continuity can also be interrupted in trivial and consistent forms like a colleague who is prepared to launch a complaint with human resources over a dirty teaspoon left in the office sink, or a simple difference of opinion over whether office doors should be left open or shut when occupied.

If extreme overvalued behaviours sound a lot like delusions, it could be because the two sit contiguously. Psychologists consider delusions to be unfounded yet tenacious beliefs. The deep beliefs that organizational members hold could operate in a similar way, but are probably properties of ordinary cognition, whereas delusions appear as symptoms of psychotic disorders. It could be a fine line between the two as studies reveal varying degrees of delusional thought in healthy individuals (Schmack et al., 2013).

Understanding—and perhaps even accepting—conflicting beliefs is a different matter entirely to simply recognizing their presence. Almost every behaviour exhibited in organizations falls under the potential repertoire of our own actions. In fact, neuroscientific studies demonstrate that a person can explicitly attribute to others any possible beliefs they can themselves entertain (Kovács, Kühn, Gergely, Csibra and Brass, 2014). At the same time, we can each only track and reflect upon a restricted belief content. Our brains seem to selectively exclude and include content without our conscious deliberation. That is not to say that each of us could succumb to extremist behaviour, but it does mean that acquiring different beliefs is possible in the right context and combination of innate disposition and socio-cultural pressure. But, interrupting a strong belief means revealing the illusion of continuity, which organizational leaders might be reluctant to do as it will inevitably lead to significant confrontation, disruption and conflict. Of course, this is exactly what some philosophies of change consider essential for genuine change to transpire, the exemplar being the critical philosophy described in Chapter 11.

CONCLUSION

Organizational change pivots on individual responses to change. In the psychological philosophy, nothing takes on more importance than managing the traumatic as well as the subtle experiences that individuals face. However, the nature of psychological change experiences means that one size will not fit all. Change agents should therefore participate in communities of practice. For the psychological philosophy, change arrives from the inside-out. Communities of practice work collaboratively to explore new options and directions. Organizational goals filter through communities with change agents acting as provocative but objective facilitators. To supplement, management structures may be appended to allow greater employee empowerment. Forms of coaching and mentoring may be introduced, while at the extremes, spiritual development can add a novel dimension. Personal development lies at the heart of the psychological philosophy.

Psychological change advocates point to OL as the key outcome from OD. OL elegantly embeds a knowledge component in order to explain how employees respond and adapt to changing demands. Knowledge management strategies provide an opportunity to implement clear policies to promote OL. However, as the literature on cognitive heuristics reminds us, individuals do not always act rationally or even in their own best interests.

Psychological theories of mind and agent causality have been employed to explain the social application of beliefs, along with their action-oriented rituals. In borrowing from cognitive psychology, we find an understanding of just how well attuned the mind is to other minds. So much so, in fact, that we tend to think in terms of agents—beings with active minds—even when they are either absent or non-existent. Our minds leap to assumptions about causes, where the intuitive response means blaming someone or something else sentient. Many of us have been heard to complain about an uncooperative photocopier or malevolent weather created exclusively for our personal inconvenience. Minds see the world through other minds; an axiom pivotal to understanding why some beliefs slide past ignored, while others linger for a lifetime.

Critics of psychologically styled programmes of change point to the problematic aspects of allowing employees to initiate change. Concerns over the uncertainty of action and timing remain common. Psychological models complicate change's implementation, and add the need for heavy investments in time and money. Most change leaders look for more tangible methods, but still may use employee empowerment and engagement. The most devastating criticism of psychological models comes from rationalist managers who believe that employees are incapable of envisioning organizational strategy. A more balanced position supports employee engagement about their experiences of change, and if possible, encourages a contribution to decision making. However, scarce resources will rarely permit the use of permanent external change agents. In fact, there can be no guarantee that talking about change will make it come about. For this reason, change should be approached from numerous angles, as we shall explore in Chapter 9 on systems.

REFERENCES

Abelson, Robert (1986), 'Beliefs are like possessions', *Journal for the Theory of Social Behaviour*, **16** (3), 223–50.

Argyris, Chris and D. A. Schon (1996), *Organizational Learning II: Theory, Method and Practice*, Reading, MA: Addison-Wesley.

Arkes, Hal R. and C. Blumer (1985), 'The psychology of sunk cost', *Organizational Behavior and Human Decision Processes*, **35** (1), 124–40.

Artinger, Florian, M. Petersen, G. Gigerenzer and J. Weibler (2015), 'Heuristics as adaptive decision strategies in management', *Journal of Organizational Behavior*, **36** (1), 33–52.

Ashmos, Donde P. and D. Duchon (2000), 'Spirituality at work: A conceptualization and measure', *Journal of Management Inquiry*, **9** (2), 134–45.

Atran, Scott (2002a), *In Gods We Trust: The Evolutionary Landscape of Religion*, Oxford: Oxford University Press.

Atran, Scott (2002b), 'Modular and cultural factors in biological understanding: An experimental approach to the cognitive basis of science', in P. Carruthers, M. Siegal and S. Stich (eds), *The Cognitive Basis of Science*, Cambridge: Cambridge University Press, pp. 41–72.

Beckhard, Richard (1969), *Organization Development: Strategies and Models*, Reading, MA: Addison-Wesley.

Bell, Vaughan and Peter Halligan (2013), 'The neural basis of abnormal personal belief', in F. Krueger and J. Grafman (eds), *The Neural Basis of Human Belief Systems*, New York: Psychology Press, pp. 191–224.

Benefiel, Margaret (2003a), 'Mapping the terrain of spirituality in organizations research', *Journal of Organizational Change Management*, **16** (4), 367–77.

Benefiel, Margaret (2003b), 'Irreconcilable foes? The discourse of spirituality and the discourse of organizational science', *Organization*, **10** (2), 383–91.

Bligh, Michelle C., J. C. Kohles and Q. Yan (2018), 'Leading and learning to change: The role of leadership style and mindset in error learning and organizational change', *Journal of Change Management*, **18** (2), 116–41.

Bokeno, Michael R. (2003), 'Introduction: appraisals of organizational learning as emancipatory change', *Journal of Organizational Change*, **16** (6), 603–18.

Boreham, Nick and C. Morgan (2004), 'A social cultural analysis of organizational learning', *Oxford Review of Education*, **30** (3), 307–25.

Bovey, Wayne H. and A. Hede (2001), 'Resistance to organizational change: The role of cognitive and affective processes', *Leadership and Organization Development Journal*, **22** (8), 372–82.

Bradford, D. L. and W. W. Burke (2004), 'Is organizational development in crisis?', *Journal of Applied Behavioral Science*, **40** (4), 369–73.

Bridges, William (1995), *Managing Transitions: Making the Most of Change*, Boston, MA: Addison-Wesley.

Bringselius, Louise (2014), 'Employee objections to organizational change: A framework for addressing management responses', *Organization Development Journal*, **32** (1), 41–54.

Bunker, Barbara B., B. T. Alban and R. J. Lewicki (2004), 'Ideas in currency and OD practice', *Journal of Applied Behavioral Science*, **40** (4), 403–22.

Burack, Elmer H. (1999), 'Spirituality in the workplace', *Journal of Organizational Change Management*, **12** (4), 280–91.

Chaves, Mark (2010), 'Rain dances in the dry season: Overcoming the religious congruence fallacy', *Journal for the Scientific Study of Religion*, **49** (1), 1–14.

Choi, Myungweon and W. E. Ruona (2011), 'Individual readiness for organizational change and its implications for human resource and organization development', *Human Resource Development Review*, **10** (1), 46–73.

Church, Allah H., J. Waclawski and S. A. Berr (2002), 'Voices from the field: Future directions for organizational development', in Janine Waclawski and A. H. Church (eds), *Organization Development: A Data-Driven Approach to Organizational Change*, San Francisco, CA: Jossey-Bass, pp. 321–36.

Connors, Michael and Peter Halligan (2015), 'A cognitive account of belief: A tentative road map', *Frontiers in Psychology*, **5**, 1–14.

Cummings, Thomas G. and C. G. Worley (2008), *Organization Development and Change*, 9th edition, Mason, OH: Thomson/South-Western.

Cunha, Miguel P., A. Rego and T. D'Oliveira (2006), 'Organizational spiritualities: An ideology-based typology', *Business and Society*, **45** (2), 211–34.

Damasio, Antonio R. (2000), 'Thinking about belief', in D. L. Schacter and E. Scarry (eds), *Memory, Brain and Belief*, Cambridge, MA: Harvard University Press, pp. 325–34.

De Val, Manuela P. and C. M. Fuentes (2003), 'Resistance to change: A literature review and empirical study', *Management Decision*, **41** (2), 148–55.

Dean, Kathy L., C. J. Fornaciari and J. J. McGee (2003), 'Research in spirituality, religion, and work: Walking the line between relevance and legitimacy', *Journal of Organizational Change Management*, **16** (4), 378–95.

Dehler, Gordon E. and M. A. Welsh (1994), 'Spirituality and organizational transformation', *Journal of Managerial Psychology*, **9** (6), 17–26.

Dent, Eric B. and S. G. Goldberg (1999), 'Challenging resistance to change', *Journal of Applied Behavioural Science*, **35** (1), 25–42.

Devendhiran, Sangeetha and J. R. Wesley (2017), 'Spirituality at work: Enhancing levels of employee engagement', *Development and Learning in Organizations: An International Journal*, **31** (5), 9–13.

Dunn, Elizabeth W., T. D. Wilson and D. T. Gilbert (2003), 'Location, location, location: The misprediction of satisfaction in housing lotteries', *Personality and Social Psychology Bulletin*, **29** (11), 1421–32.

Duveen, Gerard (2002), 'Construction, belief, doubt', *Psychologie and Societe*, **5**, 139–55.

Ellis, Albert (1973), *Humanistic Psychotherapy: The Rational-Emotive Approach*, New York: Julian Press.

Fenwick, Tara J. (2003), 'Emancipatory potential of action learning: A critical analysis', *Journal of Organizational Change Management*, **16** (6), 619–32.

Foegen, Joseph H. (1999), 'Why not empowerment', *Business and Economic Review*, April–June, 32.

French, Wendell L., C. Bell and R. A. Zawacki (2005), *Organization Development and Transformation: Managing Effective Change*, 6th edition, New York: McGraw-Hill/Irwin.

Freshman, Brenda (1999), 'An exploratory analysis of definitions and applications of spirituality in the workplace', *Journal of Organizational Change Management*, **12** (4), 318–27.

Friedman, Sheldon (2004), 'Learning to make more effective decisions: Changing beliefs as a prelude to action', *Learning Organization*, **11** (2), 110–28.

Goleman, Daniel, R. E. Boyatzis and A. Mckee (2002), *Primal Leadership: Realizing the Power of Emotional Intelligence*, Boston, MA: Harvard Business School Press.

Gormley, Helen and C. van Nieuwerburgh (2014), 'Developing coaching cultures: A review of the literature', *Coaching: An International Journal of Theory, Research and Practice*, **7** (2), 90–101.

Gray, Colin (2002), 'Entrepreneurship, resistance to change and growth in small firms', *Journal of Small Business and Enterprise Development*, **9** (1), 61–72.

Greiner, Larry E. and T. G. Cummings (2004), 'Wanted: OD more alive than dead!', *Journal of Applied Behavioral Science*, **40** (4), 374–91.

Halligan, Peter (2007), 'Belief and illness', *Psychologist*, **20** (6), 358–61.

Heaton, Dennis P., J. Schmidt-Wilk and F. Travis (2004), 'Constructs, methods, and measures for researching spirituality in organizations', *Journal of Organizational Change Management*, **17** (1), 62–82.

Holmqvist, Mikael (2009), 'Complicating the organization: A new prescription for the learning organization', *Management Learning*, **40** (3), 275–87.

Hsee, Christopher K. and R. Hastie (2005), 'Decision and experience: Why don't we choose what makes us happy?', *Trends in Cognitive Science*, **10** (1), 31–7.

Hsee, Christopher K. and J. Zhang (2004), 'Distinction bias: Misprediction and mischoice due to joint evaluation', *Journal of Personality Social Psychology*, **86** (5), 680–95.

Huber, George P. (1991), 'Organizational learning: The contributing processes and the literatures', *Organization Science*, **2** (1), 88–115.

Imran, Muhammad Kashif, C. A. Rehman, U. Aslam and A. R. Bilal (2016), 'What's organization knowledge management strategy for successful change implementation?', *Journal of Organizational Change Management*, **29** (7), 1097–117.

Irwin, Harvey J. (2009), *The Psychology of Paranormal Belief: A Researcher's Handbook*, Hatfield: University of Hertfordshire Press.

Iyengar, Sheena S. and M. R. Lepper (2000), 'When choice is demotivating: Can one desire too much of a good thing?', *Journal of Personality and Social Psychology*, **76**, 995–1006.

Joo, Baek Kyoo and J. H. Shim (2010), 'Psychological empowerment and organizational commitment: The moderating effect of organizational learning culture', *Human Resource Development International*, **13** (4), 425–41.

Jost, John T., Jack Glaser, Arie Kruglanski and Frank Sulloway (2003), 'Political conservatism as motivated social cognition', *Psychological Bulletin*, **129** (3), 339–75.

Joyce, Amy (1998), 'Career watch: Business coach', *Washington Post*, 14 September.

Kahneman, Daniel, B. L. Fredrickson, C. A. Schreiber and D. A. Redelmeier (1993), 'When more pain is preferred to less: Adding a better end', *Psychological Science*, **4** (6), 401–5.

Karakas, Fahri (2010), 'Spirituality and performance in organizations: A literature review', *Journal of Business Ethics*, **94** (1), 89–106.

Karney, Benjamin R. and R. H. Coombs (2000), 'Memory bias in long-term close relationships: Consistency or improvement?', *Personality and Social Psychology Bulletin*, **26** (8), 959–70.

King, James E. and M. R. Crowther (2004), 'The measurement of religiosity and spirituality', *Journal of Organizational Change Management*, **17** (1), 83–101.

Kirkman, Bradley L., R. G. Jones and D. L. Shapiro (2000), 'Why do employees resist teams? Examining the "resistance barrier" to work team effectiveness', *International Journal of Conflict Management*, **11** (1), 74–92.

Kirrane, M., M. Lennon, C. O'Connor and N. Fu (2017), 'Linking perceived management support with employees' readiness for change: The mediating role of psychological capital', *Journal of Change Management*, **17** (1), 47–66.

Kivetz, Ran and I. Simonson (2002), 'Self-control for the righteous: Towards a theory of pre-commitment to indulgence', *Journal of Consumer Research*, **29** (2), 199–217.

Kovács, Ágnes M., Simone Kühn, Gyorgy Gergely, Gergely Csibra and Marcel Brass (2014), 'Are all beliefs equal? Implicit belief attributions recruiting core brain regions of theory of mind', *PLoS one*, **9** (9), e106558, 1–6.

Kraus, Stephen J. (1995), 'Attitudes and the prediction of behavior: A metaanalysis of the empirical literature', *Personality and Social Psychology Bulletin*, **21**, 58–75.

Krishnakumar, Sukumarakurup and C. P. Neck (2002), 'The "what", "why" and "how" of spirituality in the workplace', *Journal of Managerial Psychology*, **17** (3), 153–64.

Kübler-Ross, Elisabeth (1969), *On Death and Dying*, New York: Simon and Schuster/ Touchstone.

Kuhnen, Camelia M. and Brian Knutson (2011), 'The influence of affect on beliefs, preferences, and financial decisions', *Journal of Financial and Quantitative Analysis*, **46** (3), 605–26.

Lamm, Eric and J. R. Gordon (2010), 'Empowerment, predisposition to resist change, and support for organizational change', *Journal of Leadership and Organizational Studies*, **17** (4), 426–37.

Lau, Kung Wong, P. Y. Lee and Y. Y. Chung (2019), 'A collective organizational learning model for organizational development', *Leadership and Organization Development Journal*, **40** (1), 107–23.

Layard, Richard (2005), *Happiness: Lessons from a New Science*, New York: Penguin Press.

Lee, Kyootai, M. Sharif, T. Scandura and J. Kim (2017), 'Procedural justice as a moderator of the relationship between organizational change intensity and commitment to organizational change', *Journal of Organizational Change Management*, **30** (4).

Loock, Moritz and G. Hinnen (2015), 'Heuristics in organizations: A review and a research agenda', *Journal of Business Research*, **68** (9), 2027–36.

Maslow, Abraham H. (1968), *Toward a Psychology of Being*, 2nd edition, Princeton, NJ: Van Nostrand.

Milfont, Taciano L., Petar Milojev, Lara Greaves and Chris Sibley (2015), 'Socio-structural and psychological foundations of climate change beliefs', *New Zealand Journal of Psychology*, **44** (1), 18–30.

Naylor, Thomas H., W. H. Willimon and R. Osterberg (1996), *The Search for Meaning in the Workplace*, Nashville, TN: Abington Press.

Norenzayan, Ara, Azim F. Shariff, Will M. Gervais, Aiyana K. Willard, Rita A. McNamara, Edward Slingerland and Joseph Henrich (2016), 'The cultural evolution of prosocial religions', *Behavioral and Brain Sciences*, **39** (e1), 1–65.

Norman, Geoffrey R. (1988), 'Problem-solving skills, solving problems and problem-based learning', *Medical Education*, **22** (4), 279–86.

Patchett, Raymond R. (2005), 'Organization development in the public sector', in Thomas G. Cummings and C. G. Worley (eds), *Organization Development and Change*, 8th edition, Cincinnati, OH: South-Western College Publishing, pp. 596–603.

Piderit, Sandy K. (2000), 'Rethinking resistance and recognizing ambivalence: A multidimensional view of attitudes towards organizational change', *Academy of Management Review*, **25** (4), 783–94.

Porth, Stephen J., J. McCall and T. A. Bausch (1999), 'Spiritual themes of the "learning organization"', *Journal of Organizational Change Management*, **12** (3), 211–20.

Pradhan, Rabindra K., L. K. Jena and S. K. Singh (2017), 'Examining the role of emotional intelligence between organizational learning and adaptive performance in Indian manufacturing industries', *Journal of Workplace Learning*, **29** (3), 235–47.

Raelin, Jonathan D. and C. G. Cataldo (2011), 'Whither middle management? Empowering interface and the failure of organizational change', *Journal of Change Management*, **11** (4), 481–507.

Rahman, Tahir, Phillip J. Resnick and Bruce Harry (2016), 'Anders Breivik: Extreme beliefs mistaken for psychosis', *Journal of the American Academy of Psychiatry and the Law Online*, **44** (1), 28–35.

Rogers, Carl R. (1972), *On Becoming a Person*, Boston, MA: Houghton Mifflin.

Rosha, Angelina and N. Lace (2016), 'The scope of coaching in the context of organizational change', *Journal of Open Innovation: Technology, Market, and Complexity*, **2** (1), 2.

Roth, Stefan, T. Robbert and L. Straus (2015), 'On the sunk-cost effect in economic decision-making: A meta-analytic review', *Business Research*, **8** (1), 99–138.

Saucier, Gerard (2000), 'Isms and the structure of social attitudes', *Journal of Personality and Social Psychology*, **78** (2), 366–85.

Saucier, Gerard (2013), 'Isms dimensions: Toward a more comprehensive and integrative model of belief-system components', *Journal of Personality and Social Psychology*, **104** (5), 921–39.

Schmack, Katharina, Ana Gòmez-Carrillo de Castro, Marcus Rothkirch, Maria Sekutowicz, Hannes Rössler, John-Dylan Haynes, Andreas Heinz, Predrag Petrovic and Philipp Sterzer (2013), 'Delusions and the role of beliefs in perceptual inference', *Journal of Neuroscience*, **33** (34), 13701–12.

Schmidt-Wilk, Jane, D. P. Heaton and D. Steingard (2000), 'Higher education for higher consciousness: Maharishi University of Management as a model of spirituality in management education', *Journal of Management Education*, **24** (5), 580–611.

Sharot, Tali, Ryota Kanai, David Marston, Christoph W. Korn, Geraint Rees and Raymond J. Dolan (2012), 'Selectively altering belief formation in the human brain', *Proceedings of the National Academy of Sciences*, **109** (42), 17058–62.

Smith, Aaron (2016), *Cognitive Mechanisms of Belief Change*, London: Palgrave Macmillan.

Smith, Alan D. and W. T. Rupp (2003), 'An examination of emerging strategy and sales performance: Motivation, chaotic change and organizational structure', *Marketing Intelligence and Planning*, **21** (3), 156–67.

Sperber, Dan (1997), 'Intuitive and reflective beliefs', *Mind and Language*, **12**, 67–83.

Sperber, Dan (2006), 'Why a deep understanding of cultural evolution is incompatible with shallow psychology', in N. Enfield and S. Levinson (eds), *Roots of Human Sociality*, Oxford: Berg, pp. 431–49.

Tempest, Sue and K. Starkey (2004), 'The effects of liminality on individual and organizational learning', *Organization Studies*, **25** (4), 507–27.

Teo, Stephen T. and J. Crawford (2005), 'Indicators of strategic HRM effectiveness: A case study of an Australian public sector agency during commercialization', *Public Personnel Management*, **34** (1), 1–16.

Turnbull, Oliver H., Helen Berry and Cathryn E. Y. Evans (2004), 'A positive emotional bias in confabulatory false beliefs about place', *Brain and Cognition*, **55** (3), 490–94.

Van Boven, Leaf and G. Loewenstein (2003), 'Social projection of transient drive states', *Personality and Social Psychology Bulletin*, **29** (9), 1159–68.

Van Boven, Leaf, G. Loewenstein and D. Dunning (2005), 'The illusion of courage in social predictions: Underestimating the impact of fear of embarrassment on other people', *Organizational Behavior and Human Decision Processes*, **96** (2), 130–41.

Van Buren III, Harry and C. R. Leana (2000), 'Building relational wealth through employment practices: The role of organizational social capital', in Carrie R. Leanna and D. M. Rousseau (eds), *Relational Wealth: The Advantages of Stability in a Changing Economy*, Oxford: Oxford University Press.

Weitz, Ely, Y. Vardi and O. Setter (2012), 'Spirituality and organizational misbehavior', *Journal of Management, Spirituality and Religion*, **9** (3), 255–81.

Wenger, Etienne (1998), *Communities of Practice: Learning, Meaning, and Identity*, Cambridge: Cambridge University Press.

Wenger, Etienne (2000), 'Communities of practice and social learning systems', *Organization*, **7** (2), 225–46.

Wilson, Timothy D. and D. Gilbert (2005), 'Affective forecasting: Knowing what to want', *Current Directions in Psychological Science*, **14** (3), 131–4.

Wilson, Timothy D., T. P. Wheatley, J. M. Meyers, D. T. Gilbert and D. Axsom (2000), 'Focalism: A source of durability bias in affective forecasting', *Journal of Personality and Social Psychology*, **78** (5), 821–36.

You, Jieun, J. Kim and D. H. Lim (2017), 'Organizational learning and change: Strategic interventions to deal with resistance', in P. Ordoñez de Pablos and R. D. Tennyson (eds), *Handbook of Research on Human Resources Strategies for the New Millennial Workforce*, Hershey, PA: IGI Global, pp. 310–28.

9. The systems philosophy: 'changing everything'

INTRODUCTION

Although it has come in and out of management theory fashion for decades, the systems philosophy has made a significant impact on organizational change thinking, leadership and methods (Dumas and Beinecke, 2018). Like many of the philosophies we have considered, the systems approach permeates numerous important theories in and around organizational change (Lowell, 2016). All of these theories have in common the assumption that change cannot be segregated or compartmentalized. When one part of an organization changes, there are corresponding implications for all the others. Systems thinking change managers avoid reductionist cause and effect, instead seeking to understand the entire organization and pursue change across its many facets, aware that even small causes in one area can lead to large effects in others. In this chapter we will explore how organizational components intertwine in complex and unpredictable ways. Approaching change from a systems philosophy means that the entire organization represents the unit of change rather than industries, strategy, structure, processes, culture, psychology or any other element that could provide a focus for change. To put it another way, the systems philosophy assumes that organizations are irreducible in that they can only be properly understood as a whole.

The systems philosophy emerged in the middle of the twentieth century as scholars from the physical and social sciences began to consider the implications of inter-disciplinary connections. These pioneering theorists thought that irrespective of the complexity that exists in various forms of organization, whether in biology or in human society, general laws describing commonly occurring patterns of behaviour could be identified. As a result, understanding any complex form of organization—what became known as systems—requires the exposition of its laws. But in order to locate universal laws, an entire system must be observed in operation with all of its interconnections, both internal and external. The conventional, linear 'Newtonian' analytical approach of reducing a system to its simpler, constituent parts does not work (Hasan, Chatwin and Sayed, 2019). The forthcoming section of this chapter will provide further background by exploring how general systems theory developed. Following on, we introduce an advanced systems theory, known as complexity theory, and assess its explanation of organizational change. We conclude the chapter by adding commentary about adaptive complex systems and their legacies for change theory.

SYSTEMS THINKING

Most formal definitions acknowledge that systems comprise a set of two or more elements where the behaviour of any individual element effects the entire system as well as the other elements (Skyttner, 1996). Put simply, a system is made up of interdependent sub-systems. Most importantly, interdependent sub-systems naturally move towards equilibrium within the entire system; systems always gravitate towards balance and stability. As we shall explore in later sections of this chapter, more recent work claims that systems of social organization may be distinguished from other types by their complex, adaptive and self-regulating features. Systems may change according to this view, but not on the basis of simple cause and effect. No amount of planning can control the complex patterns that emerge from social systems, but lessons may be learned retrospectively to guide the principles of organizational change (Dumas and Beinecke, 2018).

Too many variations on systems theories exist to provide an inventory of them all here, chiefly because each major writer in the area has championed his or her own 'school' of thought. However, systems theories connect to other philosophies we discuss in this text. For example, 'living systems theory' pioneered by James Grier Miller (1978) emanated from his work on biological sub-systems. In addition, prior to the influence of biological systems, organizational theorists such as Kurt Lewin grappled with the narrow ideas that behavioural psychology employed to explain complex organizational phenomena. Although Lewin's approach emphasized greater linearity than his successors, he nevertheless paved the way for a more dynamic perspective of organizations. Lewin's beneficiaries included Edgar Schein, who established some of the fundamental concepts around organizational culture. Those interested in using systems concepts for organizational change subsequently focused on the maintenance of equilibrium and stability through responses to negative feedback. While the introduction of feedback loops clearly delivered advantages, systems theory still needed another element to help make sense of the way organizations interact with their environments.

BIOLOGICAL AND OPEN SYSTEMS

When the early management theorists combined their thinking with biological models, systems theory found added traction. The quantum leap came in shifting the emphasis from the independent components of the system to the interrelationships between the components. Biological sub-systems encouraged organizational theorists to study dynamic interrelationships. So profitable became the sub-systems approach that it started to reveal a new phenomenon in organizational science: the emergent properties of organizational systems. These properties emerged from simple everyday behaviours, but culminated in complex, extraordinary events (Hasan et al., 2019).

Biological analogies appear commonplace in systems-based commentaries of organizations. For example, the human body can be represented as a system comprising a complex set of organs and sub-systems. Each sub-system depends upon the others, where dysfunction or pathology in one can lead to general problems in others, and even fatality. Systems theory highlights organizational components that contribute to performance but also can be affected by external factors. As a result, organizational behaviour is determined by a complex array of forces and pressures operating within a delicate equilibrium vulnerable to even a small shift in tension between variables. Times when organizations are 'far-from-equilibrium' represent an opportunity for change (Mittleton-Kelly, 2003).

Organizations may be considered open systems. Not only are their elements interrelated, they are susceptible to influence from the outside. In the case of a biological system like a human body, an external variable such as a bullet could prove a substantive influence. Equally, organizations operate subject to environmental changes in the form of legal, political, economic, technological, social and other forces. However, as Kerzner (1998) emphasized, the systems change approach predicts that solutions arrive by examining the entire picture and not just a handful of its components. Most systems theories go to some trouble to specify both the differentiation and integration of organizational parts (Robbins and Barnwell, 1998).

While systems thinking acknowledges the specialization of functional areas, it also maintains that these areas must work together in order to be effective. The heart and lungs take responsibility for separate tasks but work seamlessly in order to sustain life. Equally, organizations possess task-driven structures that meld together in order to deliver successful outcomes. Of course, change initiatives typically strive to rectify poor integration, chiefly through a shift from linear siloed solutions to a holistic systems approach that integrates all stakeholders (Dunn, Brown, Bos and Bakker, 2017). For the systems theorist, however, fixing problematic functional areas or departments constitutes only part of the problem, as meeting the bigger objective means integrating the entire organizational system. Focusing only on sub-systems sentences a change manager to failure because it will only deliver a compartmentalized resolution. Effective change must be systemic.

GENERAL SYSTEMS THEORY

Developed by Von Bertalanffy (1968), 'general systems theory' was slow to gain acceptance, and never achieved the prominence its founder anticipated. The reticence was caused, as Boulding (1956) presciently observed, because general systems theory disappoints if interpreted as a 'theory of everything'. Boulding responded by devising a hierarchy of systems based on their levels of complexity. He also proposed some of the first theoretical premises to describe general systems, which emphasized the desirability of order. Boulding's way of thinking also had other significant implications. His proposition that systems can be classified means that those within the same class can be expected to possess common properties. As a result, all organizations may be expected to exhibit the same characteristics. Furthermore, systems possess the properties of their component sub-systems. From a change viewpoint, systems theory predicts that all organizations can be managed the same way because they all possess common features. As we shall see, this claim has led to controversy.

One issue concerns the systems assumption that all organizations are heterogeneous in nature. However, many change theorists believe that all organizations cannot be usefully classified together into one generic category. Even if all organizations do share enough properties to be treated the same, theorists or practitioners would likely fail to agree upon the best actions to support change. Nevertheless, systems theorists point out that without common properties to fall back on, general management solutions to problems cannot be devised. At the same time, some of the change philosophies examined in this text advocate that no common solutions exist; all organizations possess different features, and all change interventions must be customized to meet unique circumstances. Perhaps part of the issue arises from the long-standing systems philosophy connection to biological descriptions of natural systems. Open biological systems tend towards equilibrium. Social systems like organizations, in contrast, do not operate as natural systems. Rather, the analogy contrives to make organizations appear to work like natural systems when in reality their behaviour can be inconsistent and unpredictable.

SYSTEMS AND STABILITY

The systems philosophy assumes that organizations move towards stability and equilibrium. While some evidence supports the view that organizations can seize up with inertia, other evidence indicates that organizations ensconced in turbulent environments where uncertainty and ambiguity feature prominently, can degenerate into chaos and failure. Furthermore, systems approaches struggle to separate organizations from their environments. If change managers are tasked under systems models to encourage equilibrium, then they need to be able to clearly distinguish the boundaries of their organizations. For example, businesses operating in the digital arena find their boundaries permanently blurred by rapid escalations in technological change. How can change managers take a systemic approach when the method of management becomes ambiguous? Change researchers have also encountered the boundary problem in system theories during attempts to map the effects of change interventions. The larger issue reflects a fundamental systems philosophy premise. Management occupies the control centre of change driven by the expectation that organizational change must always be controlled, and always remains controllable, subject to managers' watchful tinkering.

Another problematic aspect of the systems philosophy concerns its predilection to treat organizations as open systems. Most change studies reveal more ambiguity than sharpness. Sometimes environmental forces provide powerful stimuli for change, while at other times, external forces can be resisted or ignored. Equally, certain events within a system generate different levels of change depending on their salience to the organization (Morgeson, Mitchell and Liu, 2015). Salience is determined by an event's novelty, disruptiveness and criticality to an organization's objectives. It might be more accurate to accept that organizations move fluidly between different degrees of being partially open and partially closed.

The challenge for change managers allegiant to a systems philosophy lies with navigating the complexity of organizational systems. Add in, as Von Bertalanffy did, the importance of feedback from inside and outside the system, and it becomes exceedingly difficult to make sense of the behaviour that can be seen. For many years, systems theories languished because no one could really make sense of the behavioural patterns that organizations created. However, when general systems theory returned to biology for inspiration in the 1980s, it found a new science that had hitched aboard physics and mathematics to describe the complex chemical systems that had been uncovered. For science, it was not just the interrelationships between sub-systems that were important, but also the complex, sometimes chaotic nature of the patterns they created.

COMPLEXITY THEORY

Complexity and chaos theory have amassed a voluminous presence in scientific, and more recently organizational, literature. With this body of work, the concepts have filtered down to popular writing. Complexity theory has been proclaimed as everything from a helpful metaphor to a profound revolution in conceptualizing the workings of systems. Emanating principally from a sizable and quantitative mathematical literature, chaos and complexity have been applied with some success to physical systems. For example, Prigogine (1989) and colleagues demonstrated that under certain conditions, randomly combined chemical systems can self-organize to produce emergent structure. For this, they acquired a Nobel Prize, and stimulated a substantial interest in employing complexity theory towards resolving the mysteries of organizational behaviour (Prigogine and Stengers, 1984).

The key in complexity thinking (and chaos, which henceforth will be considered subsumed conceptually within complexity) revolves around the interaction of elements in a system. Complexity theory explains how a system can generate output greater than the sum of its parts. At its most extreme, this may be manifest as seemingly routine behaviours leading to a catastrophic accident (Hasan et al., 2019). This observation can be both contentious and misleading because it implies that progressive directionality can exist in a system; a possibility precluded by the second law of thermodynamics, which insists on entropy in a closed system (Haken, 1987). In other words, closed systems degenerate towards disequilibrium; chaos always rules eventually. But systems like economies and organizations are not closed (Byeon, 1999). They receive input, or in technical terms, energy from outside sources. Thus, complexity in this context does not represent a departure from conventional laws of physics or systems, as some writers have implied (Kelly, 1994). Information and 'energy' can enter an organization from the outside encouraging new and emergent structures and behaviours.

From a complexity theory perspective, organizations (as systems) under certain conditions exhibit normal and predictable behaviours. However, under other circumstances, they also behave strangely, where predictability fades and chaos reigns. Hence, the ubiquitous cliché that the mere fluttering of a butterfly's wings in one part of the world can account for a weather anomaly in a different part altogether. Although somewhat overdramatic, the example has a useful organizational analogy. For example, Begun (1994) noted that the apparently straightforward introduction of policy can periodically manifest in exactly the opposite practice than prescribed. Somehow, simple instructions entered into systems can magnify errant anomalies into chaos, like a rumour spreading and changing exponentially and randomly.

INTRODUCING CHAOS

In some ways, complexity theory starts with chaos. In order to understand complexity theory, we need to consider the nature of dynamic systems. Typically, systems can be observed in two states, the first stable and the second unstable (Rosenhead, 1989). In the former, the system remains at equilibrium like an undisturbed glass of water. In the latter, however, organizational change can cascade into a range of unpredictable and divergent behaviours where water spills over the edges of the glass. The cause of these behaviours is extremely difficult if not impossible to track down due to the system's complexity. However, the most interesting behaviour occurs on the cusp of stability and instability, or what physicists call the phase transition (like boiling water to steam), and Pascale (1999) calls the 'edge of chaos'. Here, causal expectations about organizational behaviour collapse.

At the heart of complexity theory lies the premise of emergence, which refers to outcomes that cannot be the result of mere random interaction, particularly when it produces unexpected outcomes in organizations. If indeed the complex meanderings of organizations can exhibit some form or pattern, then an underlying force directs its operation (Goldstein, 1999). Accordingly, successful organizational change means creating the conditions under which unpredictable self-organization can be rendered predictable. However, what looks like randomness may not actually be random at all. For example, Therrien, Normandin and Denis (2017) argued that hospitals are complex systems, but crucially can prepare for the stress of health crises by preemptively creating 'favourable order' through mechanisms such as diverse employee experience and interunit trust.

According to Dent (1999), complexity embraces acausal, non-linear interpretations of systems. Marion and Bacon (2000) helped operationalize this definition by stipulating three distinguishing characteristics. First, non-additive behaviour emerges from interactive networks; the whole is greater than the sum of its parts. Second, the emergent behaviour exhibited in a complex system unpredictably relates to underpinning causes. Finally, complex behaviour occurs in the nebulous region between predictability and unpredictability, or the 'edge of chaos' (Pascale, 1999). As a consequence, creating the conditions under which emergence might appear leads to 'surfing' the edge of chaos. For the change manager, the ability to identify the edge of chaos would appear to be a monumental advantage, even if the outcomes it produces cannot be controlled. Accordingly, recommendations are often proffered for how to reach this organizational state, but rarely about how to ensure positive outcomes (Rook and Watson, 2017).

From a change management perspective, complexity theory may be seen as a systems approach for examining the behaviour of fundamental, interacting units with the awareness that the collective activity of the units will not be fully explained by their sum. The evidence comes with novel, emergent properties of systems that defy prediction on the basis of normal cause-and-effect expectations. These properties feature spontaneous, unpredictable and self-organized patterns and behaviours. Complexity theory offers the twin benefits of describing how complex systems can generate simple outcomes while looking at the whole system and not just its components. For example, a city represents a complex system comprising millions of human beings. Similarly, a body is a complex organism made up of trillions of cells. When a proliferation of simple entities come together, they interact and new levels of operation and organization emerge.

Complexity theory provides change managers with an avenue for anticipating emergent behaviour; novel behaviour that could neither have been predicted nor deliberately introduced. Notwithstanding the counterintuitive nature of emergent organizational change, it stands in direct contrast to the rational philosophy, which insists upon strategic control. In numerous industries and fields, rational linear reduction reigns supreme (Dunn et al., 2017; Speakman, 2017). But, for many change managers comfortable with a conventional, rational approach, the idea that unpredictable, emergent change should be pursued means accepting an unpalatable and fundamentally new way of looking at the world and the systems it contains.

PLANNING COMPLEXITY

Complexity theory as a systems philosophy represents 'an approach to research, study, and perspective that makes the philosophical assumptions of the emerging worldview' (Dent, 1999, p. 5). This worldview is in contrast to the classical view, or what Dent called the traditional worldview, which depends upon the causal, reductionist interpretations of the world provided by Newtonian physics. Thus, complexity theory emphasizes acausal, holistic interpretations, which from a change management perspective refers to the point where sufficient chaos or unpredictability exists in an organization to ensure the loss of regularity and predictability, but also enough order or predictability for consistent patterns to endure. 'Edge of chaos' thinking of this kind means that undetectable variations in initial conditions (the butterfly's wings flap at different speeds or at different altitudes) can lead to outputs that seem unrelated to inputs. Herein, new and unimagined properties can emerge. For example, Peters (1987; 1992) argued that managers need to move people from complacency towards the edge of chaos. Of course, organizations move in and out of the edge of chaos all the time. Trying to keep workers in it can lead to nervous breakdowns and totally unpredictable results, which sooner or later will lead to catastrophic results (Rook and Watson, 2017). So, where does complexity theory leave change managers? After all, the edge of chaos might lead to innovation, but innovation cannot be harnessed by unstable organizations incapable of taking advantage of it.

The majority of change management literature focuses on the new behaviours and structures intended by management. In general, this reflects a desire for both stability and innovation. However, the pursuit of both does not work as well in turbulent environments. Complexity theory, in contrast, views change as the norm rather than the exception (Salem, 2002). It can almost be seen as a reverse of the punctuated equilibrium model in the biological philosophy; disequilibrium is normal, or should be normal, punctuated by odd periods of relative stability. However, since complexity theory implies that instability should be normal, staying the same can be viewed as a sign of slippage. Stability or equilibrium, to the complexity advocate, signals organizational obsolescence and death (Pascale, 1999).

Redfern and Christian (2003) acknowledged that planned change can be distinguished from emergent change, the former involving deliberate conscious reasoning and rational planning, whereas the latter features spontaneous and uncontrolled change. Studies show that change management is just as often dynamic, disorderly and uncertain as rational and linear, without the two needing to be mutually exclusive (Booth, Zwar and Harris, 2013). The environment defies rational control even by the most adept change leaders, and organizational convolution makes internal control only a little easier. Yet, like many researchers who study the process of organizational change, Redfern and Christian also observed that most managers employ change programmes in a planned, episodic way. Such an approach symptomatically reflects the dominant perception of organizational change, the benchmark for which traditionally focuses upon systems and rules, all tightly controlling the activities of employees (Dolan, Garcia and Auerbach, 2003).

NATURAL COMPLEXITY

For complex industries characterized by fickle consumers, planning linear change is paradoxical to the acknowledged reality, yet remains the dominant paradigm (Boukas and Ziakas, 2014). However, the rational standpoint has slowly ceded ground to change management perspectives that accept the presence of complexity within organizations as natural. For example, Brown and Eisenhardt (1997) examined how organizations engage in continuous change. They revealed that successful firms balance structure and chaos, and rely on a range of low-cost experimental initiatives as forays into the future. Complexity-consistent thinking proved more effective than planning for, or reacting to, unforeseen changes.

Complexity theory offers a new perspective on change management because it discourages managers from making predictions about the future, instead encouraging them to allow innovation to emerge from the bottom up. Therefore, advice for managers revolves around a greater focus on creating conditions for work, such as facilitating cooperation between stakeholders to improve learning, rather than on prescribing working practices (Dunn et al., 2017; Lowell, 2016). As a result, complexity theory does not specify a mode of change; not necessarily incremental or radical, complexity leads to spontaneous change. Neither does complexity theory make assumptions about the level or impetus for change. Whether a stimulus arrives internally or externally does not matter. Instead, where complexity exists in a system like an organization, the possibility of unexpected, emergent change also loiters. Complexity theory treats organizations as living systems co-evolving with their environments that cannot be reduced to their constituent parts, where 'management is the most highly evolved form of complexity' (Tasaka, 1999, p. 122).

From a change management perspective, emergent change does not receive much attention (Lissack, 1999), and as a result, its causes remain nebulous and its outcomes attributed to other macro phenomena. Indeed, even those involved in enacting change daily may not remember the motives or reason for why a change occurred (Booth et al., 2013). Change management commentators tend to perceive change as the transition from one equilibrium state to another, but this sort of understanding does not capture the messy reality of actual change (Pascale, 1999).

CHANGING WITH ADAPTIVE COMPLEX SYSTEMS

Armed with a growing vocabulary and an expanding portfolio of popular reading, the concept of complexity has transgressed mathematical abstraction to become a fashionable change management ideology. Like many popular fads, complexity advocates shine with optimism about the revolution that it will bestow upon organizational leaders and change agents, for whom the stalwart practices of the past few decades—strategic, rational change programmes—fade in effectiveness given the giant leaps in competitiveness in the organizational context over the same period (Lynch and Kordis, 1988).

Complexity advocates believe that organizational change needs to reflect a new conceptualization of the world. Systems like organizations behave in fundamentally complex ways, sometimes so much so that they appear to be chaotic. A complexity theory interpretation suggests that sometimes chaos springs from underlying patterns, encouraging the emergence of unpredictable organizational behaviours. Under the right circumstances, these emergent behaviours can produce powerful, albeit unpredictable, innovation (Coleman, 1999). Patterns of self-organization emerge from the turbulence of systemic interactions. Equally, as the principle of chaos theory implies, the ongoing multiplication of simple and predictable interactions can lead to radically divergent results (Lissack, 1999). The acceptance of these rules of system operation has a number of substantive implications for organizational leaders seeking to initiate change.

A first principle holds that strategic, linear change planning hopelessly founders in the context of real-world change. For example, Tetenbaum (1998) identified seven trends that help explain why complexity theory has fallen on fertile ground: technology, globalization, competition, change, speed, complexity and paradox. She wrote: 'The new world is full of unintended consequences and counterintuitive outcomes. In such a world, the map to the future cannot be drawn in advance. We cannot know enough to set forth a meaningful vision or to plan productively' (p. 24). Kelly (1998) also argued that we need new ideas, paradigms and practices to make sense of the tumultuous changes that have come about through global restructuring of the economy, radical new technologies and advances in social, political and cultural change. More recently, ever increasing globalization has further reinforced arguments (e.g. rapid technological change) for the intuitive appeal of complexity theory to managers (Lowell, 2016). According to complexity theory advocates like Kelly and Tetenbaum, the future inherently flouts predictability. Organizations function as unstable entities, from which patterns emerge from the bottom up. Top-down strategy and change planning fails from the start.

FASTER CHANGE

A staggering volume of literature proclaims that we live in times of unprecedented change, although it less often reflects upon the historical evidence indicating that every generation since the Industrial Revolution has made the same observation (Grey, 2003). Clearly, it is difficult, perhaps impossible, to remain objective about any assumptions concerning the frequency or depth of change compared to other eras. Nevertheless, we cannot ignore the experiential evidence that the rate of change feels faster than ever before, driven at least partly by technological escalation and the era of big data across the globe (Lowell, 2016). Despite the rhetoric about globalization and the 'new economy', it may not be an overstatement to suggest that the nature and role of change has shifted with the blue-chip revolution. Boundary shifting of this kind continues to be the source of great strain and uncertainty for organizations. No one disagrees that the successful introduction and management of change defines organizational success.

Complexity thinking assumes that change represents the pervasive force in organizational life. According to advocates like Peters (1987), stability and inertia combat organizational prosperity. As Rooney and Hearn (1999) suggested, complexity embraces ephemera. Yet, the organizational evidence suggests that change is the exception rather than the rule (Brown and Eisenhardt, 1998). Change management studies show that change attempts fail just as often, if not more often, than they succeed. Molinski (1999) concluded that the change process itself drives the problem. Change works in seemingly contradictory ways. Although paradoxical, change programmes themselves preclude effective change outcomes. Conversely, according to complexity advocates, instability acts as a precondition for change. Organizational leaders should work to remove inertia and security because they form barriers to change and discourage innovation. Successful change means making organizations less stable without slipping beyond the edge of chaos (Rook and McManus, 2016).

Steiner (2001) noted that change can go wrong for reasons as varied as human psychology, engrained systems and institutionalized ideas, as well as conflicting cultural standards. But as the systems philosophy emphasizes, these dimensions interact and even neutralize each other in ways that can hide the real obstacles. Most change commentators concede that change is difficult to bring about in organizations (Armenakis and Bedeian, 1999). If this holds true, then the rule is stability, rather than chaos. Moreover, to bring an organization close enough to 'surf' the tension between order and chaos might require considerable change in the first place. Complexity theory might therefore best be viewed as a metaphor only, amongst a range of others that have varying and situational applicability in the absence of an accepted and overarching change theory. The idea of applying complexity-based metaphors to organizational change allows managers to understand change in new ways (Speakman, 2017). The metaphors of complexity theory act as discursive tools reframing reality in a more comprehensible manner than can be understood from the random facts alone.

RATIONAL UNCERTAINTY

Like most nascent management paradigms, complexity attempts to fill a gap in conventional approaches to dealing with change and environmental turbulence. In particular, it leads with the assumption that linear approaches to strategic change will falter, flawed due to the faulty expectation of causality, even though the notion of strategy itself aims to ameliorate uncertainty (Foo and Foo, 2003). Complexity advocates reason that the future is unknowable. They argue that change managers waste their time with endless diagnoses of future conditions and the establishment of an organizational plan to reach a predetermined set of objectives. Planning for outcomes is a delusion, and a dangerous one at that. Uncertainty, complexity and ambiguity should not stimulate lament and combative, rational interventions. Rather, as natural consequences of organizational systems, they should be accepted and even encouraged. Stacey (1993), in his seminal work on complexity, offered the following harrowing conclusions about the legitimacy of orthodox planning techniques: analysis is no longer pre-eminent; cause and effect contingency is meaningless; long-term planning is impossible; visions are illusions; strong, unified cultures are dangerous; and statistical relationships are dubious.

Two lessons for leaders and change managers surface. First, management adjustments to activity and change programmes become critical because responsiveness must replace preparation. The ability of a leader to facilitate organizational 'readiness' is imperative (Dumas and Beinecke, 2018). Second, rather than pursuing stability and predictability, change managers should encourage the phase transition, where the edge of chaos can provide a platform for the emergence of innovative ways of looking at organizational problems. For the change manager, this means accepting that possible futures for the organization will emerge or arise, rather than being stimulated or provoked. Creative solutions will occur when the organizational system is primed; poised between equilibrium and disequilibrium. This should not imply that ordinary operational management should cease (Stacey, 1996), but the extraordinary process of strategizing and planning should be modified. As Dumas and Beinecke (2018) observed, 'As parts of the system interact, new patterns emerge over time. Facilitating this process requires a container to hold it all together' (p. 873). In essence, change leaders need to manage the boundaries that govern equilibrium, thereby encouraging an environment in which innovation and creativity will bubble up. This may even require the amplification of ambiguity and uncertainty.

Arbitrating the strategy process no longer commands priority; elaborate analysis should be a marginalized activity (Rosenhead, 1989). Complexity models downplay the importance of the rational philosophy. Lowell (2016) offered several key practices to enable a complexity-based change perspective. A change manager should set out an organizational vision for the future, rather than specific outcomes, derived from fostering a flexible operation, open communication, developing high-quality relationships between sub-systems, introducing tension to reach the edge of chaos (e.g. creating intra-organizational competition or removing behavioural constraints), and empowering individuals to solve paradoxes. However, some of its lessons may not be as novel as presented in the complexity literature, the prescriptions for new action seem vague and the recommendations against analysis and futures thinking may be questionable.

ADAPTIVE COMPLEX SYSTEMS

The observation that organizations behave adaptively, capable of developing unexpectedly creative solutions to problems, has been recorded in the change management literature for decades (e.g. Kanter, 1989; Pettigrew, 1985). It is also well established that innovations can arise from the bottom up, via self-organized groups that take it upon themselves, with little direction, to solve a problem. The total quality management movement, for example, particularly in emphasizing quality 'circles' and teams, explored this process thoroughly (e.g. Deming, 1982; Ishikawa, 1982; Juran, 1989). However, complexity advocates assume that emergent behaviour occurs from acausal processes and therefore cannot be anticipated. The evidence for this is limited (Brown and Eisenhardt, 1997). After all, although tracing activity to its beginnings might be difficult through deductive investigation, all activity has a cause in an organization, even if it is non-linear and resides at the confluence of unlikely and unexpected variables (Booth et al., 2013). As a result, the principle of emergence might not necessarily illustrate the same 'specialness' that holds in natural systems, where the sum of the parts genuinely underperforms the whole. Emergence in particular, and complexity in general, might simply be useful metaphors for describing a new set of behaviours. Although difficult to trace, the emerging behaviour does not necessarily represent order from chaos.

Viewing organizations as complex adaptive systems could be best seen as a metaphor through which to observe activity in organizations. It may even provide some suggestive evidence that socially based systems like organizations can thrive on the edge of chaos. For example, Chae (2014) adopted the complex adaptive systems metaphor to provide recommendations on how organizations can introduce information technology-enabled services, as economies transition from manufacturing to service dominance. But, this may not have as much to do with bringing about change as complexity advocates might suggest. For example, a robust body of literature, particularly from organizational psychology and human resources, demonstrates that many employees prefer looser boundaries and working conditions (Foegen, 1999; Fenwick, 2003; Stohl and Cheney, 2001). In short, the edge of chaos might be something like a proxy for an empowered work environment.

Another difficulty lies with finding a place for analytical and rational techniques like strategic planning. As Rosenhead (1989) acknowledged, complexity writers appear equivocal on the subject, even though the principles of 'hands-off' management and empowerment receive general acceptance. However, it may not be an issue of contention as much as one of oversight. For example, several writers imply that strategy might have value (McMaster, 1995) while others, like Stacey (1993), suggest that complexity equals creativity, where no place exists for the rational approach to change.

MAKING COMPLEX SYSTEMIC CHANGE

A good start might be to accept that the organizational world does sometimes operate as a non-linear and dynamic system. In such a world, the encouragement of emergence (read self-organized innovation and creativity) might well be advantageous. However, achieving this situation without resorting to a predetermined, rational crutch would be an achievement indeed. By definition, intentional organizational change requires some form of rational planning. As Rosenhead (1989) counselled, the complexity anti-analytical platform has some appeal as a counterweight to overly rational approaches to change planning, but the assertion that analysis should be supplanted entirely by incidental, reactionary, 'seat of the pants action', lacks logical, not to mention practical, appeal. Few chief executive officers would be game to present a change plan to a board of directors that argued for abandoning a change plan in exchange for surfing chaos.

Perhaps the key to understanding the appeal of the complex systems movement comes with understanding that its popularity accompanied the perception of growing uncertainty and turbulence in the environment. But if complexity thinking rules out strategic thinking, then it also marginalizes most experienced change agents. Planning, after all, seeks to diminish the uncertainty that the future presents. The fact that it might materialize unexpectedly or emergently is irrelevant. Change agents might argue that thinking about different alternatives remains a better approach to encouraging innovation than trusting to emergence and quick action, which in itself requires analysis to predict the likely outcome of the decision. Abandoning strategy in exchange for co-evolution and self-organization leaves the manager few tools to wield in an environment where they need all the help they can get.

Complexity authors tend to break their own rules. Their assumption that strategy is doomed calmly co-exists with daily rational, predictive behaviours. Few managers can genuinely abandon logical thinking. Further, the expectation that other, specific interventions such as changes to structure or culture will automatically fail, overlooks case evidence to the contrary. Change management in adaptive complex systems also tends to assume that the future will be an emergent property, when plainly the system in question might not be operating under the conditions required for emergence to occur, namely the edge of chaos. This can be seen in most organizations, which have been shown in countless studies to typically behave with reasonable predictability, hovering much closer to equilibrium than chaos (Brown and Eisenhardt, 1997).

At a more abstract level, whether the conditions in an organization, industry, economy or even the world are ripe for emergence appears to be a subject for supposition. Ironically, thinking about complexity represents a rational interpretation in itself. The future of an organization might depend upon the butterfly effect of a seemingly insignificant variable, but it could also pivot upon a macro condition, like the price of oil, which while perhaps not always predictable, remains accessible to rational preparation. Again, frameworks such as event system theory (Morgeson et al., 2015), which is based on open systems, suggest that it is possible for change managers to understand which micro- and macro-level events will generate change based on the characteristics of the event (i.e. novelty, disruptiveness and criticality).

Complexity reminds us that non-linear and dynamic systems can exhibit chaotic properties from the interaction of simple laws, and that the patterns may emerge from the apparent randomness of complex interactions. While these characteristics have been shown to exist in some natural systems, a full explanation as to how it works in organizations and social systems has not yet been presented. In short, we do not know whether complexity in a social system manifests the same as complexity in a natural system. Perhaps it is just like it? The other unanswered question concerns whether complexity operates as a metaphor or a rule. For the moment, and for the change agent, it appears to be the former rather than the latter.

FROM ABSTRACT TO INTERVENTION

We suspect that all managers involved in change would be well served by thinking of organizations as systems, including the idiosyncrasies of chaos and complexity. Recognition along these lines might be helpful in conceptualizing alternative ways of looking at change problems, as it does tend to encourage an awareness of emerging patterns. It also foreshadows an undervalued source of data in illustrating the role of bottom-up self-organization (Dumas and Beinecke, 2018). In particular, senior policy makers and managers would find it rewarding to engage in servant leadership, and consider the change possibilities advocated by those working at the 'coal face' of organizations. Lastly, conceptualizing the unit of analysis (whether organizational or world-based) represents an important step in noting relationships between variables. Complexity thinking implies that the causes of events cannot be known, but this may reflect an absence of reliable information about the systems' constituents, rather than the impossibility of the task. It would be a brave change manager indeed who discarded all rational techniques in favour of 'surfing the edge of chaos', even if how to surf chaos was well understood.

Assessing the veracity of complexity thinking in organizational change becomes more troublesome with the assumption of acausal behaviour. Because the organization in question behaves as a complex system, tracking down the initial impetus for the emergent outcomes seems hopeless. Unfortunately, despite the promise complexity theory holds as a change metaphor, further paradox and ambiguity remain in its specific implementation. Lynch and Kordis (1988) described complexity and chaos theories as earth-shaking science so powerful that those who discover its direct applications will deserve to be remembered as modern Isaac Newtons. However, despite the volume and vehemence of this kind of proclamation, the evidence still needs to be gathered about whether emergence can be empirically verified. Can organizations, under the right circumstances, operate in the mysterious realm beyond observable causality (Goldberg and Markoczy, 2000)?

According to Mittleton-Kelly (1997), complexity principles do not transfer well to social systems like organizations. At the very least, analysing complexity in action is like trying to take a photo of a cloud forming. Clearly, the most important decision for change managers revolves around how to create the conditions under which self-organized change can occur. According to Stacey (1996), change leaders should focus on managing the boundaries that govern equilibrium, with a view to encouraging an environment where innovative change will emerge unprompted. This can be as simple as instigating regular intersystem communications that may allow employees to identify new opportunities or, potentially, the mediation between chaos and stability could require a manager to deliberately incite chaos, a role few practitioners would deliberately assume (Rosenhead, 1989). Ironically, many change managers inadvertently cause chaos anyway.

CONCLUSION

Systems thinkers portray the natural world as giant systems of almost immeasurable complexity. Like biologists, their work has been appropriated by change management researchers hoping to find new ways of understanding the intricacies of organizational systems. Like changes in weather, organizations can exhibit behaviour that cannot easily be traced to logical causes. With the intention of better understanding some of this apparently emergent behaviour, general systems theory introduced some of the lessons from both the natural sciences as well as physics and mathematics to produce complexity theory.

Systems thinking through complexity has probably best been used to help explain how some organizations that seem to totter precariously between chaos and order manage to stimulate innovation (Chae, 2014; Sullivan, 2004). In the conventional worldview, planned and systematic change is seen as a prescription rather than a reality. In contrast, complexity theorists argue that change inevitably becomes messy and non-linear, and any attempt at introducing planned change is futile (Styhre, 2002; Shaw, 1997). Dealing with the future means facilitating an edge-of-chaos organizational climate where emergent innovation can react to market changes (Marion and Bacon, 2000). By consequence, the only path for change managers demands accepting this contradiction. Despite the pessimism of complexity writers like Stacey (1996) about the usefulness of tackling change in a rational manner or with specific objectives, the complexity metaphor does not have to be viewed in absolute terms.

Complexity theory serves as a reminder that non-linear and dynamic systems can exhibit chaotic properties from the interaction of simple laws, and that patterns may emerge from the ostensible randomness of complex interactions. These characteristics have been shown to exist in some natural systems. The theoretical explanation for how emergence works in organizations and social systems is still developing. In reality, very few organizations have dared to discard the rational philosophy altogether and seek the edge of chaos. Naturally, the achievement of organizational performance holds sovereign, and the implementation of complexity mires change leaders in uncertainty. For example, although complexity theory can provide a metaphorical explanation for how some parts of organizations can hover in limbo between chaos and order to deliver innovation, maintaining equilibrium between these states requires management intervention of the old-fashioned kind (Sullivan, 2004). Change *within* the complexity paradigm is non-linear and ambiguous (Styhre, 2002; Shaw, 1997), but change *to* the complexity paradigm is linear and rational.

The systems philosophy demonstrably offers advantages in appreciating the complexities of organizational change (Marion and Bacon, 2000). However, some aspects of organizational activity do not perform favourably under edge-of-chaos conditions, like legal obligations, employee remuneration and risk management. Hard complexity advocates like Stacey (1996) might object to this kind of dilution. Equally, change managers might still reject the ideas behind complex, adaptive systems as vague, ivory-tower rhetoric.

REFERENCES

Armenakis, A. A. and A. G. Bedeian (1999), 'Organization change: A review of theory and research in the 1990s', *Yearly Review of Management*, **25**, 293–315.

Begun, James W. (1994), 'Chaos and complexity: Frontiers of organization science', *Journal of Management Inquiry*, **3** (4), 329–35.

Booth, Barbara J., N. Zwar and M. F. Harris (2013), 'Healthcare improvement as planned system change or complex responsive processes? A longitudinal case study in general practice', *BMC Family Practice*, **14**, https://doi.org/10.1186/1471-2296 -14-51.

Boukas, Nikolaos and V. Ziakas (2014), 'A chaos theory perspective of destination crisis and sustainable tourism development in islands: The case of Cyprus', *Tourism Planning and Development*, **11** (2), 191–209.

Boulding, Kenneth E. (1956), 'General systems theory: The skeleton of the science', *Management Science*, **2** (3), 197–208.

Brown, Shona L. and K. M. Eisenhardt (1997), 'The art of continuous change: Linking complexity theory and time-paced evolution in relentlessly shifting organizations', *Administrative Science Quarterly*, **42** (1), 1–34.

Brown, Shona L. and K. M. Eisenhardt (1998), *Competing on the Edge: Strategy as Structured Chaos*, Boston, MA: Harvard Business School Press.

Byeon, Jong H. (1999), 'Non-equilibrium thermodynamic approach to change in political systems', *Systems Research and Behavioral Science*, **16** (3), 283–91.

Chae, Bongsug Kevin (2014), 'A complexity theory approach to IT-enabled services (IESs) and service innovation: Business analytics as an illustration of IES', *Decision Support Systems*, **57**, 1–10.

Coleman, Henry J., Jr. (1999), 'What enables self-organizing behavior in businesses', *Emergence*, **1** (1), 33–48.

Deming, William E. (1982), *Out of the Crisis*, Cambridge, MA: MIT Press.

Dent, Eric B. (1999), 'Complexity science: A worldview shift', *Emergence*, **1** (4), 5–19.

Dolan, Simon L., S. Garcia and A. Auerbach (2003), 'Understanding and managing chaos in organisation', *International Journal of Management*, **20** (1), 23–35.

Dumas, Colette and R. H. Beinecke (2018), 'Change leadership in the 21st century', *Journal of Organizational Change Management*, **31** (4), 867–76.

Dunn, Gemma, R. R. Brown, J. J. Bos and K. Bakker (2017), 'Standing on the shoulders of giants: Understanding changes in urban water practice through the lens of complexity science', *Urban Water Journal*, **14** (7), 758–67.

Fenwick, Tara J. (2003), 'Emancipatory potential of action learning: A critical analysis', *Journal of Organizational Change Management*, **16** (6), 619–32.

Foegen, Joseph H. (1999), 'Why not empowerment', *Business and Economic Review*, April–June, 31–3.

Foo, Check-Teck and C. T. Foo (2003), 'Forecastability, chaos and foresight', *Foresight*, **5** (5), 22–3.

Goldberg, Jeffrey and L. Markoczy (2000), 'Complex rhetoric and simple games', *Emergence*, **2** (1), 72–100.

Goldstein, Jeffrey (1999), 'Emergence as a construct: History and issues', *Emergence*, **1** (1), 49–72.

Grey, Christopher (2003), 'The fetish of change', *Tamara: Journal of Critical Postmodern Organization Science*, **2** (2), 1–19.

Haken, Hermann (1987), 'Synergetics: An approach to self-organization', in Francis E. Yates (ed.), *Self-Organizing Systems: The Emergence of Order*, New York: Plenum.

Hasan, Rumy, C. Chatwin and M. Sayed (2019), 'Examining alternatives to traditional accident causation models in the offshore oil and gas industry', *Journal of Risk Research*, https://doi.org/10.1080/13669877.2019.1673796.

Ishikawa, Kaoru (1982), *Guide to Quality Control*, Tokyo: Asian Productivity Organisation.

Juran, Joseph M. (1989), *Juran on Leadership for Quality: An Executive Handbook*, New York: Free Press.

Kanter, Rosabeth M. (1989), *When Giants Learn How to Dance: Mastering the Challenge of Strategy, Management, and Careers in the 1990s*, New York: Simon and Schuster.

Kelly, Kevin (1994), *Out of Control: The New Biology of Machines, Social Systems, and the Economic World*, New York: Addison-Wesley.

Kelly, Kevin (1998), *New Rules for the New Economy*, New York: Viking.

Kerzner, Harold (1998), *Project Management: A Systems Approach to Planning, Scheduling and Controlling*, 6th edition, New York: John Wiley & Sons.

Lissack, Michael R. (1999), 'Complexity: The science, its vocabulary, and its relation to organizations', *Emergence*, **1** (1), 110–26.

Lowell, Kevin R. (2016), 'An application of complexity theory for guiding organizational change', *Psychologist-Manager Journal*, **19** (3–4), 148–81.

Lynch, Dudley and P. L. Kordis (1988), *Strategy of the Dolphin: Scoring a Win in a Chaotic World*, New York: William Morrow.

Marion, Russ and J. Bacon (2000), 'Organizational extinction and complex systems', *Emergence*, **1** (4), 71–96.

McMaster, M. (1995), *The Intelligence Advantage: Organizing for Complexity*, Douglas: Knowledge Based Development.

Miller, James G. (1978), *Living Systems*, New York: McGraw-Hill.

Mittleton-Kelly, Eve (1997), 'Organisations as co-evolving complex adaptive systems', *BPRC Paper No. 5*, Business Process Resource Centre, University of Warwick.

Mittleton-Kelly, Eve (2003), 'Complex systems and evolutionary perspectives on organisations: The application of complexity theory to organisations', in E. Mittleton-Kelly (ed.), *Complex Systems and Evolutionary Perspectives on Organizations: The Application of Complexity Theory to Organizations*, Oxford: Elsevier.

Molinski, Andrew L. (1999), 'Sanding down the edges: Paradoxical impediments to organizational change', *Journal of Applied Behavioural Science*, **35** (1), 8–26.

Morgeson, Frederick P., T. R. Mitchell and D. Liu (2015), 'Event system theory: An event-oriented approach to the organizational sciences', *Academy of Management Review*, **40** (4), 515–37.

Pascale, Richard T. (1999), 'Surfing the edge of chaos', *Sloan Management Review*, **Spring**, 83–94.

Peters, Thomas J. (1987), *Thriving on Chaos: Handbook for a Management Revolution*, New York: Harper Perennial.

Peters, Thomas J. (1992), *Liberation Management: Necessary Disorganization for the Nanosecond Nineties*, London: Macmillan.

Pettigrew, Andrew M. (1985), *Awakening Giant*, New York: Prentice Hall.

Prigogine, Ilya (1989), 'Thermodynamics and cosmology', *International Journal of Theoretical Physics*, **28** (9), 927–33.

Prigogine, Ilya and I. Stengers (1984), *Order out of Chaos*, New York: Heinemann.

Redfern, Sally and S. Christian (2003), 'Achieving change in health care practice', *Journal of Evaluation in Clinical Practice*, **9** (2), 225–38.

Robbins, Stephen P. and N. Barnwell (1998), *Organisation Theory: Concepts and Cases*, 3rd edition, New Jersey: Prentice Hall.

Rook, Laura and L. McManus (2016), 'Viewing WIL in business schools through a new lens: Moving to the edge of chaos with complexity theory', *Emergence: Complexity and Organization*, **18** (2), 1–14.

Rook, Laura L. and G. Watson (2017), 'Chaotic edge thinking: Understanding why work practices fail', *Emergence: Complexity and Organization*, **19** (3), https://doi.org/10.emerg/10.17357.91cb484bde0df797bb934cebe10bd950.

Rooney, David and G. Hearn (1999), 'The zone of entanglement: Change, non-change and the new managerial ideology of ephemera', *Foresight*, **1** (2), 143–53.

Rosenhead, Jonathan (1989), *Rational Analysis for a Problematic World: Problem Structuring Methods for Complexity, Uncertainty and Conflict*, Chichester: Wiley.

Salem, Philip (2002), 'Assessment, change and complexity', *Management Communication Quarterly*, **15** (3), 442–50.

Shaw, Patricia (1997), 'Consulting from a complexity perspective: Intervening in the shadow systems of organizations', *Journal of Organizational Change Management*, **10** (3), 235–50.

Skyttner, Lars (1996), *General Systems Theory: An Introduction*, London: Macmillan Press.

Speakman, Mark (2017), 'A paradigm for the twenty-first century or metaphorical non-sense? The enigma of complexity theory and tourism research', *Tourism Planning and Development*, **14** (2), 282–96.

Stacey, Ralph D. (1993), *Strategic Management and Organisational Dynamics*, London: Pitman.

Stacey, Ralph D. (1996), *Complexity and Creativity in Organizations*, San Francisco, CA: Berrett-Koehler.

Steiner, Carol (2001), 'A role for individuality and mystery in managing change', *Journal of Change Management*, **14** (2), 150–67.

Stohl, Cynthia and G. Cheney (2001), 'Participatory processes/paradoxical practices', *Management Communication Quarterly*, **14** (3), 349–407.

Styhre, Alexander (2002), 'Non-linear change in organizations: Organization change management informed', *Leadership and Organization Development Journal*, **23** (5/6), 343–51.

Sullivan, Terence J. (2004), 'The viability of using various system theories to describe organisational change', *Journal of Educational Administration*, **42** (1), 43–54.

Tasaka, Hiroshi (1999), 'Twenty-first-century management and the complexity paradigm', *Emergence*, **1** (4), 115–23.

Tetenbaum, T. J. (1998), 'Shifting paradigms: From Newton to chaos', *Organizational Dynamics*, **26** (4), 21–32.

Therrien, Marie Christine, J. M. Normandin and J. L. Denis (2017), 'Bridging complexity theory and resilience to develop surge capacity in health systems', *Journal of Health Organization and Management*, **36** (1), 96–109.

Von Bertalanffy, Ludwig (1968), *General System Theory: Foundations, Development, Applications*, New York: George Braziller.

10. The cultural philosophy: 'changing values'

INTRODUCTION

The interpretation of organizations as cultural systems began with interest from anthropologists for whom change reflects what members of a group consider important; their values, beliefs, attitudes, assumptions and opinions. The concept of organizational culture emerged in response to an absence of explanations for how certain values and beliefs gain prominence. Just as nations possess cultures that influence their citizens, organizations generate cultures that shape how their members behave (Hayton, George and Zahra, 2002). Although elusive in definition and measurement, organizational culture has become an influential philosophical approach to change. At its heart lies the idea that organizational change transpires when the common beliefs and values held by organizational members change. A key foundation to the culture philosophy, therefore, maintains that change must be preceded by a period of careful cultural diagnosis where common beliefs and values are exposed. The cultural philosophy assumes that culture permeates all organizations, varying in strength, and exerts a powerful influence on individual behaviour and organizational outcomes (Harris and Mossholder, 1996).

Anthropology first set the concept of culture alight, developing it to become the pivotal lens used in the field. Anthropologists addressed the task of investigating, interpreting and translating the behavioural and social patterns of groups. Their efforts were directed at explaining how groups relate to their environments. One of the earliest accounts of culture was provided by Edward Tylor in 1871, where he described culture as the entire set of knowledge, beliefs and customs held by members of a society. Tylor pointed out that these complex ideas, whether in the form of customs, morals, artwork or other capabilities, are acquired and transmitted by members of a social group. Anthropologists concern themselves with making sense of how people relate to their environments through the learning and adaptation that culture orchestrates. This simple proposition exploded the way change theorists and practitioners thought about organizations. By understanding the interaction between individuals and their cultural circumstances, change theorists started to realize that the most useful interventions need to change deep values and beliefs. Changing organizational behaviour suddenly became about changing what people consider important. Since most people adjust to organizational environments in similar ways, they inevitably begin to take on shared beliefs. The cultural philosophy targets these beliefs as the key path to change. The following section of the chapter provides a conceptual overview of the culture philosophy. Next, we consider cultural diagnosis and the way cultural dimensions can be employed. Dimensions also help us to explore the natural connections to psychology, which in turn leads us to examine cultural change through symbols, rituals and identity. Finally, we assess the cultural philosophy's approach to targeting powerful cultural units as a method of organizational change.

CONCEPTUALIZING CULTURAL CHANGE

Although organizational theorists picked up on the anthropological concept of culture relatively late, the notion first entered the academic lexicon through an article by Pettigrew (1979), entitled 'On studying organizational cultures'. Pettigrew's seminal article unleashed three subsequent decades of study on organizational culture, much of it concerned with how to go about revealing common and deeply held values in order to bring about radical change. For cultural theorists, organizations operate as social systems that work according to the collective norms and priorities of its members. In the same way that individuals possess ensconced personalities, so too do organizations. However, like changing an individual personality, shifting an organization's collective mindset necessitates changes to deep and meaningful values. Cultural theorists acknowledge that while behaviour reveals underpinning attitudes, deeper and intensely personal psychological traits also drive behaviour unconsciously. Although little disagreement can be found amongst organizational theorists that deep values can act like a fulcrum for change, most also agree that the only thing more difficult than bringing values to the surface is changing them once identified. In this chapter we will emphasize the importance of correct diagnosis, along with its challenges. As Denison, Nieminen and Kotrba (2014) concluded concerning diagnostic tools for organizational culture, there are a 'number of problematic trends and remaining gaps in the types of reliability and validity evidence that support these instruments' (p. 159). We shall also pay particular attention to the impact of cultural thinking on structuring an approach to organizational change.

Understanding organizational culture proves counterintuitive for many change managers, mainly due to the influence imposed by traditional views of organizational theory, which focus on observable behaviours. In contrast, cultural theorists claim that overt behaviour can dominate and camouflage the underlying values and motivations that really drive action. Although commonality can be found in the conception and definition of organizational culture, inconsistency and controversy remain present as well. However, one influential view offered by Schein (1979) takes a psychological position, portraying culture as an unconscious phenomenon made up of deep assumptions and beliefs, and where conscious beliefs skim the surface as artefacts and symbolic representations.

Schein advised change managers to avoid the superficial. Rather, they should explore the unconsciously held and fundamental concepts of right or wrong held in an organization. These values painstakingly build up through organizational members' interactions as they gradually learn to work together to achieve their collective and individual aims (Schein, 1984). Another influential early position presented by Ouchi and Pascale (1975) took a simpler view where artefacts and tangible items, such as the office landscape, represent not just the physical manifestations of the existing culture, but the important parts of culture itself. The two presentations of culture diverge on the most significant part of its manifestation, but agree that culture commands monumental importance in managing change.

The variability in perspectives on organizational culture stems from diverging central interests ranging from the most easily perceived and visibly apparent artefacts, such as the environment, architecture, technology and audible behaviour, to its deep psychological manifestations. Some researchers tend to focus on their preferred element of culture, describing the leftovers as insignificant, or existing only as a symptom of the 'deeper' phenomenon. Beyer and Trice (1993), for example, argued that organizational rites provide the richest and deepest sources of cultural understanding, and declared all other culture sources as superficial. Drucker (1992) would have disagreed, advocating that an analysis of organizational habits offers greater revelations. Morgan (1986) prioritized the ways in which metaphors characterize organizations, and proposed that they illuminate distinctive patterns of cultures. A different approach again by Pedersen and Sorensen (1989), viewed culture as simultaneously: an analytical tool for the researcher; as managerial key tools to improve economic output; as a tool of change; and as a cognitive sense-making tool for organizational members. These four elements interrelate, indicative of the way in which researchers often combine different perspectives, and assume that the value of the concept extends beyond diagnosis to offer a launching point for organizational change.

COMMON THEMES

While organizational culture has been defined and interpreted in a variety of ways, some themes recur, and despite being established early, still endure.

First, culture resists flexibility; second it is determined by the members of an organization; third it is shared by members of an organization; and finally, while its influence on behaviour can be profound, its core assumptions frequently remain hidden from most organizational members (Hofstede, Neuijen, Ohayv and Sanders, 1990; Kilman, Saxton and Serpa, 1985; Langan-Fox and Tan, 1997; Reichers and Schneider, 1990; Schein, 1997, Siehl and Martin, 1990). For most change managers, culture operates as a collection of fundamental values, beliefs and attitudes common to members of an organization, and which subsequently guide its behavioural standards and norms (Ogbonna and Harris, 2002, Pettigrew, 1979).

Another theme embedded in the cultural philosophy proposes that culture must be appropriate to the environment or context in which an organization functions. Examples unsurprisingly suggest that organizations such as the police or military will cultivate different values and behaviours to others, such as theatre companies or schools. Equally, the research indicates that certain industrial sectors and types of organizations share common ideologies, like banking and sport, respectively. For change managers, each organization should foster a culture consistent with the challenges and expectations of its internal and external environments. Culture can therefore be used to shape the values, expectations, assumptions and norms of employees, prescribing the behaviour of the entire organization. Thus, the appropriateness of culture links to performance. For example, a 'human relations' culture (i.e. flexible, cohesive, trusting) in a clinical setting is more likely to foster employees who embrace change when compared with other cultures, because there is less fear of change amongst clinical workers, a critical characteristic of that medical context (Carlström and Ekman, 2012). Diversity in the appropriateness of cultural characteristics also makes it even more difficult for change managers to determine what to aim for, especially when cultural values fluctuate so much in strength.

Strength refers to the intensity or pervasiveness of the culture (Schein, 1985). Research suggests that strong cultures lead to appealing outcomes such as unity, commitment and coordination, thereby contributing to better performance. However, strong organizational culture can be a liability when it does not align with the context of its operating environment. Strong works well when it reinforces useful common values and beliefs, but can be debilitating when it undermines or obstructs performance. Research has indicated that a moderate strength culture is optimal because it provides values, but does not suppress other, new options to the point that innovation is crushed and group-think increases the threat of change (Ramachandran, Chong and Ismail, 2011).

An extensive range of studies demonstrates that culture significantly impacts upon organizational performance by affecting employee behaviour

(Denison, 1990; Detert, Schroeder and Mauriel, 2000; Schein, 1985). Culture has also been related to performance and innovation (Subramanian and Ashkanasy, 2001), as well as employee commitment, cooperation, efficiency, job performance and decision making (Goodman, Zammuto and Gifford, 2001). If leaders and managers can find ways of making culture more appropriate, the evidence confirms that there will be a correspondingly advantageous performance effect. To add a final dimension of complexity, evidence has demonstrated that national culture can affect organizational culture as well as overall performance (e.g. Hofstede, 2001; Hayton et al., 2002; Nazarian, Atkinson and Foroudi, 2017).

CULTURAL EXPOSURE

The cultural philosophy advocates that an organizational cultural diagnosis needs to precede a change programme. However, assessing culture can prove extremely challenging. The difficulty lies in locating and teasing out its submerged or hidden aspects. While some cultural theorists prescribe a strongly research-based, statistical or quantitative approach utilizing questionnaires and scaled responses to generate data, these methods do not guarantee that the hidden aspects of culture will be exposed. Equally, cultural studies show that change leaders who assume that they 'know' the culture of their organizations can be in for a big surprise. Further complexity can arise as the utility of instruments to measure organizational culture markedly varies depending on context, population and change manager goals (Jung et al., 2009). A different resolution calls for a detailed organizational examination using interviews, close but discrete observation of behaviour, and the systematic analysis of statements and documents. Collectively, such rich and detailed information can be used to draw out the core, but often submerged, values and beliefs that define an organization's identity.

At the same time, any kind of formal approach to unveiling culture represents a kind of contradiction. After all, culture manifests in every aspect of an organization's existence; both the chief executive officer's office and the cleaner's cupboard depict symbols of cultural meaning. Diagnosis presents a perennial problem for cultural theorists and for the cultural philosophy in general. On the one hand, culture may be understood symbolically through every observable feature of an organization. It permeates everything and literally surrounds organizational members. On the other hand, culture possesses unconscious, unspoken and concealed qualities, meaning that organizational members may be only partially aware of the deep assumptions underpinning the 'way things are done'. Assumptions, values and beliefs can be so thoroughly embedded that bringing them to the surface constitutes an immense and ongoing problem. Exposing the depth and pervasive nature of organizational culture remains one of the most formidable tasks in change management.

Another confusing issue linked to cultural diagnosis arises with the constant interchangeability of terms employed to describe different cultural characteristics. For example, culture advocates talk about norms, values, attitudes, assumptions, beliefs and mores, to name just a handful. Hofstede (1991) even provided an inventory of 51 terms that can be used to describe prevalent cultural terms. Perhaps the two most frequently used terms are values and attitudes. Despite variations in meaning, the middle ground view describes an attitude as an enduring structure of beliefs around an object or situation predisposing an individual to respond in some preferential manner. A value represents a broad tendency to prefer certain states over others. These two definitions contribute to the majority view that organizational culture operates as a kind of mental programming that differentiates members of one organization from another (Ogbonna and Harris, 2002). It also, of course, hones in on what makes members of the same organization feel connected.

The beliefs organizational members hold sovereign may be noticeable through visible artefacts such as symbols, heroes and rituals, while the more covert aspects of culture such as values and assumptions may be inferred through behavioural patterns. Patterns of behaviour collectively distinguish each organization, forming the basis for assuming all organizations possess unique cultures. However, change agents face a practical difficulty because researchers claim that a rigorous examination of culture really demands a standardized approach (Holmes and Marsden, 1996). In order to sidestep the standardization issue, both commentators writing for change managers and serious cultural scholars have devised sets of dimensions against which any organization can be mapped. The only problem is that they are all different.

MAPPING CULTURE

Any effective system for examining culture requires a common measurement scale. Using dimensions offers change managers a focal point for intervention, particularly because they can be expressed as values on a scale of opposing extremes, like risk aversity versus risk acceptance, or even stability versus change. Dimensions imply that all organizations can be diagnosed using the same set of value scales. While any set of dimensions might be usefully employed across a range of organizations, the key philosophical premise holds that every culture exudes a unique expression. At the same time, the complexity of diagnosing an organizational culture cannot be ignored, and any tool that helps the process would seem worth considering.

At first glance, a uniform set of cultural dimensions appears elusive. For example, Allen and Dyer (1980), Bettinger (1989), Denison (1990) and

Gordon (1988) all proposed differently labelled values. Van der Post and de Coning (1997) identified 114 interdependent and independent dimensions from a literature survey, and managed to conflate them to a representative 15, discovering in the process that many commonalties exist between the dimensions suggested by various researchers. A cursory examination of the mass of dimensions can be confusing. Despite the fact that common themes underpin many dimensions, they can be difficult to locate given the variable and often creative labels placed upon them. For example, Gordon's (1988) dimension, 'Clarity of direction' pivots upon the same theme as Bettinger's (1989), 'A sense of pride in the mission and objectives of the organization', notwithstanding the different terminology. Both dimensions emphasize the importance of clarity in relation to an organization's strategic focus and direction.

A number of pre-eminent themes reoccur, including stability/changeability; cooperation/conflict; short-term goals/long-term goals; and control/freedom. Each of these values may be expressed through additional sub-values and attitudes, which in turn manifest in the form of more superficial and observable behaviours or symbols such as artefacts, rituals and heroes. These more accessible aspects of culture represent the sites change managers target for manipulation.

One of the key problems surrounding the use of cultural dimensions arrives when determining what exactly they represent. For example, dimensions strive to measure values by asking questions about symbols, rituals, heroes, history, attitudes and behaviour. Is it reasonable to assume that these criteria offer suitable proxies for covert, underpinning values? Varying assumptions and terminologies make the conceptualization of organizational culture dimensions even more difficult. As a result, cultural dimensions tend to be homogeneous, where all represent an equal unit of cultural depth, but have to be described and evidenced through other characteristics. Dimensions get expressed through different hierarchical layers of the cultural 'onion', like values, attitudes, rituals and symbols. The deeper, more inaccessible core of the onion has to be symbolically interpreted through more overt, superficial layers. Layer complexities make cultural diagnosis problematic for change agents employed in the real world of organizational life where change cannot rely on endless assessment and analysis. A solution offered by popular management authors involves classifying or typologizing organizations into a handful of categories. For example, the competing values framework (Quinn and Rohrbaugh, 1983) uses two axes (flexibility versus control, and internal versus external orientation) and has become a popular model for linking culture, change and performance (Büschgens, Bausch and Balkin, 2013). Typologies can be useful in narrowing the options faced by change managers, but also tend to smooth out the novel idiosyncrasies that make organizations unique.

Most organizational culture typologies distinguish between a handful—usually four—of specified and separate cultural categories, and nearly all organizations can be neatly slotted into one of these groupings. Opponents of simple cultural classification systems argue that cultures cannot be pigeon-holed into just a few categories; since all cultures are unique by definition, there are as many organizational cultures as there are organizations. Cultures cannot be generically categorized into one of a fixed number of groups, nor can they be described by investigating only the external observable characteristics of an organization. Organizations are immersed in tradition, history, values and myths, and should be identified by these symbolic cultural indicators in addition to readily observable organizational characteristics.

In the end, the cultural problem always comes down to the same obstacles for change managers. To accurately assess organizational culture, an essential first step means comprehending the depth and breadth in which a culture can be expressed. Because culture may well contain an unconscious, hidden component, a cultural map must be devised to address organizational culture on varying levels of depth and accessibility. A cultural map summarizes the pre-dominant features of an organization's culture, and provides a means through which raw data can be interpreted into measurable criteria. Once culture has been mapped, a suitable change strategy can be determined to target cultural areas, usually in line with the rational philosophy, but with a special interest in some elements of the psychological philosophy.

THE PSYCHOLOGICAL CONNECTION

The eminent psychologist Jung (1968) provided a useful construct that can be applied to the analysis of cultural meaning. His three-level model was not originally designed with organizations in mind, but when considered as a tool to examine cultural layers, neatly revealed the psychological element in the cultural philosophy. The highest level of the Jungian model represents the conscious mind: the totality of a person's thoughts and experiences. This rational level is analogous to those readily apparent and observable qualities of an organization, such as the physical environment, the public statements of officials, the way individuals interactively communicate, the form of language used, what clothes are worn, and the content of offices. One of the most important observable qualities involves the place of organizational heroes who represent culturally rich and highly visible indicators of the dominant culture. Heroes give an insight into the culture of an organization because members select them. In addition, heroes indicate those admired and respected qualities that organizational members seek to emulate. The hero may also be charismatic, entrepreneurial or distinguished by any other feature from tenacity to temerity. By understanding the orientation of hero figures, both past and present, change managers can map the cultural change trends. Heroes can be both reactionary and progressive. For example, heroes that reinforce the dominant culture will not change the values and attitudes that the culture emphasizes. On the other hand, a hero that transcends and transforms the dominant culture will be a catalyst for change in the behaviours and values of organizational members. Often heroes deliver the most powerful change. Some theories even suggest that leaders should aspire to become heroic figures. However, there is a growing trend to encourage change leaders to adopt a distributed rather than 'all-powerful' approach to cultural change (Kempster, Higgs and Wuerz, 2014).

Also operating from Jung's rational level, tradition offers another easily observable window into the culture of an organization. Like heroes, traditions can be understood from documents and word of mouth, but the underlying values and assumptions that give meaning to heroes and traditions reside in the deeper levels of the Jungian model. Tradition may be preserved by the existing cultural identity. However, many organizations strive to cultivate a contemporary cultural personality. Acknowledging the importance of tradition and history remains crucial because they serve as cultural linchpins and stepping stones from which an organization's cultural character gains momentum.

In order to bypass the obstacles, the stereotypical views, and the superficial signs blocking an assessment of culture, most cultural analysts with a psychological interest recommend exploring natural, observable outcroppings of culture; places where cultural understandings can be exposed. Organizational rites and rituals hold a central importance because their performance can be readily accessed and observed. In addition, in performing rites and rituals, employees use other forms of cultural demonstration, such as customary language or jargon, gestures and artefacts. Rites and rituals display shared understandings, conveyed through myths, sagas, legends or other stories associated with the occasion. In practical terms they can take innumerable forms, including anything from an awards presentation to a weekly coffee and cake morning. However, in order to actively assess culture at this level, not only must observational techniques be employed, but meanings must be attached to the results. Careful interpretation requires more than a superficial level of analysis. We return to the importance of rituals in a forthcoming section.

THE CULTURE–BELIEF LINK

The second and middle level of the Jungian model represents the personal unconscious. According to the Jungian interpretation, the subconscious controls individuals through powerful drives that exist below conscious awareness. This equates to what cultural theorists call a non-rational level of culture, incorporating the beliefs, habits, values, behaviours and attitudes prevalent in an organization. An accurate assessment of the non-rational level of culture could not be more elusive for change managers, and getting it wrong can lead to catastrophic results. For example, how employees say they behave and what they state they believe must be compared to their actual behaviour. Cultural theorists advise that beliefs should be inferred from what people do, rather than what they say they believe. Of course, such a position presents challenges for leaders and change managers faced with bringing about belief change when the presence of unhelpful beliefs escapes acknowledgement. However, advocates of the cultural philosophy contend that genuine and secure behavioural change precedes and stimulates changes to underpinning beliefs. Counterintuitive though this might seem, research indicates that the key lies with changing all the observable and accessible aspects of culture to work in line, because they have a collective impact upon beliefs. Therefore, congruence is required between the cultural leader (e.g. chief executive officer), cultural carriers (e.g. middle managers), cultural artefacts (e.g. observable events), management practices (e.g. employee appraisals, recruitment processes, strategic decision making), and cultural internalization (e.g. employees identify with their organization) (Armenakis, Brown and Mehta, 2011); a task easier said than done. Cultural theorists inclined towards the psychological interpretation propose that organizational members will not continue to practise what they do not believe, leading to either departure or belief change.

Finally, the deepest level of the psyche, according to Jung, refers to the collective unconscious. Jung claimed that the collective unconscious constitutes an innate, primal, virtually inaccessible level of the mind hardwired into humans. The organizational equivalent has been labelled the archetypal level of culture, which reveals the meanings held within the history, tradition, legends, myths and stories of an organization, where the deepest objectives of the culture reside. An investigation of this level, for example, can expose core assumptions about leadership, priorities and values. Paradoxically, the archetypal level appears to overlap with the most superficial layer, the rational level. However, at the rational level, cultural traits receive acceptance and interpretation at 'face' value, whereas here the same cultural traits are recognized as the iceberg's tip; merely a physical manifestation of a deeper and more complex phenomenon. To combat the complexities of the cultural equation, we noted earlier that some change theorists construct 'ideal' categories to describe culture types. Although simplistic and narrow, some change managers find these typologies to be instrumental in understanding the culture conundrum.

CULTURAL LEVELS AS SITES FOR CHANGE

Jung believed that any psychological analysis of an individual—and by extension of an organization—should not be based simply on the perceived or spoken, but on an overall consideration of the conscious, personal unconscious and collective unconscious (Jung, 1968). Within a Jungian framework, the conscious or rational manifestations of culture can be viewed as the superficial, apparent and observable features that yield concrete, but limited information for the change agent. Looking deeper into the 'psyche' of the organization, the personal unconscious or non-rational level surrenders additional cultural information reflecting the values and beliefs of employees. The furthest and least accessible level of cognitive functioning, the collective unconscious or archetypal level, generates the most significant cultural insights. Rites, rituals, mythology, stories, history and tradition offer the units of investigation, and their hidden meanings can be exposed and decoded. Consequently, in order for a true understanding of culture to emerge, multiple levels of analysis must be undertaken, with the assumption that analysis progresses from the surface to the deep (Schein, 1984).

Using the Jungian model as inspiration, Schein (1993) conceptualized culture using three levels that interact as a hierarchy: artefacts, espoused values and basic underlying assumptions. The most easily observed cultural elements come in the forms of artefacts or visible structures and processes. Espoused values typically include the strategies, goals and philosophies that organizations put forward to justify their actions, while basic underlying assumptions include the unconscious, taken-for-granted beliefs, thoughts and feelings that provide the driving impetus for behaviour and motivation. The value of ethnographic approaches to organizational culture considering all three levels was evident in one study of care homes. Despite organizational person-centred values, observation revealed that employee-learned assumptions from experience to treat the care home 'as a workplace', actually encouraged poor behaviour (Killett et al., 2016). Hatch (1993) added the importance of symbols in the model as a way of inserting a dynamic feature that helps to explain the interactions between the levels.

A psychological approach to organizational culture emphasizes that while most researchers can isolate certain shared and culturally meaningful values, they may not always be accessible and observable by change managers who take the simple 'surface' view of culture. Equally, how does a change manager begin to address how organizational culture is influenced by the external networks employees are party to, that shape their unconscious understanding of culture (Whelan, 2016)? In fact, most practising change managers have little chance of diagnosing culture in a way that goes beyond the superficial. The variability in investigation ranges from the most easily perceived and visibly apparent artefacts, such as the environment, architecture, technology and audible behaviour, to the deep psychological manifestations of culture identified by Schein as influenced by Jung and other psychologists. Other interpretations of culture by change commentators take the psychological angle in a different direction connected to symbols and theories of identity.

CULTURAL CHANGE THROUGH SYMBOLS AND IDENTITY

Some theorists like Morgan (1986) argued that organizations operate like mini-societies that wield their own distinctive patterns of cultures and sub-cultures. Accordingly, members adapt to common patterns of beliefs, shared meanings, codes of conduct and operating standards; the cultural context guiding work and behaviour. The dominant character of the culture becomes evident as patterns of behaviour rise to the surface, and the language, themes, images and rituals become transparent, illuminating critical actions and events affecting an individual's construction of reality. In adopting this position, change managers must commit to an ongoing dialogic approach that includes all viewpoints to guide change (Jabri, 2017).

Berger and Luckmann (1967) approached culture from a sociological viewpoint, labelling it as a kind of reality reconstruction. They proposed that organizational behaviour comes about because certain actions are encouraged, reinforced and repeated until habitualized as patterns in members' minds. Culture becomes ingrained in performers' constructions of an institution's identity as well as the institution's embodiment of culture in the form of individual action. In this way, culture enjoys reinforcement through a reciprocal action where organizational members act out the patterns they believe align with the prevailing collective patterns. As a consequence, reality becomes legitimized through individuals' ongoing role playing, leading to a meaningful social reality. Of particular salience to cultural change, Berger and Luckmann (1967) suggested that legitimization transmits already established institutional meaning to a new generation of employees via systems of symbolic reference: 'Language constructs immense edifices of symbolic representation that appear to tower over the reality of everyday life like gigantic presences from another world' (Berger and Luckmann, 1967, p. 55). Within this schema, organizational artefacts like stories may be considered central to the 'social distribution of knowledge' (Berger and Luckmann, 1967, p. 146). Stories function as scripts organizational members learn in order to be apprenticed and habituated into their social reality.

An individual's perception of their organizational reality provides meaning and understanding for their own behaviour. An organization, therefore, exists both physically and symbolically, the latter within a shared reality held by organizational members. This is clear in how executives interpret organizational culture to inform mission statements, as well as in concerns about not knowing what goes on lower down in the hierarchy (Babnik, Breznik, Dermol and Širca, 2014). The construction and reconstruction of reality represents a vibrant colour in change managers' cultural palette. Organizational structure, rules, policies, goals, missions, job descriptions and work procedures serve as primary points of reference for the way employees perceive their work contexts. Add to this the symbolic elements of culture such as myths, stories and legends. Collectively, the overt, tacit and deeply buried aspects of organizational culture represent the change manager's canvas.

The premise that symbolic representations guide organizational behaviour and meaning making holds consistent with more recent claims that social behaviour is influenced by external forces as well as internal. To Scott (2001), the cognitive elements of culture reflect the internal interpretive processes that individuals experience when exposed to informal beliefs, values and norms, as well as formal legal, political and economic structures. The cultural philosophy offers an insight into the effect of formal and informal structures as seen through the covert inner workings of individuals engaged in the process of constructing meaning. The hard part remains working out what reality organizational members have already constructed and how these deep meanings might be influenced by changes to tangible things that managers can target. Cultural surveys premised on discursive reflective practice between managers and non-managers, in order to better understand constructed cultural realities at different hierarchical levels, may offer one solution (Ivolga and Booth, 2019). In the end, change managers make a difference to culture by manipulating those overt organizational elements they can access, driven by the assumption that if the right elements are selected, there will be a cumulative impact on deeper value structures. Some theorists believe that certain cultural artefacts hold greater importance than others because they provide deeper insight, and lead to a greater effect on culture when changed. Organizational rituals and organizational stories present two leading examples.

CHANGING CULTURAL RITUALS

Rituals have long been associated with an anthropological tradition placing them as pivotal contributors to social organization, cohesion and solidarity. Given the importance of social cooperation to the survival and prosperity of organizations, rituals represent an important window into understanding and modifying culture. Ritualized behaviour may be understood as both an input and output of organizational culture, through the channelling of specific forms of social interaction and behavioural custom (Anand and Watson, 2004; Beyer and Trice, 1993; Pedersen and Sorensen, 1989; Pettigrew, 1979; Schein, 1985).

In their seminal account, Trice and Beyer (1984) defined rites and ceremonies as discrete enactments with clear boundaries that symbolically express a culture's driving values and beliefs. The term rite refers to a singular and specific instance of a ritual (Grimes, 1990), although the terms historically blend interchangeably. A ceremony, on the other hand, provides the context in which a rite, or in which numerous rituals, are performed (Trice and Beyer, 1984). A pivotal differentiation to the change manager made by anthropologist Turner (1969), specified that rituals 'transform' in that they bring about changed social conditions. In contrast, ceremonies 'confirm' by bolstering existing social circumstances. Transforming and confirming beliefs and practices lie at the heart of successful organizational change. Practitioners would perhaps be best to consider organizational rituals as the study of a collection of rituals and specific individual rites, as well as their ceremonial enactment.

Anthropological research on rituals has a rich tradition of examining their meaning, structure and function. In these descriptions, rituals depict communicative actions with multi-layered meanings relative to a foundation culture. Dulaney and Fiske (1994) noted that although rituals embody distinctive and universal modes of human action, it remains unclear which actions should be considered distinctive and universal. The same observation may be made about rituals performed in organizations. Given such variety, the only reasonable starting point focuses on how organizational rituals can be differentiated from the plethora of other organizational activities. Rappaport (1979; 1999) and Boyer and Lienard (2006) offered some useful criteria. First, actions associated with rituals fail to connect with normal organizational goals where causes and effects logically associate, partly because the ritual environment is different. Second, rituals tend to be either compulsory or compulsive. Third, the actions involved in rituals remain inflexible due to the incorporation of repetition and redundancy. Finally, rituals relate, either symbolically or overtly, to a restricted set of themes. While these criteria provide a solid descriptive start to the understanding of rituals, they do not offer a detailed approach to change. In fact, this kind of prescriptive vagueness characterizes the cultural philosophy, and it gets worse.

Denison (1996) noted that organizational culture research makes a distinction between overt manifestations, of which rituals offer an exemplar, and covert assumptions and values that drive overt expressions. A typical research method for uncovering culture involves identifying overt cultural artefacts such as symbols and rituals (Detert et al., 2000) with the intention of inferring something about deeper structures such as values and meanings. As we noted earlier, Schein (1984) argued that rituals can reveal the tacit and elusive aspects of organizational life. The most easily perceived and visibly apparent artefacts include the environment, architecture, technology and audible behaviour, while the more inaccessible features include deep psychological meanings and symbols. Some researchers manage the accessibility problem by selectively choosing their particular element of culture, or describing what remains as insignificant, little more than a symptom of the deeper phenomenon. Others, like Beyer and Trice (1993), argued that organizational rites represent the richest and deepest sources of cultural understanding, dismissing more overt and tangible culture sources as superficial.

EXPOSING CULTURE TO CHANGE

Beyer and Trice (1993) acknowledged the difficulties in exposing the culture of organizations and sought to remedy the situation by exploring as many natural, observable representations as possible. They suggested that by analysing sites where cultural understandings are revealed, managers gain insights into the functioning of their organizations and can make surgical interventions accordingly. Organizational culture includes not simply the shared understandings organizational members hold, but also the communication of these understandings. The behavioural and regulatory power of organizational rites command the greatest respect, because in performing rituals, employees utilize other forms of culture to communicate, such as language, gestures, coordinated behaviour, ceremonies and artefacts. Shared understandings occurring in rites also get transmitted through myths, sagas, legends or other stories. As a result, rites and rituals can be distinguished from other organizational activities by the presence of relatively elaborate and planned sets of activities, social interaction, an audience, and predictable social consequences (Trice and Beyer, 1984). Rituals execute planned social dramas with well-defined and rehearsed roles for actors to play. They offer a rich source of cultural understanding, being tangible, visible and accessible. A distinction should also be made between full rituals and activities that are 'ritual-like', with the former being more formal, intense and infrequent (Smith and Stewart, 2011). Manipulating rituals connects organizational behaviour and performance with culture. Cultural advocates suggest that this combination offers a potent vehicle for change.

If we are to accept the early work by Beyer and Trice, rituals not only communicate and reinforce the shared understandings of an organization's culture, they also provide an entry point for its change. For example, in attempting to bolster an organizational change initiative, managers typically focus on cognitive elements of persuasion like rational argument and logical appeals. However, the emotional dimension of persuasion can be more powerful, particularly when underpinned by ceremonies reinforcing specific values and goals. A simple example can be seen in a ceremony introducing a change programme (Fox and Amichai-Hamburger, 2001). In this case decorations and adornments can fortify the importance placed on the programme, and reward behaviours that lead to the desired changes. The symbology of change-related ceremonies allows organizational members to acknowledge the soon to be discarded past.

Organizational rituals commonly commemorate significant losses, achievements and life transitions, such as weddings, birthdays, retirements and funerals. Here the past is celebrated, summarized and used to propel change. Indeed, rituals can even be used to affect innovation in organizations. For example, Jassawalla and Sashittal (2002) found that an intensive schedule of formal meetings for sharing information, ideas and conflicts became common rituals for those organizations with innovation-supportive cultures. Rituals may also be able to generate a sense of mutual obligation and emotional solidarity.

It would be dangerous to assume that rituals always provide a useful function or act to support the prevailing culture. Rituals expose a symbolic attenuation with the workplace, just as often allowing ambiguity and tension to be managed as identity develops and massages behaviour. Sometimes organizational rituals get wrongly attributed to the workplace as if the organization and its leaders were exclusively in control of them. Rituals may be imposed but they also emerge. Rituals can operate as a fierce interrogation between an organization and its employees, sometimes reinforcing prevailing cultural values and sometimes undermining them.

Introducing new rituals, or the removal of existing ones, can also prove dangerous. Change managers might intend to modify employee behaviour through a new ritual, but end up causing disaffection. Some rituals come to represent subversion or at least discontent. It is safer to support existing functional rituals. Organizational rituals demand attention because employees confer symbolic meaning to intrinsically meaningless activities. For example, 'good' rituals may be seen as those allowing participants to withdraw from normal time and space and to forge social connections. Advantageous rituals also organize and reduce uncertainty or anxiety. For examples, ritual-like activities such as inter-employee storytelling, can reinforce comradery (Erhardt, Martin-Rios and Heckscher, 2016). However, some rituals and ritual-like activities can have an ambiguous impact. For example, the removal of alcohol-based social rituals in a police force was perceived negatively by some officers on the basis of reduced comradery, and positively by others on the basis of a reduction in drinking culture (Brough, Chataway and Biggs, 2016). Such evidence reinforces how organizational members interpret rituals, and can perceive changes to rituals differently, especially with regard to their subsequent impact on organizational culture. For this reason, change theorists recommend approaching rituals with caution, instead preferring to work on interpreting culture through less complex and inflammatory mechanisms such as stories.

STORIES AND STORYTELLING

Stories involve an oral or written performance portraying two or more people interpreting past or anticipated experiences (Boje, 1991). Stories explain events, simplify behavioural expectations, provide conceptual accounts of organizational phenomena, place characters into context and generally offer examples that serve as guides. Organizational stories can be differentiated by the level of colour (i.e. engaging narrative content), fulfilment (i.e. the story satisfies employee needs), or on the basis of whether it contains a separate, descriptive, anecdotal, script or epic story (O'Neill, 2002). Each story type can be employed to serve different strategic organizational needs, including change (Beigi, Callahan and Michaelson, 2019). Contrasting or competing stories highlight points of contention and diverging cultural priorities or sub-cultures. From an organizational change perspective, stories affect behaviour by defining characters, sequencing plots, scripting events and enacting responses to change (Boje, 2001). Their consideration demands the attention of change managers because they provide insights and avenues into the complex social worlds that organizations construct. Organizational stories contain both implicit and explicit meanings that impact upon reality. Stories help individuals to enact their own script within a group (Browning, 1991). Organizations provide a 'collective storytelling system in which the performance of stories is a key part of members' sense-making and a means to allow them to supplement individual memories with institutional memory' (Boje, 1991, p. 106). Change agents can access stories that communicate deep cultural meanings but cannot access the values and assumptions that support them. Successful change therefore focuses on working with existing stories as diagnostic tools and reinforcing those containing advantageous cultural messages.

Boje (2001), like Weick (1995), argued that stories play an essential sense-making function for organizational members attempting to find their way in a complex environment infused with ambiguity and uncertainty. Often for individuals, sense making occurs retrospectively through stories and their interpretation. Organizational storytelling has conventionally been considered subservient to organizational history as a way of interpreting culture (Gabriel, 2000; 2004). But while stories do not necessarily reflect a perfect account of what happened, they remain authoritative shapers of meaning. This view has been strongly influenced by postmodern accounts of storytelling that acknowledge the presence of multiple realities and countless stories, many of which are fragile and susceptible to a myriad of interpretations (Boje, 2001; Czarniawska, 2004; Gabriel, 2004; Hardy, Lawrence and Grant, 2005). Chapter 11 on the critical philosophy picks up on this line of thinking as it applies to organizational change.

The stream of story analysis that Boje pioneered assumes that organizations cannot be registered as a single story, but rather as a plurality of stories and interpretations that compete in a struggle to represent the diverse, uncertain and sometimes chaotic organizational world. However, defining and interpreting stories hardly makes for a straightforward undertaking. Gabriel (2004), for example, considers Boje's version of stories to be fragments of more important narratives which contain a clear plot and the causal resolution to problems. Czarniawska (2004) went a step further, acknowledging the relevance of social context, story fragments and forms of emergent storytelling as important pieces in the wider context of narratives. In the narrative conception, stories precede narratives; they exist in a void between coherence and incoherence where a resolved significance constructed within the social setting remains absent or underdeveloped. Stories present accounts of incidents and events upon which narration may be layered.

Swap, Leonard, Shields and Abrams (2001) defined an organizational story as a detailed narrative of past management actions, employee interactions or other intra- or extra-organizational events. From this perspective, stories are typically communicated informally and contain a plot, characters and a resolution. Sometimes the most influential stories associated with change identify new realities, unexpected dilemmas and creative possibilities (Tyler, 2006). In addition, the setting in which a story is told adds further nuance (van Hulst and Ybema, 2020). Accordingly, change managers look for potent stories which provide symbolic reference to activities and ideas that are hard to access or specify lucidly. For example, stories about 'heroes of innovation' have been used to display desired behaviour when seeking to change an organization towards innovative practices (Hogan and Coote, 2014). In some cases, change managers try to promote stories that represent idealized future behaviour, while carefully avoiding formal methods or prescriptions to take up that behaviour. In this sense, storytelling can provide a powerful tool for gaining support for change, but it is not sufficient alone to ensure positive organizational change (Wilson, 2019).

CULTURAL SENSE MAKING

Most change researchers support the view that stories supply conduits for sense making and competing perspectives on organizational reality. Stories can further serve to reinforce inertia and prohibit change if they limit sense making (Näslund and Pemer, 2012). The degree to which organizations are stories, or are nothing more than their stories, remains more contentious. The extreme of this view holds that organizations only exist as stories in that they were created through discourse (Czarniawska, 2004). Narratives construct organizations through individual constructions of the self (Hopkinson, 2003).

Notwithstanding the symbolic or literal nature of the relationship between organizations and their stories, we suggest that they do sequence cultural history in ways that facilitate future action (Boje, 1991; 2001; Gabriel, 1995; 2000; Gardner and Avolio, 1998; Weick, 1995). Furthermore, we agree that stories stimulate vicarious experiences, reconcile the past with the present, pattern predictions for the future, encourage the projection of personal agency into organizational activity, provide interpretations of events, and channel meaning (Nair, 2002).

Understanding an organization begins with its 'genesis' story. It represents the central metaphor framing employees' perceptions of the organization (Poulton, 2005). Stories like those about the beginning of an organization allow common thoughts and messages to be repeated in novel ways, bypassing ordinary conversation and encouraging listeners to infer a general truth (Nair, 2002). Cultures that facilitate storytelling support tacit knowledge transfer between employees and managers, in turn supporting performance (Suppiah and Sandhu, 2011). Change managers can find such an approach more useful than baldly pronouncing the 'truth' or the way that members should be thinking. From this perspective, stories share norms and values, cultivate trust, communicate tacit information and stimulate an emotional connection (Denning, 2000; 2002; Gargiulo, 2005; 2006). Gabriel (2000, p. 239) wrote: 'Stories are narratives with plots and characters, generating emotion in narrator and audience, through a poetic elaboration of symbolic material'. Legitimate, formidable and influential stories: (1) involve characters in a predicament; (2) occur in a sequence which subsequently reflects the plot and the salient features of the characters; (3) employ symbolism; (4) utilize poetic embellishment and embroidery; (5) have a discernible beginning, middle and end; and (6) communicate enduring truths beyond mere facts.

Some conclusions can be drawn from the preceding discussion. First, the evidence suggests that organizational stories can be manoeuvred as units of culture containing important information about organizations and the behaviour of their members. Second, while the content of stories varies, most generic definitions (e.g. Gabriel, 2000; 2004) assume that they can exist in any context and will possess the same basic definitional properties. Third, like all aspects of culture, interpretation drives understanding. The contextual importance and meaning of organizational stories must precede any form of cultural change intervention.

SENSE MAKING AND SENSE GIVING

Every organization holds shared beliefs reflected in forms of communication that increase social cohesion and solidarity. In fact, organizational members share common beliefs and interpretations of their own experiences as well as of external events. Berger and Luckmann (1967), as we noted earlier, proposed that behaviour in institutions comes about because certain actions are encouraged, reinforced and repeated until patterned and habitualized. These behaviours become ingrained in both the performers' constructions of the institution's identity and the institution's collective activities through a multiplicity of individual actions. As a consequence, reality is legitimized through individuals' role playing, leading to a shared, plausible and meaningful social reality. That is, culture.

Of particular salience to narratives is Berger and Luckmann's (1967) suggestion that 'legitimization' helps transmit already established institutional meaning via systems of symbolic reference: 'Language constructs immense edifices of symbolic representation that appear to tower over the reality of everyday life like gigantic presences from another world' (p. 55). Within this schema, sense making and sense giving may be considered central to the 'social distribution of knowledge' (p. 146). From a cultural philosophy viewpoint, through their 'sense-making' and 'sense-giving', leaders are able to 'use the raw materials of narrative to construct new organizational sense' (Fleming, 2001, p. 34). Gioia and Chittipeddi (1991) conceptualized the sense-making/ sense-giving process as pivotal to leadership communications in articulating a new organizational identity. Leader sense giving represents a critically important activity in shaping 'the processes and outcomes of organizational sensemaking' (Maitlis and Lawrence, 2007, p. 57), because it serves to guide organizational actors' interpretations and meaning making towards a new reality. Other studies have similarly commented on the importance of leader sense giving in bringing about organizational change (Fiss and Zajac, 2006; Maitlis and Lawrence, 2007). Through language, talk and communication, 'meanings' materialize from sense giving and sense making that 'inform and constrain identity and action' (Weick, Sutcliffe and Obstfeld, 2005, p. 409). From a cultural modification perspective, the sense-making/sense-giving dynamic means replacing old ways of looking at things with new ways (Gioia and Chittipeddi, 1991).

Management plays a pivotal role in providing 'connective tissue', and in engendering social integration among senior team members and cross-functional interfaces, for knowledge and skills sharing (Turner, Swart and Maylor, 2012). Leader sense-giving and sense-making 'craft' can therefore play a significant part in shaping understandings about the organizational change process through the words, ideas and images leaders employ (Peirano-Vejo and Stablein, 2009). Accordingly, it is up to leaders to use persuasion to craft a new cultural reality. Further, acting as 'sense givers', leaders' subtle and strategic interpretation and contextualization of events, conveyed through the rhetoric of metaphor, stories and repetition, serve to construct a compelling change message. In this respect, a leader's language can reshape organizational reality by delineating acceptable modes of social engagement. In times of uncertainty and change it remains particularly important for a leader to 'develop a vision or mental model of how the environment works (sense-making) and then be able to communicate to others and gain their support (sense-giving)' (Hill and Levenhagen, 1995, p. 1057). The connection between organizational culture and open interpretations of social reality lead us to the critical philosophy, examined next.

CONCLUSION

Despite the diverse range of opinions held by researchers regarding the nature, existence and importance of organizational culture, a general consensus recognizes that it commands a significant effect on performance and behaviour. Given this opinion, organizational culture receives respect from researchers and change managers alike. Any approach to changing organizational culture faces major challenges. To begin with, trying to influence culture without a carefully constructed prior assessment means playing with fire, especially given the multiple interpretations given to workplace rituals (Brough et al., 2016). Simple surveys lead to problems because they risk taking cultural phenomena out of context and thus ignoring the more important underpinning symbolism. At the same time, any analysis capturing the complexity of organizational culture must separate the interwoven strands of organizational history and personal relationships captured in cultural expressions such as rituals and stories. Change agents face the disadvantage of interpreting the symbolism created by myths, rituals and artefacts before they can arrive at a complete understanding of the full range of human behaviour within a complex organization.

Perhaps it is because the cultural philosophy seeks to come to a deep understanding of organizational behaviour that it has proven so popular with change managers. Few can argue against the wisdom of better organizational diagnosis (despite the challenges presented by longitudinal ethnographic approaches). In this respect, the cultural philosophy has made a significant contribution to organizational change by encouraging change leaders to think carefully about the intervention mechanisms they employ. In the same way as in the systems philosophy, cultural theorists recognize that change in one part of an organization inescapably connects to other parts. For the culture advocate, this means recognizing that deeper cultural values manifest through superficial outcroppings of organizational behaviour. Access to deep values will always be a fundamental challenge, but the cultural philosophy encourages managers to accept that the most significant cultural values cannot be directly changed; a key lesson from the cultural philosophy.

Even though the change intervention must be directed at deeper and hidden levels such as values, assumptions and beliefs, it must be approached through changes to more overt and accessible levels such as rituals, stories and artefacts. Once the decision has been reached about what can be changed to affect a systemic and collective cultural response, the implementation can be achieved using conventional rational or strategic models. As problematic as an accurate diagnosis might be, cultural theorists caution that it is easy compared to delivering deep changes to values, beliefs and behaviours.

REFERENCES

Allen, Robert F. and F. J. Dyer (1980), 'A tool for tapping the organizational conscious', *Personnel Journal*, **March**, 57–63.

Anand, N. and M. R. Watson (2004), 'Tournament rituals in the evolution of fields: The case of the Grammy Awards', *Academy of Management Journal*, **47** (1), 59–80.

Armenakis, Achilles, S. Brown and A. Mehta (2011), 'Organizational culture: Assessment and transformation', *Journal of Change Management*, **11** (3), 305–28.

Babnik, Katarina, K. Breznik, V. Dermol and N. T. Širca (2014), 'The mission statement: Organisational culture perspective', *Industrial Management and Data Systems*, **114** (4), 612–27.

Beigi, Mina, J. Callahan and C. Michaelson (2019), 'A critical plot twist: Changing characters and foreshadowing the future of organizational storytelling', *International Journal of Management Reviews*, **21** (4), 447–65.

Berger, Peter L. and T. Luckmann (1967), *The Social Construction of Reality: A Treatise in the Sociology of Knowledge*, New York: Anchor Books.

Bettinger, Cass (1989), 'Use corporate culture to trigger high performance', *Journal of Business Strategy*, **10** (2), 38–42.

Beyer, Janice M. and H. M. Trice (1993), 'How an organization's rites reveal its culture', *Organizational Dynamics*, **December**, 4–26.

Boje, David M. (1991), 'The storytelling organization: A study of storytelling performance in an office supply firm', *Administrative Science Quarterly*, **36**, 106–26.

Boje, David M. (2001), *Narrative Methods for Organizational and Communication Research*, London: Sage.

Boyer, Pascal and P. Lienard (2006), 'Why ritualized behavior? Precaution systems and action parsing in developmental, pathological and cultural rituals', *Behavioral and Brain Sciences*, **29** (6), 595–613.

Brough, Paula, S. Chataway, and A. Biggs (2016), '"You don't want people knowing you're a copper!" A contemporary assessment of police organisational culture', *International Journal of Police Science and Management*, **18** (1), 28–36.

Browning, L. D. (1991), 'Organizational narratives and organizational structure', *Journal of Organizational Change Management*, **4** (3), 59–67.

Büschgens, Thorsten, A. Bausch and D. B. Balkin (2013), 'Organizational culture and innovation: A meta-analytic review', *Journal of Product Innovation Management*, **30** (4), 763–81.

Carlström, Eric D. and I. Ekman (2012), 'Organisational culture and change: Implementing person-centred care', *Journal of Health Organization and Management*, **26** (2), 175–91.

Czarniawska, Barbara J. (2004), *Narratives in Social Science Research*, London: Sage.

Denison, Daniel R. (1990), *Corporate Culture and Organizational Effectiveness*, New York: John Wiley.

Denison, Daniel R. (1996), 'What is the difference between organizational culture and organizational climate? A native's point of view on a decade of paradigm wars', *Academy of Management Review*, **21** (3), 619–54.

Denison, Daniel R., L. Nieminen and L. Kotrba (2014), 'Diagnosing organizational cultures: A conceptual and empirical review of culture effectiveness surveys', *European Journal of Work and Organizational Psychology*, **23** (1), 145–61.

Denning, Stephen (2000), *The Springboard: How Storytelling Ignites Action in Knowledge-Era Organizations*, Boston, MA: Butterworth-Heinemann.

Denning, Stephen (2002), 'The narrative lens: Storytelling in 21st century organizations', *Knowledge Directions*, **3** (2), 92–101.

Detert, James R., R. G. Schroeder and J. J. Mauriel (2000), 'A framework for linking culture and improvement initiatives in organizations', *Academy of Management Review*, **25** (4), 850–63.

Drucker, Peter F. (1992), *Managing for the Future*, Oxford: Butterworth-Heinemann.

Dulaney, Siri and A. P. Fiske (1994), 'Cultural rituals and obsessive-compulsive disorder: Is there a common psychological mechanism?', *Ethos*, **22** (3), 243–83.

Erhardt, Niclas, C. Martin-Rios and C. Heckscher (2016), 'Am I doing the right thing? Unpacking workplace rituals as mechanisms for strong organizational culture', *International Journal of Hospitality Management*, **59**, 31–41.

Fiss, P. C. and E. J. Zajac (2006), 'The symbolic management of strategic change: Sensegiving via framing and decoupling', *Academy of Management Journal*, **49** (6), 1173–93.

Fleming, D. (2001), 'Narrative leadership: Using the power of stories', *Strategy and Leadership*, **29** (4), 34–6.

Fox, Shaul and Y. Amichai-Hamburger (2001), 'The power of emotional appeals in promoting organizational change programs', *Academy of Management Executive*, **15** (4), 84–94.

Gabriel, Yiannis (1995), 'The unmanaged organization: Stories, fantasies and subjectivity', *Organization Studies*, **16** (3), 477–501.

Gabriel, Yiannis (2000), *Storytelling in Organizations: Facts, Fictions, and Fantasies*, London: Oxford University Press.

Gabriel, Yiannis (2004), 'Narratives, stories and texts', in David Grant, C. Hardy, C. Oswick and L. L. Putnam (eds), *The Sage Handbook of Organizational Discourse*, London: Sage.

Gardner, William L. and B. J. Avolio (1998), 'The charismatic relationship: A dramaturgical perspective', *Academy of Management Review*, **23** (1), 32–58.

Gargiulo, Terrence L. (2005), *The Strategic Use of Stories in Organizational Communication and Learning*, Armonk, NY: M. E. Sharpe.

Gargiulo, Terrence L. (2006), *Stories at Work: Using Stories to Improve Communication and Build Relationships*, Westport, CT: Praeger.

Gioia, D. A. and K. Chittipeddi (1991), 'Sensemaking and sensegiving in strategic change initiation', *Strategic Management Journal*, **12** (6), 433–48.

Goodman, Eric A., R. F. Zammuto and B. D. Gifford (2001), 'The competing values framework: Understanding the impact of organizational culture on the quality of work life', *Organizational Development Journal*, **19** (3), 58–68.

Gordon, George G. (1988), 'The relationship of corporate culture to industry sector and corporate performance', in Ralph H. Kilman, M. J. Saxton and R. Serpa (eds),

Gaining Control of the Corporate Culture, San Francisco, CA: Jossey-Bass, pp. 451–67.

Grimes, Ronald L. (1990), *Ritual Criticism: Case Studies in its Practice, Essays on Its Theory*, Columbia, SC: University of South Carolina Press.

Hardy, Cynthia, T. B. Lawrence and D. Grant (2005), 'Discourse and collaboration: The role of conversations and collective identity', *Academy of Management Review*, **30** (1), 58–77.

Harris, S. G. and K. W. Mossholder (1996), 'The affective implications of perceived congruence with culture dimensions during organizational transformation', *Journal of Management*, **22** (4), 527–47.

Hatch, Mary J. (1993), 'The dynamics of organizational culture', *Academy of Management Review*, **18** (4), 657–93.

Hayton, James C., G. George and S. A. Zahra (2002), 'National culture and entrepreneurship: A review of behavioral research', *Entrepreneurship Theory and Practice*, **26** (4), 33–52.

Hill, R. C. and M. Levenhagen (1995), 'Metaphors and mental models: Sensemaking and sensegiving in innovative and entrepreneurial activities', *Journal of Management*, **21** (6), 1057–74.

Hofstede, Geert (1991), *Cultures and Organizations: Software of the Mind*, London: McGraw-Hill.

Hofstede, Geert (2001), *Culture's Consequences: Comparing Values, Behaviors, Institutions and Organizations across Nations*, Thousand Oaks, CA: Sage.

Hofstede, Geert, B. Neuijen, D. D. Ohayv and G. Sanders (1990), 'Measuring organizational cultures: A qualitative and quantitative study across twenty cases', *Administrative Science Quarterly*, **35**, 286–316.

Hogan, Suellen J. and L. V. Coote (2014), 'Organizational culture, innovation, and performance: A test of Schein's model', *Journal of Business Research*, **67** (8), 1609–21.

Holmes, Scott and S. Marsden (1996), 'An exploration of the espoused organizational cultures of public accounting firms', *Accounting Horizons*, **10** (3), 26–53.

Hopkinson, Gillian C. (2003), 'Stories from the front-line: How they construct the organization', *Journal of Management Studies*, **40** (8), 1943–69.

Ivolga, Marina and S. Booth (2019), 'Beyond the figures of organisational culture surveys', Dissertation, Lund University.

Jabri, Muayyad (2017), *Managing Organizational Change: Process, Social Construction and Dialogue*, London: Palgrave.

Jassawalla, Avan R. and H. C. Sashittal (2002), 'Cultures that support product-innovation processes', *Academy of Management Executive*, **16** (3), 42–54.

Jung, Carl G. (1968), *Analytical Psychology: Its Theory and Practice*, New York: Vintage Books.

Jung, Tobias, T. Scott, H. T. Davies, P. Bower, D. Whalley, R. McNally and R. Mannion (2009), 'Instruments for exploring organizational culture: A review of the literature', *Public Administration Review*, **69**(6), 1087–96.

Kempster, Steve, M. Higgs and T. Wuerz (2014), 'Pilots for change: Exploring organisational change through distributed leadership', *Leadership and Organization Development Journal*, **35** (2), 152–67.

Killett, Anne, D. Burns, F. Kelly, D. Brooker, A. Bowes, J. La Fontaine … and M. O'Neill (2016), 'Digging deep: How organisational culture affects care home residents' experiences', *Ageing and Society*, **36** (1), 160–88.

Kilman, Ralph H., M. J. Saxton and R. Serpa (1985), 'Introduction: Five key issues in understanding and changing culture', in Ralph H. Kilman, M. J. Saxton and R. Serpa (eds), *Gaining Control of the Corporate Culture*, San Francisco, CA: Jossey-Bass, pp. 1–16.

Langan-Fox, Janice and P. Tan (1997), 'Images of culture in transition: Personal constructs of organizational stability and change', *Journal of Occupational and Organizational Psychology*, **70** (3), 273–95.

Maitlis, S. and T. B. Lawrence (2007), 'Triggers and enablers of sensegiving in organizations', *Academy of Management Journal*, **50** (1), 57–84.

Morgan, Gareth (1986), *Images of Organization*, London: Sage.

Nair, Rukmini B. (2002), *Narrative Gravity: Conversation, Cognition, Culture*, New York: Routledge.

Näslund, Lovisa and F. Pemer (2012), 'The appropriated language: Dominant stories as a source of organizational inertia', *Human Relations*, **65** (1), 89–110.

Nazarian, Alireza, P. Atkinson and P. Foroudi (2017), 'Influence of national culture and balanced organizational culture on the hotel industry's performance', *International Journal of Hospitality Management*, **63**, 22–32.

O'Neill, John (2002), 'The role of storytelling in affecting organizational reality in the strategic management process', *Journal of Behavioral and Applied Management*, **4** (1), 3–15.

Ogbonna, Emmanuel and L. C. Harris (2002), 'Organisational culture: A ten year, two-phase study of change in the UK food retailing sector', *Journal of Management Studies*, **39**, 673–706.

Ouchi, William G. and B. Pascale (1975), 'Organizational control: Two functions', *Administrative Science Quarterly*, **20** (4), 559–69.

Pedersen, Jesper S. and J. S. Sorensen (1989), *Organisational Cultures in Theory and Practice*, London: Gower Publishing.

Peirano-Vejo, M. E. and R.E. Stablein (2009), 'Constituting change and stability: Sense-making stories in a farming organization', *Organization*, **16** (3), 443–62.

Pettigrew, Andrew M. (1979), 'On studying organizational cultures', *Administrative Science Quarterly*, **24** (4), 570–81.

Poulton, Michael S. (2005), 'Organizational storytelling, ethics and morality: How stories frame limits of behavior in organizations', *Electronic Journal of Business Ethics and Organization Studies*, **10** (2), 4–9.

Quinn, Robert E. and J. Rohrbaugh (1983), 'A spatial model of effectiveness criteria: Towards a competing values approach to organizational analysis', *Management Science*, **29** (3), 363–77.

Ramachandran, Sharimllah Devi, S. C. Chong and H. Ismail (2011), 'Organizational culture: An exploratory study comparing faculty's perspectives within public and private universities in Malaysia', *International Journal of Educational Management*, **25** (6), 615–34.

Rappaport, Roy A. (1979), *Ecology, Meaning and Religion*, Berkeley, CA: North Atlantic Books.

Rappaport, Roy A. (1999), *Ritual and Religion in the Making of Humanity*, Cambridge: Cambridge University Press.

Reichers, Arnon E. and B. Schneider (1990), 'Climate and culture: An evolution of constructs', in Benjamin Schneider (ed.), *Organizational Climate and Culture*, San Francisco, CA: Jossey-Bass, pp. 5–39.

Schein, Edgar H. (1979), *Organizational Culture and Leadership*, San Francisco, CA: Jossey-Bass.

Schein, Edgar H. (1984), *Coming to a New Awareness of Organizational Culture*, San Francisco, CA: Jossey-Bass.

Schein, Edgar H. (1985), 'How culture forms, develops and changes', in Ralph H. Kilman, M. J. Saxton, R. Serpa and Associates (eds), *Gaining Control of the Corporate Culture*, San Francisco, CA: Jossey-Bass, pp. 17–43.

Schein, Edgar H. (1993), 'On dialogue, culture and organizational learning', *Organizational Dynamics*, **20**, 40–51.

Schein, Edgar H. (1997), *Organizational Culture and Leadership*, 3rd edition, San Francisco, CA: Jossey-Bass.

Scott, William R. (2001), *Institutions and Organizations*, 2nd edition, Thousand Oaks, CA: Sage.

Siehl, Caren and J. Martin (1990), 'Organizational culture: A key to financial performance?', in Benjamin Schneider (ed.), *Organizational Climate and Culture*, San Francisco, CA: Jossey-Bass, pp. 241–81.

Smith, Aaron C. T. and B. Stewart (2011), 'Organizational rituals: Features, functions and mechanisms', *International Journal of Management Reviews*, **13** (2), 113–33.

Subramanian, Nava and N. M. Ashkanasy (2001), 'The effect of organisational culture perceptions on the relationship between budgetary participation and managerial job-related outcomes', *Australian Journal of Management*, **26** (1), 35–54.

Suppiah, Visvalingam and M. S. Sandhu (2011), 'Organisational culture's influence on tacit knowledge-sharing behaviour', *Journal of Knowledge Management*, **15** (3), 462–77.

Swap, Walter, D. Leonard, M. Shields and L. Abrams (2001), 'Using mentoring and storytelling to transfer knowledge in the workplace', *Journal of Management Information Systems*, **18** (1), 95–114.

Trice, Harrison M. and J. M. Beyer (1984), 'Studying organizational cultures through rites and ceremonials', *Academy of Management Review*, **9** (4), 653–69.

Turner, N., J. Swart and H. Maylor (2012), 'Mechanisms for managing ambidexterity: A review and research agenda', *International Journal of Management Reviews*, **15** (3), 317–32.

Turner, Victor W. (1969), *The Ritual Process: Structure and Anti-Structure*, Chicago, IL: University of Chicago Press.

Tyler, Jo A. (2006), 'Storytelling and organizations: Introduction to the special issue', *Storytelling, Self, Society*, **2** (2), 1–4.

Tylor, E. B. (1871), *Primitive Culture*, London: John Murray.

Van der Post, W. Z. and T. J. de Coning (1997), 'An instrument to measure organizational culture', *South African Journal of Business Management*, **28** (4), 147–69.

van Hulst, Merlijn and S. Ybema (2020), 'From what to where: A setting-sensitive approach to organizational storytelling', *Organization Studies*, **41** (3), 365–91.

Weick, Karl E. (1995), *Sensemaking in Organizations*, London: Sage.

Weick, Karl E., K. M. Sutcliffe and D. Obstfeld (2005), 'Organizing and the process of sensemaking', *Organization Science*, **16** (4), 409–21.

Whelan, Chad (2016), 'Organisational culture and cultural change: A network perspective', *Australian and New Zealand Journal of Criminology*, **49** (4), 583–99.

Wilson, Antoinette Ophelia (2019), 'The role of storytelling in navigating through the storm of change', *Journal of Organizational Change Management*, **32** (3), 385–95.

11. The critical philosophy: 'changing realities'

INTRODUCTION

According to commentators such as Drucker (1989) and Harvey (1989), the Western, capitalist world underwent a transformative shift in cultural mood and economic expectations during the 1970s. That a change transpired in one way or another seems relatively uncontentious, but the nature of the change, its content and implications, fuel ongoing debate. For some, the change skimmed the surface, characterized by a rise in fads, fashions, advertising and shallow spectacle, while for others the changes foreshadowed a pervasive new force that undermined the search for universal truth and meaning (Huysens, 1984). Accepting transformative change as a social constant, the critical philosophy of organizational change consistently challenges conventional ways of thinking, from ideas about power and politics to constructions of social reality. We use the critical philosophy as an umbrella to encompass those change theories that seek to contradict and confront.

Notwithstanding the continuing arguments about exactly how Western society changed, some consistency appeared about the kinds of cultural and commercial issues making headlines. One obvious area focused on the way so-called conventional boundaries of thinking had been overthrown. The rules governing the ways things had always been done loosened almost to the point of chaos. For example, artists, designers, architects and intellectuals began experimenting with new concepts and ideas that not only challenged the traditional approaches, but discarded them altogether. It seemed as though society had become more than a complex assemblage of values and cultural imperatives. Instead, ambiguity and contradiction were the new norm, and assumptions about absolute truth, meaning and value became reclassified as individual issues. Cultural universality began to give way to cultural relativism.

At the same time, organizations started to soften their management philosophies and sought to capitalize on changing patterns of consumption (Firat, Dholakia and Vinkatesh, 1995). The 'postmodern' organization emerged (Bergquist, 1993), which established a newfound emphasis on more fluid and customized ways of delivering products to consumers, in response to the growing disfavour with bureaucracy and homogenized, mass production. The business world tested the boundaries of culture and commerce. Art, sport, literature, film and tourism all blurred into a synthesis of entertainment-driven capitalism where nothing was sacred and everything became a legitimate vehicle for making money. The literature of the 1980s and 1990s included a feast of commentary about the shameless rise of the post-industrial postmodern age (Crook, Pakulski and Waters, 1992; Jameson, 1991).

Ideas about organizational change were substantially influenced by the emergence of the postmodern era. Popular but conventional rational, systems and cultural philosophies of organizational change became the subjects of severe criticism. Like contingency approaches, the postmodern view rejects singular or grand theories. However, the postmodern view differs considerably in that it insists that change functions as a socially constructed view of reality contributed by multiple players (Buchanan, 2003). Organizational change can therefore be considered no more than unfolding the linguistic processes that construct meaning and inform management practice. If change remains subservient to the social realities of players, then innumerable legitimate views exist about what constitutes the right kind of changes and how they should be introduced. As a result, a moderate interpretation of the postmodern change approach remains comfortable with ephemerality, fragmentation, discontinuity and chaos, but also seeks to act rationally towards ongoing improvement (White and Jacques, 1995).

We shall deal with this postmodern aspect of the critical change philosophy in the early part of the chapter. A more radical view of postmodernism introduces notions of power and politics, following a line more consistent with the social theory emanating from Marx and Foucault. Trends in changing modern working environments sold as liberating for employees, such as flexible working, can actually be considered surveillance mechanisms that reinforce hegemony between employers and employees. We shall venture into this area in the latter part of the chapter. An instructive beginning, however, sets the scene with a brief overview of that which is being challenged—modernism.

CHANGE MANAGEMENT IN A CHANGING WORLD

Nothing about postmodernism makes sense until viewed with reference to its departure from modernism (Brown, 1995). Most commentators agree that modernization emerged from the Age of Discovery associated with fifteenth-century Europe, culminating in the scientific and commercial progress of the Enlightenment several centuries later (Lyon, 1994; Ruccio, 1991). The feudal and religious conventions that had overlorded decision making for centuries succumbed to a rapid process in industrial development, international trade, urbanization and bureaucratic governance (Spencer, 1998). It also introduced the need for more efficiency and specialization in the workforce. So was born the modern organization driven by a new dedication to mechanistic specialization and the production of homogenized commodities.

Galbraith's (1969) seminal book on the new industrial state described the function of these 'techno-structures' in terms of managing demand. A centralist corporate planning system sat at the heart of management activities. Organizational change revolved around the maximization of productivity, spurred by the fervent assumption that material progress accompanied getting things done faster, cheaper and with economies of scale (Grant, 1998). Management 'Taylorism' aimed to remove the uncertainty and chaos from the equation. Organizational change held no place for human irrationality; the way forward fell to reason, logic, stability and certainty, while a watchful eye cast over all those who might undermine progress by introducing unnecessary and destructive creativity, or worse, insist that monopoly capital exploited social relations (Mannheim, 1936).

Organizational change fell subject to the complete authority of senior managers for whom regulated markets exemplified progress. Change managers constrained themselves to the pursuit of rationality and order. Standardization and uniformity drove objectives (Brown, 1992), underpinned by a powerful conviction that change should deliver certainty and stability, which would in turn deliver uninterrupted prosperity. But then, the world changed, and certainty evaporated along with the success of Taylorism.

The post-war boom of the 1950s and early 1960s inevitably gave way to a series of economic crises and a new kind of boom, this time in social permissiveness and a powerful counter-culture movement. Taylorism faltered and the Keynesian model of economic structure came under pressure. With the Organization of the Petroleum Exporting Countries oil crisis of 1973, where the price of oil quadrupled followed by rampant unemployment and inflation, accompanied by a growing chorus of anti-capitalist sentiment echoed through political activism, unionism and anarchism, it became clear that the environmental stability that had characterized the modern period was being replaced by a new, more turbulent economic and social context (Johnson, 1983). Regulation acceded to free markets. Globalization and cultural diaspora rallied against technical-bureaucratic rationality. And, for the first time, the leaders and senior managers in all forms of enterprise were faced with the imperative to change. In fact, change became an ever present demand in the quest to accommodate a market that was not only morphing, but demanding a voice in the development and delivery of new products and services.

THE POSTMODERN EXPERIMENT

Businesses began to experiment with novel structures and systems, sometimes including lower-level employees in the decision-making process. Perhaps, most importantly, organizational leaders started to recognize that satisfied employees were productive and creative. In order to meet the needs of increasingly fickle consumers, organizations started to employ post-Fordist structures emphasizing flexible specialization where innovation played a key part of the change agenda (Piore and Sobel, 1984; Hirst and Zeitlan, 1991). The custom-built product emerged and it required a flexible and talented workforce. Market segmentation arrived as well, and in the space of little more than a decade, the consumer had gone from being an amorphous and distant figure to a customer with individual needs and a unique profile. The services economy increased exponentially at the same time as marketers found new leadership roles at the expense of engineers.

Change managers encountered unforeseen problems during this period of radical change. With the increased significance of services, the timescale of delivery had become immediate. Tangible products were being subsumed by fleeting experiences, and change managers had to find ways of ensuring that disposable services were worth paying for again and again. But the challenge expanded beyond dealing with a transition in the methods of production and delivery. Social expectations had changed as well. Increasingly, consumers seemed prepared to dispose of inconsequential products and experiences, and displayed less connection to rigid ideas about values, lifestyles and people. For postmodern change management theorists, the changing attitudes to material culture indicated the need for a different perspective on some fundamental issues in organizations. No longer would anything stand the test of time or deliver universal application. Values and truth no longer held sway as insolvent social elements. In fact, the forceful escalation in marketing and advertising showed that consumers' appetites could be manipulated by the right images and ideas.

At the same time, organizational leaders realized that their workforces were equally susceptible to symbolic imagery and galvanizing slogans. Companies like Coca-Cola and Nike forged the foundations of life-long consumption habits by changing their ideology from selling to branding. No markets seemed off limits. In the postmodern world, everything including sex, religion, art, music and ideas possessed a market value. It is perhaps no surprise then that organizations designed to protect against marketization, such as student unions, themselves adopted consumerism to survive (Brooks, Byford and Sela, 2016). Change managers were charged with navigating a volatile and fast-moving world of consumerism.

THE RISE OF THE CONSUMER

The growth of consumerism had three implications for organizational change, all of which proved pivotal to the postmodern approach. First, the substitution of essential, standardized products for a pluralistic array of unnecessary products and services meant that organizations purveyed personal identity as much as daily needs. The consumer and the consumed connected in a way far more pervasive and powerful than a simple exchange of money for products or services. Brands commanded emotional meaning, which meant that organizational leaders held custodianship of a workforce capable of not only generating immediate economic value, but also immense, long-term loyalty. Change had to be sensitive to the value woven into the fabric of organizations and collectively wielded by employees who could either deliver tremendous success or catastrophic ruination. Overly mechanistic models of change management that dealt with the workforce as a single, undifferentiated group no longer performed acceptably.

Second, with the experience economy came a reduced distance between perceptions of high and low culture. Traditional cultural priorities were undermined by the denial of universal value and a preference for cultural relativism. Art was not different to sport, and popular music was just as good as classical. An absence of meaning and value hierarchies became an essential tune in the postmodern change theorist's song-sheet. If consumers could have anything they liked, then so could employees. The search for personal meaning and identity through work emerged as another variable that the postmodern-savvy change agent had to consider. Work no longer simply put bread on the table. Rather, work represented a key to personal satisfaction, and good employees exercised free agency, taking their services to more ideologically rewarding companies.

Third, the world seen through the postmodern lens was packed with sensory stimulation and a fluid combination of reality, simulation and fantasy. So-called hyper-reality replaced authenticity as a key feature of entertainment in a 'Disneyfied' realm of consumption, where the only certainty came in the form of shameless marketing. The reconstructed experience exceeded the original. In fact, French postmodern theorist Jean Baudrillard claimed that the simulation of reality was more real than reality itself. For the change agent operating under the postmodern philosophy, the manipulation of reality represented both an opportunity and an ever present danger, because the content and method of change communication impacted radically on its effect. From this launching point of postmodern thinking, change theorists ventured into 'discourse' analysis as a way of understanding the implications of communication. We examine this stream of change later in the chapter.

THE POSTMODERN CHANGE AGENT

The postmodern approach to change is less concerned with overarching, grand theories describing social behaviour, and more interested in the indeterminacy, ambiguity and contradiction of organizational life. Contradictions can manifest discursively as dilemmas, conflicts, critical conflicts and double binds, all with separate implications for change managers (Engeström and Sannino, 2011). For a change agent, rejecting conformity and certainty in exchange for paradox and doubt (Cooper and Gibson, 1989) introduces a range of new challenges. The textbook postmodernist accepts the changing face of capitalism, and feels comfortable with the superficial and crass juxtaposed against the traditional and revered. Of course, such a perspective provides little guidance about the best way to introduce organizational change. The postmodern rejection of rigid processes characterizes its philosophical position. However, for most post-modern thinkers, organizational change will never work if it conforms to the uptight demands of rationalist leaders seeking to impose corporate objectives and performance measures. However, some principles can be advantageously wielded by the judicious, postmodern-sympathetic change agent who wishes to translate some esoteric ideas into the real world.

To begin with, a postmodern change manager does not seek to standardize the workforce or throw slogans at underperforming employees until they perform or leave. From a postmodern perspective, this is why standard organizational managerial practices developed under a Western philosophy do not translate effectively into other, non-Western management contexts with their own distinct cultures (Nwagbara, 2011). The postmodern view permissively accepts novel ways of approaching change, reticent to declare one approach more valuable than another. Notwithstanding the obvious predicament that a completely permissive change manager can find him or herself in, cultivating innovative thinking by deconstructing barriers and removing traditional impediments to change can offer advantages. Part of the postmodern way of thinking about change can be encapsulated in the concept of pastiche.

THE PASTICHE AS A CHANGE LEVER

Practising pastiche requires the fusion of opposites into a new form. As it evolved in popular culture, pastiche involved juxtaposing clashing ideas or symbols until they took a novel life of their own as something new and original, rather than a compromise or something in the middle. The use of pastiche found a home in the arts, proliferating in music and architecture, as well as in marketing. Baudrillard described something similar to the pastiche in his use of the term 'implosion'. For him it represented the conflation of opposites into a fused category or experience. Although pastiche is not exactly a word thrown around by many change managers, the fundamental idea behind it has made an impact on the organizational world beyond imaginative advertising campaigns. For change managers, pastiche means experimenting with a unique combination of products, structures and values in a way that traditional, conservative change methods would never accommodate. Organizational 'changing' (i.e. organizations conceptualized as emerging processes) is therefore a discursive process as employees constantly vie to give new practices meaning (Jian, 2011). In a similar way, companies like Google and Apple have embedded constant change into their cultures, coming to terms with a certain degree of uncertainty and instability as a consequence.

The problem with pastiche—and all principles of postmodernism for that matter—comes in its commitment that no rules guide change because change itself simultaneously functions as the journey and destination. After all, postmodernism rejects the modern imperative of control and continuity. As the organizational world became turbulent and uncertain, the modernist's natural inclination led to working even harder at control. The result took the form of complex variations on the rationalist philosophy. As we have shown, change theorists started to see organizations as systems, organisms, cultures and minds, for example, in an attempt to find better ways of bringing change to a constantly shifting landscape. Order was restored by changing the way leaders and managers thought about their organizations, which led to more subtle methods of intervening and counteracting the deleterious impact of an indeterminate external environment. In contrast, postmodern change theory takes a different approach where the 'chaotic currents of change' (Harvey, 1989, p. 44) represent the only certainty. Rather than finding better metaphors and models for understanding organizations, the postmodern approach looks for better ways of dealing with change itself. Rather than trying to counter change, the key lies in embracing it, because there can be nothing more certain than the obliteration of the past.

Taking a postmodern change approach can also help to assuage the mayhem of fickle markets. McLuhan's (1962) term 'global village' was appropriated by postmodern writers as a way of expressing the contradiction of competing in a bigger pond at the same time as being better connected to any part of it. Exemplified by the explosion of the internet, the notion of the global village has been seized by postmodernists as evidence that organizational change should mirror the fluidity of the world in which organizations operate. However, fragmentation of this nature seems to be an unwise way to manage an organization seeking to achieve harmonized goals and realize profits. As a result, while the postmodern ideal waxes lyrical about pastiche and paradox, real-world leaders stay obsessed with performance and profit. There may be some useful lessons in creating a working environment in which employees can experiment, innovate and even get caught up in a kind of hyper-reality, but inevitably, some modernist thoughts about getting things done will surface. Postmodern theory evolved in numerous directions in an attempt to tease out more tangible ideas. For our purposes, the most pertinent developments intersect at the confluence of social and political theories of organizations, where conflict, power, knowledge and discourse drive change management.

POLITICS, POWER AND CHANGE

The social theories of Marx and Hegel injected a different spin on organizations, emphasizing their political dimensions as change forces. For political theorists, change management means pursuing power through political means. Sometimes referred to as the dialectical model (Van de Ven and Poole, 1995), political explanations of change describe clashing ideologies or belief systems (Morgan, 1986). Conflict signifies the most important variable driving change. As a result, introducing a political dimension means assuming that clashing political forces will lead to change. Dialectical management actively harnesses organizational conflict to find creative solutions (Seal and Mattimoe, 2014). When one group with a political agenda gradually gains power, they challenge the status quo in the hopes of shifting the organization towards their own interests. The concept of organizational politics rests on the notion that change can elicit internal conflict that potentially leads to both positive and negative outcomes, depending on the skills of managers (Cacciattolo, 2015). Change processes inevitably revolve around activities such as bargaining, consciousness raising, persuasion, influence and power, and social movements (Bolman and Deal, 1991). Ideology stimulates dissention about the existing organizational composition, and political manoeuvring, manipulation and conflict guide the resolution. Victory goes to the most powerful group.

Some organizational theorists focus on power, having drifted away from the Marxist interpretation that emphasized the exploitative ownership of productive capital, in favour of an approach inspired by Foucault. For those studying organizational change, Foucault's ideas stimulated a novel way of looking at how and why change occurs. Known as discursive analysis, change arrives through 'discourse' within organizations, and its application has triggered significant debate and contention (Alvesson and Karreman, 2000; Hardy, Palmer and Phillips, 2000).

Discursive, or discourse, analysis concerns the ways language helps to reveal social phenomena (Clegg, Courpasson and Phillips, 2006; Grant, Hardy, Oswick and Putman, 2004). Discourse analysis fits as a sub-set of the critical philosophy due to the importance it places on the analysis of organizations and their members as social units that compete for power and ideological priority. As we shall see, the discourse approach shares an implementation challenge with the postmodern outlook. Both have plenty to say about change, but less to say about how change should be introduced in practice. Extreme versions of both discourse and postmodern interpretations take an anti-theoretical position in that they resist generalization and categorization to the point that little tangible advice about change management can be elicited.

The term 'discourse' refers to conversation or dialogue. Discursive analysis begins with the premise that language—whether written, spoken, heard or read—plays an active role in creating the social worlds that organizational members inhabit. Some theorists like Oswick, Keenoy and Grant (2000) argued that in addition to language, other forms of representation may be considered kinds of discourse, such as art, music and architecture. Accordingly, the systems of representation employed within an organization create the social world in which change transpires or stalls. In fact, most discourse theorists suggest that reality itself is a social construction laid down by the discourses in operation. Although other philosophical approaches to organizational change privilege meaning, discursive approaches to change actually attempt to explain the construction of new meanings underpinning change (Phillips and Oswick, 2012).

Like assumptions within postmodern theory, every individual holds a different perception of their own organization. Also common with postmodernism, discourse theory discards universal ways of looking at organizations, change and reality in general. Instead, every individual possesses a unique set of perceptions built up over time as a consequence of their unique experiences. To the discourse theorist, this uniquely constructed social reality arrives via discourse with other organizational members. To the change manager adopting a discourse perspective, 'Change requires a type of conversation that challenges taken-for-granted understandings, while enabling productive conflicts to reshape the meanings guiding organizational life' (McClellan, 2011, p. 477). To make sense of how the idea of a constructed social reality through discourse influences thinking about organizational change, we need to go back to the contribution made by Michel Foucault. We shall then return to the role of discourse thinking in the critical philosophy of change.

THE FOUCAULDIAN VIEW

French social theorist, Michel Foucault, explored the relationship between power, knowledge and discourse. He claimed that power and knowledge intertwine, but are mediated by discourse. Every organizational member possesses a unique mental model about the way things work and what changes need to occur. As a result, individuals possess 'knowledge' about what reality encompasses. At an organizational level, knowledge includes common ideas about mission, vision, objectives, appropriate conduct, instructions and rules, and who holds responsibility for certain duties.

Change theorists adopting the Foucauldian style of interpretation claim that each organization uniquely produces and reproduces knowledge through what is written, spoken, heard and read. The key to organizational change therefore lies in interpreting written documents (such as mission statements, strategic plans, email correspondence, reports and press releases to name a few) and verbal interactions (including speeches, casual 'talk', meetings, interviews and phone calls). These forms of discourse collectively represent an organizational truth or reality influencing how power is acquired and discharged. For example, Fairclough (1995) argued that parties with the power to control discourse—its production, distribution and consumption—also maintain the power to uphold certain ideologies and enforce change despite resistance.

To Foucault (1982; Foucault and Gordon, 1980), the exercise of power through the control of discourse underpins the ability to introduce change. For example, the simple application of a new policy in an organization will affect the behaviour of employees. Furthermore, when groups of policies and other organizational discourses, such as strategic plans containing objectives and performance measures, or the speeches of leaders, are aggregated, the social reality of a workplace changes. In fact, the processes that created the existing social reality may have been long forgotten, having been unspoken for some time. Social reality is habitual, routinized and familiar. Covert forms of power can also become virtually unrecognizable because its mechanisms have subtly embedded in the way organizational members see themselves and the roles that they play.

Foucault (1982) assumed that power can be wielded directly when a manager shapes an employee's role through domination. For the discourse change theorist, organizational members are players on stage, reading scripts that they did not write, and being directed by managers who do not permit anyone else to interpret scenes. Conventional treatments of power look for overt expressions, such as confrontations or directives. Discourse analysis takes a more liberal view where power manifests as an ever present script-prompter hovering in the stage wings. Power operates most of the time through the delimitation of behavioural choices. Not only can correct and incorrect behaviours be specified, but normal and right actions funnel to a limited choice. Organizational leaders and change agents do not own or possess power; rather, they apply power.

Although it might sound subtle, accepting the idea that power is not owned but exercised has a substantial effect on change management approaches. To begin with, change agents and leaders do not automatically possess power; they must acquire or assume it. Having the positional authority to introduce a change is not the same as wielding the power to make it happen. For

Foucault, and discourse theorists after him, the fluid movement of power directly contrasts with Marxist averments that power can only be held by those with the ownership of productive means. Where Marx thought that power resides with control of economic resources, Foucault saw power as far more ubiquitous, existing in the relationships between people.

To the discourse change theorist, the relationships between people in organizations legitimize an imbalance of power, supported tangibly through systems that facilitate the subordination of one over another. While the systems tend to be formal as determined by such factors as legislation, status, economic factors, hierarchical configurations, imbalances in skill, cultural or language differences, and customs, they can also operate unconsciously, giving 'permission' for one party to act upon others: 'it incites, it induces, it seduces, it makes easier or more difficult; in the extreme it constrains or forbids absolutely' (Foucault, 1982, p. 220). Where Marx saw power as repressive—something which restricts what people can do—Foucault thought it could also be permissive and productive, encouraging people to behave in novel ways (Clegg et al., 2006).

CONTROLLING ORGANIZATIONAL CHANGE

From the late 1980s onwards, a second generation of Foucault-inspired work appeared, drawing on a series of essays on what was called 'governmentality' (e.g. Foucault, 1991; Miller, 1990; Miller and Rose, 1990; Rose, 1991). The common threads drawn from these authors indicated that Foucault's theories of governmentality centred on: (1) a conception of power operating at multiple points throughout the social network; (2) a conception of the management of populations as central to the task of government; and (3) a conception of continuous surveillance as a means of control. Collectively, these three principles carry decisive implications for the critical philosophy because they shape the way that power is understood as a mechanism to enact change. In the modern working environment, societal change promoting employee empowerment has been accompanied by increased employee responsibility, serving as a form of surveillance to maintain power relations.

As we noted earlier, issues of power are pivotal in understanding Foucault's theory of governmentality. For Foucault (1979, p. 93), 'power is everywhere', but can be hidden in the discursive practices of organizations. Power in this context, however, is always shifting and inherently unstable, as discursive expression is subject to the changing networks and alliances forged through a desire for similar organizational outcomes (Clegg, 1989). As a result, discursive communications between organizational stakeholders lead to the positioning and repositioning of stakeholders, and demonstrates how the relative and changing nature of power comes to manifest itself in certain components of the organization. Further, the key expression of power in the change process arrives via management. The process of management to achieve desired ends is central to the notion of governmentality, wherein management devises policy as an instrument of control.

Management through policy remains a feature of all kinds of organizational change. If the main task of leaders is the management of the organization and its members through policies, it follows that an analysis of the policies should reveal the ways in which leaders enact change. For example, in healthcare settings, policies that decentralize power to workers are accompanied by policies that increase 'accountability upwards', such as work-quality assessments, changing responsibility rather than power (Ferlie, Mcgivern and FitzGerald, 2012). Miller and Rose (1990, p. 3) proposed that governmentality can offer insights into the ways in which organizational policies work to render 'aspects of existence thinkable and calculable, and amenable to deliberated and planful initiatives'. Policy can be seen as a tool for directing organizational change.

GOVERNMENTALITY AND THE PANOPTICON

Policy development within organizations reveals how 'authorities of various sorts have sought to shape, normalise and instrumentalise the conduct, thought, decisions and aspirations of others in order to achieve the objectives they consider desirable' (Miller and Rose, 1990, p. 8). From this perspective, it is possible to view policies as part of the technology of governmentality; that is, the way policies are designed to determine the type, direction and desired outcomes of organizational change.

Governmentality theory fits with the idea of a 'panopticon', as the former assumes the presence of continuous surveillance. Foucault used the metaphor of the panopticon to characterize and describe the technology of control. The idea of a panopticon came from Jeremy Bentham's design for a prison. It comprises an annular building surrounding a central tower. The panopticon itself is an apparatus for the continual, one-directional observation of those in custody, with the intention that the incarcerated should eventually come to internalize the watching eye as being ever present, and thus regulate their own conduct without need for further coercion.

A panopticon is designed so that its prisoners inhabit small cells built on the perimeter of a circular building, with an observation tower at the centre. The cells have windows on both the inner and outer walls of the ring, so that their every movement is in view. Conversely, the tower stays in darkness so that the observers are hidden. The regime aimed towards reform so that the prisoner's sentence depends not on a fixed retributive scale but on the degree of penitence and personal change perceived by the prison governor (or his or her representatives, as the prisoners would never know the difference). The inmates, unable to tell when they were being watched, would have to continuously behave as reformed characters in order to have the best chance of early release. It was believed that being forced to behave in this way would lead the prisoner to repent and become fit to be released back into society.

Although Bentham's design was intended to be taken literally as a form of prison, the panopticon has since been interpreted as a metaphor for the power of control by scrutiny, and for the internalization and normalization of control mechanisms. More important than surveillance by the supervisor, however, is the development of self-surveillance by the prisoners themselves, and the acceptance of the naturalness of the self-surveillance. As Foucault (1979) observed, the panopticon induces 'a state of conscious and permanent visibility that assures the automatic functioning of power' (p. 201). Ultimately, the external application of surveillance becomes unnecessary as an individual 'inscribes in himself the power relation in which he simultaneously plays both roles, he becomes the principal of his own subjection' (p. 202). It is cheaper and more efficient if employees can be convinced to police themselves than to pay supervisors to crack the whip. Surveillance thus becomes a technique for self-control or self-discipline. When this aspect of Foucault's work is applied to organizational change, where policies stand in for self-surveillance, the panoptic quality looms large.

CHANGE AS POWER

As a technology of power, management operates like the panopticon both providing techniques for surveillance and requiring the internalization and naturalization of certain 'truths'. Furthermore, according to Ball (1990), it offers 'a system of normalisation, whereby a resister is normalised through coercive or therapeutic means' (p. 158). This form of regulatory control is therefore not just imposed from the outside but is threaded through the organization in the everyday work that members perform. Foucault (Foucault and Gordon, 1980) described such control methods as a capillary form of power, 'which reaches into the very grain of individuals' synaptic regime of power, a regime of its exercise within the social body, rather than from above it' (p. 39). For example, a study of organizational change in an Italian car manufacturing plant demonstrated how change sold as enabling worker flexibility and autonomy served as an 'electric panopticon' to reinforce control over employees (Iacono, De Nito, Martinez and Mercurio, 2017). Foucault emphasized that when normalization is combined with the exercise of surveillance, it assists in reducing inconsistent organizational performance through the creation of a one-dimensional indicator for the desired outcomes of the change process—the strategic plan. Later management theorists picked up on the panoptic nature of change. For example, Considine (1988) argued that corporate management represents a shift in the technologies of power within organizations, rather than major paradigm shifts. He suggested that one of the effects of corporate management is that it tightens the control function that leaders and senior managers wield.

While current policy formulation and implementation can be seen as expressions of governmentality, this does not necessarily mean that policy directions and intentions are unable to be challenged, or unable to be reinterpreted. Although the written texts of policy may not change over time, their interpretation and re-creation are constantly shifting. According to Derrida's (1982) mode of 'deconstruction', when organizational members begin to decipher a policy document it is the interpretation of the text that proves instrumental in justifying their understanding of it. These differing interpretations of policy documents can be used to expose the reasons why organizational change outcomes can contradict those suggested in the policy documents. Moreover, it provides an understanding of why the actions of certain sub-units may not be consistent with the desired strategic direction of the organization's senior management.

Readers of policy documents—organizational members—allow their own biases to influence their interpretations, changing its nature and therefore their own responses. As a consequence, although policy documents are designed to provide a framework for compliance, they might actually lead to resistance. In addition, lower-level management may choose to follow a certain organizational direction that supports their own interpretation of the text within the policy documents. For this reason, later critical philosophy theorists started to see the value of studying organizational change primarily from a language or 'discourse' perspective.

DISCOURSE AND CHANGE

Most discourse change theorists commit to the assumption that reality is a social construction (Clegg, 2005). A starting point for change acknowledges that how individuals make sense of things determines their reality. As we introduced at the end of Chapter 10, when confronted with jolts that challenge taken-for-granted routines, such as an employee confronted with new work responsibilities due to organizational change, they must engage in sense making (Maitlis and Christianson, 2014). If their sense making changes, so does their reality. As a result, organizational change transpires when members change their sense of the organizational situation. In turn, sense making change necessitates an understanding of how individuals make sense of their organization, including its objectives and problems.

Sense making in an organization involves three dimensions: history, power and imagination (Clegg, 2005). The first dimension, history, refers to the way the rules for interpreting meaning were established in the past and have been maintained through tradition. This part of discourse thinking strongly connects to the cultural philosophy in that both acknowledge the seminal importance of the way things have been done in the past.

The second dimension affecting sense making is power. Traditions persevere through reinforcement, reproduction and practice, which requires the application of power through choices about communication content and delivery. The perceived 'fundamentals' in conservative disciplines, such as finance, are one example of how change is stifled through communication of tradition (Gendron and Smith-Lacroix, 2015).

Imagination constitutes the third dimension influencing sense making, referring to the capacity to envisage a difference; an essential ingredient in planned change. The imagination component provides direction. However, imagination cannot be equated with vision, which lies at the heart of the rational philosophy. Imagination is less about a change leader's vision, and more about how any given organizational member can see a positive result coming from a change programme.

To theorists such as Clegg, the three dimensions of sense making provide some tangible guidance about the circumstances under which organizational change transpires. Change is not inevitable. In fact, successful change only comes about when history, power and imagination all line up with an organization's contextual circumstances. Clegg summarized this idea elegantly when he commented that planned change occurs when the capacity to conceive a difference (imagination) meets the capacity to make a difference (power). Unplanned change occurs when context meets imagination. Organizational context can be understood as the conditions or circumstances of operation, including external factors, such as the global and national situation, the nature of the industry, culture, legislation and so on, as well as the internal setting, such as the employees, processes and structures. Changes stimulated by context may therefore come from external or internal sources.

Accepting a change management relationship incorporating power, history and imagination leads to a new interpretation of both power and resistance, both of which have tended to be seen in a negative light as obstructers of change. A discourse approach suggests that in order to leverage imaginative change, organizational members need to be able to reflect on how power functions in their organization. Allocentrism captures an employee's ability to recognize that their power over change is dependent on the actions of others as well as their own, and this will shape sense making in response to organizational change (Lockett, Currie, Finn, Martin and Waring, 2014). Most importantly, it leads members to envisage new ways of being and working in the organization. Equally, 'deeply embedded practices, sticky prior accounts, or top team attention that is focused on alternative issues' (Maitlis and Christianson, 2014, p. 91) can impede employees' ability to remedy change with their realities.

Power, when reconceptualized as a mobilizing force, frees imagination to tackle problems in novel ways, having shifted perceptions about boundaries and options. Foucault, however, clung to resistance as the best lens through which power can be understood. All organizations have power relations, and where power exists, so too does resistance.

Returning to a central axiom of discursive thinking, Ford, Ford and McNamara (2002) proposed that resistance is not found within individuals, but within their constructed realities, which have been challenged. Conventional models of resistance assume that all employees in an organization share a common reality, and therefore will react similarly about prospective change. From this perspective, the change agent need only determine the source of resistance and remove it in order to proceed with the change programme. From a discursive angle, employee emotions, such as resistance, emerge when confronted with change, and can be treated as social constructs (Bisel and Barge, 2011). However, if resistance represents a challenge to an individual's social construction of reality, then resistance must be a systemic and ever present phenomenon within all levels of organization. It must also be unique to each individual. Furthermore, as Butcher and Atkinson (2001) noted, language and communication shape organizational change because they influence perceptions of reality. In discourse between senior and middle management, the style of communicative practices can be the difference between the emergence of innovative change and stand-offs (Thomas, Sargent and Hardy, 2011). Once again, through the instrumental nature of language and communication, the discourse approach strikes a consonant note with the cultural philosophy tune.

CONCLUSION

The notion of postmodernism accompanied the transition from industrial to post-industrial society; from manufacturing and materials to knowledge and information. Postmodernism juxtaposes the old and new, characterized by a change management approach emphasizing diffusion, empowerment, flexibility, trust and market responsiveness (Clegg, 1992). However, the practical implementation of postmodern change ideas involves a refocusing of the social boundaries established in modernism, rather than a transcendence of them. Nevertheless, a pure view of postmodern thinking would implicitly reject universal management truths (Gephart, Thatchenkery and Boje, 1996), which in turn makes practical recommendations for change management interventions problematic. Identification of discursive paradoxes might be one starting place for the change manager utilizing a critical approach (Engeström and Sannino, 2011).

It would be presumptuous to talk of postmodernism as if it were one unified field of thought. It is, in fact, notoriously fragmented. Some proponents claim that postmodernism represents a departure from the modernist tendencies of mechanization, hierarchy and centralization, and therefore supports the decentralized, empowered, team-centred, network-based, flexible, technologically adept organization. Another interpretation of postmodern change management connects with the quest for novelty, innovation and better ways of doing things that do not necessarily fit with the past (De Cock, 1998). However, unlike the systems perspective that encourages best practice thinking, a postmodern analysis precludes the use of an overarching theoretical approach. For this reason, it tends to fall short as a popular tool for change, at best informing the way change agents think about their approaches, rather than specifying best practices for the successful implementation of change.

Discursive models of organizational change similarly discard the conventional pursuit of universal patterns of change management, and focus instead on the individual social construction of reality. In order to tackle these divergent social realities and the prospects of entrenched resistance, discursive models of change suggest that the background discourses in organizations— the ongoing conversations—need to be made transparent so that power relations can be examined. Of course, all of this seems a bit vague and uncertain for most leaders and managers involved in the day-to-day implementation of change. After all, who has time to consider the innumerable social realities that must exist within each organization? And, which leaders are prepared to spend their time bringing 'background discourses' out into the open where power can be scrutinized and change delayed in favour of reducing the challenges to employees' fragile social constructions of the world in which they work? Like all theories that fall under the critical philosophy, discourse analysis offers the critical contribution that change, power, conflict and imagination all intersect.

REFERENCES

Alvesson, Mats and D. Karreman (2000), 'Varieties of discourse: On the study of organizations through discourse analysis', *Human Relations*, **53** (9), 1125–49.
Ball, S. (1990), 'Management as moral technology: A Luddite analysis', in S. Ball (ed.), *Foucault and Education: Disciplines and Knowledge*, London: Routledge, pp. 153–66.
Bergquist, William H. (1993), *The Postmodern Organization: Mastering the Art of Irreversible Change*, San Francisco, CA: Jossey-Bass.
Bisel, Ryan S. and J. K. Barge (2011), 'Discursive positioning and planned change in organizations', *Human Relations*, **64** (2), 257–83.
Bolman, Lee G. and T. E. Deal (1991), *Reframing Organizations: Artistry, Choice, and Leadership*, San Francisco, CA: Jossey-Bass.
Brooks, Rachel, K. Byford and K. Sela (2016), 'Students' unions, consumerism and the neo-liberal university', *British Journal of Sociology of Education*, **37** (8), 1211–28.
Brown, Doug (1992), 'Institutionalism and the postmodern politics of social change', *Journal of Economic Issues*, **26** (2), 547–9.

Brown, Stephen (1995), *Postmodern Marketing*, London: Routledge.
Buchanan, David (2003), 'Getting the story straight: Illusions and delusions in the organizational change process', *Tamara: Journal of Critical Postmodern Organization Science*, **2** (4), 7–21.
Butcher, David and S. Atkinson (2001), 'Stealth, secrecy and subversion: The language of change', *Journal of Organizational Change Management*, **14** (6), 554–69.
Cacciattolo, Karen (2015), 'Organisational politics: The positive and negative sides', *European Scientific Journal*, **11** (1), 121–9.
Clegg, Stewart R. (1989), *Frameworks of Power*, London: Sage.
Clegg, Stewart R. (1992), 'Postmodern management?', *Journal of Organizational Change Management*, **5** (2), 31–49.
Clegg, Stewart R. (2005), 'The bounds of rationality: Power/history/imagination', *Critical Perspectives on Accounting*, **17** (7), 847–63.
Clegg, Stewart R., D. Courpasson and N. Phillips (2006), *Power and Organisations*, London: Sage.
Considine, M. (1988), 'The corporate management framework as administrative science: A critique', *Australian Journal of Public Administration*, **47** (1), 4–18.
Cooper, Robert and B. Gibson (1989), 'Modernism, postmodernism and organisational analysis: An introduction', *Organization Studies*, **9** (1), 94–9.
Crook, Stephen, J. Pakulski and M. Waters (1992), *Postmodernization: Change in Advanced Society*, London: Sage.
De Cock, Christian (1998), 'It seems to fill my head with ideas: A few thoughts on postmodernism, TQM and BPR', *Journal of Management Inquiry*, **7** (2), 144–53.
Derrida, J. (1982), *Margins of Philosophy*, trans. A. Bass, Chicago, IL: University of Chicago Press.
Drucker, Peter F. (1989), *The New Realities*, New York: Harper and Row.
Engeström, Yrjö and A. Sannino (2011), 'Discursive manifestations of contradictions in organizational change efforts', *Journal of Organizational Change Management*, **24**, 368–87.
Fairclough, Norman (1995), *Critical Discourse Analysis*, London: Longman.
Ferlie, Ewan, G. Mcgivern and L. FitzGerald (2012), 'A new mode of organizing in health care? Governmentality and managed networks in cancer services in England', *Social Science and Medicine*, **74** (3), 340–7.
Firat, A. Fuat, N. Dholakia and A. Vinkatesh (1995), 'Marketing in a postmodern world', *European Journal of Marketing*, **29** (1), 40–56.
Ford, Jeffrey D., L. W. Ford and R. T. McNamara (2002), 'Resistance and the background conversations of change', *Journal of Organizational Change*, **15** (2), 105–21.
Foucault, Michel (1979), *Discipline and Punish: The Birth of a Prison*, trans. A. Sheridan, New York: Vintage Books.
Foucault, Michel (1982), 'The subject and power', in Hubert L. Dreyfus, P. Rabinow and M. Foucault, *Michel Foucault, Beyond Structuralism and Hermeneutics*, Chicago, IL: University of Chicago Press, pp. 208–26.
Foucault, Michel (1991), 'Governmentality', in G. Burchell, C. Gordon and P. Miller (eds), *The Foucault Effect: Studies in Governmentality*, Hemel Hempstead: Wheatsheaf, pp. 87–104.
Foucault, Michel and C. Gordon (1980), *Power/Knowledge Selected Interviews and Other Writings 1972–1977*, New York: Pantheon.
Galbraith, J. K. (1969), *How to Control the Military*, New York: Doubleday.

Gendron, Yves and J. H. Smith-Lacroix (2015), 'The global financial crisis: Essay on the possibility of substantive change in the discipline of finance', *Critical Perspectives on Accounting*, **30**, 83–101.

Gephart, R. P., T. J. Thatchenkery and D. M. Boje (1996), 'Conclusion: Reconstructing organizations for future survival', in D. Boje, R. Gephart and T. Thatchenkery (eds), *Postmodern Management and Organization Theory*, Newbury Park, CA: Sage, pp. 358–64.

Grant, David, C. Hardy, C. Oswick and L. L. Putman (2004), *The Sage Handbook of Organizational Discourse*, London: Sage.

Grant, Ian H. (1998), 'Postmodernism and politics', in Stuart Sim (ed.), *Postmodern Thought*, Cambridge: Icon Books, p. 29.

Hardy, Cynthia, I. Palmer and N. Phillips (2000), 'Discourse as a strategic resource', *Human Relations*, **53** (9), 1227–48.

Harvey, David (1989), *The Condition of Postmodernity*, Oxford: Blackwell.

Hirst, Paul and J. Zeitlan (1991), 'Flexible specialisation versus post-Fordism', *Economy and Society*, **20** (1), 1–45.

Huysens, Andreas (1984), 'Mapping the postmodern', *New German Critique*, **Autumn** (3), 5–33.

Iacono, Mario P., E. De Nito, M. Martinez and R. Mercurio (2017), 'Exploring the hidden aspects of organizational change: The constellation of controls at a Fiat-Chrysler automotive plant', *Studi Organizzativi*, **2**, 69–89.

Jameson, Fredric (1991), *Postmodernism: The Cultural Logic of Late Capitalism*, London: Verso.

Jian, Guowei (2011), 'Articulating circumstance, identity and practice: Toward a discursive framework of organizational changing', *Organization*, **18** (1), 45–64.

Johnson, Paul (1983), *A History of the Modern World: From 1917 to the 1980s*, London: Weidenfeld and Nicholson.

Lockett, Andy, G. Currie, R. Finn, G. Martin and J. Waring (2014), 'The influence of social position on sensemaking about organizational change', *Academy of Management Journal*, **57** (4), 1102–29.

Lyon, David (1994), *Postmodernity*, Buckingham: Open University Press.

Maitlis, Sally and M. Christianson (2014), 'Sensemaking in organizations: Taking stock and moving forward', *Academy of Management Annals*, **8** (1), 57–125.

Mannheim, Karl (1936), *Ideology and Utopia*, New York: Harcourt Brace.

McClellan, John G. (2011), 'Reconsidering communication and the discursive politics of organizational change', *Journal of Change Management*, **11** (4), 465–80.

McLuhan, Marshall (1962), *The Gutenberg Galaxy: The Making of Typographic Man*, 1st edition, Toronto: University of Toronto Press.

Miller, P. (1990), 'On the interactions between accounting and the state', *Accounting Organisations and Society*, **15** (4), 315–38.

Miller, P. and N. Rose (1990), 'Governing economic life', *Economy and Society*, **19** (1), 1–31.

Morgan, Gareth (1986), *Images of Organization*, Newbury Park, CA: Sage.

Nwagbara, Uzoechi (2011), 'Leading a postmodern African organisation: Towards a model of prospective commitment', *Journal of Economics and Business*, **14** (2), 75–92.

Oswick, Cliff, T. Keenoy and D. Grant (2000), 'Discourse, organizations and organizing: Concepts, objects and subjects', *Human Relations*, **53** (9), 1115–23.

Phillips, Nelson and C. Oswick (2012), 'Organizational discourse: Domains, debates, and directions', *Academy of Management Annals*, **6** (1), 435–81.

Piore, Michael J. and C. F. Sobel (1984), *The Second Industrial Divide*, New York: Basic Books.

Rose, N. (1991), 'Governing by numbers: Figuring out democracy', *Accounting, Organisations and Society*, **16** (7), 673–92.

Ruccio, David F. (1991), 'Postmodernism and economics', *Journal of Post Keynesian Economics*, **13** (4), 499–500.

Seal, Will and R. Mattimoe (2014), 'Controlling strategy through dialectical management', *Management Accounting Research*, **25** (3), 230–43.

Spencer, Lloyd (1998), 'Postmodernism, modernity and the tradition of dissent', in Stuart Sim (ed.), *Postmodern Thought*, Cambridge: Icon Books, pp. 158–9.

Thomas, Robyn, L. D. Sargent and C. Hardy (2011), 'Managing organizational change: Negotiating meaning and power-resistance relations', *Organization Science*, **22** (1), 22–41.

Van de Ven, Andrew H. and M. S. Poole (1995), 'Explaining development and change in organizations', *Academy of Management Review*, **20** (3), 510–40.

White, Robert F. and R. Jacques (1995), 'Operationalizing the postmodernity construct for efficient organizational change management', *Journal of Organizational Change Management*, **8** (2), 45–71.

12. The innovation philosophy: 'changing ideas'

INTRODUCTION

A common cliché declares that we are living in 'new times' (Hall, 1996) and in 'new spaces' (Appadurai, 1996); that is, the shifting social and technical landscapes of the so-called global liquid modernity are bringing inexorable change (Bauman, 2004; Castells, 2000, Giddens, 2000). This period is characterized by: (1) rapid transformations in scientific and technological knowledge producing fast and continual social, economic and cultural changes; (2) high-speed flows of information, ideas, images, people and money across increasingly porous territorial borders as capitalism goes global; (3) identities increasingly produced by patterns of consumption rather than ascribed attributes of social class, ethnicity and gender; (4) the emergence and 'changing morphology' of new online and offline worlds; and (5) a merging of global and local ('glocal') as global flows of cultural products are reworked and reinscribed (cultural reconversion) into local settings (Robertson, 1995). All of these factors have produced, and continue to produce, irreversible changes in society. Indeed, some theorists question whether the term 'society' is still appropriate given the 'brittleness, breakability, ad hoc modality of inter-human bonds' (Bauman, 2004, p. 19), instead preferring the term 'liquid-modern sociality' to capture the transient nature of social frames that now guide global and life politics (Bauman, 2004). Whatever the terminology used to describe these 'new times', there is little doubt that we are all expected to negotiate multiple and diverse economic and social worlds. This chapter introduces a relatively new philosophy of organizational change that emphasizes the centrality of responding to the new time in new ways. Accordingly, innovation—or the capacity to create something new that can produce value—therefore constitutes an organization's best approach to bringing about successful change.

According to the innovation philosophy, in turbulent fields an organization's long-term survival and success has less to do with efficiency and productivity, and more to do with its ability to adapt and innovate. Organizations therefore need to improve their adaptive capacities and transform themselves in order to stay ahead of their competitors. Many organizations face intense pressures to innovate in order to meet customer requirements and produce radical product improvements that will capture significant market share. Change that facilitates innovation leads to the generation of new ideas and their implementation into new products and services, processes and procedures. This means that incremental change can be punctuated by periods of transformational change. Actual or anticipated disruption requires organizations to change fundamentally, and how it adapts will determine how best it will be able to deal with disruption (Day, 2020). Change through innovation provides an approach that allows organizations to react to market uncertainty and volatility in creative ways, develop new products and services and establish an organizational framework for the development of innovation. These elements are addressed in the forthcoming sections of this chapter.

LIQUID MODERNITY

Liquid modernity may signal the death of older forms of society, but new forms of sociality are being actively forged. In the shifting terrain of liquid modernity, flexibility, resilience and invention are required in abundance in order to cope (Harris, 2004). Arguably, the most pertinent issue confronting organizations is globalization. Piecing together the threads of the various definitions of globalization, it can be described as a process in which the world is becoming increasingly interconnected through a growing exchange across trade and the diffusion of culture. In turn, the interconnections have led to the emergence of a global economy that the world has become increasingly dependent upon. Further, it has led to the free movement of capital, goods and services (Giddens, 2000). As such, the process of globalization is disrupting the market as a greater cultural mix of populations means markets are no longer homogenous, but are culturally and socially heterogeneous. The philosophical assumption underpinning the approach is neoliberalism. Neoliberalism is rooted in the classical literal ideals of British philosophy such as Adam Smith (1723–90), David Ricardo (1772–1823) and Herbert Spencer (1820–1903). Neoliberalism constitutes an economic system and philosophy based on laissez-faire free market values, and the freedom of the globalized players within that market. It enshrines values of competition, entrepreneurialism, market participation, privatization, lack of state intervention, individual responsibility, surveillance, assessment, managerialism and innovation (Birch, 2017).

As societies and economies become more complex and interconnected, they start to assume the properties of organized complexity, becoming more unpredictable and turbulent. Organizational theorists coming from a range of different theoretical traditions have experienced difficulty in articulating coherent theoretical notions about turbulent fields. However, it is generally agreed that in turbulent fields, organizations are more likely to experience discontinuous and disruptive changes in their environments (Day, 2020). Disruptions may also be a consequence of new competitors in the market. Competitors that prove disruptive begin by successfully targeting overlooked segments, gaining a foothold by delivering a product or service that is acceptable to consumers, but at a lower price or a higher quality. Incumbents tend not to respond aggressively as they are servicing more demanding market segments that offer greater profitability. When new competitors decide to move into the up-market segment, and take a significant number of core customers away from the incumbent while preserving their existing market, disruption has occurred. The theory of disruption predicts that when a new competitor tackles an incumbent's competitor front on, offering better products or services, the incumbents will accelerate their innovations to protect their business. They will either challenge the new market competitor by offering better services or products at comparable prices, or one of them will seek to acquire the new competitor.

Disruptive change is therefore a non-localized, irreversible change that affects organizations, caused by transitions in market trends and demanding a shift in the mode of production to fit new customer demands. A good example of disruptive change was seen during the introduction of mobile phones when wired analogue phones were the standard. At first, mobile phones had poor sound quality and were expensive. As time passed, innovations to the mobile phones made them cheaper with improved sound quality, and as they were also portable, they eventually displaced the analogue phones. The disruption caused through innovation, coined 'disruptive innovation', fundamentally changes markets and customers. In this example, a few entrepreneurial companies started to refine and improve a product, but finally ended up reshaping the entire industry. Other examples include long-distance video calls (Skype), record stores (iTunes), local stores (eBay), taxis (Uber) and accommodation (Airbnb) (Lindmark and Meisner, 2016).

IDEATION AND CREATIVITY

Ideation is the process of forming ideas with others. Change through innovation is the result of planting seeds of new ideas, which then grow over time through contributions from multiple individuals and varying perspectives. Good ideas can also come from knowledge spillovers (Aghion and Jaravel, 2015), which take place through the interactions of individuals working for different organizations, and often different industries. An emphasis on interconnectivity provides a valuable rubric for facilitating idea creation internally within the organization, as well as through collaboration and knowledge exchange with individuals situated in the broader environment. An environment where ideation and creativity are encouraged generates the organizational context where the opportunity for value can be added. Opportunity can be measured by parameters such as the size of the market, the demand, or the market structure; parameters that differentiate an opportunity from an idea. Timmons and Spinelli (2007) argued that, 'the more imperfect the market the greater the opportunity. The greater the rate of change, the discontinuities, and the chaos, the greater is the opportunity' (p. 90). The opportunity therefore has a lot to do with gaps in the market, and changes in the environment in which the organization competes.

The next element is the 'resources', which can be defined as a procedure or a means to accomplish a task. Every idea needs an effective deployment of its resources so that it can be exploited into a tangible opportunity. Making the most of the opportunity requires having the right people working efficiently. An effective team is necessary for creating new market niches and opportunities. The degree to which the team actively participates in the creativity process will depend on a number of factors, such as the complexity of the organization, relevant expertise areas and the nature of the problem and solution required. While managing innovation requires a great deal of attention towards internal teams and group members, there should also be ample focus given to the external environment.

In order to change through innovation, change leaders need to learn from other organizations that have a higher dependence on creativity. Sherwood (2002) suggested that for organizations with lower levels, creativity needs to be introduced steadily over time. Creativity starts with input measures (most importantly, the number of people trained, and the amount of time devoted to idea generation and evaluation), then should encompass process measures (monitoring the flow through the idea pipeline) and, finally, should lead to output measures. By adopting a staged approach, organizations can reduce complexity and minimize the burden of new systems. As a result, they will be best placed to stimulate innovation through new, espoused behaviours and values.

THE CULTURAL LINK

Espoused values represent an organization's declared set of 'values norms'. These values affect how members interact and represent the organization (Schein, 2010). In this case, change managers are most interested in the values underpinning the innovation paradigm; the approach that organizational leaders or members take to identify innovative solutions to problems. The most important aspect of espoused values relates to the way they sculpt entrenched ways of thinking. From an innovation change perspective, some espoused values can transform into automatic behavioural responses; influential cultural levers that can be seen during the formation of new working groups. Typically, the group defines certain issues or problems it was tasked to resolve. One or more individuals generate proposed solutions to the problems, doing so on the basis of their espoused values, or the assumptions they make about the best way of tackling the problem at hand. Espoused values explain why newly formed group dynamics exhibit greater complexity compared to the interactions of more mature groups. In the latter, the group has created its own espoused values, which serve as 'rules of engagement' for the successful resolution of problems. The key lies in finding ways to infuse values associated with innovation into the thinking that dominates group problem solving, such as creativity, experimentation, comfort with ambiguity, the safe sharing of ideas and a user-customer-oriented perspective (Schein, 2010).

In the early and uncertain stages of group development, some individuals make an over-representative contribution, thereby influencing group behaviour and its espoused values. Although the views of group leaders may receive greater prominence, their potential solutions have little validity until the remainder of the group has accepted them. The social validation process offers the mechanism through which innovation values can be implanted. Change leaders determine the espoused values they want to communicate throughout the organization to facilitate change, and then reinforce them during the recruitment, induction and training of new staff. Social validation provides an insight into how culture affects behaviour. Those behaviours fitting an organization's espoused values are more easily adopted, while those failing to align are removed, resisted or rejected. Similarly, employees fitting the espoused values advance swiftly, while those who do not find themselves unwelcome or unsuccessful.

Espoused values play a central role in innovation-driven change because their credibility relies upon a shared conception of success. Leaders should focus their efforts on aligning their organization's definition of success with the idea of constant innovation as a natural way of working and thinking. Basic underlying value assumptions reflect the deepest, most ingrained form of culture. Sometimes, basic underlying assumptions have existed for so long in an organization that no one thinks to question their utility. As a result, deep levels of culture tend to be covert, subtly permeating organizations through intangible concepts and tacit beliefs that guide members' behaviours, even without their conscious consideration. Underlying assumptions reside so deeply that affecting them directly will likely prove problematic.

Rather than trying to directly influence these subterranean assumptions, the best response is to bring them to the surface of conscious awareness, exposing them to discussion and interrogation. This way, organizational members can collectively go through the process of socially validating competing assumptions consistent with innovation values. During the process, valuable assumptions also become tacit, and can be built upon and reinforced by supportive values and artefacts (Skinner, Smith and Swanson, 2018). In this respect, the innovation philosophy adopts many of the principles core to the cultural phi-losophy, which we encountered in Chapter 10.

From a philosophical viewpoint, change that facilitates innovation begins with disequilibrium. The acceptance of a new, displaced 'normal', where change towards innovation becomes an inexorable reality, leads to a series of cultural consequences. It initially means that avoiding decisions that decrease or remove uncertainty may undermine the innovative, non-additive—that is, emergent—behaviours emerging from the interactive networks comprising all of an organization's stakeholders. Controlling all the inputs does not necessarily lead to the best outputs. Change that enables innovation accepts enough 'chaos' or unpredictability to ensure that creativity is encouraged, but also enough order or predictability for consistent patterns of activity to endure. Herein lies a key innovation philosophy intersection with the complexity theories embedded in the systems philosophy. The opportunity at the intersec-tion reflects all the undetectable and emergent ideas, possibilities, accidents, options and variations that can lead to novel outcomes. New and unimagined products, or other forms of innovation, can be revealed.

Leaders need to transform their organizations by encouraging—even 'stretching'—their members to be more creative, in so doing playing an important stimulus by embracing change and demonstrating commitment to the creative process themselves. For example, leaders can communicate a vision of creativity, and focus group member attention on the collective goal of developing innovative solutions. They have a pivotal role in creating an environment conducive to developing new ideas for practical application. Leaders who have the capacity to continually stimulate new ways of thinking will be well positioned to infuse innovation into the organizational environ-ment. Other practices such as crowdsourcing can also assist in facilitating idea generation.

CROWDSOURCING

Crowdsourcing, as a mechanism for enhancing and creating new ideas, is a relatively new phenomenon. Howe (2008) described crowdsourcing as taking a job traditionally performed by a designated agent and outsourcing it to an undefined, generally large group of people in the form of an open call. In the same vein, Sheehan (2010) defined crowdsourcing as 'the ability to gather a large group of people around your brand and get them working to develop products and/or solutions' (p. 107). Blohm, Leimeister and Krcmar (2013) extended the definition and distinguished two forms of crowdsourcing: collaborative and competitive. In collaborative crowdsourcing a common solution is developed in a collective way. Competitive crowdsourcing is based on collecting and transmitting independent solutions. Aitamurto, Leiponen and Tee (2011) suggested that although the term 'crowdsourcing' continues to be debated, particularly in relation to other concepts like co-creation and user innovation, the collaborative-based crowdsourced approach is best used when innovations are based on past advances. However, they counselled that competitive market-based approaches—those relying more on competition among participants for creating the 'best' solution—are more appropriate when widespread and parallel experimentation is needed.

Both collaborative-based and competitive market-based crowdsourcing forms are commonly related to the concept of open innovation crowdsourcing (Chesbrough, 2003). Here, organizations search for innovative ideas in an open environment instead of relying on their internal staff to generate creative ideas or solutions. Gassmann and Enkel (2004) presented three open innovation processes: (1) outside-in; (2) inside-out; (3) and the coupled process strategy. The outside-in process enriches the expertise of an organization by integrating external resources into the innovation process. In contrast, the inside-out process makes internal knowledge accessible to external actors. The coupled process merges external resources and actors with internal knowledge, to leverage the knowledge from each group.

Similar to the crowdsourcing approach to innovation, Litvin, Goldsmith and Pan (2008) proposed that many customers recognize their own power as a form of collective intelligence, and may be useful in propelling innovation. Organizations also consider customers to be a valuable market research tool (Schmallegger and Carson, 2008) in order to obtain business intelligence about their products, services and trends. Diversity is beneficial both when customers collaborate to come up with a collective decision or solution, as well as when individuals work independently of each other, but inputs are aggregated. Marjanovic, Fry and Chataway (2012) noted that organizations are interested in crowdsourcing models because customers are motivated to contribute with creative ideas at no cost. Hence, organizations adopting a crowdsourcing philosophy have a greater capacity to learn, and are more sensitive to market tendencies and changes. Moreover, they can anticipate changes more rapidly than their competitors. Crowdsourcing can have a positive impact on innovation capacity, since tacit and explicit knowledge obtained from the customers can be used to create new products and services (Ku, 2014).

Crowdsourcing may be seen as a problem-solving and task realization approach used to facilitate change through innovation. It is driven by the possibility of harnessing a collective intelligence to find a solution to a complex problem. Due to its success, organizations seeking change through innovation are placing greater emphasis on the practice. Caution however needs to be exercised as organizations that embrace crowdsourcing practices need to maintain intellectual property rights, competitive advantage and strategic fit by complementing existing products and services in a useful way (Poetz and

Schreier, 2010). The more precisely a set of complementary assets coincides, the more marked the specificity of the intangible assets will become. However, crowdsourcing must be integrated alongside other innovation capabilities and entrepreneurial activities in order to create new ideas (Xu, Ribeiro-Soriano and Gonzalez-Garcia, 2015). Crowdsourcing can provide a mechanism for change that facilitates idea generation and provides a platform for experimentation.

EXPERIMENTATION, PROTOTYPING AND BOOTSTRAPPING

In the innovation philosophy, experimentation is not necessarily an isolated phenomenon, instead representing part of a larger organizational effort towards change. The excessive use of rules can lead to a workforce averse to thinking independently and reluctant to either suggest or initiate innovative solutions. Innovation change managers provide looser boundaries that give employees at all levels the space and flexibility to take responsibility for innovation themselves. The result is room for experimentation, and the potential emergence of innovations that could not have been forced or prescribed through didactic, top-down impositions.

The degree to which communication and coordination linkages exist between different parts of the organization can also be important to the experimentation process. Dialogue between domains, and functional specializations within the organization, amplify innovation by building social capital and a safe environment in which experimentation can occur (Taylor and Helfat, 2009). Where a minimal threshold of coordination is maintained, organizational members can improvise, flexing around the needs of other functional areas as well as those of external customers and clients. In addition, human resource management support mechanisms such as rewards, play a central role in enabling change managers to feel more comfortable with experimentation, and to encourage imaginative thinking (Swart, Turner, van Rossenberg and Kinnie, 2016).

Berglund and Grimheden (2011) maintained that experimentation and prototyping consist of iterations of 'trial and error', directed by needs that at times may be difficult to distinguish. Studies have shown that iterative trial and error features in several aspects of new product development and design (Ulrich and Eppinger, 2007; Wheelwright and Clark, 1992), technology integration (Iansiti, 1997), manufacturing (Liou, 2008) and service delivery (Blomkvist and Holmlid, 2011). Prototyping generates organizational capabilities where flexibility and 'requisite variety' are integral to product and service processes, and also operates as an antidote to bureaucratic rigidities by introducing new methods for solving problems (Leonard-Barton, 1995).

Prototyping means making an idea more concrete (Fulton Suri, 2008). Prototypes allow ideas to merge in more accessible formats for developers and customers to better understand. They can also influence learning where existing and new technologies, routines and skills are integrated into the problem-solving mode (Petroski, 1996). Idea generation and prototyping can be merged together into a single 'hands-on' activity. In parallel to idea generation methods, prototyping incorporates lateral thinking where divergence and systematic thinking match up (von Hippel, 1994).

Prototypes should represent product, technological and social interactions (Kurvinen, 2007). They can quickly and cost-effectively communicate a service proposition and prompt questions concerning technical feasibility, consumer desirability and business viability (Samalionis, 2009). Successful prototypes, however, are rarely fully functional. In fact, to get to this point would be considered a waste when a more unsophisticated version would suffice. A prototype aims to provide a user—a prospective customer—with a simulation of what the product experience might be like. Promising innovations can then be supported by strong proof-of-concept prototypes that can be disaggregated into discrete chunks or 'staged gates', where exits can be taken, discontinuing, divesting, spinning in/out or commercializing the new product or service.

Prototyping allows innovation-driven change to be 'smarter' because it shifts the concentration from whether an innovation might work in theory to whether it will work in practice, thereby allowing an organization to scale experimental products into commercially viable offerings. However, to achieve sustainable commercial scale, an organization must deploy its financial resources cautiously. As a result, many innovation-savvy organizations aim to shift prototypes into commercial development through low-risk internal support where a very small amount of capital is allocated in order to 'bootstrap' the project. Sometimes the support comes in the form of human capital, where a small project team contributes some extra time in the hope that profits from early sales arrive before it becomes unsustainable.

Bootstrapping enables an organization, in particular small and medium-sized enterprises, to secure financial resources and grow a market at the lowest cost possible (or at no cost) without relying on long-term financing. The motives for financial bootstrapping include the need to lower costs, to compensate for a lack of capital and to reduce risk. Other motives include product development without external finance, speed-to-market time improvements, increased work satisfaction, freedom of action, a desire to learn and legitimacy (Freear, Sohl and Wetzel, 1995; Winborg, 2009). Bootstrapping has become particularly important in the rapid growth stages of start-up enterprises.

FAST FAILURE

Perhaps more than most of the other philosophies, change through innovation risks failure. Change managers can be left with a serious dilemma when they conclude that innovation is necessary for ongoing prosperity or even survival, but remain aware that the potential for failure is high and consequently so are their chances of hastening their own demise. The innovation approach to change risks a high failure rate for a number of reasons.

First, the key to achieving and sustaining significant innovation lies with changing the basic values, beliefs and ways of thinking that dominate within an organization, but this is extremely difficult to achieve and sustain as we detailed in Chapter 10 on culture. Organizations can resist new truths and the need for experimentation. Second, innovation requires coordinated leadership. Even the most skilful leaders can make matters worse when they confront their employees with the need for transformative change. Third, after leaders decide what to do and when, they still have to work out how to make their objectives and activities sufficiently transparent to encourage employees to take some calculated risks, and to convince them that they know what they are doing. Fourth, some leaders are too impatient or do not realize that innovation must take place over a lengthy cultural transition. Innovation takes hold over the long term, with careful attention needed to its disruptive aspects, as well as consideration for when to consolidate. For example, periods of intense innovation programmes tend to be best followed by periods of stability, where the new ideas can be consolidated and converted into meaningful outcomes. Skipping essential cultural change steps in the pursuit of innovation creates only an illusion of speed and does not produce sustainable productivity. Finally, given the need to conduct 'normal' business during an intense innovation period, the importance of the existing structures and practices remains. Instead of creating new pockets of unfettered innovation, most organizations tend to implement trivial innovations into the existing systems, which at best only yields incremental improvements.

Failure carries a heavy economic and human toll. In organizations where change is shaped by innovation, the focus should shift to study how and when failure occurs. The findings can then be used to avoid mistakes and increase performance and competitiveness. Innovation-driven change aims to build organizations that embrace failure and learning, in turn, enhancing the process by supporting ideas and knowledge sharing, risk taking, as well as internal and external assessment. Failures can shed light on issues seldom addressed (Ghezzi, Balocco and Rangone, 2010). Failure analysis focuses on the unsuccessful processes deployed by researching the source(s) of the mistakes and the strategies used. While understanding failure requires a review of those strategies driving the decisions, it needs to move beyond a conservative approach and focus on understanding which organizational practices are conducive to innovation.

ENTREPRENEURIAL APPROACHES TO CHANGE

Since the early work of Schumpeter (1934), the concepts of 'entrepreneurship' and 'innovation' have been strongly related. Baumol (2002) noted that entrepreneurship drives innovation, and therefore change facilitated through innovation is created by entrepreneurial activities. Pinchot (1985) was the first to mention entrepreneurship as a tool for creating new innovation in established organizations (Dess and Lumpkin, 2005; Kuratko, Montagno and Hornsby, 1990), naming it 'intrapreneuring'. More recently, the term has been subsumed by the concept of corporate entrepreneurship. Corporate entrepreneurship can either take the form of internal or external activities, and tends to be presented as a combination of environmental factors and the individual characteristics of the intrapreneur (MacMillan, Block and Subba Narasimha, 1986).

The innovation change philosophy incorporates many notions from corporate entrepreneurship, which emphasizes the importance of change agents, encourages creative ideas and aims towards entry in new markets (Kuratko and Hodgetts, 1998). Adopting an entrepreneurial orientation can facilitate innovation by helping to recognize opportunities through new ideas. Promoting corporate entrepreneurship and creating new opportunities requires the ability to manage the duality of entrepreneurial activities, where organizations must balance the need to exploit existing knowledge to attain competitive advantage while learning and integrating new entrepreneurial actions into their existing practices (Burgelman, 1983). The challenge to be 'ambidextrous' requires a balance between the exploitation of opportunities through formal and informal entrepreneurship, against learning and integrating new knowledge that will extend into new markets or niches.

Organizations embracing an entrepreneurial orientation tend to generate a large number of ideas internally. More ideas leads to a greater utilization of problem-solving knowledge, in turn delivering an improved deployment of human capital and existing capabilities. However, encouraging people to create with new ideas is not enough. In order to yield innovation, an entrepreneurial orientation needs to integrate practices that convert creativity into commercial success (Lee, Hallak and Sardeshmukh, 2016). For example, Kanter (1985) and Sathe (1985) each stressed the importance of an effective reward system. Such a system must take into consideration goals, results-based incentives, individual responsibility and feedback, since these elements fuel the entire entrepreneurial process. Change managers play a central role in corporate entrepreneurship. Their acceptance of new initiatives, ideas and projects are of particular importance since they manage the shift from one set of operating routines to another. A fundamental challenge in corporate entrepreneurship lies with managing the conflict between the new and the old, and in overcoming the inevitable tensions that such conflict produces for management (Dess et al., 2003).

Unlike bootstrapping, corporate entrepreneurship requires a significant commitment of resources, since it involves both experimentation and risk taking (Burgelman and Sayles, 1986). Large organizations might possess the ideas and the resources to create innovation, but may not have the human resources capable of converting these ideas into commercially viable products and services. Some evidence suggests that the most effective entrepreneurial organizations tend to be supportive, flat in hierarchy and have a close relationship between the employees and the management team. It is also important to allow information to flow through the organization openly, through decentralized authority, and a low span of managerial control. Entrepreneurial organizations constantly learn and evolve their business models (Srivastava and Agrawal, 2010). Moreover, the most innovative organizations possess high levels of flexibility and agility (Rule and Irwin, 1988). Large organizations face greater difficulties in achieving change through an innovation philosophy because the established processes have often been in place for decades. In contrast, highly entrepreneurial organizations readily display risk taking.

The practices considered in this section contribute to an organization's entrepreneurial culture. Organizations with an entrepreneurial culture are usually willing to take on high-risk projects with the chance of high returns, and tend to be more aggressive in pursuing new opportunities (Barringer and Bluedorn, 1999). Change leaders within these organizations have created an environment encouraging calculated risk, but at the same time have a more robust tolerance for failure. While entrepreneurial cultures provide the bedrock for innovation, there often remains a challenging implementation gap in deploying ideas rapidly, cost-effectively, and getting them to market quickly (Pinchot and Pellman, 1999).

SPEED TO MARKET

Speed to market describes how quickly an idea moves from conception to its first commercialization or introduction into the marketplace. At the organizational level, speed to market measures the capability to move quickly from ideas to actual products in the marketplace, increasing the potential to realize first-mover or fast-follower advantages. For new product development, it is commonly thought that those who are first to market tend to have a better chance of outperforming competitors. The first to market in an unaddressed segment faces less competition and therefore commands better profit margins.

Getting fresh and relevant products to market quickly attracts customers. Product innovation also leads to increased brand recognition and perceived value.

For existing products, speed to market with product updates is an equally important objective. When facing margin pressure, organizations seek to pinpoint areas of underperformance in their product portfolios and then quickly implement pricing or other product changes to protect profitability. The ability to make timely updates to cover new, competing offerings that have more attractive pricing can help protect profitability when unfavourable trends emerge. Finally, achieving speed to market has become increasingly important in the global competitive environment. Competition for market share is fierce, and the commoditization of products leads to thinner profit margins, which in turn requires greater volumes and lower operating costs to achieve profit targets.

A key obstacle in achieving speed to market is the lack of a consistent, repeatable approach to product management. Inconsistent approaches, and the lack of collaboration between operating units, can lead to product proliferation. This redundancy and duplication increases costs. Organizations therefore need to maintain a disciplined approach to product life-cycle management, view the product portfolio holistically, proactively engage the right resources at the right times, and regularly monitor the performance of the product portfolio as well as the product development teams.

The innovation philosophy emboldens organizations to collaborate in order to build a foundation for achieving speed-to-market aspirations. To become more agile in the marketplace, organizations should try to balance consistency and flexibility in product management, from product design to the deployment of products (Carbonell and Escudero, 2010). One outcome of this kind of thinking can be seen in the popularity of incremental systems of innovation, which prescriptively take advantage of structured processes designed to streamline ideation, manufacturing or product development. Project management methods such as 'Agile'—devised for swifter and simplified software development—and 'Lean'—originating in the efficiency-driven manufacturing sector—have become standard practices in many companies. Although we would not necessarily classify these methodologies as change philosophies, they, like the quality and reengineering movements of the 1980s, exemplify a managerial response to change. Unlike the broader innovation philosophy which embraces disruption, project management methods and techniques seek to control change through micro innovations, often guided by software systems. As such they have implications for strategy, structure and culture.

Speed to market may be accelerated by contributions made by other partners or contributors in the organization's environment. The pharmaceutical industry offers an instructive case where there has been a willingness by large firms to engage much smaller biotechnology firms in marketing alliances, co-development programmes and equity investments, as new product successes from traditional chemical-based methods have diminished. Such traditional methods can be complex, costly and time-consuming, which has resulted in an upsurge in rapid prototyping and concept testing.

Rapid prototyping can increase the speed in which a product can be put on the market. As with prototyping, rapid prototyping comprises a method of testing an innovation under real-world market conditions with the aim of finding out whether investing additional resources into its feasibility, or finalization, is warranted. Rapid prototyping sidesteps the costly development lag that follows the excitement around an initial idea. It works by seizing the momentum that emerges from the possibility of converting the idea immediately into something tangible that can be trialled by the very people who will end up using it (Berglund and Grimheden, 2011). Similarly, concept testing involves testing a product prototype. Here, a prototype can be as simple as a basic sketch or flowchart, a handful of 'wireframes' illustrating the sequence of pages in a website or mobile application, a 'mock-up' product or an unrefined but fully functional technology or physical item. Through instant feedback an idea can be improved and tested again, until it inspires confidence or is abandoned as a failure. From this perspective, innovative organizations embrace failure because fast and cheap product disappointments allow for more ideas to be designed and tested, ultimately leading to superior speed to market.

DESIGN THINKING

Design thinking gained prominence in the change management literature because it promises increased innovation through a more user-centred approach, prioritizing the way that designers think and work (Brown, 2008; Martin, 2009). Lockwood (2010) described design thinking as a human-centred innovation process that emphasizes observation, collaboration, fast learning, visualization of ideas, rapid concept prototyping and concurrent business analysis. Hobday, Boddington and Grantham (2012) further suggested that design thinking contributes to an organization's innovation capability by offering a collective approach to 'wicked' problems; those that are ill-defined or tricky, enabling new opportunities for problem solving and solution generation. For an organization seeking to change through innovation, the design-thinking approach seeks to minimize the uncertainty and risk of innovation by using the collective intelligence of users themselves. Design thinking engages with customers and prospective users by constructing a series of prototypes to learn, test and refine concepts that lead to a deeper customer understanding, and therefore more attractive products. Unlike conventional market research, insight comes with customer insights from tangible, real-world testing, rather than on the basis of perceptions about hypothetical situations. A design-thinking framework can help an organization find viable, feasible and desirable ideas where user-centricity becomes a core element of the approach.

Design thinking utilizes a non-linear iterative approach that focuses on user needs, articulating frameworks and formulating a strategy to constantly reassess the direction, design and development of a product. This process is sometimes referred to as a 'fast acting–learning' cycle. The learning cycle ensures that the direction, design and development of a product constantly loops back to validate against user needs (Tschimmel, 2012). The process specifies an initial exploratory phase focused on data gathering to identify user needs and define the problem, followed by a second stage of idea generation, and then a final phase of prototyping and testing. It constitutes a process corresponding to what Seidel and Fixson (2013) described as 'need finding, brainstorming, and prototyping'. All descriptions of the process emphasize iterative cycles of exploration using deep user research to develop insights and design criteria, followed by the generation of multiple ideas and concepts, and then prototyping and experimentation to select the best one by working closely with users.

Design thinking relies on the designer's capacity to simultaneously consider: (1) human needs and new visions of living well; (2) available material and technical resources; and (3) the constraints and opportunities of the organization designing the product. The integration of these three factors demands that the designer be equally analytical and emphatic, rational and emotional, methodical and intuitive, organized and spontaneous (Pombo and Tschimmel, 2005). Some design researchers call this kind of dualistic reasoning 'abductive thinking', to differentiate it from rational deduction and from inductive reasoning (Cross, 2011). Abductive reasoning is a concept developed by the philosopher Charles Sander Pierce, who argued that no new idea could be produced by either deduction or induction of past data (Martin, 2009). Thus, abductive thinking considers future possibilities, which do not fit into existing models. The innovation approach to change provides a comfortable philosophical home for design thinking as they strengthen each other in an upward spiral (Carlgren, 2013).

CONCLUSION

The innovation philosophy of organizational change can be understood as a consequence of global liquid modernity and a response to the rapid upsurge in globalization that has forced organizations to find new ways to remain viable and competitive. While most organizations possess a general awareness of the importance and necessity of innovation and change in general, there is a gap when it comes to understanding how innovation can drive change.

The long-term growth of organizations will stem from their ambidextrous ability to continually develop and produce innovative products and services, while simultaneously protecting their existing business from competitors and a declining market (Anthony, Gilbert and Johnson, 2017). In this respect, the traditional concept of 'managing change' has become an oxymoron, as embracing innovation has become a natural part of the change process. There is a need for organizations to be as strategically adaptable as they are operationally efficient. Organizations embracing the innovation paradigm will need to be flexible, agile, intuitive, imaginative, resilient and creative in order to stimulate new ideas in the face of increasing complexity and turbulence (Schiuma, 2011).

Sustaining innovation-driven organizational change requires a cultural shift. A first step is to develop a contextualized understanding of creativity, and identify the benefits of innovation for the specific work team, organization or broader collaboration. The necessity for creativity and innovation stems in large part from keeping pace with competition. When group members collectively appreciate the need for innovation, and are actively involved with incorporating it into organizational strategy and objectives, a sense of ownership will engender support for the creative mindset. Further, comfort with 'risk experimentation' (Borgelt and Falk, 2007) requires the courage to accelerate through failure by building momentum and speed through new learning. Accepting risk also requires a willingness to embrace failure as learning opportunities that would ordinarily inspire uncertainty. Communicating that innovation can proceed as a gradual process of smaller leaps can be helpful, rather than one creative idea of transformational proportion (Kuyatt, 2011). However, potential shortfalls in an organization's innovation capabilities may detract from its capacity to implement ideas rapidly and cost-effectively, and to design a process that will accelerate the product to market (Pinchot and Pellman, 1999).

In this chapter, we noted that design thinking offers a process to enhance an organization's innovation capabilities, although the concept and its applicability to change management is not necessarily easy (Tonkinwise, 2011). While powerful in concept and potential, implementation tends to be far more challenging (Persson, 2005). As with all organizational change philosophies, innovation can take different forms, and can therefore lead to different change outcomes depending upon their implementation.

REFERENCES

Aghion, P. and X. Jaravel (2015), 'Knowledge spillovers, innovation and growth', *Economic Journal*, **125** (583), 533–73.

Aitamurto, T., A. Leiponen and R. Tee (2011), 'The promise of idea crowdsourcing: Benefits, contexts, limitations', *Nokia Ideas Project White Paper*, June.

Anthony, S. D., C. G. Gilbert and M. W. Johnson (2017), *Dual Transformation: How to Reposition Today's Business while Creating the Future*, Boston, MA: Harvard Business Review Press.

Appadurai, A. (1996), *Modernity at Large: Cultural Dimensions of Globalization*, Minneapolis, MN: University of Minnesota Press.

Barringer, B. R. and A. C. Bluedorn (1999), 'The relationship between corporate entrepreneurship and strategic management', *Strategic Management Journal*, **20**, 421–44.

Bauman, Z. (2004), 'Zygmunt Bauman: Liquid sociality', in N. Gane (ed.), *The Future of Social Theory*, London: Continuum, pp. 17–46.

Baumol, W. J. (2002), *The Free-Market Innovation Machine*, Princeton, NJ: Princeton University Press.

Berglund, A. and M. Grimheden (2011), 'The importance of prototyping for education in product innovation engineering', in Amaresh Chakrabarti (ed.), *Research into Design: Supporting Sustainable Product Development*, Bangalore: Research Publishing, Indian Institute of Science, pp. 737–49.

Birch, K. (2017), *A Research Agenda for Neoliberals*, Cheltenham, UK and Northampton, MA, USA: Edward Elgar Publishing.

Blohm, I., J. M. Leimeister and H. Krcmar (2013), 'Crowdsourcing: How to benefit from (too) many great ideas', *MIS Quarterly Executive*, **12** (4), 199–211.

Blomkvist, J. and S. Holmlid (2011), *Existing Prototyping Perspectives: Considerations for Service Design*, Helsinki: Nordic Design Research.

Borgelt, K. and I. Falk (2007), 'The leadership/management conundrum: Innovation or risk management?', *Leadership and Organization Development Journal*, **28** (2), 122–36.

Brown, T. (2008), 'Design thinking', *Harvard Business Review*, **86** (6), 84–92.

Burgelman, R. A. (1983), 'A model of the intersection of strategic behaviour, corporate context, and the concept of strategy', *Journal of Management Review*, **8**, 61–9.

Burgelman, R. A. and L. R. Sayles (1986), *Inside Corporate Innovation: Strategy, Structure and Managerial Skills*, New York: Free Press.

Carbonell, P. and A. I. R. Escudero (2010), 'The effect of market orientation on innovation speed and new product performance', *Journal of Business and Industrial Marketing*, **25** (7), 501–13.

Carlgren, L. (2013), *Design Thinking as an Enabler of Innovation: Exploring the Concept and Its Relation to Building Innovation Capabilities*, Doctoral dissertation, Chalmers University of Technology, Sweden.

Castells, M. (2000), *The Rise and Fall of the Network Society*, Malden, MA: Blackwell.

Chesbrough, H. W. (2003), *Open Innovation: The New Imperative for Creating and Profiting from Technology*, Boston, MA: Harvard Business School.

Cross, N. (2011), *Design Thinking: Understanding How Designers Think and Work*, London: Berg.

Day, A. (2020), *Disruption, Change and Transformation in Organisations: A Human Relations Perspective*, Oxford: Routledge.

Dess, G. G. and G. Lumpkin (2005), 'The role of entrepreneurial orientation in stimulating effective corporate entrepreneurship', *Academy of Management Executive*, **19**, 147–56.

Dess, G. G., R. Duane Ireland, S. A. Zahra, S. W. Floyd, J. J. Janney and P. J. Lane (2003), 'Emerging issues in corporate entrepreneurship', *Journal of Management*, **29** (3), 351–78.

Freear, J., J. E. Sohl and W. E. Wetzel, Jr. (1995), 'Who bankrolls software entrepreneurs?' In *Proceedings, Babson College Entrepreneurship Research Conference*, 9–13 April, London Business School.

Fulton Suri, J. (2008), 'Informing our intuition: Design research for radical innovation', *Rotman Magazine*, **Winter**, 53–5.

Gassmann, O. and E. Enkel (2004), 'Towards a theory of open innovation: Three core process archetypes', *Proceedings of the RADMA Conference*, Lisbon, 7 July, 1–18.

Ghezzi, A., R. Balocco and A. Rangone (2010), 'How to get strategic planning and business model design wrong: The case of a mobile technology provider', *Strategic Change*, **19**, 213–38.

Giddens, A. (2000), *Runaway World: How Globalization Is Reshaping Our Lives*, New York: Routledge.

Hall, S. (1996), 'Who needs "identity"?', in S. Hall and P. du Gay (eds), *Questions of Cultural Identity*, London: Sage, pp. 1–17.

Harris, A. (2004), *Future Girl: Young Women in the Twenty-First Century*, New York: Routledge.

Hobday, M., A. Boddington and A. Grantham (2012), 'An innovation perspective on design: Part 2', *Design Issues*, **28**, 18–29.

Howe, J. (2008), *Crowdsourcing: Why the Power of the Crowd Is Driving the Future of Business*, New York: Crown Publishing.

Iansiti, M. (1997), *Technology Integration: Making Critical Choices in a Turbulent World*, Boston, MA: Harvard Business School Press.

Kanter, R. M. (1985), 'Supporting innovation and venture development in established companies', *Journal of Business Venturing*, **1**, 47–60.

Ku, E. C. S. (2014), 'Putting forth marketing competencies strength with collaborating partners in the hotel industry', *Service Business*, **8** (4), 679–97.

Kuratko, D. F. and R. M. Hodgetts (1998), *Entrepreneurship*, New York: Thompson.

Kuratko, D. F., R. V. Montagno and J. S. Hornsby (1990), 'Developing an intrapreneurial assessment instrument for an effective corporate entrepreneurial environment', *Strategic Management Journal Special Issue: Corporate Entrepreneurship*, **11**, 49–58.

Kurvinen, E. (2007), *Prototyping Social Action*, Helsinki: Gummerus Printing.

Kuyatt, A. (2011), 'Managing for innovation: Reducing the fear of failure', *Journal of Strategic Management*, **3** (2), 31–40.

Lee, C., R. Hallak and S. R. Sardeshmukh (2016), 'Innovation, entrepreneurship, and restaurant performance: A higher-order structural model', *Tourism Management*, **53**, 215–28.

Leonard-Barton, D. (1995), *Wellsprings of Knowledge: Building and Sustaining the Sources of Innovation*, Boston, MA: HBS Press.

Lindmark, A. and H. Meisner (2016), *Get your Head in the Game*, Masters dissertation, Uppsala University.

Liou, F. W. (2008), *Rapid Prototyping and Engineering Applications: A Toolbox for Prototype Development*, New York: CRC Press.

Litvin, S. W., R. E. Goldsmith and B. Pan (2008), 'Electronic word-of-mouth in hospitality and tourism management', *Tourism Management*, **29** (3), 458–68.

Lockwood, T. (ed.) (2010), *Design Thinking: Integrating Innovation, Customer Experience, and Brand Value*, New York: Allworth Press.

MacMillan, I. C., Z. Block and P. N. Subba Narasimha (1986), 'Corporate venturing: Alternatives, obstacles encountered, and experience effects', *Journal of Business Venturing*, **1**, 177–91.

Marjanovic, S., C. Fry and J. Chataway (2012), 'Crowdsourcing based business models: In search of evidence for innovation 2.0', *Science and Public Policy*, **39**, 318–32.

Martin, R. (2009), *The Design of Business: Why Design Thinking Is the Next Competitive Advantage*, Boston, MA: Harvard Business Press.

Persson, S. (2005), *Toward Enhanced Interaction between Engineering Design and Industrial Design*, PhD thesis, Chalmers University of Technology, Gothenburg.

Petroski, H. (1996), *Invention by Design: How Engineers Get from Thought to Thing*, Cambridge: Cambridge University Press.

Pinchot, G. (1985), *Intrapreneuring: Why You Don't Have to Leave the Company to Become an Entrepreneur*, New York: Harper and Row.

Pinchot, G. and R. Pellman (1999), *Intrapreneuring in Action: A Handbook for Business Innovation*, San Francisco, CA: Berrett-Koehler.

Poetz, M. and M. Schreier (2010), 'The value of crowdsourcing: Can users really compete with professionals in generating new product ideas?', *Journal of Product Innovation Management*, **29** (2), 245–56.

Pombo, F. and K. Tschimmel (2005), 'Sapiens and demens in design thinking: Perception as core', in *Proceedings of the 6th International Conference of the European Academy of Design EAD '06*, Bremen: University of the Arts Bremen.

Robertson, R. (1995), 'Glocalisation: Time-space and homogeneity-heterogeneity', in M. Featherstone, S. Lash and R. Robertson (eds), *Global Modernities*, London: Sage.

Rule, E. G. and D. W. Irwin (1988), 'Fostering intrapreneurship: The new competitive edge', *Journal of Business Strategy*, **9** (3), 44–7.

Samalionis, F. (2009), 'Can designers help deliver better services?', in S. Miettinen and M. Koivisto (eds), *Designing Services with Innovative Methods*, Helsinki: Kuopio Academy of Design, pp. 124–35.

Sathe, V. (1985), 'Managing an entrepreneurial dilemma: Nurturing entrepreneurship and control in large corporations', *Frontiers of Entrepreneurship Research*, **37** (2), 636–56.

Schein, E. H. (2010), *Organizational Culture and Leadership*, Hoboken, NJ: John Wiley & Sons.

Schiuma, G. (2011), *The Value of Arts for Business*, Cambridge: Cambridge University Press.

Schmallegger, D. and D. Carson (2008), 'Blogs in tourism: Changing approaches to information exchange', *Journal of Vacation Marketing*, **14** (2), 99–110.

Schumpeter, J. (1934), *The Theory of Economic Development: An Inquiry into Profits, Capital, Credit, Interest, and the Business Cycle*, Cambridge, MA: Harvard University Press.

Seidel, V. and S. Fixson (2013), 'Adopting design thinking in novice multidisciplinary teams: The application and limits of design methods and reflexive practices', *Journal of Product Innovation Management*, **30** (1), 19–33.

Sheehan, B. (2010), *Basic Marketing: Online Marketing*, London: AVA Publishing.

Sherwood, D. (2002), *Creating an Innovative Culture*, London: Capstone.

Skinner, J., A. C. T. Smith and S. Swanson (2018), *Fostering Innovative Cultures in Sport*, London: Palgrave Macmillan.

Srivastava, N. and A. Agrawal (2010), 'Factors supporting corporate entrepreneurship: An exploratory study', *Journal of Business Perspectives*, **14** (3), 163–71.

Swart, J., N. Turner, Y. van Rossenberg and N. Kinnie (2016), 'Who does what in enabling ambidexterity? Individual actions and HRM practices', *International*

Journal of Human Resource Management, http://dx.doi.org/10.1080/09585192 .2016.1254106, 1-28.

Taylor, A. and C. E. Helfat (2009), 'Organizational linkages for surviving technical change: Complementary assets, middle management, and ambidexterity', *Organization Science*, **20** (4), 718–39.

Timmons, J. and S. Spinelli (2007), *New Venture Creation: Entrepreneurship for the 21st Century*, 8th edition, London: McGraw-Hill.

Tonkinwise, C. (2011), 'A taste for practices: Unrepressing style in design thinking', *Design Studies*, **32** (6), 533–45.

Tschimmel, K. (2012), 'Design thinking as an effective toolkit for innovation', *Proceedings of the XXIII ISPIM Conference: Action for Innovation: Innovating from Experience*, Barcelona.

Ulrich, K. T. and S. D. Eppinger (2007), *Product Design and Development*, 4th edition, Singapore: McGraw-Hill.

von Hippel, E. (1994), '"Sticky information" and the locus of problem solving: Implications for innovation', *Management Science*, **40** (4), 429–39.

Wheelwright, S. C. and K. B. Clark (1992), *Revolutionizing Product Development: Quantum Leaps in Speed, Efficiency, and Quality*, New York: Free Press.

Winborg, J. (2009), 'Use of financial bootstrapping in new businesses: A question of last resort?', *Venture Capital: An International Journal of Entrepreneurial Finance*, **11**, 71–83.

Xu, Y., E. Ribeiro-Soriano and J. Gonzalez-Garcia (2015), 'Crowdsourcing, innovation and firm performance', *Management Decision*, **53** (6), 1158–69.

13. The dualities philosophy: 'changing tensions'

INTRODUCTION

We argued at the outset of this text that traditional approaches to organizational change follow a linear, rational model where control and strategy are delivered by strong leaders. The underlying premise guiding this classical version of organizational change assumes that it involves a series of predictable, reducible steps that can be planned and managed. The evidence from case after case of failed change implementations indicates, however, that the reality of change defies simple, planned responses. The rational philosophy not only represents a limited, one-dimensional approach to change, but it also ignores the messy, complex and iterative nature of change. Perhaps more importantly, it fails to accommodate the fact that change and continuity work in a dynamic tension. Organizations cannot prosper at either extreme of rapid change or intractable inertia. As a result, change leaders struggle to instigate change from the top while the operational bottom demands continuity. In response, the dualities philosophy advocates for the ostensibly paradoxical pursuit of both change and stability at the same time.

From the classic, rational perspective, change management decision making comes down to an either-or choice between change and continuity, such as innovation and efficiency; collaboration and competition; freedom and accountability; or new and old. However, according to the dualities philosophy, organizational change cannot always be a matter of reducing one kind of activity to offset another kind. For example, often organizations need more of *both* top-down leadership and bottom-up empowerment; a dual ambition.

A duality is not a dilemma, which can be assessed against positives and negatives, but is better understood as two opposing poles that can vary between conflicted and complementary as context changes (Stoltzfus, Stohl and Seibold, 2011). Understandably, some change practitioners would reject one approach for the other because they seem to represent diametrically opposite views. But, the dualities philosophy asks us to consider the advantages of an organizational culture that might be described as both loose and tight. Its non-hierarchical management approach and entrepreneurial spirit encourage high levels of autonomy and discretionary power, within a strong risk and performance management framework.

Ironically, change management cannot be only about change. One interpretation of organizational change research suggests that the underlying duality change manager is balancing continuity and change without trade-off or compromise (Nasim and Sushil, 2011). The need for both continuity and change means becoming comfortable with the ever present dilemma of tension between the two. It also means managing the dynamics of human interaction and responses to external perturbations alongside institutionalized structures, systems and routines, and harnessing this dynamic to challenge existing practices where they are no longer appropriate (Smith, Sutherland and Gilbert, 2017).

The dualities philosophy maintains that managing change demands balancing and conciliating what often appear as conflicting dilemmas. That is, merging: (1) rational strategic planning with adaptive strategic thinking. Rational strategic planning sets the direction, considers resources and budgeting and provides a clearly defined focus and vision of future possibilities. Adaptive strategic thinking treats strategy as a trial-and-error learning process, including the ability to change and adapt in an unknown and turbulent environment; (2) cultural renewal in the form of surfacing and challenging the core values, beliefs and assumptions, or 'the way we do things around here', with structural change in the form of improving operational efficiencies through tangible changes to existing work processes, systems and reporting structures. An innovative, creative culture depends on equally dynamic, adaptive and thoughtfully designed systems and structures to sustain and support it; (3) empowerment with strong leadership. The need for strong leadership that provides a clear overarching vision and focus seems particularly critical in the boundary-less organization, which needs autonomy and interdependence. The focus of a leader's role must also be balanced between power and control, and using new skills as teachers, counsellors and negotiators. Leaders need to integrate the hard rational, analytical, planning, organizing and controlling skills with the soft human relations skills; (4) continual, incremental adaptation with radical transformation, when sudden, unexpected environmental shifts occur that require decisive, unilateral action; and (5) social goals with economic goals. This chapter explores each of these dualities, highlights the challenges, examines what 'dualities thinking' comprises, considers the challenges of converting thinking into tangible change action, and presents some defining dualities characteristics.

THE STABILITY–CHANGE DILEMMA

Change might easily be seen as an inconvenient truth to be wrestled under control as expeditiously as possible. Katz and Kahn (1966, p. 449), for example, argued that organizations seek to maintain stability through 'authority structures, reward mechanisms, and value systems'. As cultural theorists remind us, these structures and values become embedded in an organization's psyche, and represent the taken-for-granted 'way we do things around here' that notoriously evades challenge. Organizations sometimes seem preoccupied with maintaining inertia, as stability can be seen as essential to survival (Kilduff and Dougherty, 2000). The preconception that change inopportunely forces instability underlies the assumption that implementing change involves a series of corrective steps, driven by senior management and rolled out in a systematic, orderly manner. Invariably, the goal is regaining the certainty of equilibrium at a new set-point.

A focus on re-establishing order and stability challenges the idea of change as a naturally occurring, ongoing phenomenon affirming continuity. Traditional frameworks for change ignore the dynamic, complex and contradictory nature of organizations as well as the diverse people working within them, with their individual needs and idiosyncrasies. And, ironically, the intersection of stability and change—what complexity theory advocates refer to as the 'edge of chaos'—reveals where opportunities for organizational development lie. As Tsoukas and Chia observed, 'If change is viewed as the exception, the occasional episode in organizational life, we underestimate how pervasive change already is' (2002, p. 568). The dualities philosophy takes the view that a better approach means coming to terms with simultaneous change and stability.

Duality theory proposes that the tension, or 'dynamic synthesis', between contradictory forces within organizations provides a catalyst for self-renewal (Pascale, 1990). Writing around half a century ago, Cyert and March (1963) and Thompson (1967), claimed that plurality offers an essential ingredient in performance. To be effective therefore requires an appreciation of the pluralistic extremes that exist in organizations, such as centralization and decentralization, teamwork and individual accountability, and long-term vision and short-term performance management. Other contradictions inherent in organizations include the need to increase efficiency and creativity, build individualistic teams, provide strong leadership and support empowerment, include hierarchy and networks, ensure cost control and quality, and think globally while acting locally (Cameron and Quinn, 1988; Evans, 1999; Lewis, 2000). These dualities are present and interact at every level of an organization, from the intra-individual level within an employee's identity, to the overarching organizational-level mission statement (Ashforth and Reingen, 2014).

SIMULTANEOUS EXTREMES

Most change philosophies based on 'either/or' thinking would try and resolve the paradoxical tension between these 'conflicting truths' by pursuing one extreme (Lewis, 2000, p. 761). However, prioritizing the stable dimensions (e.g. control and stability) over the less certain dimensions (e.g. flexibility and change) dilutes the 'enlightening' potential of paradox (p. 763). For example, Stoltzfus et al. (2011) noted that in order to make organizational change work, 'it is necessary to include stakeholders who intend to and will subvert the process' (p. 362). In contrast, exploring the links between opposing dimensions and exploiting the tensions that arise from paradox provides scope for rich insights into the complexities, ambiguities and nuances of the change management process.

A dualities perspective proposes that once we recognize organizations as dynamic rather than static entities, we can begin to appreciate and accommodate their complex and contradictory natures. Rather than trying to resolve opposing forces, managers need to learn how to tap into the creative potential of these tensions (Evans, 1999). Organizational exploration processes designed to generate innovation and insight will naturally contain elements and processes that exploit existing knowledge, and vice versa (Farjoun, 2010). In addition, the resulting shift in focus from organizational similarity to plurality may introduce a more nuanced understanding of institutional dynamics (Glynn, Barr and Dacin, 2000). For example, Cameron and Quinn (1988, p. 13) claimed that contradictions do not need reconciliation 'because paradoxes are not necessarily dialectical'. Indeed, they argued 'perfect fit or congruence' would likely result in a 'tensionless state' and cause systemic inertia. A more holistic way of thinking leads to the conclusion that, 'Opposites cease to be opposites' (Schumacher, 1977, p. 126).

Change managers benefit when they find comfort with 'paradox management', which entails 'exploring rather than suppressing' the dual tensions that exist (Lewis, 2000, p. 764). An important first step involves recognizing merit in each of the opposing elements (Morgan, 1997). Most organizational features possess a complementary quality, even if they appear to be opposing. Excessive focus on one pole of a duality leads to stagnation and decline, while overcompensating in the other direction leads to disruptive and discontinuous crisis (Evans, 1992). Change managers have to find a balance between order and disorder (Pettigrew and Fenton, 2000). This is also consistent with the reality of success and failure, which is more commonly manifest in a duality form too, such as close calls or just surviving (Farjoun, 2010).

If change management should be thought of as a 'fuzzy, deeply ambiguous process' (Collins, 2003, p. v), then we need a new philosophy that moves away from the uni-dimensional approach. After all, it would be a form of 'blindness' to regard one perspective as superior to all others (Van de Ven and Poole, 2005, p. 1395). In fact, drawing on diverse philosophical perspectives offers different, albeit partial, interpretations, enabling researchers and managers to accommodate the contradictory nature of change.

CONCEPTUALIZING DUALITIES

Traditional approaches view change management as an exception, a passing irritation to be overcome quickly before returning to stability. We can easily fall into the trap of assuming that organizations behave as rational entities subservient to a change leader's instrumental, prescriptive intentions. Leaders also tend to drift towards stability and conformity because control intuitively connects to improved performance. Yet, as we have noted throughout this text, careful case analyses reveal that change resists prescriptive logic. We have argued that change is never simple, sometimes emergent, often uncertain, typically complex, value-laden and always messy. Biological and systems approaches help remind us that organizations can operate as living systems, dynamically shifting, growing, morphing and sometimes even dying.

While stability bolsters organizational effectiveness, the irony remains that performance can be paradoxical because it demands the presence of dual attributes that appear to be simultaneously contradictory, including: stability–change, control–flexibility and efficiency–creativity (Quinn and Rohrbaugh, 1983; Cameron, 1986; Evans, 1992). To be effective means appreciating how such dualistic forces shape change. Prescriptive logic seeks to resolve the contradiction by selecting one extreme over another. The duality philosophy encourages a tension between opposing dimensions. In fact, duality theory suggests that what appear to be opposing dimensions should be seen as essential complements that must co-exist in order to account for the nuanced and textured management of change. Change management actually reflects continuity–change management. Indeed, evidence suggests that where duality thinking exists, so does efficiency and effectiveness, however, the direction of this relationship remains unclear (Biloslavo, Bagnoli and Figelj, 2013). Although it sounds peculiar, we shall explore in this chapter how duality theory encourages the potential for complementarity within contradiction.

Duality theory—originally a by-product of Giddens' (1984) structuration theory—suggests that dualism elements may be independent and conceptually distinct, rather than opposed. Thus, theorists who employ duality theory 'can maintain conceptual distinctions without being committed to a rigid antago-nism or separation of the two elements being distinguished' (Jackson, 1999,

p. 549). In a management context within an organization, this kind of thinking implies that pairs like stability and change, order and disorder and predictability and unpredictability operate by 'mutual specification' rather than mutual exclusivity (Ford and Backoff, 1988, p. 100). When organized correctly, 'golden dualities' can emerge that gain the best of seemingly opposite poles, such as enabling creative freedom within mainstream management principles (Sugarman, 2014). But how then do managers accommodate these contradictions and balance the dualistic tensions that accompany a commitment to either continuity or change? To put the issue simply, how can organizational change be about change *and* continuity at the same time?

The duality philosophy offers managers conceptual guidance in identifying the tensions of change, as well as their power (Graetz and Smith, 2008). A dualities-aware approach depends on understanding the composition of duality characteristics. In the forthcoming sections, we explain the form and function of five duality characteristics and their application in managing the tensions, uncertainties and ambiguities that dictate the relationship between continuity and change. We present a conceptual framework of the five duality characteristics and continuity–change dualities that managers must face.

Operationalizing the duality characteristics makes explicit, and forces consideration of, competing continuity–change goals. In turn, the interacting, iterative nature of duality characteristics encourages a bi-modal approach, helping managers to appreciate the interplay between apparently competing continuity–change goals. A dualities approach to organization change can also sharpen researchers' interpretive schema and provide a broader framework for exploring complex phenomena, which simultaneously seem confusing and understandable, common and surprising, and predictable and unpredictable (Cameron, 1986; Lewis, 2000).

UNDERSTANDING DUALITIES: A DUALITIES-AWARE PERSPECTIVE

How can change managers deal with the paradox of continuity and change? Part of the answer lies in allowing a state of tension to emerge (Lewis, 2000). A dualities lens allows researchers to explore paradox in organizations, as it compels sensitivity and receptiveness to the complexities, ambiguities and contradictions that are intertwined in day-to-day routines. A dualities approach that embraces numerous philosophies of change can liberate managers (Johnston and Selsky, 2006). Yet, as Sanchez-Runde and Pettigrew (2003) observed, we know little about dualities, their antecedents and how they should be managed. Seo, Putnam and Bartunek (2004, p. 102) similarly noted that while ambiguity needs to be recognized as a 'valued asset', organizations 'are not generally equipped to cope with fragmentation and high ambiguity'. The challenge for senior management involves integrating the functionality of the different forms into a coherent whole (Quinn, Anderson and Finkelstein, 1998, p. 162).

By developing a 'dualities-aware perspective', change managers can identify and exploit the two oppositional poles simultaneously (Graetz and Smith, 2008). A dualities-aware approach is born of paradox and sees merit in each position along the duality continuum. Consequently, rather than seeking resolution towards one position, a dualities-aware approach encourages a constructive tension (Evans, 1999; Evans, Pucik and Barsoux, 2002) between extremes of adaptive and manipulative acts (Hedberg, Nystrom and Starbuck, 1976). Tension can manifest in different ways. For example, Ashforth and Reingen's (2014) study of an organization structured as a co-operative demonstrated how decisions 'oscillated' between the duality of commercialism and idealism as circumstances changed, rather than reflecting a compromise between them. Equally, a more efficient long-term response to dualities would involve adopting fluid organizational forms that support both poles concurrently by providing conditions for workers to comfortably co-exist with ambiguity (Smith, Gilbert and Sutherland, 2017). A dualities-aware approach depends, however, on an understanding of dualities characteristics. Lewis (2000) confirmed the value of understanding duality characteristics suggesting that a paradox framework could be a vehicle for exploring *what* sorts of tensions exist, *why* they might trigger reinforcing cycles and *how* change managers might deal with the paradoxes accompanying dualities.

The demise of 'linear causality' thinking in social systems has encouraged more interest in the tensions and 'oppositions' evident in change management (Johnston and Selsky, 2006). Dualities are not simply alternatives. The problem arises when an organization chooses to focus on one of the poles at the expense of the other, thus making it difficult to enact both ends of the continuum simultaneously (Seo et al., 2004, p. 74), leading to a paradox of sorts. This simultaneous existence of two inconsistent states has been described as a duality of co-existing tensions (Eisenhardt, 2000, p. 703). Inconsistency, however, is a matter of interpretation (Johnston and Selsky, 2006). Paradox seems to exist in the duality of inconsistent, co-existing tensions present in environments characterized by complexity, ambiguity and uncertainty. Change managers see paradox when oppositional tendencies like control and flexibility are brought together (Ford and Backoff, 1988).

A paradox represents a range of contradictory, yet interrelated, elements such as perspectives, feelings, messages, identities, interests or practices. As 'constructed' entities, they explain the efforts made by change managers to simplify and make sense of the complexities and uncertainties in the work environment; attempting to resolve rather than embrace contradictory elements (Lado, Boyd and Hanlon, 1997, p. 112). The desire to resolve seemingly contradictory elements might be natural to change managers but it is also unhelpful. The dualities philosophy encourages change managers to fight their urge to reconcile different approaches to change. While messier, dualities show that greater advantages for change reside in a little ambiguity. One research example highlighted the ability to capture the growth value of both global integration and local responsiveness by having two headquarters in different locations that were laterally related (Birkinshaw, Crilly, Bouquet and Lee, 2016). In order to understand how dualities can be put into practice, we next attempt to explain the form and function of duality characteristics, and their value in managing the tensions of organizational continuity and change.

DUALITY CHARACTERISTICS

We use the term 'characteristic' to describe a prominent aspect or a definable, differentiating and universal feature, trait or property (Graetz and Smith, 2008). Understanding the characteristics of dualities reveals the implications of change management interventions and subsequent choices in support systems. Both continuity and change need to be encouraged, but this requires a new mindset. The following discussion identifies and describes five duality characteristics: (1) simultaneity; (2) relational; (3) minimal thresholds; (4) dynamism; and (5) improvisation. The dualities philosophy argument hinges on the importance of considering the five duality characteristics as a harmonized unit.

It helps to perceive duality characteristics as escalating. Simultaneity is the most basic property. But the simultaneous presence of competing change and continuity goals is a necessary but not sufficient condition for dualities to emerge. Because organizing forms are interdependent and relational, minimal levels of competing forms create a benefit and ensure that organizations can enjoy the advantages afforded through the complementary forces of continuity and change. However, thresholds change with contextual pressure, so for dualities to endure they must also possess a dynamic property. Ultimately, improvisation characterizes dualities because the previous conditions do not arise without some form of intervention and management (Graetz and Smith, 2008).

Simultaneity

The foundational duality characteristic is simultaneity. Dualities represent the simultaneous presence of what conventionally have been considered contradictory if not mutually exclusive elements (Cameron and Quinn, 1988; Van de Ven and Poole, 1988). In their early work, Lawrence and Lorsch (1967) presciently argued that organizations would be increasingly expected to manage heterogeneous environments in which highly dynamic sectors operate simultaneously alongside relatively stable sectors. Similarly, Abernathy (1978) observed that an organization's competitive survival over time depends not only on its ability to increase efficiency, but also on its ability to be efficient and innovative simultaneously. The importance of dualistic simultaneity further underlines Pascale's (1990) claim that the tension or 'dynamic synthesis' between contradictory opposites provides the catalyst for long-term organizational effectiveness and self-renewal. Social systems like organizations rely on both chance and necessity, and situations of instability and bifurcation (Fuchs, 2003).

Simultaneity and contradiction reveal the push–pull tension of organizational dualities, such as accountability and freedom, individuality and teamwork, action and reflection, and competition and cooperation (Evans, 1992; Evans et al., 2002; Pettigrew et al., 2003). While 'apparent' opposites, they operate through 'mutual specification' as complementary and interdependent activities (Ford and Backoff, 1988, p. 102). A dualities-sensitive approach therefore does not attempt to resolve or eliminate these inherent contradictions, but instead encourages a complementary interplay between simultaneously operating forces. In this sense, poles in a duality are not contradictory or antagonistic because they can be reconciled as mutually beneficial, which distinguishes dualities from other types of tension such as trade-offs and dialectics (Gaim, Wåhlin, e Cunha and Clegg, 2018). The interactive, 'operational' characteristics of 'simultaneity' also highlight the relational nature of duality characteristics.

Relational

The bi-modal nature of dualities, integral to simultaneity, also manifests in its relational, interdependent nature. Clegg, da Cunha and e Cunha (2002, p. 494), for example, stressed the importance of a bi- rather than uni-directional relationship between opposite poles. Bi-directional relationships involve not only simultaneous, but also mutual feedback: 'when these relationships are symmetrical, we are in the presence of a synthesis—a synthesis that emerges in the *relationship* between the two opposite poles rather than their merger into a schizophrenic entity'. This relationship becomes most important when considering the fundamentally different logics of exploration and exploitation that create tensions between the simultaneous need to explore new possibilities while exploiting 'old certainties' (He and Wong, 2004). Recognizing the bi-directional relationship between exploration and exploitation is critical to survival and prosperity because it ensures a dual focus on short-term viability and long-term growth (He and Wong, 2004).

The relational characteristic illustrates that organizations are not independent of the other practices they house (Graetz and Smith, 2008). Dualities often relate to other dualities (Pettigrew et al., 2003). These relationships exist as bi-polar, interrelated tensions where certainty–uncertainty entwines with expected–unexpected and routine–non-routine in a larger system of bi-polar pairs (Seo et al., 2004). Dualities involve bi-polar systems of thinking and acting (Pettigrew and Fenton, 2000). As relational interdependence suggests, a change to one can affect all of the others as well (Graetz and Smith, 2008).

Minimal Thresholds

Dualities need a minimal threshold. Clegg et al. (2002) argued that the poles must be kept above a minimum to ensure that a centrifugal (enabling) rather than centripetal (constraining) force emerges. However, a certain level at each pole creates the tension necessary to stimulate a duality. In this respect, while Clegg et al. sensibly caution that too much at each pole of change and stability leads to a collision that constrains, a minimal threshold of desirable attributes is also essential. A minimal consensus ensures that the status quo is not implacable and unchallenged (Hedberg et al., 1976). Thus, minimal contentment and minimal affluence encourages commitment, yet also mediates against complacency and inertia. Minimal consistency and minimal rationality are both needed so that exploration and exploitation work hand in hand within the framework of a self-designing organization (Graetz and Smith, 2008). A degree of ambiguity, contradiction and incoherence provides the catalyst for organizational learning, diversity and renewal.

Pettigrew et al. (2003) proposed that success no longer depends on having the best strategic plan or organizational structure in place, but on having the capability to continuously reinvent them. Change managers need to recognize and embrace the need for ongoing learning, strategizing and structuring to avoid the constraints and inertial qualities of embedded systems. The arrival of the 'knowledge age' has proven decisive to competitive advantage, extending to this valuable and unquantifiable resource a fluidity and elusiveness that requires continuous effort (Pettigrew et al., 2003). The 'dynamic' becomes evident in the relationship between the two 'different logics' of exploration and exploitation, where a minimal dynamic ensures a healthy tension between the forces of exploration and exploitation.

Dynamic capabilities come with streams of innovation that simultaneously exploit and explore (Ancona, Goodman, Lawrence and Tushman, 2001). The characteristic 'minimal thresholds' depends upon a corresponding dynamic between the 'simultaneity' and 'relational' duality characteristics to establish a healthy tension between the two opposing poles. The purposeful, active connection between characteristics leads us to consider the role of 'dynamism'.

Dynamism

In discussing the simultaneous, relational nature of dualities, its dynamic and flexible quality can be seen. The duality characteristic of dynamism underlines the bi-modal, interactive nature of dualities relationships. Here, energy and feedback are pivotal to competing but simultaneous criteria (Cameron and Quinn, 1988). In this way, dynamism demonstrates how duality thinking invokes a complementary force that encourages a dynamic interaction between duality poles such as integration and differentiation. In essence, organizations never reach a state of balanced equilibrium (Evans and Doz, 1992), primarily because the simultaneous need for freedom and order within social systems means that these two poles often act against each other. If dynamic capabilities play a central role in flexibility, creativity and timing (Galunic and Eisenhardt, 2001), then maintaining a healthy balance between simultaneously contradictory truths becomes critical. Some argue that duality thinking places the concept of time at the heart of change (Evans, 1992; Evans et al., 2002). The simultaneous presence of competing tensions invokes an engine of adaptation, which powers the 'dynamic' role they play in mediating a balance between continuity and change, and order and disorder (Galunic and Eisenhardt, 2001).

The tension between the two opposing poles needs to be managed on a continuous basis to ensure an ongoing interaction between constraining and enabling forces. Senior leaders should instigate practices that enable lower-level management to appreciate tensions as salient to organizational behaviour at all levels (Knight and Paroutis, 2017). Connectivity between the dynamic characteristic of dualities and their relational properties also acknowledges how minimal thresholds ameliorate potential dangers associated with extreme poles. The 'dynamism' characteristic works with its counterparts, simultaneity, relational and minimal thresholds, to maintain a 'constructive' tension, 'a state where there is sufficient tension to mobilize change and action, but not so much as to engender politicization or perverse, unintended consequences' (Evans, 1999, p. 330).

Improvisation

The dynamic and symbiotic properties of dualities suggest the centrality of improvisation (Graetz and Smith, 2008). Improvisation represents a fusion of intended and emergent action, which manifests as a mix of control with innovation, exploitation with exploration, and routine with non-routine (Weick, 1998). In this sense, improvisation represents a dynamic but integral component of dualities, intrinsically embedded as a consequence of its emergent potential (Tsoukas and Chia, 2002). Similarly, Clegg et al. (2002) observed that paradox and contradiction infuse organizational life and need to be managed accordingly. In organizations that differentiated exploration and exploitation poles, but did not integrate poles (and the reverse), tensions led to further conflict. It was only by utilizing both differentiation and integration of poles that organizations sufficiently shifted attention to maintain an adaptive decision-making approach over time that supported strategic paradoxes (Smith, 2014).

Improvisation illustrates the value of a bi-directional relationship between two opposing poles by encouraging activities that alter, revise, create and discover rather than simply shift, switch or add (Weick, 1998). A dynamic interplay emerges between duality poles. For example, plans and action (representing continuity and change) are not separate. Rather, plans become amended through improvisation as the result of changing circumstances, before being enacted (Clegg et al., 2002). As a mediating action, improvisation reinforces how two organizing dualities can work dynamically to shape decision making. Improvisation can therefore be seen as an ongoing, iterative action which works in sync with the characteristics of simultaneity, relational, minimal thresholds and dynamism to manage continuity and change.

CONTINUITY AND CHANGE: COMPETING AND COMPLEMENTARY FORCES

Figure 13.1 provides a framework of the five duality characteristics and typical continuity–change dualities that managers must deal with daily. It shows the nature and role of each characteristic and how they operate in tandem to manage simultaneously operating dual approaches to management such as control and flexibility, and hierarchy and networks. It also aims to depict their role in arbitrating between the competing continuity–change goals. Simultaneity, which captures the heterogeneous, qualitative nature of dualities, represents the starting point for understanding and managing organizational dualities. The relational duality characteristic points to the interactive, symbiotic attributes of the dualistic tensions that arise from continuity and change. In addition, relational interdependence within these dual forms of organizing highlights the advantages that come from managing contradictions as complementarities. This in turn illustrates the importance of a 'both/and' rather than 'either/or' mindset, facilitated through a dynamic balance of minimal levels along the continuity–change continuum. The characteristic dynamism keeps the minimum thresholds in tune to ensure the organization stays poised on the competitive cusp (Deephouse, 1999) between order and disorder, and that an enabling tension is maintained between exploration and exploitation. Improvisation serves as the arbiter between the intended and the emergent by encouraging simultaneity, interdependence, minimal thresholds and dyna-

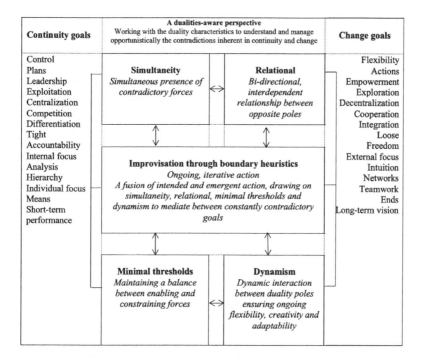

Continuity goals	A dualities-aware perspective Working with the duality characteristics to understand and manage opportunistically the contradictions inherent in continuity and change	Change goals

Figure 13.1   Duality characteristics: arbitrating continuity and change

mism. It works deliberately and extemporaneously to ensure that contradictions become complementarities.

Enabling the five characteristics requires an almost paradigmatic mind-shift. Seo et al. (2004) offered five ways to manage dualities ranging from 'selecting' one pole and rejecting the other, to 'connecting' poles to allow equal space for both to thrive. However, the characteristics do suggest boundary principles that can be placed around management activity which encourage dualities. For example, simple heuristics can work effectively as guidelines around which minimal thresholds can be safely established. That is, a high degree of flexibility can be introduced in certain areas whilst still maintaining high levels of control. For example, Macintosh and Maclean (2001) have shown how pockets of innovation can be cultivated without compromising the stability that comes through performance management.

Duality boundary heuristics can also help to implement change in complex, non-linear systems where the innovation that accompanies putative 'edge-of-chaos' conditions can be approached without fear of degenerating into random chaos. Equally, by deliberately introducing a minimal threshold through, for example, teams, managers can offset the chances of overbureaucratic order. Change managers must have tension awareness to monitor tensions created by themselves or by stakeholders advocating for opposing poles, as well as interrelated tensions created between dualities such as scope of change (small–large) and implementation style (incremental–big bang) (Boonstra, van Offenbeek and Vos, 2017). In so doing, rather than seeking to find an awkward balance between two forms of organizing, managers can increase or decrease the levels of each type relative to situational contingencies. This is, of course, where the role of improvisation comes into play.

A simple example regarding the structure of office environments provides a useful illustration of how boundary heuristics can be employed. Haynes and Price (2004) showed that organizations with high levels of bureaucracy have high levels of order but low levels of connectivity between employees; a relationship underpinned by a closed, segmented and regimented office environment. On the other hand, open-plan office structures were correlated with high levels of inter-employee connectivity and low levels of order. Duality heuristics would encourage managers to keep in mind that the best of both worlds is not necessarily a function of finding equilibrium somewhere in the middle where every employee gets an office with moveable partitions. Boundary heuristics would be used in this example by experimenting with the ideal critical densities of each configuration. In the end, for example, Haynes and Price (2004) observed that it is desirable to find a tension between the 'frozen' order of walls and doors and the 'erratic' stimulation of interruption and distraction. Instead of a compromise with a little of each, the best approach came with the informal connectivity of both walls and interruption, encouraged by some guidelines that maintained boundaries (and precluded continuous interruption), but also allowed for emergent interaction. From the viewpoint of duality theory, office structure is 'synchronistic' in that the two conditions (solitude and interaction, or in metaphoric terms, stability and change) connect through a random factor generated as a consequence of the iteration of simple heuristics. Managerial cognitive framing of apparent paradoxes, such as vicious, virtuous or ambivalent paradoxes, will influence the ability to find an adequate emergent heuristic (Karhu and Ritala, 2020).

DYNAMIC CONTROL

Boundary heuristics can provide guidance one step removed from operational activity and therefore are less likely to be obstructed by contextual variables. In some cases, the combination of a minimal threshold, simultaneity and dynamism means that managers seek to introduce deliberately destabilizing influences or order-infusing mechanisms depending on the circumstances.

Research in group dynamics has revealed, for example, that formal structures set around work teams prior to their formation can be particularly helpful in ensuring high levels of both creativity and focus (Okhuysen and Eisenhardt, 2002). Boundary heuristics such as these operate a little like Grint's (1998) notion of 'strange attractors', which act to pull a system back towards dynamic equilibrium. While the price for reaching the destination is uncertainty about the nature of the journey (Stacey, 1996), boundary heuristics offer a mechanism for enabling dualities to work in organizations.

Figure 13.1 highlights dualities that can be stimulated by observing the characteristics, and manipulated through boundary heuristics. For example, consider the duality fixed/dynamic where the presence of a duality implies that both poles are represented, and that the opportunity to pivot around either/and both is critical to success. When a chief executive officer (CEO) deliberately fails to provide senior management with any plans other than a broad vision in the hope that it would stimulate their own strategic imagination, he or she is providing a boundary heuristic governing several dualities including plan/action and centralization/decentralization.

Boundary heuristics can amplify the properties of a duality. For example, a simple heuristic establishing one hierarchical relationship in an organization can also liberate all other relationships as well. To illustrate, if the CEO of a small firm is the only real 'boss' to whom performance is reported, then there are no obstructions to the evolution of cross-functional teams and networks. Similarly, rules establishing broad objectives but without clarifying specific methods or mechanisms, while contrary to conventional strategic planning wisdom, can stimulate emergent and innovative solutions. Decision making can follow a paradoxical process approach incorporating the poles of rationality and intuition to enable the decisions considering financial and non-financial factors that are often required in innovation (Calabretta, Gemser and Wijnberg, 2017).

Dualities can be pursued with boundary heuristics which set strict guidelines that cannot be exceeded, but simultaneously allow many possibilities within their confines. The limitation for most managers is that it may be easier to create new activities on one side of the dualities ledger than on the other. Goals, budgets and definitive reporting relationships are simple and uncontroversial to introduce. Fewer managers would be prepared to create project teams, informal groups and allow resources to be deployed without careful approval. If organizational innovation needs flexibility and a critical mass of connective density between responsible employees and managers, then the minimal threshold for cross-functional groups, ad hoc meetings, task teams and other informal mechanisms that encourage unpredictability needs to be developed.

Managers cannot control organizations the same way that an operator can control a machine made of moving, but inanimate parts. This means that it might be more effective for leaders to encourage dualities and help establish boundary heuristics, but to remain less involved in operational activities. Excessive rules to help employees problem-solve can communicate that they are considered incapable of solving problems, and can lead to a workforce averse to thinking for themselves and initiating innovative solutions. Equally, no rules implicitly abandons the need for any kind of efficiency and planning towards predetermined goals. However, dualities imply that there is greater potential for emergent creativity and innovation when they are as close to disorder as they are from order. The minimal threshold comes about in the achievement of goals within order-generating rules.

CONCLUSION

According to the dualities philosophy, traditional, positivist approaches that view management and organizational change as a troublesome diversion and a simple case of unfreeze-move-refreeze have little conception of the 'unfolding, emergent qualities' of change (Tsoukas and Chia, 2002, p. 568), or of the complex, competing dynamics change managers confront. While organizations may view stability as the antidote to risk, it really presents an Achilles' heel, which may lead to 'blindness' when new insights and opportunities arise because they contradict, or threaten to destabilize, the existing 'steady state'. Yet, as Pascale (1990) suggested, the potential for self-renewal and long-term sustainability lies in responding positively and constructively to the dynamic tension between opposites. Even if ignored, the tension between conflicting goals such as creativity and efficiency, flexibility and control, individuality and teamwork are not going to disappear. Instead, they will become a toxic force constraining critical reflection, revitalization and development.

Rather than dismissing or trying to resolve opposing forces, the benefits for change managers come in learning how to tap into the creative potential of the tensions. The dualities philosophy encourages building 'both/and' constructs that accommodate contradictory elements of management as simultaneously operating truths. Change management therefore represents a form of paradox management. The management of continuity and change intricately aligns with finding a balance between order and disorder. The five duality characteristics provide a framework for managing a constructive tension between dualities, arbitrated by improvisation around boundary heuristics.

This chapter sought to develop a dualities-sensitive framework that provides a foundation to better understand and respect the tensions and ambiguities that come with managing continuity and change. As Figure 13.1 illustrated, a dualities-aware perspective makes explicit competing continuity–change goals. In turn, the interacting, iterative nature of duality characteristics shows the complementarities within contradictions. Paradox and ambiguity are revealed as healthy sites for innovation and change. Dualities theory illustrates how tensions are managed not through definitive resolution towards one pole or the other, but through the application of boundary heuristics that establish a broad conforming imperative while opening up enabling mechanisms. The concept also reinforces the need to discard assumptions about opposing values, instead replacing them with an appreciation of complementary concepts. The change–stability and order–flexibility paradoxes do not need to be interpreted as uni-dimensional choices. Flexibility might be essential in a turbulent environment in order to find new paths to innovation, but order is also necessary to ensure that innovation is focused and relevant. The utility of dualities-based heuristics is evident in some of the most pressing contemporary challenges organizations face, such as integrating seemingly incompatible economic, environmental and social tensions in sustainable development (Hahn, Pinkse, Preuss and Figge, 2015).

REFERENCES

Abernathy, William J. (1978), *The Productivity Dilemma: Roadblock to Innovation in the Automobile Industry*, Baltimore, MD: Johns Hopkins University Press.

Ancona, Deborah G., P. S. Goodman, B. S. Lawrence and M. L. Tushman (2001), 'Time: A new research lens', *Academy of Management Review*, **26**, 645–63.

Ashforth, Blake E. and P. H. Reingen (2014), 'Functions of dysfunction: Managing the dynamics of an organizational duality in a natural food cooperative', *Administrative Science Quarterly*, **59** (3), 474–516.

Biloslavo, Roberto, C. Bagnoli and R. R. Figelj (2013), 'Managing dualities for efficiency and effectiveness of organisations', *Industrial Management and Data Systems*, **113** (3), 423–42.

Birkinshaw, Julian, D. Crilly, C. Bouquet and S. Y. Lee (2016), 'How do firms manage strategic dualities? A process perspective', *Academy of Management Discoveries*, **2** (1), 51–78.

Boonstra, Albert, M. A. van Offenbeek and J. F. Vos (2017), 'Tension awareness of stakeholders in large technology projects: A duality perspective', *Project Management Journal*, **48** (1), 19–36.

Calabretta, Giulia, G. Gemser and N. M. Wijnberg (2017), 'The interplay between intuition and rationality in strategic decision making: A paradox perspective', *Organization Studies*, **38** (3–4), 365–401.

Cameron, Kim S. (1986), 'Effectiveness as paradox: Consensus and conflict in conceptions of organizational effectiveness', *Management Science*, **32** (5), 539–53.

Cameron, Kim S. and R. E. Quinn (1988), 'Organizational paradox and transformation', in Robert E. Quinn and K. S. Cameron (eds), *Paradox and Transformation: Toward a Theory of Change in Organization and Management*, Cambridge, MA: Ballinger Publishing.

Clegg, Stewart R., J. V. da Cunha and M. P. e Cunha (2002), 'Management paradoxes: A relational view', *Human Relations*, **55** (5), 483–503.

Collins, David (2003), 'Guest editor's introduction: Re-imagining change', *Tamara: Journal of Critical Postmodern Organization Science*, **2** (4), iv–xi.

Cyert, Richard M. and J. G. March (1963), *A Behavioral Theory of the Firm*, New York: McGraw-Hill.

Deephouse, David L. (1999), 'To be different, or to be the same? It's a question (and theory) of strategic balance', *Strategic Management Journal*, **20**, 147–66.

Eisenhardt, K. M. (2000), 'Paradox, spirals, ambivalence: The new language of change and pluralism', *Academy of Management Review*, **25** (4), 703–5.

Evans, Paul A. L. (1992), 'Balancing continuity and change: The constructive tension in individual and organizational development', in Warren Bennis, R. O. Mason and I. I. Mitroff (eds), *Executive and Organizational Continuity: Managing the Paradoxes of Stability and Change*, San Francisco, CA: Jossey-Bass, pp. 253–83.

Evans, Paul A. L. (1999), 'HRM on the edge: A duality perspective', *Organization*, **6** (2), 325–38.

Evans, Paul A. L. and Y. Doz (1992), 'Dualities: A paradigm for human resource and organizational development in complex multinationals', in Vladimir N. Pucik, N. M. Tichy and C. K. Barnett (eds), *Globalizing Management: Creating and Leading the Competitive Organization*, New York: Wiley, pp. 85–106.

Evans, Paul A. L., V. Pucik and J. L. Barsoux (2002), *The Global Challenge: Frameworks for International Human Resource Management*, New York: McGraw-Hill/Irwin.

Farjoun, Moshe (2010), 'Beyond dualism: Stability and change as a duality', *Academy of Management Review*, **35** (2), 202–25.

Ford, Jeffrey D. and R. W. Backoff (1988), 'Organizational change in and out of dualities and paradox', in Robert E. Quinn and K. S. Cameron (eds), *Paradox and Transformation: Toward a Theory of Change in Organization and Management*, Cambridge, MA: Ballinger Publishing.

Fuchs, Christian (2003), 'Structuration theory and self-organization', *Systemic Practice and Action Research*, **16** (2), 133–67.

Gaim, Medhanie, N. Wåhlin, M. P. e Cunha and S. Clegg (2018), 'Analyzing competing demands in organizations: A systematic comparison', *Journal of Organization Design*, **7** (1), 6.

Galunic, D. Charles and K. M. Eisenhardt (2001), 'Architectural innovation and modular corporate forms', *Academy of Management Journal*, **44** (6), 1229–49.

Giddens, Anthony (1984), *The Constitution of Society: Outline of the Theory of Structuration*, Cambridge: Polity Press.

Glynn, Mary Ann, P. S. Barr and M. T. Dacin (2000), 'Pluralism and the problem of variety', *Academy of Management Review*, **25** (4), 726–34.

Graetz, Fiona and A. Smith (2008), 'The role of dualities in arbitrating continuity and change in forms of organizing', *International Journal of Management Reviews*, **10** (3), 265–80.

Grint, Keith (1998), 'Determining the indeterminacies of change', *Management Decision*, **36** (8), 503–8.

Hahn, Tobias, J. Pinkse, L. Preuss and F. Figge (2015), 'Tensions in corporate sustainability: Towards an integrative framework', *Journal of Business Ethics*, **127** (2), 297–316.

Haynes, Barry and I. Price (2004), 'Quantifying the complex adaptive workplace', *Facilities*, **22** (1/2), 8–18.

He, Zi-Lin and P.-K. Wong (2004), 'Exploration vs. exploitation: An empirical test of the ambidexterity hypothesis', *Organization Science*, **15** (4), 481–94.

Hedberg, Bo L. T., P. C. Nystrom and W. H. Starbuck (1976), 'Camping on seesaws: Prescriptions for a self designing organization', *Administrative Science Quarterly*, **21**, 41–65.

Jackson, William A. (1999), 'Dualism, duality and the complexity of economic institutions', *International Journal of Social Economics*, **26** (4), 545–58.

Johnston, Stewart and J. W. Selsky (2006), 'Duality and paradox: Trust and duplicity in Japanese business practice', *Organization Studies*, **27** (2), 183–205.

Karhu, Päivi and P. Ritala (2020), 'The multiple faces of tension: Dualities in decision-making', *Review of Managerial Science*, **14**, 485–518.

Katz, Daniel and R. L. Kahn (1966), *The Social Psychology of Organizations*, New York: Wiley.

Kilduff, Martin and D. Dougherty (2000), 'Change and development in a pluralistic world: The view from the classics', *Academy of Management Review*, **25** (4), 777–82.

Knight, Eric and S. Paroutis (2017), 'Becoming salient: The TMT leader's role in shaping the interpretive context of paradoxical tensions', *Organization Studies*, **38** (3–4), 403–32.

Lado, Augustine A., N. G. Boyd and S. S. Hanlon (1997), 'Competition, cooperation and the search for economic rents: A syncretic model', *Academy of Management Review*, **22** (1), 110–41.

Lawrence, Paul R. and J. W. Lorsch (1967), 'Differentiation and integration in complex organizations', *Administrative Science Quarterly*, **12** (1), 1–47.

Lewis, Marianne W. (2000), 'Exploring paradox: Toward a more comprehensive guide', *Academy of Management Review*, **25** (4), 760–76.

Macintosh, Robert and D. Maclean (2001), 'Conditioned emergence: Researching change and changing research', *International Journal of Operations and Production Management*, **21** (10), 1343–57.

Morgan, Gareth (1997), *Images of Organization*, Thousand Oaks, CA: Sage.

Nasim, Saboohi and Sushil (2011), 'Revisiting organizational change: Exploring the paradox of managing continuity and change', *Journal of Change Management*, **11** (2), 185–206.

Okhuysen, Gerardo A. and K. M. Eisenhardt (2002), 'Integrating knowledge in groups: How formal interventions enable flexibility', *Organization Science*, **13** (4), 370–86.

Pascale, Richard T. (1990), *Managing on the Edge: How Successful Companies Use Conflict to Stay Ahead*, New York: Viking Penguin.

Pettigrew, Andrew M. and E. M. Fenton (2000), 'Complexities and dualities in innovative forms of organizing', in Andrew M. Pettigrew and E. M. Fenton (eds), *The Innovative Organization*, London: Sage, pp. 279–300.

Pettigrew, Andrew M., R. L. Whittington, L. Melin, C. Sanchez-Runde, F. A. J. Van Den Bosch, W. Ruigrok and T. Numagami (2003), *Innovative Forms of Organizing*, London: Sage.

Quinn, James B., P. Anderson and S. Finkelstein (1998), 'New forms of organizing', in Henry Mintzberg and J. B. Quinn (eds), *Readings in the Strategy Process*, 2nd edition, Upper Saddle River, NJ: Prentice Hall, pp. 162–74.

Quinn, Robert E. and J. Rohrbaugh (1983), 'A spatial model of effectiveness criteria: Towards a competing values approach to organizational analysis', *Management Science*, **29**, 363–77.

Sanchez-Runde, Carlos J. and A. M. Pettigrew (2003), 'Managing dualities', in Andrew M. Pettigrew, R. Whittington, L. Melin, C. Sanchez-Runde, F. A. J. Van Den Bosch,

W. Ruigrok and T. Numagami (eds), *Innovative Forms of Organizing*, London: Sage, pp. 243–50.

Schumacher, Ernst F. (1977), *A Guide for the Perplexed*, New York: Harper and Row.

Seo, Myeong-Gu, L. L. Putnam and J. M. Bartunek (2004), 'Dualities and tensions of planned organizational change', in Marshall S. Poole and A. H. Van de Ven (eds), *Handbook of Organizational Change and Innovation*, Oxford: Oxford University Press, pp. 73–107.

Smith, Aaron C. T., D. H. Gilbert and F. Sutherland (2017), 'The explore–exploit tension: A case study of organizing in a professional services firm', *Journal of Management and Organization*, **23** (4), 566–86.

Smith, Aaron C., F. Sutherland and D. H. Gilbert (2017), *Reinventing Innovation: Designing the Dual Organization*, London: Springer.

Smith, Wendy K. (2014), 'Dynamic decision making: A model of senior leaders managing strategic paradoxes', *Academy of Management Journal*, **57** (6), 1592–623.

Stacey, Ralph (1996), 'Emerging strategies for a chaotic environment', *Long Range Planning*, **29** (2), 182–9.

Stoltzfus, Kimberly, C. Stohl and D. R. Seibold (2011), 'Managing organizational change: Paradoxical problems, solutions, and consequences', *Journal of Organizational Change Management*, **24** (3), 349–67.

Sugarman, Barry (2014), 'Dynamic capability seen through a duality-paradox lens: A case of radical innovation at Microsoft', *Research in Organisational Change and Development*, **22**, 141–89.

Thompson, James D. (1967), *Organizations in Action*, New York: McGraw-Hill.

Tsoukas, Haridimos and R. Chia (2002), 'On organizational becoming: Rethinking organizational change', *Organization Science*, **13** (5), 567–82.

Van de Ven, Andrew H. and M. S. Poole (1988), 'Paradoxical requirements for a theory of organizational change', in Robert E. Quinn and K. S. Cameron (eds), *Paradox and Transformation: Toward a Theory of Change in Organization and Management*, Cambridge, MA: Ballinger Publishing, pp. 19–61.

Van de Ven, Andrew H. and M. S. Poole (2005), 'Alternative approaches for studying organizational change', *Organization Studies*, **26** (9), 1377–404.

Weick, Karl E. (1998), 'Improvisation as a mindset for organizational analysis', *Organization Science*, **9** (5), 543–55.

14. Conclusion: 'changing futures'

INTRODUCTION

Change can be understood as the movement away from a present state towards a future state. But this statement hides the fact that change is rarely easy or painless. At the same time, the capacity to change to meet environmental challenges is essential for organizational survival. However, the best approach—what we have termed 'philosophy'—for approaching change has become heavily complicated by cautious behavioural researchers who frequently do not get beyond describing the complexity of change, and zealous business consultants who discard all theoretical discussion in favour of simplistic but authoritative solutions. The choices for change management practitioners are further obfuscated by the variety of common management practices and tools that can be used to initiate and manage change, such as structural variations, strategic shifts, systems or process revisions, cultural modifications, technological solutions and project management methods. In this chapter, we strive to review the divergent philosophies addressed in this book, as well as offer some comments on a productive direction forward.

One starting point for observing and conceptualizing change is to establish its driving force. The force for change may be monumental or it may be small and subtle. In each case, though, the force may act as an impetus for change. This 'impetus' or 'catalyst' may then be classified according to its source. Thus, an internally driven change such as a creative design or administrative process initiative by management can be contrasted with an involuntary change made by an organization as a result of a radical change in trade practices legislation, or a sudden jolt. In other words, change can be considered on the basis of whether it is planned or unplanned. Planned or premeditated changes may display certain characteristics, which are uncommon in planned changes. A commitment to planning change, therefore, can prove decisive to the way a philosophy advocates action.

Irrespective of the stimulus for change, there is a general consensus that change involves having to overcome some form of organizational inertia; the ubiquitous problem of being stuck in a rut and immobile as a consequence of the way things have always been done. As a result, most change philosophies embrace some form of challenge to conventional wisdom, while seeking to find the awkward balance between stability and dynamism. This elusive equilibrium is typically considered in the context of a match between an organization and its environment. To find success, an organization must have a 'fit' between its primary products and services, and the needs of the marketplace. This view, of course, arrives from the domain of 'strategic' change.

Within philosophies we discover that the rapidity with which an organization should be capable of responding to the need for change is the subject of some debate. For example, some external disturbances can be so prodigious that unless organizations respond immediately and profoundly, they may be permanently incapacitated or worse. At the same time, some philosophies assume that most change is incremental, and should be implemented with a slow and steady mindset. Others take the middle ground, arguing that successful change comes from both swift action and steady improvement. To complicate matters further, every philosophy adopts a different perspective concerning how an organization should respond to imposed, external change.

Separating out change forces, their magnitude and organizational responses is extremely complex. First, the change impetus may be significant or weak in magnitude. Second, it may originate from inside the organization, the immediate organizational environment or from the industrial sector. Finally, an organization may be differentiated based on its response to the change imperative. Responses may vary between complete disinterest and strategic proactivity. It is also appropriate to note that the change may proceed or not proceed irrespective of the desires and actions of organizations and their leaders.

Different change philosophies advocate a range of sophisticated conceptual models to explain the nature of change both within industries and organizations. One way of understanding the complexities of each approach is to consider them against two dimensions: type and level. Type refers to the size and rapidity of the change, while level describes whether the change is proceeding within a specific organization or as part of a broader sector-wide reform. A philosophy can favour small or large change, and/or focus on change inside or outside an organization. As a result, philosophies can emphasize incremental change, or push for radical change. In addition, they can concentrate on change directed from within the organization, or change that is imposed from outside it. Of course, the character of the emphasis tends to determine whether a philosophy is proactive or reactive, and whether it prefers sweeping changes or modest ones. Moreover, if a philosophy's pre-eminent concern is the outside industrial environment, it likely downplays the importance of planned, internal action. In some cases, a philosophy assumes that an organization has complete control of its own change agenda, while another philosophy can presuppose that the choices are bounded, sometimes severely. We have also examined philosophies premised on a view that very little if anything of importance ever really changes, as well as those that begin with individuals as change agents rather than organizations.

Different philosophies predict that the scale of the change will have an impact on the nature of the obstacles an organization will encounter. For example, massive environmental chaos, uncertainty and even catastrophe can shift organizations whether they like it or not. In other, more stable times, organizations can barely manage any change at all despite concerted efforts. Some philosophies prioritize internal resistance to change, while others become preoccupied with the tide of industrial and external forces as the key levers. A further distinction between philosophies concerns how they perceive resistance, as for some it manifests in the psychological responses of organizational members, while for others it plays out through organizational systems, structures, policies and procedures. The middle ground sees culture, power or resources as the linchpin of change.

A REVIEW

In this text we have described and assessed 12 philosophies of organizational change. Our approach was to examine each of the philosophies by detailing and critiquing their methods for change. In Chapter 2, dealing with changing theories, we noted that philosophies express their methods for change through inferences about the most effective ways of thinking about change, which in turn leads to recommendations for interventions, tools and techniques to bring about change in a practical sense. At the core of each philosophy are 'theories', or the conditional generalizations that a philosophy builds its change inferences and assumptions upon. In Chapter 2, we considered how the theory philosophy places emphasis not only on the importance of change theories, but also on how theories change over time, whether refined, updated, expanded or replaced. Rather than advocate for one type of theory, the theories philosophy assumes that change can be explained by developing or connecting theories over time to deliver an increasingly comprehensive, overarching theory of change. By implication, the theory philosophy links understanding change with the development of more accurate, inclusive and far-reaching theories. Here, the key to successful organizational change can be traced back to the most fundamental unit there is for its understanding—theories. Furthermore, in order to accommodate the shifting nature of the organizational environment, change managers should be on the lookout for better theories all the time.

Chapter 3 addressed the rational philosophy, which remains the enduring approach upon which change management practitioners primarily rely. Part of its popularity emanates from the strategic alignment the rational philosophy encourages between an organization's competencies and environmental opportunities. In addition, the rational philosophy makes the compelling case that change pivots upon leaders' whims because they wield the power to make best use of resources in the pursuit of objectives. Change is only limited by a leader's capacity to envision a new future. Once a vision and accompanying objectives have been determined, the change becomes a mechanical and clinical process. Sound planning and execution can bring about any change. Firmly in the hands of leaders, success reflects a capacity to translate objectives into stepwise actions. Change is only a plan away.

Rational approaches assume that intention and outcome connect in a causal and linear manner. Change predictably results from simple steps in the strategic process. Any prescriptive, logical and simple advice for introducing change tends to be well received by change managers. After all, navigating the uncertainties of organizational behaviour will be aided by a decent map. Because rational models provide piecemeal steps for implementing change, they can be bolted on to most change philosophies. However, rational models seldom recognize the complexities of change and the impact of external, unplanned circumstances. Reality can quickly diverge from even the best plans. As a result, the rational philosophy has moved to incorporate strategy-as-action approaches to change that give more attention to leaders and practice than to organizations and planning.

While the rational philosophy dominates the practical introduction of change, the biological philosophy examined in Chapter 4, and the metaphors it has generated based on the natural world, enjoy the longest history of use. Biological approaches seem intuitive because change represents a normal response to dynamic environmental circumstances. For business organizations in particular, metaphors emphasizing the ruthless struggle for survival and reproduction, as well as the need for constant adaptation, seem fitting. Population ecologists treat industries like biologists treat species. Industries evolve incrementally in response to the most forceful environmental pressures. As a result of this evolutionary process, organizations within the same industry assume similar configurations in order to maximize their chance of prosperity.

Non-incrementalists favour the punctuated equilibrium model of organizational evolution where radical change interjects between periods of stability. Both incremental and rapid change can be seen in organizations, and both metaphors have proven useful in revealing the way external forces mould change. Another biological metaphor, the life-cycle theory, offers a linear interpretation of the way individual organizations evolve. This approach considers change from the perspective of individual organisms as they are born, grow, mature and ultimately die. Similarly, an organization goes through start-up, expansion, maturity and divestment. Change merely follows the transition along its natural curve of progression, but at least the common problems at each stage are foreshadowed for managers to anticipate. The biological philosophy reveals change to be inevitable but nevertheless predictable. More recently, the biological philosophy has expanded to include the concept of 'ecosystems', where networks of actors, agents, organizations and stakeholders create a synergistic system that collectively delivers greater value than independent activity. Ecosystems offer a glimpse into what happens when two philosophies intersect, as it imports a systems concept into the biological philosophy.

The models philosophy, outlined in Chapter 5, also readily accepts the appropriation of parts of one approach for use in a change intervention model. In the chapter, we explored the kinds of change prescriptions advocated—and sold—by consultants. We used the term 'models' because consultants most often present ready-made, one-size-fits-all approaches that place an exclusive emphasis on one particular concept, idea or framework. For both efficiency and market-positioning reasons, consultants employ the same change model for every client that employs them. The chapter did not aim to provide a comprehensive catalogue of every major change model offered by consultants. Instead, it sought to show how the models philosophy uses a particular kind of organizational change approach that is heavily dependent on predetermined frameworks and concepts. It also reveals the pivotal models that started the change-consulting movement, and upon which most contemporary models have used as inspiration.

From the most practical of philosophies in Chapter 5, we turned to one of the most theoretical in Chapter 6, focused on the institutional philosophy. Like population ecology from the biological philosophy, the institutional philosophy concerns industries rather than organizations. Change comes through the shaping forces of the institutional environment, which pressure organizations to conform. The pressure upon organizations towards commonality—also known as isomorphism—means that change managers cannot choose from an unlimited set of choices determined by managerial strategy. Unlike the rational philosophy, strategy is constrained to the alternatives imposed by institutional conditions emanating from competitors, regulatory agencies, social conventions and so on. 'New' institutionalism goes further, recognizing that institutional forces can come from diverse sources, such as new management techniques. Understanding that power accompanies institutional norms confers several advantages to change managers. For example, changes to institutional circumstances can be anticipated, helping managers select better future structures and practices. When change managers better appreciate the forces impelling conformity, they can respond accordingly. Of course, any proactive change response might legitimately be considered a rational action. However, as clever as any change response might be, organizations still require the resource building blocks essential to delivering competitive advantages.

In Chapter 7 we switched from the institutional environment to the availability of organizational resources as the key precipitant of change. The resource philosophy, presented in Chapter 7, which has delivered resource dependence and resource-based theory, views the acquisition and deployment of resources as critical to survival and prosperity. Organizations acquire, grow and utilize resources, changing accordingly. How organizations cluster their resources determines competitive success. The central tenet of the resource philosophy holds that resources—human, financial, knowledge-based and others—represent pivotal assets that can be combined in unique and powerful ways in order to bring about change. Managers charged with organizational change therefore focus on reconfiguring existing resources and obtaining new ones in ways that exploit unique advantages.

Since resource deployment and utilization fall under the control of leaders, management competence ranks amongst the most important of assets. In fact, successful change reflects leaders' capacities to organize their resource assets in more powerful configurations. Like the institutionalist position, the environment plays a critical role in affecting the availability of critical resources. Change managers should develop strategies for reducing environmental uncertainty. As a strong theme in strategic management, the resource-based view intersects with the rational philosophy under conditions of organizational change. However, the strategic management of resources adds a novelty in assuming that each organization possesses a unique composition, founded upon resource assets, or perhaps even resource liabilities. While change might necessitate strategy, successful strategic change will be different in every organization. At this point the rational and resource philosophies diverge, because the former insists that strategic planning will always bring about successful change. But some organizations will be incapable of shifting their unique, difficult-to-imitate, non-substitutable resources towards a desired goal, particularly if the necessary resources for change are unavailable from the environment. Some organizations endure severe resource deficiencies within unforgiving environments where no amount of planning will introduce change. For example, a strategic plan may not be enough to bring about change in organizations mired in deeply entrenched circumstances, or which are bottled up by institutional pressures to conform. Unlike the institutional perspective, the resource perspective best explains deviance, in the form of a resource configuration leading to a competitive advantage, rather than conformity. Similarly, the resource view can be differentiated from a purely rational view of change where the strategy process itself represents a conformist approach, and it is assumed that the resources essential for change already reside within an organization.

In Chapter 7 we also considered behaviourist modes of change thinking, such as contingency theory, which may be usefully applied to the resource philosophy. Here, the degree of fit between different organizational components, relevant to the situation at hand, should be the ones considered for change.

As with the resource philosophy, the efficiency demands that accompany competitive environments force managers to change composition. However, unlike institutionalists, contingency theory views conformity as one of numerous, competing pressures. Contingency advocates are natural adversaries of rational change as they contend that the best approach cannot be planned or forced. Contingency and resource theorists accept that human responses to change defy predictability. A complete account of organizational change therefore needs to accommodate the human dimension.

Rational models portray change as a perfunctory process where human beings comprise another construction material to be shaped and placed in the correct location. In contrast to a mechanical interpretation of people in the change process, organizational (and industrial) psychology and social psychology claim that individual responses to change determine its success. As a result, the psychological philosophy presented in Chapter 8 addressed the human side of the change equation. Where biological and institutional metaphors focus on industries, and the rational and resource perspective on organizations, the psychological philosophy holds individuals to be the most important unit to study.

In Chapter 8, we explained how, emerging from the psychological philosophy, organizational development (OD) and change transitions provide theories seeking to explain personal change experiences. OD employs knowledge from the applied behavioural sciences in order to understand individuals' experiences of change through 'action' research and intervention. According to OD, resistance to change can be managed with care and sensitivity. Similarly, change transitions theory begins by acknowledging that change incurs psychological and emotional trauma for employees. Transitions means approaching change like a psychiatrist treats mental illness, constantly evaluating, diagnosing and treating, until change can be transitioned from rejection to acceptance. All psychological approaches seek to understand the personal feelings and emotions of employees, in some cases to the point of 'empowerment' in decision making. As an approach to change management, the psychological perspective can help us understand general disaffection and even ameliorate the destructive impact of resistance. As part of the chapter, we further examined the importance of the 'cognitive' dimension of organizational change. A cognitive perspective demonstrates how the beliefs and thinking modes of organizational members can moderate their responses to change initiatives.

Treating individuals as the carriers of change leads to a weaker position when dealing with the systems organizations rely upon for the delivery of their products and services. To theoretical expansion, strategic thinking, evolutionary development, institutional pressure, resource deployment and personal responses, the astute change manager should add an appreciation of how systems change organizations. To that end, in Chapter 9, we explained the systems philosophy. Systems thinking and general systems theory treats organizations as complex machines, where change means tinkering with the convoluted interaction of dynamic parts. Simple causality does not work because organizations behave as open systems, influenced by the environment, as well as any number of internal conditions. In fact, even small changes to one part of an organization will have multiple and cascading effects across the rest of the organization. As a consequence, change must be undertaken across every organizational part or sub-system.

Systems theories overlap with biological models that observe the natural world as a giant system of almost immeasurable complexity. Like the biological philosophy, the systems philosophy borrows from natural systems to help explain the intricacies of complex and dynamic organizations. Part of the attraction lies with extending theories beyond causal relationships. Like changes in weather patterns, organizations exhibit changes difficult to trace to logical causes. As a result, complexity theory explains how organizations seem to totter precariously between utter chaos and rigid order. Such 'chaordic' (chaos-order) change shows how organizations can seem to possess incompatible characteristics at the same time. For complexity systems theorists, neatly planned change exists only in textbooks; change is messy and non-linear. The best way to view change is from a holistic viewpoint, with organizations accounting for more than the sum of their parts. Successful change accompanies the 'edge of chaos', a point where disorder produces unexpected innovation and control ensures that it can be put to good use.

Where complexity theory explains emergent change, chaos theory explains how the combination of simple systems can lead to chaos and unpredictability. From this perspective, organizations are in a constant state of flux, tempered by occasional bouts of stability and order, representing the complete opposite to the biological philosophy's punctuated equilibrium model. While systems like organizations may appear to be random and chaotic, they actually begin with simple rules that have the potential to get out of hand. Notwithstanding the limited practical dimensions of complexity and chaos theories, systems approaches have succeeded because they offer prescriptions for change. The variations on total quality management and best practices illustrate the enduring popularity of systems approaches that provide clear guidelines for change action. However, few can agree on what these guidelines should be. While some have proved useful in certain circumstances, many systems-based change models are faddish and flimsy. As a result, theorists with an affinity for both the systems and psychological philosophy began to explore deeper and murkier territory in the hope of revealing what it is that makes organizations 'tick'. From this anthropological dig emerged the cultural philosophy.

The cultural philosophy, described in Chapter 10, receives its inspiration from anthropology, the social science that studies the origins and social relationships of human beings. Cultural thinking approaches change as a process of interpreting and influencing the behavioural and social patterns of individuals within an organization and their responses to the environment. Culture represents the collection of values and attitudes common to organizational members. Because these values and attitudes set the behavioural standards and norms for all members, they offer a potent target for change. However, change managers face the challenging task of diagnosing cultural values before they can be changed. While most researchers believe that cultural meaning permeates every aspect of an organization, they also acknowledge the impossibility of directly accessing deep values. Change, therefore, has to be targeted at multiple, superficial manifestations of culture in the hope that it can affect hidden or protected values.

Like the psychological philosophy, culture takes an interest in personal responses to the change experience. However, while psychologists examine the behaviour of individuals, culturalists assess the common behaviours of individuals operating within groups and the organization in general. The shared behaviours and experiences generate the most attention because they are shaped by prevailing cultural norms. Although cultural theorists acknowledge that individuals freely choose their own behaviour, the reasons why they choose to behave like everyone else stimulates far more interest. Culturally oriented change managers try to challenge the shared values they consider dysfunctional or unhelpful in realizing goals. However, doing this badly can create substantial conflict and disaffection. Culture powerfully shapes behaviour and there can be little argument that its diagnosis plays a role in understanding how certain changes will be received. On the other hand, cultural change is slow and difficult; its introduction requires a rational and systemic approach in order to cover the whole range of cultural outcroppings around an organization. Critical theorists think that cultural change cannot be undertaken without manipulating the power relationships that govern an organization. After all, if leaders want change they have to make it happen.

As we revealed in Chapter 11, critical philosophy advocates approach organizational change from the viewpoint of power and conflict. Change comes with winning the fight for organizational control leading to a new ideological or positional agenda; change and politics are inseparable. Change managers attempt to introduce new philosophies, approaches or ideas into an organization. Since this means displacing an existing status quo, change begins with the acquisition of sufficient power to make a challenge, and inevitably culminates in conflict stimulated by clashing beliefs.

Political theorists from the critical philosophy expect change to be a conflict-driven phenomenon where interventions take the form of bargaining, lobbying, persuasion, propaganda, manipulation, influence, intimidation, posturing and the application of various types of power. A connection might be seen here with the psychological philosophy as politics introduces an intensely social agenda. It remains impossible to escape the human inclination to seek influence while assuming that one's own beliefs are correct. Change becomes an adversarial event where success relies on power. Another view in the form of postmodernism, however, suggests that any form of universal explanation for change will prove unsatisfactory.

The prevailing modern view of organizational change embraces the rational perspective that sufficient analysis will ultimately reveal everything important. Postmodernism rejects such certainty, arguing that the world is fragmented, messy and contradictory. Accordingly, knowledge is relative rather than absolute, determined by social reality rather than some universal truth. Postmodern interpretations of change reject universal theories. Instead, change should be understood through the social realities constructed by organizational members. Given its recognition of different, co-existing social realities, postmodernism shares some ground with the cultural perspective and systems-based complexity theory. Postmodernism departs from other philosophies of change in claiming that language, symbols and organizational artefacts remain distant from real-world experience. Discourse analysis has taken this perspective much further by showing how language uncovers important social phenomena.

'Discourse' refers to conversation or dialogue, and discursive analysis assumes that language (written, spoken, heard and read) creates the social worlds in which organizations attempt change. Since systems of representation influence social worlds, 'reality' itself is a social construction. The way the world appears to one organizational member will not be common to all. Furthermore, the absence of a universal social reality means that introducing organizational change will be different for every organization. Change managers therefore must find ways of understanding and assessing their organization's constructed reality because it is the only real window into lasting change. Although the constructed reality concept appears similar to the cultural philosophy, it emphasizes discourse as the best mechanism to affect change, usually through the application of some form of power.

In contrast to the critical view, Chapter 12 on the innovation philosophy highlighted a new but increasingly popular approach to organizational change that places the power across all levels of the organization, based on a firmly realist notion that there is only one reality, and it demands change by doing things differently. The innovation philosophy of organizational change arrived in response to a rapid, global transformation in commerce and technology forcing organizations to find new ways to remain competitive. Innovation theorists maintain that in radically turbulent environments, an organization's performance has less to do with efficiency and productivity and more to do with its capacity to adapt and innovate. Accordingly, innovation-driven change focuses on the generation of new ideas and their scaling into new products and services, processes and procedures.

The chapter noted that the innovation philosophy recommends an entrepreneurial mindset, which encourages comfort with risk, experimentation and accepting fast and cheap failures as excellent learning investments. A more recent trend has introduced the practice of design thinking as a tool to supplement an organization's innovation process. Design thinking rallies around a user-centric approach to new ideas and product testing. By working directly with prospective consumers, design methods sidestep the conventional but expensive and lengthy use of market research and product refinement. Advocates claim that innovation-driven change allows organizations to react to market volatility in creative ways, develop new products and services and establish an organizational framework for continual rejuvenation. However, they also acknowledge that sustaining innovation-driven organizational change requires a deep culture shift. In addition, potential shortfalls in an organization's innovation capabilities may detract from its capacity to implement ideas rapidly, cost-effectively, and design a process that will accelerate the product to market. As a result, innovation-inspired change tends to be viewed as powerful but risky.

At the outset of Chapter 13, which detailed the duality philosophy, we reminded the reader that traditional approaches to organizational change follow a linear, rational model where control and strategy emanate from a strong leader. The underlying premise assumes that change involves a series of predictable, reducible steps that can be planned and managed. The evidence from case after case of failed change attempts indicates, however, that the reality of change defies simple, planned responses. The rational philosophy not only represents a limited, one-dimensional approach to change, but it also ignores the messy, complex and iterative nature of change. Perhaps more importantly, it fails to accommodate the fact that change and continuity work in a dynamic tension. Organizations cannot prosper at either extreme of rapid change or intractable inertia. As a result, change leaders struggle to instigate change from the top while the operational bottom demands continuity. The dualities philosophy attempts to respond to this fundamental dilemma.

From the classic, rational perspective, change management decision making comes down to an either-or choice between change and continuity, such as innovation and efficiency; collaboration and competition; freedom and accountability; and new and old. However, according to the dualities philosophy, organizational change cannot always be a matter of reducing one kind of activity to offset another kind. In fact, often organizations need more of *both* top-down leadership and bottom-up empowerment. Understandably, some change practitioners would reject one approach for the other because they seem to represent diametrically opposite views. But the dualities view argues that change agents should consider the advantages of an organizational culture that might be described as both loose and tight. Its non-hierarchical management approach and entrepreneurial spirit encourage high levels of autonomy and discretionary power, within a strong risk and performance management framework.

The dualities philosophy further claims that, ironically, change management cannot be only about change. The need for both continuity and change means becoming comfortable with the ever present dilemma of tension between the two. It also means managing the dynamics of human interaction and responses to external perturbations alongside institutionalized structures, systems and routines, and harnessing this dynamic to challenge existing practices where they are no longer appropriate. A dualities approach concludes that managing change demands balancing and conciliating what often appear as conflicting dilemmas.

PHILOSOPHIES IN NARRATIVE

We started our 12-part philosophy journey with the premise that organizational change should be understood through theoretical constructs that explain and predict its character. Over time, these constructs become more comprehensive and powerful, delivering superior theoretical understanding, and therefore better practical guidance. Our first philosophy, 'theories', therefore focuses on *changing theories*. However, for most change agents, the prospects of building a better theory is just too abstract to be useful. As a result, most change practitioners rely on the 'rational' philosophical tradition; organizational change is about *changing plans*. While plans, and the strategy underpinning them, are undoubtedly helpful, they can fail to capture the evolutionary, animated nature of organizations, which suggests that organizational change can also be about *changing organisms*. According to the 'biological' philosophy, treating organizations as if they are natural living organisms invites a greater appreciation for their dynamic properties.

With the rational and biological philosophies assuming that change can simply be planned or grown respectively, a gap emerges between the two popular approaches. With the commercial opportunities in mind, organizational change consultants propose 'models' for change purportedly designed to control its introduction. These stepwise models promise organizational change by *changing consultants*. At the same time, other theorists reject the idea that change can be delivered by predetermined, linear models. Rather, they point to evidence indicating that organizations succumb to 'institutional' forces funnelling them towards a similar composition. Organizational change is therefore also about *changing conformity*. But, of course, change aims to improve organizational performance, which holds relative to competitors. In order to secure a competitive advantage, organizations must possess unique attributes that are difficult to duplicate. The importance of acquiring and configuring pivotal 'resources' implies that organizational change is about *changing opportunities*.

So far, none of these philosophies acknowledges the role that organizational members play as enablers and obstructers of change. Enter the 'psychological' philosophy to remind managers that organizational change must also be about *changing minds*. But, given the difficulties in navigating the innumerable personal responses to change, some argue that we need a 'systems' philosophy, which shows that success accompanies organizational-wide interventions where *changing everything* holds the key.

Combining a systems vision with a psychological edge delivers a 'cultural' philosophy. Organizational change demands that deep aspects of identity are challenged, and *changing values* introduces new behaviours and superior performance. But this might not be enough, because any realistic approach to change accepts that power must be wielded, if only to empower employees. A more 'critical' interpretation proposes that change has to account for the individual constructions of social reality and that organizational change is akin to *changing realities*.

In the opposite corner to those who want to change social reality are those who think that reality is fixed and organizations need to be the ones to adapt. Adaptation for the 'innovation' philosophy means *changing ideas*, which in turn can be converted into new products and ways of performing. Finally, the 'cake and eat it too' 'duality' philosophy argues for the simultaneous pursuit of the old and new; of rational strategy and of creative innovation, or *changing tensions*. Just because doing both at the same time seems contradictory is no reason not to aim for the best of both worlds. One conclusion must be certain: organizational change cannot be encapsulated by a single philosophy. A more comprehensive, inclusive philosophy seems warranted, which returns us to the problems inherent in the first 'theories' philosophy.

CHANGING FUTURES

The contemporary business environment, characterized by globalization, deregulation and the information age, has spawned a variety of new angles on existing philosophies of change. To at least some extent, these current trends attempt to deal with the need for added flexibility, responsiveness and adaptability. They also tend to shift in focus away from traditionally 'hard' management approaches with their associated machine bureaucracies and divisional structures, to 'softer', more people-focused approaches, with flexible structures that have the capacity to respond swiftly and effectively to change, and that give priority to organizational innovation.

Along with the new business imperative for change to deliver innovation has come an increased willingness to mix and match philosophies, conflating previously impermeable boundaries and experimenting in order to test out what works. For example, new change agendas have been constructed around concepts like design thinking, networking, virtual teams, collaboration, synergies and prototyping. In addition, change managers can consider numerous project management methods like Six Sigma, Lean Manufacturing and Agile. However, these concepts have been imported from other disciplines, and as a result have not yet integrated into any of the more established philosophical approaches.

Part of the challenge lies in reconciling the contradictions that accompany change in the contemporary organizational environment. For example, change has become a perpetual process best approached by recognizing the existing business operations that are working, while simultaneously developing creative strategies and identifying new opportunities. However, most entrenched philosophies do not accommodate contradictory assumptions or ambitions when it comes to change. Yet, organizational leaders stand the greatest chance of negotiating the contemporary business environment when they discard unilateral philosophical assumptions and adopt a more flexible approach to change.

More and more, the human side of organizations is being supplemented or supplanted by artificial structures like artificial intelligence that are more efficient or inexpensive. This trend has implications for the change management of human resources. For the most part, the trends driving organizational change are those associated with technology, competition and industrial reform. In concert with an increasingly educated marketplace of customers calling for greater responsiveness and customization, organizations are under enormous pressure to change lumbering practices into more flexible ones that possess the capacity for greater learning, adaptation and responsiveness.

Another major issue confounding the development of new and more flexible change philosophies is the question of what the next generation of leadership should focus on. There is little understanding about how excellent leaders can maintain their competitive advantage over time, and during the most rapidly changing business environment ever experienced. Establishing a sustainable competitive advantage through leadership and its development therefore represents a change management philosophy opportunity. Different forms of change demand different types of leadership styles. Some emerging evidence suggests that leadership at different levels of organizational life may be entirely different. Leadership competencies may not be as hierarchical and cumulative as an organization itself. The increasing need for leadership direction during defining events is a gap in change philosophies. This, of course, is largely an outcome of international events and the pace of organizational activity in a globalized, technologically impelled economy.

A final problem with conventional philosophies of change is their ability to make strategic measurements during the change process in order to provide critical information to organizational managers. Without the feedback obtained from monitoring the right variables at the right time, there is no information upon which to evaluate philosophical approaches and to adjust, making effective measurement tools a valuable commodity. However, having implemented a measurement programme, the evaluation of change data is difficult, with managers often unable to separate numerous variables in the change programme. The measurement and evaluation of change is therefore an important consideration with two related issues: the identification of reliable measurement variables, and the development of effective evaluation methods. The problem is that each philosophy prioritizes different measures, tools and feedback methods.

Three common methods for measuring change are (1) financial indicators, (2) strategy-driven measures and (3) benchmarks. All three have advantages and disadvantages but financial indicators are perhaps the most common due to the ease with which they can be identified, and their 'tangibility'. Financial measures do, however, have several disadvantages including the need for long-term data, an inability to distinguish causality and their backward-looking nature. Strategy-driven measures include organizationally unique critical success factors such as customer satisfaction or safety data, and looking forward, evaluating present performance against future targets. There are concerns attributed to these measures, however, including the difficulties of including the divergent interests of multiple stakeholders, and problems establishing how data from key performance indicators flow back into 'bottom-line' financial measures. Of more concern, these conventional organizational measures—while universally considered of pre-eminent importance—are also poorly attuned to what some philosophies view as most significant, including personal responses to change, as well as the messy confluence of inputs that stimulate innovation.

CONSEQUENCES OF CHANGE INITIATIVES: THE RISK OF FAILURE

Risk is inherent in any organizational activity, but those associated with serious and substantial change typically have the least likelihood of success of any organizational ambitions, and therefore carry the burden of significant risk. Part of the mystery of change has been its perception as a nebulous process. Even if organizational leaders are sufficiently visionary to clearly articulate their long-term objectives and can specify the way they see their organizations behaving and performing after a change, it is unusual for these performances to be defined by objective criteria beyond those associated with financial imperatives. Other goals such as efficiency, cost-effectiveness, customer and employee satisfaction, and responsiveness have often been omitted from the equation or considered implicit within financial indicators. Measuring and evaluating change has traditionally been a weakness of popular change methods. The complexities of change demand measurement that is correspondingly flexible. In fact, the veracity of planned change has been questioned, with studies examining change management initiatives reporting that the majority fail and bring with that failure a heavy economic and human toll. The chances of failure reinforce the importance of measurement, especially during the change process rather than at its conclusion, in order to provide as much feedback as possible to suggest essential corrective action.

As a result, organizations are often left with a serious dilemma: they recognize that change is necessary for ongoing prosperity or even survival, but remain aware that the potential for failure is high and consequently so are their chances of hastening their organization's demise. Why is the failure rate so high? There is no shortage of suggested answers to this conundrum. After all, successful change is the 'Holy Grail', particularly for large organizations. According to the philosophies we have reviewed in this book, a synthesis of reasons for failure include the following.

First, the key to achieving and sustaining significant change is affecting the basic values, beliefs and ways of thinking within the organization, but this is extremely difficult to achieve and sustain, as we have noted. Organizations resist new truths with a great deal of vigour. It is analogous to convincing someone of changing his or her spiritual beliefs or religion.

Second, change management requires coordinated leadership. This in itself poses both personal and organizational stresses and challenges, because each person can respond differently to different leadership styles and methods. One person's charismatic leader is another's dictator. Even the most skilful leaders can make matters worse when they confront their employees with the need for fundamental change. Matters can go from bad to worse if leadership is 'weak', disunited or unclear in its intentions.

Third, even when leaders can decide what to do and when, they still have to work out how to make their objectives and activities sufficiently transparent to encourage employees to take some calculated risks, and to convince them that they know what they are doing.

Fourth, most organizations are too impatient or do not realize that change must take place longitudinally. Change needs to be implemented over the long term, with careful attention to its disruptive aspects, and consideration for when to consolidate. For example, periods of intense change tend to be best followed by periods of stability. This means that in practical terms, organizations probably need to plan for years of concerted effort to accomplish a major transformational change. Skipping essential steps in the change process creates only an illusion of speed and does not produce lasting change. Critical mistakes in any of the phases can have a devastating impact, slowing momentum and negating previous gains.

Fifth, and finally, because of the need to maintain the ability to conduct business during the change period, the existing structures and practices remain important. Rather than overcome this immense problem of system 'rollout' and exchange without losing customers and credibility, most organizations implement change around the existing systems, merely giving them a fresh coat of paint rather than changing them wholesale. One result is a general agreement that it might be easier to create the necessary conditions in new organizations than in existing organizations. This shifts the onus towards the development of new organizational divisions that are structured the 'right' way from the beginning. Change is subsequently deferred or avoided.

CONCLUSION

Philosophies of organizational change management are diverse, complex and contradictory. Even at the most fundamental level, different philosophies of change cannot even agree as to its nature, let alone any form of intervention. As we have seen, depending upon the philosophy, the impetus for change is argued to come from inside or outside an organization, or both. In consequence, the change can be received by an organization with open arms or with raised fists, or even both. And, the ultimate change that occurs may be massive, proceeding with vigour, or it may be feeble, and proceed cautiously. Intractable distinctions between philosophies ensure that there can be no agreement about whether organizations are internally resistant to change, or whether lasting change mainly comes from rapid but relatively uncontrollable environmental shifts. Similarly, some philosophies propose that change is not dependent on an environmental trauma, but rather can be managed systematically once the machinations of an organization are fully understood. That is, for some, change can be 'managed'. In particular, the barriers to change can be deconstructed in order to facilitate successful change.

The change process is also complicated by diverging views on the sources of resistance. Some philosophies caution that the principal cause of change barriers is a natural human disinclination for change. This psychological model may be contrasted with the systems model, which presupposes that individuals are not the cause of change barriers, but are merely trapped in unworkable systems that discourage change. Overwhelmingly, the weakness in the literature on organizational change management is a lack of integrated and universally accepted theory. The precise mechanisms for implementing change with consistent success remains a subject of contention, and is chiefly a factor of the fundamental assumptions made about the nature of change and its obstacles. In the absence of a unifying theory, we think it instructive to understand the fundamental philosophies of organizational change.

Index

Printed and bound by CPI Group (UK) Ltd, Croydon, CR0 4YY

01/10/2024

14566733-0001